Revolution of the Mind

Studies of the Harriman Institute

Columbia University

The Harriman Institute, Columbia University, sponsors the Studies of the Harriman Institute in the belief that their publication contributes to scholarly research and public understanding. In this way, the Institute, while not necessarily endorsing their conclusions, is pleased to make available the results of some of the research conducted under its auspices. A list of the Studies appears at the back of the book.

Revolution of the Mind

HIGHER LEARNING AMONG THE BOLSHEVIKS, 1918–1929

MICHAEL DAVID-FOX

Studies of the Harriman Institute

CORNELL UNIVERSITY PRESS
ITHACA AND LONDON

First published 1997 by Cornell University Press.

Library of Congress Cataloging-in-Publication Data

David-Fox, Michael, 1965–
Revolution of the mind : higher learning among the Bolsheviks, 1918–1929 / Michael David-Fox.
p. cm. — (Studies of the Harriman Institute)
Includes bibliographical references (p.) and index.
ISBN 0-8014-3128-X (cloth : alk. paper)
1. Education, Higher — Soviet Union — History. 2. Communism and education — Soviet Union — History. 3. Communism and culture — Soviet Union — History. I. Title. II. Series.
LA831.8.D37 1997
378.47 — dc21 96-47757

Printed in the United States of America.

Cornell University Press strives to utilize environmentally responsible suppliers and materials to the fullest extent possible in the publishing of its books. Such materials include vegetable-based, low-VOC inks and acid-free papers that are also either recycled, totally chlorine free, or partly composed of nonwood fibers.

Cloth printing 10 9 8 7 6 5 4 3 2 1

For Sanford and Vivian
who give much but ask little

The cultural revolution, which we write about and speak about so much—it is above all a "revolution of the mind."

—*Revoliutsiia i kul'tura*, 1928

Contents

Preface

While this project was in the making, the Soviet Union and Soviet communism collapsed, the party and state archives in Russia were opened, and the field of Russian history was transformed. There is no simple correlation, of course, between this transformation and my views of the revolutionary period I studied. Even so, it seems to me that my present, so to speak, has influenced my past in several ways. In part this book has been my attempt to contribute to an understanding of the Soviet 1920s, largely centering on the years of the New Economic Policy (NEP, 1921–28), which stresses that period's pivotal, transformational, often revolutionary, yet above all contradictory nature. The move away from the hoary dichotomies between an alternative to Stalinism and the straight line to totalitarianism, change from above versus change from below, seem at least partly due to a historical heightening of critical distance—a fading of present-day urgency invested in a NEP model, the Bolshevik Revolution, and communism. Second, the way in which many dimensions of systemic transformation are interconnected, driven home to me through very different kinds of "revolutions" since 1989, seems in retrospect one reason I expanded this book and changed its focus. It was to be about the making of a "socialist intelligentsia" in Soviet Russia. Yet I soon realized that the attempt to mold a new intelligentsia was only one part of a constellation of Bolshevik missions on the "third front" of culture. Finally, and most concretely, the opening of the Communist Party and Soviet state archives made it possible for the first time to write the history of the relatively little known Bolshevik institutions of higher learning dedicated to remaking the life of the mind.

Along the way, I have incurred many debts which it is my pleasure to acknowledge. Like many first monographs, this book began as a dissertation. During my graduate work at Yale in the early 1990s, and in many cases well after I had defended the dissertation, I was aided above all by Ivo Banac, Paul Bushkovitch, Katerina Clark, Mark Steinberg, and Mark von Hagen.

My work has also developed within the orbit of Columbia University's Harriman Institute, first in a semester as an exchange scholar, later as a frequent pilgrim from the provinces, and finally as a postdoctoral fellow. I have had the opportunity to present my work on the 1920s several times at the institute in recent years. The generation of younger historians I grew up with there has influenced me in ways that would be difficult to unravel.

I was first introduced to Russian studies by an extraordinary group of scholars at Princeton in the mid-1980s, including the late Cyril Black, Stephen F. Cohen, and Robert C. Tucker. Although since then some of my views have diverged from some of theirs, my studies of those years were a formative experience.

At the Kennan Institute for Advanced Russian Studies I was able to spend a crucial year of research and writing as a Research Scholar, and I am grateful that since then I have been welcomed back many times.

I am also grateful to several other sources of support, without which this work could not have been written. I received research grants or fellowships from Fulbright-Hays, the American Council of Teachers of Russian, the Spencer Foundation, the Javits fellowship program of the U.S. Department of Education, and on two occasions from the International Research and Exchanges Board (IREX). In the final stages, I was a fellow at the Swedish Collegium for Advanced Study in the Social Sciences in Uppsala.

I have also been fortunate to have been able to conduct research in some great libraries, including the Russian State (formerly Lenin) Library, INION (which inherited the library of the Communist Academy), the Library of Congress, the New York Public Library, the Bayerische Staatsbibliothek, and the libraries of Columbia, Harvard, and Yale Universities. I thank the staffs of these institutions, and a great many Russian archivists from each of the archives listed in the bibliography, for their spirit of cooperation.

Other debts have been both scholarly and personal. Susan Gross Solomon has been a source of support, tactful criticism, and inspiration. Nikolai Krementsov and I found out right away that we had much in common, and our exchanges have left their mark on my work. Peter Holquist has been a font of provocative ideas during our ongoing conversation in New York, Moscow, Washington, and points beyond. I have greatly valued my close association with György Péteri, and he has pushed me, at times with a well-deserved scholarly shove, into several new areas.

All the aforementioned scholars have critiqued parts or all of this work; for the same generosity in commenting on parts of it in various incarnations I also thank Julie Cassiday, Charles Clark, Katerina Clark, Paul Josephson, Peter Konecny, Woodford McClelland, Daniel Todes, and Vera Tolz. Still, I and I alone bear the responsibility for its deficiencies.

I thank my colleagues at the University of Maryland at College Park, especially George Majeska and James Harris, for their strong encouragement. Also in Washington, Zdeněk Václav David, historian and librarian, has over the years shared his unconventional wisdom and showered me with materials of the most diverse kind.

Sergei Kirillovich Kapterev, self-styled vulgar culturologist, has usually been around when I needed him.

Katja David-Fox, my wife and sharpest scholarly critic, has built a foundation of love and understanding without which the whole enterprise would have been impossible.

PORTIONS of the chapter on the Institute of Red Professors were published as "Political Culture, Purges, and Proletarianization at the Institute of Red Professors, 1921–1929," *Russian Review* 52 (January 1993): 20–42. I thank the Ohio State University Press for permission to incorporate them here.

From 1989 until the completion of this book I spent a total of about two years on five research trips to the archives in Russia. By a stroke of fortune I was able to make a bit of history myself, when in the fall of 1990 I became one of the first Western researchers admitted to the former Central Party Archive and, I was told, the second foreigner to work at the former Moscow Party Archive. Since new archival documentation comprises a large part of this study, I have developed a method of citation different from the standard Soviet and Russian practice, which has in general been adopted by Western historians. Rather than citing a document only by collection, list, folder, and page, I have preceded this information with the official title or heading of the document in quotation marks and its date. I believe specialists will gain invaluable information from the full identification of archival material, instead of just facing an "alphabet soup" of abbreviations and numbers. In many cases I (or the archivists themselves) dated the document either from internal evidence or by material in the folder surrounding it. In such cases, and in cases when the day, month, or year are not certain, that is indicated in the citation. Occasionally, when I have cited many documents of the same type, I have for reasons of space omitted the document title. It is my hope that the benefits of this methodology will be quickly apparent, and that it will attract attention to problems of source criticism in a new era in the study of Soviet history.

MICHAEL DAVID-FOX

Washington, D.C.

Glossary of Terminology, Abbreviations, and Acronyms

AN	Akademiia nauk (Academy of Sciences)
Agitprop TsK	Agitation-Propaganda Department/Central Committee
agitprops	Agitation-Propaganda departments of regional party committees
aktiv	activists
BSE	*Bol'shaia Sovetskaia Entsiklopediia* (Great Soviet Encyclopedia)
byt	everyday life, lifestyle, existence
diamat	dialectical materialism
doklad	paper, report
FONy	Fakul'tety obshchestvennykh nauk (social science departments)
GUS	Gosudarstvennyi uchennyi sovet (State Scholarly Council) of Narkompros
GPU	secret police, successor to Cheka
Glavlit	Main Administration on Literature and Presses, the Soviet censorship agency
Glavprofobr	Main Administration on Professional Education of Narkompros
Glavpolitprosvet (GPP)	Main Committee on Political Enlightenment
Glavrepertkom	Main Committee on Repertoire, censorship agency for public performances

gubkom	regional party committee
higher school	vysshaia shkola (higher educational institution)
IKP	Institut krasnoi professury (Institute of Red Professors)
ikapist(y)	student(s) of IKP
intelligent	member of intelligentsia
istmat	historical materialism
KUNMZ	Communist University of the National Minorities of the West
KUTV	Communist University of the Toilers of the East
Kadet	Constitutional Democratic Party
Komakademiia (KA)	Kommunisticheskaia akademiia (Communist Academy)
Komsomol	Communist Youth League
Komvuzy	Communist universities
kruzhok/kruzhki	study circle(s)
MK	Moskovskii Komitet (Moscow Committee of the Communist Party)
MKK	Moscow Control Commission
narkomaty	commissariats
Narkompros	Commissariat of Education (Enlightenment)
nauka	science, scholarship
Orgburo	Organizational Bureau of Central Committee
Proletkul't	Proletarian Culture movement
Profintern	Trade Union International
PSS	Pol'noe sobranie sochinenii (complete collected works)
PUR	Political Administration of the Red Army
partiinost'	party-mindedness, "partyness"
PZM	*Pod znamenem marksizma*
politgramota	political literacy
politprosveshchenie	political enlightenment
pravlenie	administration (of educational institution)
proverka	verification; used synonymously with purge
rabfak	workers' faculty (preparatory section)
raikom	district party committee
raion	district
RANION	Russian Association of Social Science Scientific Research Institutes

SAON	Sotsialisticheskaia akademiia obshchestvennykh nauk (Socialist Academy of Social Sciences)
SR	Socialist Revolutionary Party
sluzhashchie	white-collar employees
social minimum	mandatory courses in Marxist social science
sotrudniki (nauchnye)	researchers, research associates
sovpartshkoly	soviet-party schools
studenchestvo	student body
Sovnarkom (SNK)	Council of People's Commissars
spetsy	abbreviation of spetsialisty; specialists
Sverdlovets/Sverdlovtsy	student(s) of Sverdlov University
Sverdloviia	nickname for Sverdlov Communist University
TsKK	Central Control Commission
third front	cultural front, as opposed to military and political fronts
ukom	uezd party committee
VKA	*Vestnik Kommunisticheskoi akademii*
VKP(b)	All-Union Communist Party (bolsheviks)
VSA	*Vestnik Sotsialisticheskoi akademii*
VSNKh	All-Union Council of the National Economy
VTsIK	All-Union Central Executive Committee of Soviets
VUZy	vysshie uchebnye zavedeniia (higher educational institutions)
velikii perelom	Great Break
Vpered	"Forward" group of the Russian Social-Democratic Labor Party (RSDRP)
vydvizhensty	socially promoted cadres

Revolution of the Mind

INTRODUCTION / THE BOLSHEVIK REVOLUTION AND THE CULTURAL FRONT

In the years after 1917 the institutions of party education and scholarship the new regime founded in the wake of the Revolution were dedicated to molding a new intelligentsia, refashioning education and science (*nauka*), building a new culture, transforming everyday life, and ultimately creating a New Man. These institutions, notably Sverdlov Communist University, the Institute of Red Professors, and the Communist Academy, rose to become the most prominent centers of Bolshevik training and thought in the 1920s.

Bolshevik higher learning, as it embraced such quests, evolved along the contours of a particular—and particularly consequential—conjuncture in the Russian Revolution.[1] Fundamental revolutionary missions, most of which predated the Bolshevik Party and remained broader than Bolshevism, were channeled through the Party and its institutions. As a result, the concern with creating "new people," for example, part of the program of revolutionary and student movements since Chernyshevskii and the nihilists in the 1860s, began in part to mean making Bolsheviks; developing a new science came, in part, to imply spreading party Marxism. In a similar fashion, building a socialist culture and cultivating Bolshevik mores, molding a new intelligentsia and training red special-

1. I use the phrase "higher learning" to encompass all higher education, research institutes, and academies. *Nauka* (science), like its equivalents in other European languages, encompasses all fields of knowledge; thus I distinguish it from "natural science" throughout.

ists—all became connected, for each overarching mission could be refracted through a "party" lens. This Bolshevik particularizing of universalistic revolutionary goals, and this universalizing of specific Bolshevik agendas, took place during an extended historical moment, after the October Revolution of 1917 but before Stalin's Great Break of 1928–29, a moment in which the emergent party-state was still exploring the relationship between power and further revolutionary change.

It is the centrality of the party in power that makes the missions to be explored here, as they were pursued in the institutions of communist higher learning, part of an influential and distinctive revolutionary enterprise. These quests—in scope, intensity, and number greater than before—were pursued all at once and often under the same roof. They were for the first time carried out by a political party in control of a state. Thus Bolshevik higher learning, as it became an established, institutionalized enterprise in its own right, was at the same time integrated into the party polity, developed within an inner-party system of power relations, and, in no small part because virtually all the leading Bolshevik intellectuals were involved, placed near the center of high politics. In these newly created Bolshevik institutions—unified in a new system of education and research that in the 1920s at once became a countermodel to prerevolutionary, "bourgeois," and Soviet state-run systems—the attempt to revolutionize the life of the mind, along with all other attendant transformations, was therefore filtered through evolving communist practices and concerns. And the objects here were not the benighted masses, but the Bolsheviks themselves, giving party education, like the Party itself, simultaneously a mass and elite character. The Bolshevik Party carried out a project of self-transformation, experimenting on itself more intensively and, in the case of higher learning, at least a step ahead of the society it was attempting to build.

This book is thus not merely about communist visions and theories (although those were ubiquitous) but about the contested and messy attempts to implement them within new institutions. What held these diverse missions together was that they were all pursued as the result of an expansion of the Bolshevik revolutionary project to the "third" or "cultural" front. This new battleground was declared open around 1920–21, just as revolutionary and party agendas were being made inseparable. The cultural arena was widely proclaimed the next locus of revolutionary activity in the wake of Bolshevik victories on the first two "fronts," the Party's military and political struggles in the civil war.[2]

Nascent institutions of Bolshevik higher learning emerged as an intrinsic part of this third front enterprise. Their goals, to bring the revolution into the realms of culture, science, education, and ideology, became in their heyday—the 1920s—a linchpin of the Bolshevik project.

Institutionalizing Revolution

The mingling of revolutionary missions and Bolshevik agendas both reflected and advanced one of the great co-optations of revolutionary history, as the Party deliberately and successfully identified itself with the revolution as a whole.[3] This stage of the Russian Revolution, to be sure, had its roots in October, but it emerged full-blown from a discrete historical conjuncture that roughly corresponded to the red victory in the civil war. As the other socialist parties were suppressed and party leaders began to disparage the "declassed" proletariat that had turned against them or melted into the countryside, top Bolsheviks in a time of unusual candor openly justified the dictatorship of a party "vanguard."[4] To effect this dictatorship the Party added the reconstruction of its own base of support to its list of primary missions. Equally important, between 1919 and 1921 "the relationship between party and state in Soviet Russia underwent a profound change," not at all fully foreordained, as the former assumed dominance over the latter.[5] It was at the same time as well that the Party with supreme assurance put itself forward as the model for all foreign communist parties, which were to be "bolshevized," and October as the prototype for all "proletarian"

2. Samuel N. Harper recognized the link between the third front and party education many years ago, when he wrote that "a forced retreat on the economic front [i.e., NEP] led to special emphasis on education, and particularly on Communist training." Harper, *Making Bolsheviks* (Chicago: University of Chicago Press, 1931), 108.

3. Although no single work fully explores this epochal shift in the Russian Revolution, its importance and its links to the Bolsheviks' ability to create effective new institutions are underlined in Stephen Kotkin's *Magnetic Mountain: Stalinism as a Civilization* (Berkeley: University of California Press, 1995), 13–14, 292.

4. Sheila Fitzpatrick in "The Bolsheviks' Dilemma: Class, Culture, and Politics in the Early Soviet Years," *Slavic Review* 47 (Winter 1988): esp. 609–11. The "self-conscious reorientation of the regime's justification" as a party-dominated dictatorship of the proletariat by mid-1920 is analyzed by Neil Harding in "Socialism, Society and the Organic Labour State," in Harding, ed., *The State in Socialist Society* (Albany: SUNY Press, 1984), 22–25.

5. T. H. Rigby, *Lenin's Government: Sovnarkom, 1917–1922* (Cambridge: Cambridge University Press, 1979), 185.

revolutions.[6] Indeed, in the scope of its pretensions this moment around 1920–21 might be considered the bolshevization of the Russian Revolution. The birth of a unified system of party education and research—which was part of this same historical conjuncture—ensured that party higher learning would combine a specifically Bolshevik identity with universalistic aspirations for revolutionizing the life of the mind.

This great bid for hegemony also corresponded to the elaboration of a full-fledged Bolshevik engagement in the cultural arena. The proletarian culture (Proletkul't) movement—a mass organization that had tried to maintain independence from the Party, yet had attracted those Bolshevik intellectuals most concerned with creating a new culture—was stripped of its autonomy, and the impetus for a full-fledged communist cultural mission was set in place. Certain key terms were invoked as the cultural front was constituted: enlightenment (*prosveshchenie*), education (*obrazovanie*), and upbringing (*vospitanie*). All three imply both long-term tutelage and cognitive transformation. Indeed, "enlightenment," understood not merely as propagandizing for short-term benefit but as the transformation of people and the popular "consciousness," emerged as such a fundamental feature of the new regime that Soviet Russia might with justification be called the enlightenment state.[7] From the start enormous resources and energies were devoted to transforming "consciousness" in what had become an overwhelmingly didactic revolution. Even labor camps formed departments of "political," later "cultural" upbringing.[8]

The Bolshevik Revolution, following what was in many ways a chaotic explosion of educational and "enlightenment" movements during the first years after 1917, turned more systematically toward both culture-building and institution-building in the evolving order of the 1920s. One scholar, perhaps the first, to clearly identify this "cultural" program as the beginning of a new stage in Lenin's Bolshevism and, implicitly, of the revolution was Robert C. Tucker. By 1920, he argued, Lenin "had reached the point of conceptualizing Soviet Russia as the scene of a culture-building culture."[9]

6. As famously and formally codified in the "21 Conditions" adopted by the Second Congress of the Comintern, which opened in July 1920.

7. Peter Kenez gives an overview of activities referred to at the time both as agitation-propaganda and as political enlightenment in *The Birth of the Propaganda State: Soviet Methods of Mass Mobilization, 1917–1929* (Cambridge: Cambridge University Press, 1985).

8. See chapter 18 of Alexandr Solzhenitsyn, *The Gulag Archipelago*, trans. Thomas Whitney (New York: Harper & Row, 1975), 2:468–501.

9. Robert C. Tucker, "Lenin's Bolshevism as a Culture in the Making," in Abbott Gleason

Lenin's endorsement, indeed, was instrumental in raising the profile of the Bolshevik cultural mission, which had hitherto been the special province of the Vperedist wing of the Party. Yet the opening of the third front was a larger phenomenon; virtually the entire top leadership agreed on its importance. By the early 1920s Bolshevik leaders across factional lines came to portray cultural transformation, educational work, and the creation of a Bolshevik intelligentsia as pivotal to the fate of regime and revolution. Trotskii declared, "The upbringing of youth is a question of life and death for the Republic." Bukharin claimed that only a "cultural reworking" by means of state power could produce the cadres the proletarian dictatorship demanded, and that this was important enough to determine "our fate and historical path." He added that "the cultural question" is "a central problem of the entire revolution." Lunacharskii, referring to these statements by Bukharin and Trotskii in 1924, reformulated the question as the creation of "our own intelligentsia" and suggested there could be only one point of view within the Party on its exceptional importance.[10]

In this book I trace the roots and evolution of this push to bring the revolution into new realms and show how the many third front missions became tightly linked to party institutions. The creation of a system of party education and, under its auspices, the pursuit of revolutionary quests became major components of the "third front" agenda. The rise of a network of party educational and scholarly institutions followed from the constitution of this new revolutionary arena. Yet clear-cut victory on the battlefield of the mind proved more elusive than either military triumph or the consolidation of political power.

The story of Bolshevik revolutionary missions is filled with irony, unexpected yet pervasive constraints, and sudden turns. The third front missions endorsed in 1920 were followed by the New Economic Policy (NEP) in 1921. The transformational urge was tempered not only by the enormous weight of "Russian reality" and a decided deficit in the plasticity of man and culture that defied all revolutionary rhetoric but also by urgent considerations forced upon the new regime by the implosion of revolution and the collapse of "war communism." A preserva-

---

et al., eds., *Bolshevik Culture: Experiment and Order in the Russian Revolution* (Bloomington: Indiana University Press, 1989), 36.

10. L. Trotskii, "Polozhenie respubliki i zadachi rabochei molodezhi (Doklad na V Vserossiiskom s"ezde RKSM 11 oktiabria 1922 g.)," in *Sochineniia* (Moscow: Gosizdat, 1927), 21:308; N. Bukharin, *Proletarskaia revoliutsiia i kul'tura* (Petrograd: "Priboi," 1923), 9, 25; A. V. Lunacharskii, "Novoe studenchestvo," *Narodnoe prosveshchenie*, no. 2 (1924): 7–8.

tionist, stabilizing complex of tendencies—which in their cultural manifestation Richard Stites has aptly called anti-iconoclasm—was bolstered by certain features of NEP.[11] Such tendencies found justification chiefly in the need to rebuild the economy and reach a *modus vivendi* with the "bourgeois specialists" upon whose survival industry, education, and the state bureaucracy depended. They also included moves to maintain higher education, specialist training, and nonparty scholarship, to reach a working accommodation with the overwhelmingly nonparty professoriat, and, as it was frequently phrased, to adopt the best of the culture of the past.

In much of the literature on the postrevolutionary order as it relates to education, cultural policy, and the intelligentsia, "1921" has overshadowed "1920," just as a post hoc notion of a "NEP in culture" has overshadowed the third front.[12] I contend that the 1920s order in higher learning was only partly the product of the New Economic Policy. It was initiated by an aggressive Bolshevik "advance" on the third front and only then modified by a particular "retreat" associated with NEP. Moreover, NEP the policy could not be disengaged from NEP the concept, as the acronym itself became linked with images of degeneracy and corruption. The very phrase "NEP in culture," a Western coinage denoting accommodation and moderation, would have at the time implied the insidious cultural influence of NEPmen and class enemies. Still, the NEP era, which largely coincided with the settling of an academic order that coalesced after 1922, unquestionably imposed constraints on communist intellectuals, party scholarship, and myriad forces on the Bolshevik Left. In part this was due to the circumstance that the "old" (prerevolutionary) and other (nonparty) universities, higher educational institutions (VUZy), research institutes, and academies administered under Soviet state auspices were now slated either for long-term, gradual "reform" or ceded their own spheres of influence outright. The great paradox of NEP was that such constraints led almost immediately not only to a resurgence of long-term Bolshevik visions and strategies but also to attempts to transcend "retreat" in new areas, in part stimulating the attempt to realize revolutionary goals first and foremost within the

11. Richard Stites, *Revolutionary Dreams: Utopian Vision and Experimental Life in the Russian Revolution* (New York: Oxford University Press, 1989), 76–78.

12. In a significant branch of historiography in the 1970s and 1980s, the cultural "compromises" were taken out of context, mistaken for the whole of the new regime's cultural and educational policy, and reified under the title "NEP in culture." For an example, see Timothy O'Connor, *The Politics of Soviet Culture: Anatolii Lunacharskii* (Ann Arbor: UMI Research Press, 1983).

Communist Party. NEP with all its ambiguities and contradictions was a revolutionary era, a phase of the revolution of a particular kind.

Many of the tensions built into the academic order during the NEP period flowed along the contours of this fundamental contradiction at its birth. Among the outcomes least anticipated was the fate of the very institutions of party higher learning I examine here. In a decisive yet ultimately Pyrrhic victory they triumphed over their nonparty rivals at the end of the 1920s, but in the process spiraled into decline and deprived themselves of a primary raison d'etre, setting the stage for their own demise.

Mirrors, Structures, Symbols: An Approach

By 1928, on the cusp of the Great Break, which altered the organization and ethos of all higher learning in the country irrevocably, one party activist had come to the striking reformulation that comprises the epigraph to this book: the transformative third front missions, now most frequently regrouped under the rubric of cultural revolution, were really about the creation of a new mind. Despite the barrage of plans in this epoch to invent virtually everything *ab novo*—including, in the widespread phrase, a "new world"—such a modification itself was hardly new. The proposal for a new mind was but one brightly colored thread in an entire tapestry of attempted transformations.

Taking in this sweeping range of the third front of culture requires a broad angle of vision from the historian. Indeed, central categories that generations of scholars of the early Soviet experience have generally considered stable and to a large degree analytically discrete were all profoundly intertwined on a front that advanced a barrage of missions and harbored totalizing aspirations.[13] Indeed, a remarkable feature of the age was how categories like "culture" were expanded in a revolutionary way. In party usage in the early Soviet period, *kul'tura* was increasingly understood not only as high culture but—in what until then had been an ethnographic sense—as encompassing all habits, traditions, customs, and everyday life (*byt*).[14] Better known, but equally in need of exploration, is the explosive expansion of the "political" in the 1920s into realms previously unmarked or private.

13. I prefer to speak of totalizing aspirations rather than totalitarianism in order to emphasize the decisive gap between plans and achievement.

14. I. Luppol, "Problema kul'tury v postanovke Lenina," *Pechat' i revoliutsiia*, no. 7 (October–November 1925): 14–28.

A major theme of this book, then, is the interconnectedness of activity on the third front. In broadest terms, this characteristically revolutionary sweep can be related to a communist inversion of the fundamentally liberal axiom that such spheres as the economic, political, scientific, and cultural are separate and autonomous. After all, conceptualizing in terms of the entire "superstructure" and "base"—in the midst of social revolution and the attempt to build a radically new society—led to an inveterate proclivity to aggregate and to link. The Bolsheviks' Marxism dictated the primacy of class; the Leninist tradition placed political struggle at the center of all revolutionary tasks; the Party had belatedly adopted a cultural mission as it embarked on revolutionary state-building to prepare a "backward" society for socialism. The resulting merger of spheres, the intertwined missions, became a perennial feature of the "cultural" front. This was not simply an enlightenment state, but, however imperfectly realized, a system with an organic thrust.

The holistic texture of the Bolsheviks' "third front" has several implications. It suggests that its manifold agendas—from creating a new social group, a socialist or proletarian intelligentsia, to reworking science, pedagogy, and education—are fruitfully explored in tandem. It implies, as well, that "ideology" is best examined in conjunction with the practices of the new regime.[15] Reflecting on ideology and social revolutions, a historian of the French Revolution, William Sewell remarked upon the ubiquity of a "hierarchical" strategy of "asserting the primacy of some type of cause over the other," which tends to subordinate the roles of other factors or conflate them with "the chosen causal factor." The same might be said about the treatment of causality in early Soviet Russia, a problem also caught up, of course, with an overriding question of the origins of Stalin's "second revolution." The nature of the "cultural front" has suggested that reductionist approaches, those that rush to privilege a single category, are less likely to capture overlapping dimensions of revolutionary change.[16]

15. I know of no *Begriffsgeschichte* of ideology in the early Soviet period, which in general was shifting from a classical Marxist, demystifying notion of ideology as "false consciousness" to a positive notion of codified doctrine and worldview. See, for example, the discussion and citations in V. V. Adoratskii, "Ob ideologii," *Pod znamenem marksizma* (henceforth cited as *PZM*), no. 11–12 (November–December 1922): 199–210. Because I am concerned with institutions of party-Marxist thought and education which used *ideologiia* to refer to Marxist-Leninist doctrine, and more broadly to self-conscious worldviews, I restrict the term to those connotations.

16. William Sewell, "Ideologies and Social Revolutions: Reflections on the French Case," *Journal of Modern History* 57 (March 1985): 57–58. Of the most visible examples of such a

In each of the four extended inquiries into which this book is divided, I attempt to show how third front missions were woven into the history of Bolshevik higher learning, its institutions, and the groups of party intellectuals and students involved. Having said that, I take special aim at capturing and integrating two of the dimensions of postrevolutionary development that have been—to make a large but not unfounded generalization—less deeply probed in the early Soviet period and in the history of Bolshevism: the cultural and the institutional.

These party institutions are mirrors that reflect many processes that flowed from the establishment of the third front. For example, the effort to live a new communist lifestyle or everyday life (*byt*) at Sverdlov Communist University; the search to create a truly "red" specialist at the Institute of Red Professors; and the championing of a planned, "practical," collectivist, orthodox party Marxist science at the Communist Academy were preoccupations of communist students, red professors, and Bolshevik scholars at these three institutions and shaped the development of the institutions where they were pursued most intensively.

In the context of early Soviet Russia, it is clear, institution-building in higher learning following the Revolution was no consolidation of long-prepared cognitive changes or cultural shifts; rather, it occurred simultaneously with such changes. These centers of party higher learning were a new breed of specifically Bolshevik Party institution. As such, they refined distinctive practices and policies that shaped life within their walls. These practices and policies were highly novel for the academic enterprise. Among the most important of these were the activities of the party cell, purge and promotion policies, and the attempts to regulate social origin. By tying such practices to the broader context of the Soviet state and Communist Party—in areas such as purges, proletarianization, the *nomenklatura* system, and what I call the Party's disciplinary regime—I explore the participation of party higher learning in Bolshevik institutional organization not only for general insight into

strategy in the Russian field, one can mention Martin Malia's "agenda" of "reassert[ing] the primacy of ideology and politics" (Malia, *The Soviet Tragedy: A History of Socialism in Russia, 1917–1991* [New York: Free Press, 1994], 16), with heavy emphasis on the first of the dyad; Richard Pipes's characterization of the "decisive and immediate factors making for the [old] regime's fall and the resultant turmoil" as "overwhelmingly political," in *Russia under the Bolshevik Regime* (New York: Alfred A. Knopf, 1993), 491; and Ronald Grigor Suny's identification of "social polarization" as the "key to a new paradigm" in his landmark survey, "Toward a Social History of the October Revolution," *American Historical Review* 88 (1983): 31–52. Certainly it is also possible, in a similar way, to come to a cultural essentialism that seeks a cause of causes in Russian or Soviet culture.

much broader phenomena connected to party political practices and Bolshevik state-building but also for particular understanding of the influential results of the practices for the new Bolshevik academic enterprise.

Further, these Bolshevik centers were also actors in the struggles of the day in higher education, culture, pedagogy, and scholarship. During the 1920s, the world of postrevolutionary higher learning was small, and scholars and intellectuals were overwhelmingly centered in Moscow and Leningrad.[17] The central Moscow party institutions under the microscope here, as a result, played a decisive role in a decade-long rivalry with the state-run system of old universities, institutes, and the Academy of Sciences, all still dominated to one degree or another by members of the nonparty academic intelligentsia. These rivalries, both constrained and maintained by the dualistic NEP academic order, culminated in the Great Break assault on the chief nonparty institutional rivals.

Finally, these party institutions assumed the status of models and symbols of progress on the third front. The Moscow institutions founded first quickly became prototypes for an entire country-wide system of party education; soon afterward, they began to be explicitly portrayed in the party-Marxist camp as "model" (*obraztsovye*) institutions for further revolutionary change in the social sciences and, frequently by implication, in higher learning as a whole. In an academic world in which Bolsheviks were a small and parvenu minority, party institutions quickly became symbolic representations of the revolutionary. In this way the very structures of the new party-state, as they were developing, were imbued with meaning. The decade-long experience of party academia therefore took on decisive implications during a Great Break upheaval that attempted to bring the revolution to unreconstructed realms.

In the attempt to scratch beneath the surface of an often secretive communist world, I have paid special attention to the rise and formative

17. According to 1922 and 1923 census data, up to 90 percent of all professors, lecturers, and scholars lived in Moscow or in the cities of the Moscow *guberniia*; analogous figures for various kinds of professionals and "literati" ranged between 70 and 80 percent. Figures on scholars and scientists at the end of the 1920s show that the vast majority of these groups had not budged from the large cultural centers of Moscow and Leningrad. See L. A. Pinegina, "Nekotorye dannye o chislennosti i sostave intelligentsii k nachalu vostanovitel'nogo perioda (po materialam perepisei 1922 i 1923 gg.)," *Vestnik Moskovskogo Universiteta*, 8th ser., no. 3 (1979): 12–20, and V. S. Sobolev, "Uchet kadrov issledovatel'skikh uchrezhdenii i vuzov (1918–1934)," *Vestnik akademii nauk SSSR*, no. 11 (1989): 87–91.

years of party institutions and their everyday practices, not just to penetrate the walls of Bolshevik institutions, but to uncover the framework, the cultural underpinnings, that informed activity within them. Communist conventions, refined in the power politics of this "party of a new type," combined to form a powerful crucible for initiating people. Party schools were explicitly portrayed as "weapons" of "Bolshevik upbringing." Despite the fact that an institutional framework was, broadly speaking, not primary in Marxist or Bolshevik thought, it is interesting to note how quickly party educational institutions became—and, just as important, were perceived as—primary vehicles of cultural transmission. Andrei Bubnov, powerful head of the Central Committee's Agitprop department, which oversaw the party schools, gave a very clear indication of this to a group of students from Sverdlov Communist University in 1922: "This is not merely a building, into which new people are packed each year; this is a university, which possesses a defined system of regulations, certain defined internal interrelationships. . . . An institution—with its basic tone, character, customs, everyday life [*byt*]—all of this creates a certain succession from one graduating class to the next."[18]

This book explores Bolshevik culture and culture-building in several different settings and among key groups comprising the milieu of party higher learning: Old Bolshevik intellectuals and Marxist theoreticians, rising groups of "red professors" of the early and late 1920s, and the activists and rank and file of the communist *studenchestvo*. Taking into account the attributes of such groups, I attempt to portray Bolshevik culture as potent and increasingly conventionalized in many of its manifestations, but itself caught in the throes of change and never static or fully unified.

Because the branch of academia under consideration was part and parcel of the Party, and practices derived from inner-party politics and Bolshevism pervaded the life of party scholarship and education, Bolshevik political culture is critical to this inquiry.[19] What has stood out

18. "Zasedanie 26/I-23 goda. Agitprop Otdel TsK RKP," RTsKhIDNI f. 17, op. 60, d. 500, l. 47.

19. Sidney Verba's classic definition of political culture refers to that "system of empirical beliefs, expressive symbols, and values which defines the situation in which political action takes place. It provides the subjective orientation to politics." Lucian Pye and Sidney Verba, eds., *Political Culture and Political Development* (Princeton: Princeton University Press, 1965), 513. By using the term I hope to capture not only that system of values and norms informing approaches to politics but also those expressed in the canon of "cultural" activities developed in the Soviet state as part of political education, such as "political-enlightenment work."

above all is the ritualistic, scripted, and even theatrical quality of Bolshevik political culture in the 1920s. Commonalities across various settings have emerged which, I believe, show how this political culture acquired mass, depth, and an expanded currency in the 1920s; it thus has to be reckoned with in accounting for change. For example, the intense environment of the red professors' theory seminars exhibit similarities to staged performances of agitational trials, and telltale traces of the rites of party cell meetings are shown to be present in the social science writings of party Marxists. The written word was not isolated from the many other modes of transmission. This explains the special interest here in the development of Soviet Marxism less as a philosophy or system of ideas—for this has been examined many times before and in some fine studies—but as a prominent part of a broader political-cultural idiom. Among the implications for the party intellectuals were that central ideas such as class conflict and methodologies such as unmasking reinforced modes of action and helped crystallize a party style in intellectual life.[20]

The Bolsheviks, including the intellectuals among them, prided themselves on being tough customers and hard-headed political operators. Some might dismiss the nuances of their political culture as of secondary importance. I do not agree, for the web of stylized conventions they wrought, and which in turn wrought them, became a prominent feature of the communist modus operandi on the third front. Their methods, and the ways of acting and thinking that accompanied them, formed a crucial component of their rise to the commanding heights of organized intellectual life. Bolshevik culture was not only evolving but spreading rapidly outward in the 1920s. In higher learning attempts were made to impose forcibly its conventionalized manifestations, most violently of course at the end of the decade. Here one can cite only one example when the worlds of party and nonparty scholarship clashed, during the bolshevization of the Academy of Sciences in 1929. It is striking how transparently party emissaries attempted to inject well-worn inner-party methods—specific methods of denunciation, self-criticism, purge sessions, and exegesis of the political meaning of one's biographical past—into a hitherto completely nonparty institution. The quintessentially

20. Karl Mannheim first adopted the concept of style as developed in art history to his notion of "styles of thought," denoting constellations of patterns that become meaningful in social context. See his "Conservative Thought," in *Essays in Sociology and Social Psychology* (London: Routledge & Kegan Paul, 1953), 74–164.

nonparty scientific community at first reacted defensively and collegially and then, under immense pressure, broke ranks.[21]

As this suggests, Bolshevik political culture informed action; it was no ethereal abstraction but a phenomenon linked by a thousand threads to the emerging system. This linkage requires us to rethink some of the features of party politics and inner-party struggles of the 1920s. The constitution of the "third front" and the formative political and conceptual conflicts from which an regulatory bureaucracy emerged suggest a new appreciation of the permeable boundaries of party-state dualism. Probing this ambiguous party-state dualism on the emergent third front administrative apparat clarifies some of the contradictory impulses of cultural and higher educational policy in the 1920s. The connection of everyday life with party cell politics at Sverdlov University leads us into the Party's highest organ of discipline, the Central Control Commission. Both the single party cell and the top organ reflected the pervasive concern with lifestyle deviations as part of an emerging communist disciplinary regime. This, in turn, formed part of a top-heavy system of power relations that was challenged during the height of the Trotskyist opposition of 1923–24 and suddenly if temporarily turned topsy-turvy in Stalin's Great Break. The scripted and theatrical unmasking of deviations at the Institute of Red Professors forces a consideration of the "Right" in 1928–29 as an "invented opposition" and the birth of "Stalinism" in party intellectual life as a lengthy, gradual process stimulated by this shock. In each of these cases, and in others, immersion in the workings of the Bolshevik political-cultural system as it operated in a single environment can open up perspectives on the broader communist polity and the course of the revolution in the shift from the NEP to the Stalin eras.

The NEP Era and a New Elite

The leading educational and theoretical centers of Bolshevism in the 1920s were not only engaged in the making of red specialists, theoreticians, publicists, and social scientists. In this era above all, those activ-

21. "Stenogramma zasedaniia Plenuma komissii po proverke apparata Akademii Nauk SSSR, 24 avgusta 1929," GARF f. 3316, op. 1, d. 15, l. 479–84; "Komissiia po chistke apparata Akademii Nauk. Zasedanie 21 oktiabria 1929 g.," ibid., l. 488–95; "Stenogramma zasedaniia obshchego sobraniia sotrudnikov Akademii Nauk," 19 August 1929, ibid., l. 411–15, and 27 July 1929, ibid., l. 8–11.

ities went hand in hand with the project of training a successor generation of party leaders, often referred to as the "changing of the guard," or *smena*. A party education in the Marxist social sciences in this period was a classic career path for well-connected, up-and-coming young cadres, whereas higher technical education largely supplanted it as the primary path for rising party cadres during the industrialization drive after 1928.[22] The study of party higher education in the 1920s, then, especially its most prestigious central institutions, brings us into the heart of the protracted first phase of the making of a new elite—a central problem about the Soviet order that has interested observers of communism since Trotskii's *Revolution Betrayed* and Djilas's *New Class*.

The formation of a postrevolutionary political elite also needs to be appreciated as a mission of the new regime, yet another deliberate project inextricably tied to the third front. Institutionalized party education had come to occupy a position of overriding importance within Bolshevism in no small part because it originated in the underground party schools of 1909–11 as a means of producing both "proletarian intellectuals" and educated Marxists as well as sorely needed, loyal political agents. These goals were not rigorously distinguished either at the birth of party education or in the 1920s.

The younger generation of party members working in the central party institutions in the 1920s came from diverse national, geographical, and social backgrounds and were bound together by certain special ties. For one thing, they were nominated, mobilized, monitored, recommended, and distributed by the party-state in an elaborate appointment and promotion system developed in this same period and extended to higher education and especially the party members in it. Cadre politics was thus fundamental in structuring the training of both party scholars and politicians, and the rising generation of cadres was party-recruited and party-registered. It was as part of a new cadre system, as well, that efforts to regulate social composition and "proletarianize" the Party and the intelligentsia were first launched.

Yet perhaps the most fundamental aspect of creating a new elite took place after the promotion of cadres—the phenomenon of Bolshevik acculturation. Outlooks were molded, groups made, and identities remade by the extraordinarily intensive enviroment in which party members

22. See Harley Balzer, "Engineers: The Rise and Decline of a Social Myth," in Loren Graham, ed., *Science and the Soviet Social Order* (Cambridge: Harvard University Press, 1990), 141–67.

were educated—an environment that included the new institutions created to train them, the kind of education they received, and the powerful grip of the Bolshevik political culture into which they were initiated. This period was one of formative flux, since the project of training a party elite, the institutions created to train it, and the culture and outlook of groups that belonged to it were all evolving simultaneously.

The "new class" discussion has a full-fledged history in its own right and has been pursued in contexts ranging from the international Left, Sovietology, and social history. Here it can only be suggested that in several of these contexts over the decades social origin or social position has frequently been accepted as determinative of culture, whereas the opposite possibility—that Bolshevik culture in fundamental ways shaped the new class—has not been fully considered. At the same time, sweeping and global treatments of the place of the "new class" or political elites in the Soviet order have overshadowed the specific milieus from which its members emerged, and preoccupation with the Stalin and post-Stalin periods has tended to camouflage the sizable contribution of the NEP experience.

The debate that racked the international Left over the "bureaucracy" or "new bourgeoisie" since the 1930s—which in fact can be directly traced to the theoretical disputes of inner-party opposition groups in the USSR during the 1920s—engaged the problem of the new class above all as it affected classification of the socioeconomic nature of the regime.[23] Whether an exploiting class, or class in the Marxist sense, could exist in the Soviet mode of production comprised the heart of early debates about the nature of the Soviet system under Stalin; yet the striking result was the anonymity of elite depicted. The kind of people rising to the top, in particular their education, culture, and mentality, has long been overshadowed by disputation about their class position in Soviet society and efforts to use class analysis to categorize Soviet communism as a system. Totalitarianism theory, replacing the Marxist debates about class with the primacy of political control, was also interested in the place of elites as part of a global schema. In the decades that followed, the cottage industry that sprang up within Sovietology to analyze, much more empirically, the nomenklatura and high-ranking po-

23. I have explored aspects of the genealogy of these debates in "Ante Ciliga, Trotskii and State Capitalism: Theory, Tactics, and Reevaluation during the Purge Era, 1935–1939," *Slavic Review* 50 (Spring 1991): 127–43, and "Trotskii i ego kritiki o prirode SSSR pri Staline," *Voprosy istorii*, no. 11–12 (1992): 33–45. A comparative analysis is contained in Michael M. Lustig, *Trotsky and Djilas: Critics of Communist Bureaucracy* (Westport, Conn.: Greenwood Press, 1988).

litical figures, while often reaching back into the early years of the revolution for origins, was overwhelmingly oriented around Stalin-era and post-Stalinist developments.[24]

Western historical study of the making of a new elite, like many of the other topics addressed in this book, has been dominated by the pathbreaking work of a single scholar, Sheila Fitzpatrick. Her work privileged a single dominant generational dynamic—the formation of the "Brezhnev generation"—during massive social promotion of proletarian cadres into higher technical education during the Great Break. By far the most important period in her narrative, in which the definitive element was the social mobility of a single "cohort" during the Stalin era, was the first Five-Year Plan. Indicative of a broader tendency to put class or social origin first as determinative even of great cultural-ideological shifts was a concluding suggestion that the "Great Retreat" of the mid-1930s to hierarchical and conservative cultural values was "really the secondary consequence of a successful social revolution: the mass promotion of former workers and peasants into the Soviet political and social elite."[25]

The opening of formerly closed Soviet repositories has made it possible to study the history of the project of training a new elite by probing much more deeply the specific settings that shaped it. This study, with its locus in central party schools, is only one contribution to such an endeavor. Even so, the 1920s, as a time of cultural transformation and formative institution-building, emerges much more clearly as a period of qualitative (rather than quantitative) importance in the project of training what Bolsheviks sometimes called a new ruling stratum. What I mean by this is that the experience of the 1920s produced far fewer "cadres" than the several million beneficiaries of the breakneck proletarianization policies and expansion of higher education during the industrialization drive. Yet the fact that an unquestionably new era of massive social promotion began during the Great Break tells only a part of the story. From the 1920s on, after all, "red specialists" and a new

24. For a valuable but in its focus unrepresentative example, see Mervyn Mathews, *Privilege in the Soviet Union: A Study of Elite Life-Styles under Communism* (London: Allen & Unwin, 1978); for a survey of other works, see especially 9–10.

25. Sheila Fitzpatrick, in *Education and Social Mobility in the Soviet Union, 1921–1934* (Cambridge: Cambridge University Press, 1974), 254. Such a reductive view is questionable particularly in light of Fitzpatrick's own later work, which presses for an interpretation of Soviet social origin statistics as reflecting a highly political process of creating a kind of Marxist estate system. See Fitzpatrick, "Ascribing Class: The Construction of Social Identity in Soviet Russia," *Journal of Modern History* 65 (December 1993): 745–70.

generation began to be groomed and shaped by a new communist educational enterprise. Party cadres began to be trained in ways that integrated them into a certain culture and promoted a certain specifically Bolshevik institutional milieu. The initial stage in the making of a Soviet elite in the 1920s, then, emerges partly as a time of influential transformation in the project, as a distinctive first step that was both a precedent for and swamped by a much larger effort following on its heels.

From the first, the attempt to raise up a new ruling stratum in an age of social revolution and proletarian dictatorship was anything but an unproblematic endeavor. Indeed, the very notion of an elite was anathema to communists—yet elitism was also ever present among the professional revolutionaries in the proletarian "vanguard." The tensions and taboos, pressures and peculiarities, resulting from the rise of an anti-elitist elite were one of those central ambiguities—along with the phenomenon of what I call anti-intellectual intellectuals—plaguing Bolshevik missions in higher learning in the early years of Soviet power. In the end, so strong was the experience of acculturation in the new party education that it seems to have been capable of producing common bonds among very diverse groups of students. This is especially striking in the combative brand of Bolshevik political culture cultivated by students at the Institute of Red Professors (IKP). Records of student meetings both from the regular IKP departments (where the number of "intelligentsia" or white-collar students was high) and from the two-year IKP preparatory section designed to proletarianize the institute show strong commonalities emerging among *ikapisty* of highly variegated social and national backgrounds. In the 1920s, an age when the *smena* being trained by the Party asserted its proletarian nature most insistently, the irony was that such cadres were held together above all by political and cultural bonds; the elite being trained in top Moscow institutions in this period might be seen in many ways as a supraclass and supranational entity.

The Party Academic Sector and the Social Sciences

Party higher learning can also be seen as a network of institutions, comprising a system of higher education, a sector of academia, and a party-Marxist movement in scholarship and science. This "sectoral" perspective holds implications in particular for the history of Soviet science and higher education. Historians of higher education have rarely if ever considered party schools as an intrinsic part of postrevolutionary higher education. Yet the title "higher party school"—bestowed in 1920 on Sverdlov Communist University when that institution first moved from a six-month training program to a three-year course of study—clearly represented the party equivalent of a "higher school" or university. The title then became a standard designation written into the charter of all the communist universities, and special institutions such as the graduate-level Institute of Red Professors and the Communist Academy's "courses in Marxism." Yet perhaps because the history of these party institutions was relatively inaccessible, or because party education was largely not considered outside the context of political propaganda—in a time when, as has been emphasized, the very concepts of propaganda, enlightenment, and education were blurred—the Party's attempt to create an alternative form of higher education has in general not been taken seriously.[26] If the 1920s academic order is recognized as bifurcated along the lines of the party-state divide, as it is here, it creates a new picture of NEP-era policy and practice as structured not only by deep divisions but by a contradiction at its core.

Of the major academic sectors in the 1920s—principally the old universities, the VUZy and research institutes under Narkompros, the uniquely autonomous Academy of Sciences, and the commissariat-based institutes—party higher learning faced the greatest challenges, but also held unusual advantages.[27] Growing up under the wing of the Party gave it special powers yet also special vulnerability; it represented the revolutionary and the new regime, yet this very closeness subjected it to perennial suspicions and dangers. Not least of its advantages when it faced its academic rivals, however, was that its leaders were often politicians and academic administrators of the highest rank. The institutions examined here, as a result, formed a kind of Moscow nexus of rising party scholarship. The party camp was indeed riddled by divisions in

26. For example, Christopher Read derides Sverdlov Communist University as "more akin to a seminary devoted to the study of dogma rather than a university" where "half-educated people were being filled with pre-packaged, crude dogma." Read, *Culture and Power in Revolutionary Russia: The Intelligentsia and the Transition from Tsarism to Communism* (London: Macmillan, 1990), 137–40. Yet Read's conclusions were based almost exclusively on materials before 1921, that is, before Sverdlov emerged as a communist university; it is just as significant that the reluctance to accord communist universities a place in higher education closes off entire avenues of analysis.

27. For an introduction to the major divisions of postrevolutionary higher learning, see Alexander Vucinich, *Empire of Knowledge: The Academy of Sciences of the USSR, 1917–1970* (Berkeley: University of California Press, 1984), 72–91, and Klaus Meyer, "Wissenschaftpolitik," in Oskar Anweiler and Karl-Heinz Ruffmann, eds., *Kulturpolitik der Sowjetunion* (Stuttgart: Alfred Kröner Verlag, 1973), 145–89.

each discipline and in the inner-party disputes, but it cannot be overlooked that as a sector party higher learning developed and frequently acted as a unified entity.

At the same time, this movement *cum* sectoral base, so powerful politically yet such a parvenu force academically, evolved in tandem with nonparty higher learning, that is, with the institutions and values of the nonparty academic establishment as a principal referent. Thus the history of the Communist Academy, in particular, is unintelligible when divorced from the history of the Academy of Sciences. Party scholars prosecuted a decade-long rivalry with "bourgeois" science, but also emulated and at times imitated their established nonparty counterparts. Even when they deliberately turned their backs on anathematized features of nonparty academia—above all the twin standards of pure science and institutional autonomy—the very definition of themselves as opposite was a backhanded tribute, a form of inverted influence. In part, then, the relationship can be considered not simply antagonistic, but symbiotic.[28] Just as postrevolutionary higher education cannot be fully understood outside the context of party education, so the camp of party-Marxist scholarship cannot be fully comprehended apart from its relationship with "bourgeois" or established "academic science." The underbelly of 1920s revolutionary iconoclasm and the party camp's struggle in academia was a good dose of covert respect for the nonparty establishment.

Yet the deep-seated rivalry the party camp felt with nonparty forces was animated not by a striving for a stable accommodation, despite the degree of symbiosis in the 1920s, but by what I have called in the case of the Communist Academy the quest for hegemony. No matter how modest their initial situation, they fully expected dominance and even monopoly at the end of the struggle. The party camp's sense of struggle made the stakes high not only for the immediate actors involved. Ultimately, it helped in no small way to determine the fate of social and humanistic knowledge under Soviet communism. While party institutions did make limited but notable excursions into natural sciences in

28. Susan Gross Solomon first developed a similar thesis in her depiction of an evolving, complex interaction between agrarian Marxists (centered at the Communist Academy after 1926) and the organization-production school led by Chaianov in "Rural Scholars and the Cultural Revolution," in Sheila Fitzpatrick, ed., *Cultural Revolution in Russia, 1928–1931* (Bloomington: Indiana University Press, 1978), 128–53. I am also indebted to Fitzpatrick's suggestive remarks on the Communist Party and the nonparty intelligentsia as interdependent elites in the introduction to her collection, *The Cultural Front: Power and Culture in Revolutionary Russia* (Ithaca: Cornell University Press, 1992).

the 1920s, their overwhelming focus was on the social sciences. It was here, as well, that hegemonic aspirations were given the freest reign, and here that party Marxism can be said to have had the deepest impact (by any measurement, from effects on core methodologies to the number of party members involved).

The resulting devastation can hardly be exaggerated. Moshe Lewin, whom few would accuse of excessive antisocialist or anti-Marxist biases, recently referred to the social sciences under Stalin as utterly "destroyed," as social studies assumed the role of abstract, arid mythmaking geared explicitly to celebrating the system that spawned it.[29] Yet, strictly speaking, the adoption of such a celebratory, justificatory role did not represent destruction, but rather a remarkable transformation of the purpose and nature of social science. It is this great shift the historian must understand. It involved a fundamental revision of the purpose and position of social knowledge, as well as the place of social research in academia and its relationship with the regime. In both areas, the significant evolution of party scholarship within the most prominent bastions of the "Marxist social sciences" in the 1920s played a pivotal role.

The October Revolution can be seen as an extraordinary moment in the twentieth-century history of the social sciences—not merely for its ultimate destructiveness, but for the remarkable impetus it gave to their standing in the 1920s. In tsarist Russia, during the rise of social science after the 1860s, not only were Marxists virtually excluded from academia, but as Vucinich has shown, the search for a "science of society" and "most of the systematic sociological thought" was developed to a great extent outside the academic world. Instead, a major locus was the political-ideological movements of populism, anarchism, and Marxism.[30] Despite academic advances after the turn of the century, it was only the revolutionary state, in which Marxism was declared the official scientific ideology, which initially took an unprecedented interest in promoting social science in academia.

The Bolshevik scholars, theoreticians, and intellectuals in the new party sector in academia considered their camp synonymous with the Marxist social sciences, and in fact this primary supradisciplinary identity came to encompass the Marxist branches of disciplines such as liter-

29. Moshe Lewin, "Concluding Remarks," in Lewis H. Siegelbaum and Ronald Grigor Suny, *Making Workers Soviet: Power, Class, and Identity* (Ithaca: Cornell University Press, 1994), 381.

30. Alexander Vucinich, *Science in Russian Culture, 1861–1917* (Stanford, Calif.: Stanford University Press, 1970), 424–88, and his *Social Thought in Tsarist Russia: The Quest for a General Science of Society* (Chicago: University of Chicago Press, 1976).

ature and history, which in other academic worlds have been classified as humanities.[31] The new party academic institutions were hardly the only locus of social research involving Communists and Marxists in the 1920s. Yet the Bolshevik scholars and theoreticians there frequently equated their camp with the "Marxist social sciences" as a whole. These Bolshevik intellectuals in the 1920s viewed their *nauka* as the highest, most rigorous science and most privileged form of Marxism in a system that began to disseminate Marxist social knowledge in an entire hierarchy of settings. The paradox was that along with this rarified "scientific" self-conception, however, they embraced a cult of "practicality" and "current tasks" in their definitions of the purpose of scholarship and education; they were highly troubled by a scholarly, professorial, or even intellectual identity; and they became preoccupied with developing a service function that would directly harness scholarship for the Revolution and the party-state.

Such problems in the history of the Marxist social sciences reflect a particularly influential spectrum of tensions that plagued the nature and purpose of party scholarship in the 1920s, and especially the new party centers that were the heart of the growth in academic social science. These tensions ultimately had to do with reconciling the iconoclastic, outsider, even anti-academic proclivities of party scholarship with its new role as prestigious academic enterprise; with balancing revolutionary, proletarian, Bolshevik roles with the new status of scholars and academics; and with harmonizing their abstract Marxist theory with an embrace of practicality and service. None of these issues is simple or transparent. Yet in each case a significant evolution took place in the 1920s. Ultimately the delicate balancing act that party scholarship attempted to perform in each of these realms either broke down or led to wrenching adjustments within its own camp.

Power and the Bolshevik Intellectual Enterprise

It is no exaggeration to say that consideration of any kind of intellectual, scholarly, or cultural activity under communism must confront the relationship of the enterprise to the political system. One is confronted at each and every turn with relationships so central they have become encapsulated in convenient shorthand: power and culture, the Party and

31. Marxist social science had had as its core the three disciplines of political economy, history, and social philosophy ever since the rise of Marxism in Russia in the 1890s; not coincidentally, these disciplines were institutionalized in the three original departments of the Institute of Red Professors when it was founded in 1921.

the intelligentsia, politics and science. While the questions raised by them are hardly unique to Soviet studies, the dilemma here has always been how to grapple with what is ostensibly the extraordinarily overt predominance of the first of each pairing.

The history of Bolshevik higher learning provides a particularly interesting window into these problems because it comprises a distinct enterprise subject to party control, yet at the same time is itself so evidently a component of the Party, power, and politics. As a result, the manifestations of power and politics reveal themselves far beyond yet clearly involving intervention and control. In short, in this enterprise the underlying, everyday, implicit, systemic manifestations of power have seemed particularly unavoidable (while they can be more subtly disguised elsewhere); it is perhaps for this reason that the history of this enterprise can highlight a broader necessity of distinguishing between what might be called the pervasive and focused ramifications of power, politics, and polity.

Brute political Diktat played an unmistakable role. In fact, the extent of party-state intervention in higher learning emerges as more intrusive than often imagined, as it does in cultural and educational policy during NEP. However, such explanations—the "focused" aspects of power and politics—only advance our understanding so far. Bolshevik higher learning, it is impossible to forget, was integrated into the Party, functioned as part of the larger system, yet in its sphere represented a radical movement in its own right. The effects of intervention pale in comparison to the "pervasive" and frequently more subtle effects of power and politics as it affected its own enterprise—how patterns of authority, the Party's power hierarchy, and the extended environment of the communist political order in general influenced activity.

With this in mind, the process of change in Bolshevik higher learning—the many-layered transformation of the 1920s that is the central motif of this work—appears less frequently imposed than self-inflicted and unforeseen within this new enterprise, as, ever eyeing those it marked as rivals, the Bolshevik camp launched the first attempts to realize its own potent yet elusive aspirations.

Revolution of the Mind

The title of the book is emblematic of the Bolsheviks' transformative missions on the third front during the 1920s, in particular as they relate to higher learning. In its way such a simple slogan, the phrase, like the 1920s order that gave rise to it, harbors conflicts and contradictions. On the one hand, the phrase suggests that the life of the mind was revolutionized; on the other, it raises the possibility that the revolution itself brought to this realm was to a degree thought up, in that it was subject to imagination and revision. Both meanings assume importance in terms of a very particular dynamic with which the book is concerned. The institutions the Party erected on the third front attempted to bring the Revolution to the life of the mind; as the Bolshevik intellectuals embarked on the quest to achieve their many missions, however, they could not foresee how the very definition of the revolutionary was subject to a continual and often subtle process of reformulation. No matter how ultimately elusive the goals, the attempt to implement them began the process of associating the revolution in higher learning not solely with visions of the future, even while those persisted, but with the substantial strides the Party was already making. The Revolution was being filled with content on a new front.

1 / COMMUNIST INSTITUTIONS AND REVOLUTIONARY MISSIONS IN HIGHER LEARNING

From the first tentative innovations of the revolutionary underground to the rise of a unified system of party learning after 1920, the creation of educational institutions under Bolshevik Party auspices underwent a transformation of enormous scale and velocity—one that cuts to the heart of the relationship between Bolshevik missions and party institutions in revolutionary Russia. This historical vantage point affords some unexpected vistas.[1] The goals of party education, no matter how often overshadowed by utilitarian political concerns (the desperate need to train loyal party cadres), in a succession of widely differing periods consistently blended visions of long-range transformation with imperatives of the most immediate practical utility. This potent mix, embedded in this learning of a new type, allowed the making of party schools to play a decisive role in broadening the Bolshevik project on the third front.

Yet party education was reborn after 1917 as only one of several educational and academic movements whose various impulses had been

1. In the rare cases when party education has been examined at length by non-Soviet historians, it has invariably been put in the context of mass propaganda or examined separately as political education, that is, in contexts that isolate it from higher learning as a whole and tend to minimize its cultural dimensions. See Zev Katz, "Party-Political Education in Soviet Russia" (Ph.D. diss., University of London, 1957), and Kenez, *Birth*, 121–44. The best-known discussion of postrevolutionary higher education, Fitzpatrick's *Education*, is only peripherally concerned with party institutions.

well established in opposition to tsarist policies, and which seized the revolutionary moment to expand and institutionalize lower-class, mass, and adult education. In the civil war period, moreover, party education arose as one of the least visionary of several forms of education that became alternatives to prerevolutionary institutions, since short-term crash training programs dominated its agenda. Yet by 1920–21 party learning, from remedial to advanced, was constituted as both a unified academic system and a cultural-ideological movement, as a Bolshevik agenda on the third front was endorsed and linked to party institutions.

Just as revolutionary missions may lead to the creation of new institutions, those new institutions may in turn shape revolutionary missions, channeling and, in a sense, re-creating them. This dynamic, fraught with irony and subversion of intent, was an intrinsic part of the post–civil war rise of communist education as a vehicle for Bolshevik missions on the third front. As new communist institutions became entrenched in the 1920s, codifying their own type of learning and scholarship, and consolidating their own evolving culture and place in the party polity, they increasingly provided the basis for the model that Bolshevism had lacked in higher learning when the revolution came. Party education was traveling on a trajectory from a vehicle to a shaper of missions, from a revolutionary alternative to a part of the Soviet establishment.

For a crucial period in the 1920s, however, party academia remained an alternative challenge at the forefront of revolutionary missions on the cultural front. The rise of this party system bifurcated higher learning, in policy as in perception, as the Party created Bolshevik equivalents of academies, research institutes, universities, middle schools, and so on. It was party schools—more Marxist, more communist, and more proletarian than the old institutions—which claimed the mantle of revolution. Despite decisive changes the new order had brought to the old universities and VUZy, many policymakers began to analyze higher learning in terms of binary oppositions between old and new, state and party, universities and party schools, bourgeois and proletarian.

In the successive political-cultural shifts of the Great Break, the Great Retreat, and the Great Purges in the 1930s, all of higher education was at least outwardly Sovietized and Stalinized; the dual educational system of NEP lost its significance. With the early Soviet polarity between "bourgeois" and "red" muted if not obliterated, party education no longer commanded its extraordinary position of the 1920s. To be sure, party schools had become a permanent part of the system; in the 1930s, and especially after the reorganization of 1946, party education came to represent a vast training network encompassing higher schools for party cadres and political training for millions of adults. But never again were party institutions in a position directly to rival the conventional higher learning, and to influence the direction of organized intellectual life and central communist missions in so powerful a fashion.[2] In this sense, the heyday of Bolshevik party education was when the making of institutions was still intertwined with revolutionary attempts to jettison the old and define the new.

Capri, Bologna, and Longjumeau: Origins of Bolshevik Culture-Building, 1909–1911

Bolshevik education, given its singular importance for recruitment, inculcating rudimentary theory, and achieving "consciousness," had roots in practices in the revolutionary movement that predated the notion of an alternative "party" education and, for that matter, the existence of political parties in Russia. The incipient social-democratic movement of the 1880s inherited underground study circles, or *kruzhki*, as the most durable means of transmitting revolutionary ideas. For generations of expelled students and workers with little formal education, they also provided makeshift apprenticeships in the techniques of agitation and conspiracy.[3]

The Bolshevik wing of Russian Social-Democracy, formed in 1903 and almost immediately thrust into the Revolution of 1905, faced crisis and attrition in "period of reaction" following the suppression of the revolutionary movement and the Stolypin coup d'etat. Yet just as a system of party education was largely created amid perceptions of a post-revolutionary "retreat" in the 1920s, the first party schools emerged in post-1907 exile to attempt the transformation of workers into party leaders, intellectuals, and agents. The reversal of open revolutionary of-

2. As one study, referring to changes begun in the Stalin period, sums it up: "In most cases, a party education is remedial in nature, of low prestige, and a handicap to political mobility. The Soviet elite are for the most part trained in technical institutes and universities." Kenneth C. Farmer, *The Soviet Administrative Elite* (New York: Praeger, 1992), 32. See Tatjana Kirstein, "Das sowjetische Parteischulsystem," in Boris Meissner et al., eds., *Einparteisystem und bürokratische Herrschaft in der Sowjetunion* (Cologne: Markus Verlag, 1979), 199–230, and Ellen Propper Mickiewicz, *Soviet Political Schools: The Communist Party Adult Instruction System* (New Haven, Conn.: Yale University Press, 1967).

3. On social democratic *kruzhki*, see D. El'kina, *Ocherki po agitatsii, propagande i vneshkol'noi rabote v dorevoliutsionnoi Rossii* (Moscow-Leningrad: Gosizdat, 1930), 76–96, 105–20.

fensive thus led, in both experiences, to a decisive broadening of Bolshevik revolutionary goals in education, culture, and science.

No matter how short-lived the three party schools of 1909–11 proved, the experience that created them influenced the Bolshevik tradition. The maximalist dreamers of this epoch, the Left Bolshevik (Vpered) group led by the philosopher of proletarian culture, Aleksandr Bogdanov, were effectively defeated by the hardheaded "centrist" Leninists by 1912. But the victors proved susceptible to elements of the cultural dreams of their rivals, just as the Vperedists were no strangers to hardheaded politics and utilitarian cadre production. As a result, the Vperedists' innovative and organicist missions were wedded to the creation of party schools, even as the creation of party schools became enmeshed in Bolshevik high politics.

The German, French, and Belgian Social-Democratic parties were the first to found "higher party schools," the Germans in 1905, and this precedent was duly noted by Lenin's group after it had founded its own school at Longjumeau.[4] But the impetus behind the first Bolshevik schools was rooted in Russian circumstances that linked the enterprise not just to politics and culture but also to the making of a new intelligentsia. Such phenomena as the rise of adult education in industrial neighborhoods and the passage of several generations of lower-class revolutionaries through student *kruzhki* had led to widespread recognition of an intermediate stratum of educated "worker-intellectuals" after the turn of the century, who, by their very existence, bridged the venerable social gulf revolutionaries had so often yearned to span.[5] It was a self-educated rank-and-file worker organizer from the Urals known as comrade Mikhail (N. E. Vilonov) who proposed the idea of a "party university" to Maxim Gor'kii in 1908, and the idea gained support among several delegates traveling from Russia to the Fifth Party Conference a short time later.[6] Since a central political fact resonating throughout the entire Bolshevik faction in this period was the "flight of the intelligentsia" from the movement in the wake of 1905, calls were wide-

4. "Otchet pervoi partiinoi shkoly v Lonzhiumo," *Istoricheskii arkhiv*, no. 5 (September–October 1962): 43; N. A. Semashko, "O dvukh zagranichnykh partiinykh shkolakh," *Proletarskaia revoliutsiia*, no. 3 (March 1928): 143.

5. The worker-intellectuals have been explored especially in the work of Reginald Zelnik, most prominently in "Russian Bebels: An Introduction to the Memoirs of the Russian Workers Semen Kanatchikov and Matvei Fisher," *Russian Review* 35 (July 1976): 249–89, and 35 (October 1976): 417–47.

6. Ralph Carter Elwood, "Lenin and the Social Democratic Schools for Underground Party Workers, 1909–11," *Political Science Quarterly* 81 (September 1966): 371–75.

spread to replace the much-denounced fickle intellectuals with a new group of workers educated in Marxist theory and party organizational skills.[7] In July 1909 Bogdanov and the engineer-turned-insurrectionist Leonid B. Krasin issued a call for a "new type of party school" that would prepare "reliable and conscious" working-class leaders, endowing them with the knowledge and the discipline of mind that *intelligenty* received in higher schools.[8] From here it was but a step to associating the handful of workers attending the "underground" schools with the birth of "our own" proletarian intelligentsia. Party education began as an attempt to replace wayward *intelligenty* with reliable workers, a modest effort immediately endowed with grandiose symbolic resonance; it blossomed after 1917 into a quest ultimately to supplant the "old intelligentsia" *tout court*.

The Leninists and Vperedists teetered on the verge of a split in Bolshevism; Lunacharskii later dubbed it a "semi-schism."[9] Yet the recent rediscovery of the political, philosophical, and cultural dimensions of the prewar ferment have identified it as a major development in the history of the revolutionary movement and Russian Marxism. Politically, the phenomenon of "anti-Leninist Bolshevism" has called attention to early Bolshevism's nonmonolithic character. Philosophically, the new trends embraced by Bogdanov and colleagues gave more weight to the role of consciousness and culture than Lenin's Plekhanovian orthodoxy.[10] Left Bolshevism thus emerged as a Marxist parallel with modernist cultural movements that aimed at a kind of "secular religion of

7. Ibid., 371; Jutta Scherrer, "Les écoles du Parti de Capri et de Bologna: La formation de l'intelligentsia du Parti," *Cahiers du monde russe et soviétique* 19 (July–September 1978): 259 and passim; V. Kosarev, "Partiinaia shkola na ostrove Kapri," *Sibirskie ogni*, no. 2 (May–June 1922): 63; Semashko, "O dvukh," 143–44.

8. "Otchet tovarishcham-bol'shevikam ustranennykh chlenov rasshirennoi redaktsii Proletariia," 3 July 1909, in N. S. Antonova and N. V. Drozdova, comps., *Neizvestnyi Bogdanov* (Moscow: ITs "AIRO-XX," 1995), 2:175–76 (hereafter cited as *Neizvestnyi Bogdanov* by volume and page numbers).

9. A. V. Lunacharskii, introduction to S. Livshits, "Partiinaia shkola v Bolon'e (1910–1911 gg.)," *Proletarskaia revoliutsiia*, no. 3 (March 1926): 111. One of the best accounts of the many dimensions of the Left Bolshevik challenge is Robert C. Williams, *The Other Bolsheviks: Lenin and His Critics, 1904–1914* (Bloomington: Indiana University Press, 1986).

10. Aileen M. Kelly, "Red Queen or White Knight? The Ambivalences of Bogdanov," *Russian Review* 49 (July 1990): 311, and "Empiriocriticism: A Bolshevik Philosophy?" *Cahiers du monde russe et soviétique* 22 (January–March 1981): 89–118; Andrzej S. Walicki, "Alexander Bogdanov and the Problem of the Socialist Intelligentsia," *Russian Review* 49 (July 1990): 293–304. On the ideological and philosophical dimensions of the Vperedism, see especially Jutta Scherrer, "La crise de l'intelligentsia Marxiste avant 1914: A. V. Lunačarskij et le bogostroitel'stvo," *Revue des études slaves* 51, no. 1–2 (1978): 207–15, and "'Ein gelber und ein blauer Teufel': Zur Entstehung der Begriffe 'bogostroitel'stvo' und 'bogoiskatel'stvo,'" *Forschungen zur osteuropäischen Geschichte* 25 (1978): 319–29.

the one."[11] The creed of these innovative Bolsheviks intertwined making revolution with the creation of a collectivist, proletarian culture that would usher in a new kind of art, literature, and science.

Yet these origins of what later became central communist cultural missions in the 1920s have been interpreted, like the NEP era when many of them were mobilized, largely through a constricting choice between counterfactual "alternatives" and the seeds of totalitarianism. Bogdanovism has appealed to some as a lost choice, a libertarian program for worker self-empowerment that contrasts with the authoritarian tutelage of Lenin's professional revolutionaries; to others, the Vperedist vision of the socialist intellectual, as arbiter of the group's new theories of collective consciousness and proletarian culture, sowed the seeds of totalitarian domination in realms passed over by the Leninists.[12]

This rigid dichotomy has slighted both Vperedist and Leninist practice and interaction. Despite the voluminous literature on Bogdanov and Vperedism, the major organizational achievement of the Left Bolsheviks, the party schools at Capri and Bologna, have not been analytically compared to Lenin's school at Longjumeau. I suggest a degree of cross-fertilization occurred, that distinctively Vperedist innovations passed into and informed Bolshevik traditions even as party education and cultural agendas remained at a nascent stage. I argue that party education, since it in many ways transcended factional lines, was flexible enough to accommodate both ambitions for cultural revolution and the pressing political tasks of providing a crash program for loyal cadres. Not only did such a blend of utopian vision and cadre politics become quintessential Bolshevism; the dual emphasis endowed party education with a lasting importance to those Leninists who emphasized political instruction above all and those former Vperedists who especially yearned for

11. Katerina Clark, *Petersburg, Crucible of Cultural Revolution* (Cambridge: Harvard University Press, 1995), 17. Little-known Vperedist connections to avant-garde groups—in particular to those attempting to create an "academy" of artists and revolutionaries around 1912—are discussed in John Biggart, "The 'Russian Academy' and the Journal *Gelios*," *Sbornik*, no. 5 (Summer 1980): 17–27. In addition to their links with Vperedists concerned with proletarian cultural revolution, at least one of these modernists involved in this venture, Oskar M. Leshchinskii, also reportedly helped organize the Lenin's Longjumeau school outside Paris (21).

12. The libertarian aspects of Vperedism have been promoted most forcefully by Zenovia Sochor in *Revolution and Culture: The Bogdanov-Lenin Controversy* (Ithaca: Cornell University Press, 1981); Kelly and John Eric Marot, from different angles, underline the authoritarian potentialities of Vperedism. See Marot, "Alexander Bogdanov, Vpered, and the Role of the Intellectual in the Workers' Movement," *Russian Review* 49 (July 1990): 242–48, and responses, 283–315.

the advent of a new culture through the vehicle of a proletarian intelligentsia.

The two schools for "party propagandists" that the Vpered group organized at Capri and Bologna, and Lenin's counter-school in the Paris suburb of Longjumeau, despite their brief existence and limitation to several dozen workers sent by party committees in Russia, had a far greater impact than their size or longevity suggest. Lenin attempted successfully to "disorganize" his rivals by provoking splits among their students, by luring them to Paris, and by using all the means at his disposal to have the Capri and Bologna schools branded "factional" and even "anti-party." This, combined with the Vpered group's natural inclination to use the schools to train its own loyalists, ensured that party high politics in these years revolved around the schools.[13] One result was that party education was assured a place of permanent importance in the Bolshevik tradition.

It was significant for the making of this tradition, however, that Capri, Bologna, and Longjumeau schools were in fact not completely "factional" institutions. The schools were founded amid endless maneuverings and negotiations, which broke down in mutual recriminations, to create a nonfactional "general-party school."[14] As a result both groups attempted to give their own schools an "all-party" rather than just a factional list of lecturers; Lunacharskii, for example, lectured on art and culture at all three institutions.[15] Most important, all established educational agendas combining similarly defined realms of party theory, current politics, and practical revolutionary training. The utilitarian and party-political aspects of education were no less present at the Vperedist schools.

None of the schools can be understood without keeping in mind a

13. V. I. Lenin, "Uchenikam Kapriiskoi shkoly," in *Pol'noe sobranie sochinenii* (henceforth cited as "*PSS*") (Moscow: Politizdat, 1964), 47:202. The most detailed accounts of the political maneuvering surrounding the schools are in two articles by S. I. Livshits, "Kapriiskaia partiinaia shkola (1909 g.)," *Proletarskaia revoliutsiia*, no. 6 (June 1924): 33–73, and "Partiinaia shkola v Bolon'e."

14. "Sekretar' gruppy 'Vpered' Maksimov (A. A. Bogdanov). V Komitet shkoly pri Ts.K. ot gruppy 'Vpered,'" 7 June 1910, RTsKhIDNI f. 338, op. 1, d. 1, l. 1, and d. 4, l. 5; Andrei B. Rogachevskii, "Social Democratic Party Schools on Capri and in Bologna in the Correspondence between A. A. Bogdanov and A. V. Amifteatrov," *Slavonic and East European Review* 72 (October 1994): 673.

15. Lunacharskii and another Vperedist, the philosopher Stanislav Vol'skii, participated at Longjumeau along with a Bundist, a Polish Social Democrat, a Menshevik, and two "nonfactional" Russian Social Democrats. Similarly, the Bologna school boasted the participation of such non-Vperedists as Trotskii, Aleksandra M. Kollontai, and the Menshevik Vel'tman-Pavlovich (Volonter). "Otchet pervoi partiinoi shkoly," 47; Livshits, "Bolon'e," 132.

basic fact later discussed by one of the Capri students, a certain Kosarev: he and his group were being prepared in the space of a few months to set off to do illegal party work in a provincial Russian city, where after three to six months they could expect arrest or at best relocation to a new assignment.[16] At a time when the connections of the émigré revolutionaries to the empire were strained, it was obvious that the schools offered a great opportunity to cultivate loyalist followers. One is struck by the repeated assertion that for the Vperedists a major goal behind the schools was to train their own corps of agents (*agentura*). Lunacharskii later recalled, "Above all Bogdanov wanted to organize this whole top echelon of Vperedism as a strong propaganda center with its own journal and its own *agentura*. The *agentura* had to be recruited . . . with the help of these schools."[17] The charge dated back to June 1909, when the Bolshevik Center claimed that "the initiators of this [Capri] school . . . are organizing their own *agentura*."[18]

The accuracy of this accusation was in a sense unimportant, for Lenin not only believed the story but admired the example. In a letter to Rykov in 1911, Lenin enviously referred to the Bogdanovites' strength in maintaining a school and a group of agents. While Kosarev later claimed "Bogdanov's group from the beginning conducted affairs so that during class time there was never talk of empirio-monism or of recallism," he acknowledged that "this measure did not change anything." A schism occurred at Capri when students leaning toward Lenin protested about factional instruction, and after being expelled by the school soviet five students made their way to Paris.[19]

In the summer of 1911 in Longjumeau, Lenin was certainly no less assiduous in using his school to recruit workers loyal to his faction. The Bolshevik Center, as Krupskaia noted in her obituary of Longjumeau lecturer Inessa Armand, was above all concerned with strengthening its ties within Russia, a motivation which also led to its relocation to Kraków in 1912. The best-known alumnus of Longjumeau, the future Politburo member and commissar of heavy industry in the 1930s, Sergo

16. Kosarev, "Partiinaia shkola."

17. Lunacharskii, introduction to Livshits, "Bolon'e," 113. See also St. Krivtsov, "Pamiati A. A. Bogdanova," *PZM*, no. 4 (April 1928): 183.

18. V. I. Lenin, "O partiinoi shkole, ustraivaemoi za granitsei v NN," in *PSS*, 19:41.

19. John Biggart, "Predislovie: 'Antileninskii bol'shevizm,'" in Antonova and Drozdova, *Neizvestnyi Bogdanov*, 2:18; Kosarev, "Partiinaia shkola," 69; "Doklad v Shkol'nyi Komitet RSDRP," no date, RTsKhIDNI f. 338, op. 1, d. 5, l. 3–11; Livshits, "Kapriiskaia partiinaia shkola," 56. "Recallism" (*otzovizm*) refers to opposition to participation by Bolshevik deputies in the Duma, "empirio-monism" or "empiriocriticism" to Bogdanov's philosophy.

Ordzhonikidze, thus accepted in 1911 the "obligatory condition" for participation in the school, which was to return to Russia on party work upon completion of the course. With Bogdanov's Left Bolshevism already faltering in 1911, Lenin turned the potentialities of the Longjumeau school to use in his struggle with the Mensheviks. Of the eighteen delegates to the all-Bolshevik Sixth Party Congress Lenin convened in Prague on 18 January 1912, eight had been present at Longjumeau and the rest had been recruited by Longjumeau graduates.[20]

While cadre production exerted strong appeal to all those involved in Bolshevik party education, it was the Vpered group which from the first attached the enterprise firmly to a project of cultural transformation. Clark observes, "Marx and Lenin saw a socioeconomic revolution as a precondition of any spiritual revolution; most non-Marxist anticapitalists (and some Bolshevik intellectuals) insisted that this sequence had to be played in reverse."[21] Those Bolsheviks struggling to reconcile the primacy of culture and consciousness with Marxism were, of course, the Vperedists and their heirs. The Vpered platform of 1909 first advanced the "slogan" of proletarian culture. Bourgeois culture, it maintained, had shaped contemporary science, art, and philosophy, and to accept it meant to "preserve the past within us." Under the rubric of the new socialist culture that would be "created" and "spread among the masses" a new science, a new art, and a new philosophy would emerge. In such a way the Vperedists recast socialist "consciousness" as a sociocultural as well as a political phenomenon; through revolution the proletariat would achieve not just political predominance but cultural hegemony.[22] The Vpered platform thus suggested the deliberate reconstruction of the entire "superstructure"; even its preoccupation with replacing the very "habits" of bourgeois individualism presaged the communist movement's attempt to introduce a new everyday life. The means of conveying this new culture would be a "total [*tselostnoe*] socialist upbringing." The notion that "socialist proletarian culture" would flow from the "spiritual unity" of the "living, complete organism" of the proletariat was developed by Bogdanov in 1910; the organic metaphor led to a definition of a "new *nauka*," which would triumph

20. Nadezhda K. Krupskaia, "Inessa Armand (1875–1920)," no date, 1920, RTsKhIDNI f. 12, op. 1, d. 47, l. 29; Kosarev, "Partiinaia shkola," 70; "V komitet partiinoi shkoly pri TsKRSDRP," signed "Sergo," no later than 6 May (23 April) 1911, RTsKhIDNI f. 338, op. 1, d. 16, l. 1; Elwood, "Underground Party Workers," 390–91.

21. Clark, *Petersburg*, 21.

22. The point is underscored by John Biggart, "'Anti-Leninist Bolshevism': The *Forward* Group of the RSDRP," *Canadian Slavonic Papers* 23 (June 1981): 134–53.

over specialization and "strive toward simplification and unification of science."[23]

Party educational institutions found a major place in this transformative agenda from the first. Moving from cultural quest to institution-building, the Vpered platform called for the "elaboration of a higher form of institution" in order to create an "overall and complete" socialist "upbringing." The heavy-handed organicism may have been particularly Vperedist at this time, but there is evidence that Leninists echoed the Vperedist rhetoric of creating a new proletarian intelligentsia.[24]

Reflecting the several levels of aspirations built into their mission, the curricula of all three schools mixed abstract theory with practical skills. In 1909, the revolutionary worker-students gathered at Capri, in the incongruous setting of Gor'kii's aristocratic villa on the island resort of Roman emperors. There they devoted a major portion of their time, not only to lectures on political economy and other subjects, but also to such "practical" topics as "approaches and methods of agitational influences over the masses," practice polemics with representatives of other political parties, techniques of underground publishing, and ciphers and codes. Aside from the practical training and main section of theoretical studies, the newest concerns of the Vperedists were reflected in a smaller section on literature, art, socialist culture, and "societal worldviews" (these subjects comprised a cycle on the "philosophy of the proletarian struggle") and study of the current political situation. With much of the abstract talk at Capri apparently going over the heads of the worker-students, however, the Vperedists took steps to make the second, Bologna school, held in part at the Garibaldi University, include more of such "practical" training and a less theoretical approach. The champions of proletarian culture, who at times heroicized the proletariat in their writings as more authentically intellectual than the intelligentsia, were forced from the very outset to modify their enterprise by the living objects of their theories.[25]

The Longjumeau studies, conducted largely in a metalworkers' shop

23. "Sovremennoe polozhenie i zadachi partii. Platforma, vyrabotannaia gruppoi bol'shevikov," in Antonova and Drozdova, *Neizvestnyi Bogdanov*, 2:37–61, and A. A. Bogdanov, "Sotsializm v nastoiashchem," in Antonova and Drozdova, *Neizvestnyi Bogdanov*, 2:93–95.

24. "Sovremennoe polozhenie," 61, and "Otchet tovarishcham-bol'shevikam," in Antonova and Drozdova, *Neizvestnyi Bogdanov*, 2:175; "Mitglieder der Schulkommission an die Depositäre," Paris, 5 August 1911, in Dietrich Geyer, ed., *Kautskys russische Dossier: Deutsche Sozialdemokraten als Treuhänder des russischen Parteivermögens, 1910–1915* (Frankfurt: Campus Verlag, 1981), 430.

25. Livshits, "Kapriiskaia partiinaia shkola," 59–63; Scherrer, "Les écoles," 271; Elwood, "Underground Party Workers," 378; Clark, *Petersburg*, 19, 83.

Mikhail Nikolaevich Pokrovskii, Anatolii Vasil'evich Lunacharskii, and Martyn Nikolaevich Liadov (first row, second, third and fourth from left respectively) with former students of the Capri School—the first Bolshevik party school, organized in Maxim Gor'kii's villa on the island of Capri in 1909 by the Vpered group of the Russian Social-Democratic Labor Party. The photo was taken in 1926. Reprinted by permission of the Museum of the Revolution, Moscow, Russia.

rented by Inessa Armand in the one-street village south of Paris, were similarly divided into theory, tactical problems, current party life, and practical work. The practical training included such projects as producing a mock-up of a trade union journal. But if anything, the Longjumeau school was *less* concerned than its Vperedist counterparts with imparting the techniques and skills of the underground; as Ralph Carter Elwood notes, "Some of the students later criticized this lack of practical training." Of the major components initially included in party education—theory, practical training, and current politics—the Vperedist schools stressed the first two elements, with a special excursion into culture, whereas Longjumeau especially emphasized political instruction. Lenin's lieutenants Zinov'ev and Kamenev, for example, focused their lectures on Duma tactics, the programs of various parties, and current political problems.[26] All elements, however, were represented at all three schools.

The allocation of time for the "academic" or theoretical portions of the program at all three schools, moreover, reflected a common hierarchy of concerns. At Bologna, for example, they were dominated by Bogdanov's lectures in political economy, followed by several lecturers' courses on the history of socialism in Europe and Russia; next were the lectures by Martyn N. Liadov and Mikhail N. Pokrovskii on party and Russian history, followed by topics considered more specialized, such as the agrarian question and international politics. Lunacharskii held eight lectures, the fewest of any course, on the history of Russian literature. Lenin's Longjumeau school structured lecture time in a manner quite similar to the schools at Capri and Bologna: Lenin gave most of the lectures on political economy, followed by Zinov'ev and Kamenev on Social Democracy in Russia and the political parties, and concluding with more specialized topics such as the national and agrarian questions. Lunacharskii taught literature and art at Longjumeau as well, but in only four lectures, which he supplemented by leading his students on tours of the Louvre.[27]

The parallels between Longjumeau and the Vperedist institutions suggest that Lenin's school was deliberately modeled on the Vperedist experiments. The Longjumeau school, founded in the wake of the school on Capri, faced the task of proving to a party audience that the Leninists were as capable in proletarian education as in political maneuvering; in retrospect it seems that the Leninists had scrutinized their rivals' activities so intensely that some degree of emulation was unavoidable, whether fully deliberate or not. For example, the Central Committee's School Committee, dominated by Lenin through his proxy Zinov'ev, received a report of a defecting student from Bologna that catalogued that school's activities and organization down to the contents of breakfast (coffee, rolls, and butter).[28]

The vital importance the Bolshevik leaders placed on party education,

26. Elwood, "Underground Party Workers," 387, Semashko, "O dvukh," and "Partiinaia shkola pod Parizhem," *Proletarskaia revoliutsiia*, no. 14 (1923): 605–7.

27. Livshits, "Bolon'e," 132–33, and "Kapriiskaia partiinaia shkola," 58; "Otchet pervoi partiinoi shkoly," 46–47.

28. "Doklad v Shkol'nyi komitet RSDRP" (cited in full at n.19).

the reasons the factions debated the schools so hotly, rested not on the education itself, but on the manifold results expected from it. Bolshevik party education, whether Leninist or Vperedist, was expected above all to produce loyal cadres, if not, in some sense, new men—whether professional revolutionaries or proletarian intellectuals.

At the same time, the common hierarchy of academic topics indicates strongly held assumptions about how to impart theory and hence higher consciousness; despite the preponderance of utilitarian goals, the curricula suggest that the transformational value of theory (if not culture) was accepted by the Leninists' school as well as by the Vperedists. Party education was launched with a preponderance of extra-academic goals defining its importance, and, simultaneously, a scholastic belief that proper party education required acquisition of a body of theory that was intrinsically necessary for all educated Bolsheviks. The curriculum, designed as a program in general party education, preserved a distinct hierarchy of "party" subjects that were in their own way specialized. Latent tensions can therefore be detected in the nascent party education between general education and specialization, theory and practice, scholasticism and revolutionary practicality.

For Leninists and the Vperedists, in the end the question of cadres carried with it the promise of a future social transformation. Lenin's conceptualization of this revolved around his well-known ideal of a stratum of professional revolutionaries (although, it has been pointed out, his condemnation of slavish, passive Russian "Oblomovism," and related yearning for a *homo novus* inherited from Chernyshevskii, can be regarded as a precursor to his call for cultural revolution in the early 1920s).[29] For the Vperedists, the social dimension of pedagogy was linked to the concept of a workers' intelligentsia, a collectivity of proletarian culture-creators. The two concepts, however different ideologically (their differences were not so great that they prevented Lenin's reconciliation with Gor'kii and Lunacharskii, if not Bogdanov) overlapped in certain key respects. Both assumed a hierarchical ladder of consciousness. Both proposed to overcome the division between intelligentsia and workers through a new identity. In both cases party education was to be the basis for the formation of a new social group, a stratum of model leaders. A major divergence in the two approaches—

29. Mikhail Agursky, "Nietzschean Roots of Stalinist Culture," in Bernice Glatzer Rosenthal, ed., *Nietzsche and Soviet Culture* (Cambridge: Cambridge University Press, 1994), 258–59. Unfortunately, the author's treatment of Lenin is skewed toward attempting to prove parallels with Nietzscheanism.

the Vperedist insistence that a new culture be built as a precondition for socialist revolution—became less significant although not irrelevant after 1917.

Longjumeau, however, marked Lenin's only significant involvement in a party school. The greater concern of the Vpered group with cultural questions attracted them both to the proletarian culture movement and to party education, where they had far more impact than Lenin's immediate entourage. Leading Vperedist intellectuals—Bogdanov, Gor′kii, Lunacharskii, Pokrovskii, Liadov, Lebedev-Polianskii, as well as the Bogdanov-influenced Bukharin—later founded and played leading roles in the foremost institutions of proletarian and party education. Of the participants at Longjumeau only Krupskaia, the Bolsheviks' leading pedagogical writer, and the "nonfactional" Marx scholar David Borisovich Riazanov made major commitments to party education.

The Vperedists' overriding concern with education and culture was novel to Bolshevik movement, but became an integral part of Bolshevism that broadened the scope of the Party's agenda. As party education was launched, it embodied a combination, or perhaps conflation of immediate party-political concerns and long-term transformation. It therefore retained its vitality for those, like the Vperedists, who placed primary emphasis on sociocultural aspirations, and for others, like Lenin, who demanded above all political action. As yet lacking were a mass movement, the taste of social revolution, and confrontation with a genuine representation of the old society rather than the posturing of a semi-schism.

Co-opt and Conquer: People's, Proletarian, and Party Education

The Bolsheviks came to power with few concrete plans for higher learning's postrevolutionary future and a lengthy experience of viewing Russia's universities with profound ambivalence. The student movement had proven a prime recruiting ground for the revolutionary parties, but was also steeped in communitarian traditions that did not necessarily revolve around the revolutionary struggle.[30] The academic intelligentsia's obsession with pure science and institutional autonomy

30. See especially Susan Morrissey, "More 'Stories about the New People': Student Radicalism, Higher Education, and Social Identity in Russia, 1899–1921" (Ph.D. diss., University of California at Berkeley, 1993).

had been forged in a half-century of skirmishes with tsarist authorities, but many Bolsheviks, particularly after 1905, derided such concerns as the illusions of a bourgeois elite. Nevertheless, these primary values of the mainstream professoriat (in sharp contrast to its more elitist model, the German professoriat) were tempered by a commitment to social reform and popular enlightenment. This provided some common ground with revolutionaries also caught up in an enlightenment movement. Moreover, for several months after October the new regime was too weak and preoccupied to take any substantive initiatives in academia. In the first half of 1918 top Narkompros officials Lunacharskii and Krupskaia seemed actually to endorse the venerable ideal of institutional autonomy.[31]

The October Revolution thus seemed initially to hold an uncertain or ambiguous meaning for the world of higher learning. But between 1918 and 1920 a program took shape that made the mass education of workers and party members an essential part of the communist revolutionary agenda—and again began to link culture-building to institution-building, systems of education to systems of thought. This transformation, however, was by no means an inexorable progression. Since the war effort and economic crisis prevented full-fledged Bolshevik initiatives in the cultural realm in general and prevented much more than a cycle of threats and standoffs with the nonparty professoriat in the old universities, "war communism" witnessed a chaotic flowering of trends that had reformist prerevolutionary roots but had remained stymied before 1917. Indeed, many of the academic causes of the civil war period can be understood in this light. The exuberant mushrooming of new institutions (many of which never survived or existed only on paper), the move in the midst of dire hardship toward specialized and applied scientific-research institutes, initiatives in long-slighted higher technical education, and above all the explosion of general educational opportunities for adults and the underprivileged all came out of long-standing impulses that were quickened by revolution. In 1917 and after, for example, almost every province and major city tried to found its own university, and the number of new higher educational and academic institutions of all kinds shot upward (only to be sharply restricted in the fiscal austerity of NEP). At the same time, a militarized and centralized Bolshevik party was growing in the womb of this de facto decentraliza-

31. On the above points, James C. McClelland, "The Professoriate in the Russian Civil War," in Diane P. Koenker et al., eds., *Party, State, and Society in the Russian Civil War* (Bloomington: Indiana University Press, 1989), 243–56.

tion and these various initiatives of the nonparty intelligentsia—which would in turn have an impact on the Bolshevik agenda once the red side achieved victory and turned its attention to the cultural front. There is an analogy here with the manner in which avant-garde cultural groups seized the opportunity of revolution to shape the mass festivals and revolutionary art that in many ways defined war communist culture.[32]

Party education emerged in particular proximity with adult and working-class educational initiatives, above all the people's university and proletarian culture movements. The first had its roots in the enlightening ethos of the liberal academic intelligentsia; the second was left socialist and linked to the Vperedists tradition and Proletkul't, the ex-Bolshevik Bogdanov's new mass movement for proletarian culture.

The "people's universities" arose in 1905 and after as a response and alternative to the contradictory foundations of late imperial higher educational policy. In broadest terms, tsarist policy attempted to increase the numbers of qualified candidates to the bureaucracy and professions while maintaining the social hierarchy of the estate (*soslovie*) order and to expand or diversify higher education without conceding more autonomy to the universities and intelligentsia.[33] The new institutions and their sponsors aspired to provide education to people from all estates, to become institutions free of state intervention, and to spread science and enlightenment among the masses. They emerged on the heels of several decades of organized secular general education for adults in "Sunday schools" and elsewhere, and in fact the very term "people's universities" apparently originated in the Russian translation of an 1897 book on university extension programs in England and the United States.[34] People's universities were initially made possible by allocation of funds from city dumas, the first in Nizhnii-Novgorod in 1905; St. Petersburg followed in 1907 and Kharkov in 1909.

The best-known people's university and the leader of the movement, however, was Moscow's Shaniavskii University. It was founded by a retired officer who had made a fortune in the gold industry and had

32. N. I. Cheliapov, "Vysshee uchebnye zavedeniia RSFSR," in *Pedagogicheskaia entsiklopediia* (Moscow: Rabotnik prosveshcheniia, 1930), 3:183–95; James von Geldern, *Bolshevik Festivals, 1917–1920* (Berkeley: University of California Press, 1993).

33. This idea is developed by Peter H. Kneen, "Higher Education and Cultural Revolution in the USSR," CREES Discussion Papers, Soviet Industrialization Project Series, no. 5, University of Birmingham, 1976, 4–27.

34. David Currie Lee, *The People's Universities of the USSR* (New York: Greenwood Press, 1988), 20–22.

previously donated large sums to women's medical education. This link was not coincidental: the movement to create university-level courses for women, still barred from the universities, was an integral part of the "social-pedagogical" movement that intensified in the late nineteenth century to create a "free" (*vol'nyi*) university outside state control, independent of state subsidies, open to both sexes, and free of restrictions by nationality and estate. Conservatives in the Ministry of Education and professoriat were the main opponents of this movement, and virtually all but the most famous "women's university," the Bestuzhev Courses in Petersburg, were closed down during the era of counterreforms. But when the tsar lifted the ban on opening private higher educational institutions at the end of the revolutionary year 1905, a spurt of growth in both higher women's courses and people's universities began which lasted until the war. Shaniavskii University opened its doors in 1908 after a lengthy battle with tsarist authorities, admiting 975 students in its first year and 5,372 in 1914. It accepted all students over sixteen years of age without requirements, offered tuition waivers, and featured lectures (always in the evening) by some of the outstanding liberal academic figures of the age.[35]

Politically, the school was reportedly dominated by liberals and Kadets, who rejected the notion of "class" institutions. At the first Congress of People's Universities and Other Institutions of Private Initiative in 1908, trade-union calls to orient the institutions primarily toward the working-class were voted down. Yet future Bolshevik controversies were prefigured in the split between Shaniavskii organizers, who wished to "democratize access to scientific knowledge without compromising that knowledge" and others in the movement who viewed the popularization of knowledge as the beginning of "the very democratization of science itself." Despite the generally liberal and liberal-populist orientation of the movement, however, social-democratic factions were organized within the institutions, and one source claims that involvement in the people's universities was the first legal educational activity in Russia in which the Bolsheviks were involved.[36]

35. V. G. Kinelev, ed., *Vysshee obrazovanie v Rossii. Ocherk istorii do 1917 goda* (Moscow: NII VO, 1995), 131–38; S. N. Valk et al., eds., *Sankt-Peterburgskie Vysshie zhenskie (Bestuzhevskie) kursy (1878–1918 gg.). Sbornik statei* (Leningrad: Izdatel'stvo Leningradskogo Universiteta, 1965); Morrissey, "More Stories," 325–84.

36. Lee, *People's Universities*, 26–29, 46–47, 39 n. 29; El'kina, *Ocherki po agitatsii*, 209–15; V. R. Leikina-Svirskaia, *Russkaia intelligentsiia v 1900–1917 godakh* (Moscow: Mysl', 1981), 104–5; James C. McClelland, *Autocrats and Academics: Education, Culture, and Society in Tsarist Russia* (Chicago: University of Chicago Press, 1979), 93–94; Kinelev, *Vysshee obrazovanie*, 139–44.

People's education and certain of its cherished goals influenced all the socialist parties, including the Bolsheviks. Early Soviet decrees opened higher education to all citizens over sixteen years of age free of charge; Pokrovskii's first pronouncement on higher educational reform adopted the rhetoric of the "democratization" rather than proletarianization or party control of higher learning.[37] The special concern with adult or "extramural" education after 1917 also had obvious prerevolutionary roots.

Behind the dramatic civil-war era expansion of higher education several movements coexisted. Not only did the well-established impulses of the people's education movement flourish; newly invigorated tendencies of proletarian and party education emerged. Yet these educational movements, all alternatives to the established academic system, must be identified as ideal types, because in many newly created institutions they seem invariably to have been mixed.

The founding of new people's universities gained the approval of Narkompros immediately after 1917, for example, and one source claims 101 such institutions existed in the RSFSR in 1919. If "people's" education came to represent general education for all classes, however, "proletarian" education championed class principles; its ideals were not placed in "general enlightenment" but in the controversial notion of the proletarianization of culture and science. In practice, however, when people's universities came under attack for their apolitical character and "liberal" stress on enlightenment for its own sake, many simply changed their names to proletarian universities.[38]

The Proletkul't universities, part of Bogdanov's mass movement for proletarian culture which attempted to retain its independence from the Communist Party, were the most visible exemplars of civil war proletarian education; however, Bogdanov himself complained that many of the lesser-known Proletkul't institutions that sprang up in this period, such as the Karl Marx University of Proletarian Culture in Tver', in fact retained traditional curricula similar to those of the prerevolutionary people's universities and for his taste were not nearly proletarian enough in social composition. He made similar criticisms even about the first Proletarian University in Moscow, which was jointly opened by Proletkul't, the Moscow city soviet, and the local Narkompros division in the

37. "O pravilakh priema v vysshie uchebnye zavedeniia. Dekret SNK RSFSR ot 2 avgusta 1918," in N. I. Boldyrev, ed., *Direktivy i postanovleniia sovetskogo pravitel'stva o narodnom obrazovanii. Sbornik dokumentov za 1917–1947* (Moscow-Leningrad: Izdatel'stvo Akademii Pedagogicheskikh Nauk RSFSR, 1947), 3–4; Domov [M. N. Pokrovskii], "Reforma vysshei shkoly," *Narodnoe prosveshchenie*, no. 4–5 (1918): 31–36.

38. Lee, *People's Universities*, 50–51; M. Smit, "Proletarizatsiia nauki," *Proletarskaia revoliutsiia*, no. 11–12 (December 1919): 27–33.

spring of 1918, but soon fell prey to conflicts among its sponsors. In March of 1919, Proletkul't began anew by opening the Karl Liebknecht Proletarian University; its 400 students were mostly workers and peasants and the curriculum bore the imprint of the interdisciplinary tenets of Bogdanovian proletarian science.[39]

Party education, which can be understood as educational endeavors under the auspices of Communist Party organizations, stressed the party affiliation of its students and at first was almost exclusively associated with crash courses. But party education maintained its original combination of practical, political, and theoretical training and at this time also began to orient itself toward both mass enlightenment and the proletarianization of the higher school.

To be sure, courses for party workers set up under party auspices initially revolved mostly around rapid training of agitators and apparatchiks rather than the birth of a new kind of learning, and in these endeavors there was very little centralization until late 1920. Moreover, the efforts of party organizations were hardly cordoned off from the efforts of other Soviet organizations, most notably the Red Army. Like the local party committees, the largest "school of socialism" was deeply involved in organizing short-term instructional courses and training for party members, but chaotic conditions hindered centralization before 1920. Virtually all the Central Committee Secretariat could do was issue warnings about such matters as the reliability of the teaching staff.[40] The Central Committee sponsored its own institution, which became the most prominent party educational institution in this period, the future Sverdlov Communist University. Nevertheless, some party institutions, like the adult education movement, emphasized general education, teaching courses in natural sciences and literary skills, as well as aspiring to give precedence to students of proletarian origin and transmit Marxist and Bolshevik doctrine. In short, party education in this

39. Lynn Mally, *Culture of the Future: The Proletkult Movement in Revolutionary Russia* (Berkeley: University of California Press, 1990), 165–73; Sheila Fitzpatrick, *The Commissariat of Enlightenment: Soviet Organization of Education and the Arts under Lunacharsky, October 1917–1921* (Cambridge: Cambridge University Press, 1970), 101–4, 106; Read, *Culture and Power*, 131–33; S. Zander, "Vysshaia shkola i proletarskii universitet," *Proletarskaia kul'tura*, no. 20–21 (January–June 1921): 19–27; and "Pis'mo A. A. Bogdanova neustanovlennomu adresantu," 24 November 1920, RTsKhIDNI f. 259, op. 1, d. 68, l. 1–3.

40. A. F. Ryndich, *Partiino-sovetskie shkoly: k voprosu o metodike zaniatii so vzroslymi* (Moscow-Leningrad: Gosizdat, 1925), 5–6; Lira S. Leonova, "'Perepiska Sekretariata TsK RSDRP(b)-RKP(b) s mestnymi partiinymi organizatsiiami' kak istochnik osveshcheniia problemy podgotovki partiinykh kadrov v pervye gody sovetskoi vlasti," *Vestnik Moskovskogo Universiteta*, 8th ser., no. 6 (1987): 3–14.

period cannot be neatly distinguished from other Soviet efforts or rigidly separated from peoples' and proletarian education.

The Lenin Communist University in Tula, for example, was founded by the Tula party organization on the anniversary of the revolution in 1918. Four-month courses were offered in a former women's gymnasium for 31 Communists, 28 "sympathizers," and 31 nonparty students. The eight-hour daily schedule combined general education (Russian language, mathematics, geography, history of the region, accounting) and political education (political economy, the Soviet constitution, history of the revolutionary movement, the Bolshevik party program, and so on). The party university also showed some affinity with the proletarian education movement by its proclaimed goal of training proletarians for future leadership positions and its attempts to "merge labor and science." By 1920 there were 183 party members, 47 nonparty students, and 5 sympathizers.[41]

In 1920 the Bolshevik victory in the civil war coincided with the political-ideological justification of the one-party monopoly on power and a much tighter equation of the goals of the Party with the aims of the revolution. As one aspect of this great hegemonic claim, people's and proletarian education ceased to exist as autonomous forces and educational movements; the schools themselves were disbanded and often their buildings and resources were appropriated by institutions of party education. Given Lenin's prerevolutionary experience with Bogdanov's Capri and Bologna schools, it is not surprising that the hostile takeover of the Proletkul't universities—and of Proletkul't itself—proved cause not simply for denouncing a "deviation" but for appropriating aspects of the condemned organization's mission into the party program.

Many leading Bolsheviks, some of them former Vperedists, did not regard proletarian education as incompatible with party education, in the same way that Proletkul't leaders liked to portray their organization as a bastion of proletarian purity not incompatible with the activities of the Communist Party. Bukharin and Lunacharskii spoke at the opening ceremonies of the Karl Liebknecht University, Bukharin taught there, and the proletarian university apparently commanded some support in the Narkompros collegium. But the president of Liebknecht University, N. V. Rozginskii, from the Adult Education Division of Narkompros, soon defied Bogdanov and many of the students by proposing a merger

41. "Kratkii obzor uchebnoi deiatel'nosti Tul'skogo Kommunisticheskogo Universiteta im. Lenina," no earlier than March 1921, GARF f. A-2313, op. 1, d. 1, l. 434–38.

with Sverdlov. The Central Committee ordered the proletarian university "temporarily" shut down in July 1919.[42] When the Party moved against Proletkul't as a whole the next year, some of the party supporters of proletarian culture would transfer to party channels their project of building a new culture through a new kind of university.

The Politburo formulated plans in October 1920 to effect Proletkul't's "subordination to the Party." This, again, was arranged through motions from within the organization itself. For this purpose the Politburo enlisted Proletkul't leader Lebedev-Polianskii—whose participation foreshadowed his rise to head of the Soviet censorship agency Glavlit. Proletkul't lost its autonomy, Bogdanov resigned, and much of the movement's vitality passed to what soon became a better-funded, politically important, and ideologically approved movement of party education. Between the fall and winter of 1920—at precisely the same moment that Proletkul't was stripped of its autonomy—the Party moved to invigorate party education and unite it into an educational system. For example, at the Ninth Party Conference in September 1920, Preobrazhenskii announced plans to consolidate existing party and Red Army schools and develop a unified (*edinaia*) program for party institutions formed into a single hierarchical "ladder."[43]

The launching of this centralized educational system in 1920 followed on the heels of an act of great symbolism: the Party's new flagship institution, Sverdlov Communist University, absorbed both the Proletkul't university and Shaniavskii University. As the Party commandeered or abolished the leading institutions of people's and proletarian education, it became the de facto avatar of educational opportunities for adults, proletarians, and revolutionaries; it became heir to the deep-seated motivations that had fueled the educational explosion during the civil war. In 1921, for example, a Proletkul't writer on the higher school, while making the radicals' standard claim that the very contents

42. Mally, *Culture of the Future*, 165–73; Fitzpatrick, *Commissariat*, 101–4, 106; Read, *Culture and Power*, 131–33.

43. "Protokol No. 49 zasedaniia Politicheskogo Biuro Ts.K. ot 9 oktriabria 1920 goda," RTsKhIDNI f. 17, op. 3, d. 113, l. 1, and on measures taken to restrict Bogdanov's publishing and teaching, d. 75, l. 3; "O proletkul'takh," *Izvestiia TsK RKP(b)*, 26 December 1920, reprinted in A. Ia. Podzemskii, ed., *Direktivy VKP(b) po voprosam prosveshcheniia* (Moscow-Leningrad: Narkompros RSFSR, 1930), 250–52; *Deviataia konferentsiia RKP(b). Sentiabr' 1920 goda. Protokoly* (Moscow: Politizdat, 1972), 124–25; Podzemskii, *Direktivy*, 33, 250–52. In December 1921 the Party publicized a decision to enlarge the network of party schools "at the expense" of theatrical, art, and other schools that "do not have direct educational [*vospitatel'nogo*] significance for the working class." *Vserossiiskaia Konferentsiia R.K.P (Bol'shevikov). Biulleten'*, no. 3, 21 December 1921, 36.

of *nauka* remained to be reworked from a collectivist point of view, allowed that Sverdlov University was realizing the idea of the proletarian university. At the same time, as part of a newly broadened mission in general education, the natural science courses of Shaniavskii were integrated into the higher party school.[44] Party institutions thus coopted not just the resources but also the aspirations of movements that had been alternatives to the traditional university system.

The widening ambitions of party education were also linked to the fact that the university system was proving highly resistant to Bolshevik incursions. Most old professors were reelected when that became mandatory, and few Marxists or communist sympathizers materialized even in the social sciences. But the irony of the "war communism" period in academia was that while the Party made relatively few inroads, threatening Bolshevik gestures suggested imminent, apocalyptic change (whereas under NEP conciliatory gestures accompanied far-reaching change). Arrests of leading scholars tainted by former membership in the Kadet party, humiliatingly incarcerated in connection with the Cheka's "Tactical Center" affair, swept up even such cooperative moderates as academician Sergei F. Ol'denburg. The self-styled protector of the intelligentsia and Soviet patron extraordinaire in this period, Maxim Gor'kii, fulminated to Lenin on 6 September 1919 that the "mind of the people" was being destroyed; Lenin retorted that the intelligentsia was not the mind but the "shit." Five days later, however, the Politburo considered the protest of Gor'kii, Lunacharskii, and Kamenev about "the latest mass arrests" of scholars and professors and authorized the three to reevaluate cases in cooperation with Bukharin and Dzerzhinskii.[45]

The professoriat continued to block efforts to bring Communists and Marxists into their institutions. The Moscow University historian Got'e, who situated himself well to the right of the Kadets politically, noted in his diary that "our young people" showed "solidarity with us" in the reelections of 1919; only one professor, Pavel N. Sakulin, was blackballed, "for his currying favors with the Bolsheviks, of course." Early Narkompros efforts to alter the social and political composition of the

44. GARF f. 5221, op. 4, d. 71, l. 8; Lee, *People's Universities*, 51; Antonova and Drozdova, *Neizvestnyi Bogdanov*, 1:238 n. 224, citing Orgburo decision in RTsKhIDNI f. 17, op. 60, d. 27, l. 52; Zander, "Vysshaia shkola," 26; Kirstein, "Das sowjetische Parteischulsystem," 205 n. 34.

45. "Protokol No. 1 Zasedaniia Politicheskogo Biuro TsK ot 11 sentiabria 1919 goda," RTsKhIDNI f. 17, op. 3, d. 26, l. 2; S. G. Isakov, "Neizvestnye pis'ma M. Gor'kogo V. Leninu," *Revue des études slaves* 64, no. 1 (1992): 143–56; Lenin quoted in Dmitrii Volkogonov, *Lenin: Politicheskii portret* (Moscow: Novosti, 1994), 2:184, citing RTsKhIDNI f. 2, op. 1, d. 11164, l. 7–8.

student body were outright failures, leading Pokrovskii in March 1919 to mandate a regularized system of workers' faculties (*rabfaks*), preparatory sections attached to every higher school. (The *rabfaks* were also bulwarks of pro-Soviet support.) The conservative wing of the professoriat, while frequently putting up less overt resistance than liberals and leftists conditioned to struggle under the tsars, often linked the appearance of rabfak students, Jews, commissars, and Communists together as the harbinger of the decline of Russian science and civilization.[46]

As the standoff deepened at the universities, and with Communists weak there even as animosities sharpened, even the first signs of an incipient system of party education increased the temptation to view higher learning in the Manichaean terms that the civil war exacerbated in Bolshevik thought. Almost before the party schools moved from crash courses to longer-term training, the notion grew that there had emerged two hostile educational worlds, one revolutionary and communist, the other "bourgeois" and reactionary.

The *ABC of Communism*, written by Preobrazhenskii and Bukharin as the first communist textbook and instantly transformed into a widely studied classic, treats higher education in such dualistic terms as early as 1919. The fate of the universities is uncertain: "At the present time it is still impossible to foresee precisely what character the higher schools for the training of specialists will assume under communism." Nevertheless, the present universities have "ceased to be serviceable institutions" and "most of the students" in the future will have to be workers. In sharp contrast, the soviet-party schools represent a revolutionary alternative, "a new type of school, which is intended to be serviceable to the revolution now in progress."[47]

The first congress of Soviet-Party Schools and Communist Universities, held after the introduction of NEP, demonstrated that what had begun in emergency conditions had blossomed into a full-fledged movement with pretensions of building a new higher learning. The resolution passed by the congress noted that the "old party schools underground" had attempted to train agitators with some knowledge of Marxist the-

46. Terrence Emmons, ed., *Time of Troubles: The Diary of Iurii Vladimirovich Got'e* (Princeton: Princeton University Press, 1988), 251–52; "Protokol zasedaniia kollegii Nauchnoi Sektsii NKP ot 24 marta 1919," ARAN f. 1759, op. 2, d. 5, l. 5–7. On the combined anti-Semitism and anti-Bolshevism of Got'e's university milieu, see Emmons, *Time of Troubles*, 249 and passim, and Mary McAuley, *Bread and Justice: State and Society in Petrograd, 1917–1922* (Oxford: Clarendon Press, 1991), 330, 350.

47. Nikolai Bukharin and Evgenii Preobrazhenskii, *The ABC of Communism* (Ann Arbor: University of Michigan Press, 1966), 239–40.

Participants of the first congress of Soviet-Party Schools and Communist Universities, 1922. Identified are Adrian Filippovich Ryndich (first row, first to left), V. N. Meshcheriakov (first row, sixth from left), G. I. Okulova (Teodorovich) (second row, fifth from left), and Emelian Mikhailovich Iaroslavskii (second row, eighth from left). Reprinted by permission of the Museum of the Revolution, Moscow, Russia.

ory; in the civil war, the overwhelming need was for short-term training for party and state cadres. Now the opportunity was at hand to produce loyal new specialists, theoreticians capable of battling the bourgeois worldview, leaders for the proletariat, and genuine scholars to advance Marxist science.[48] If party education always encompassed both

48. "Rezoliutsiia I s"ezda sovpartshkol i komvuzov," in A. F. Ryndich, ed., *Metodika i or-*

immediate political imperatives and visions of long-term transformation, its postrevolutionary rebirth under the "utopian" war communism had paradoxically accentuated the utilitarian impulse, while the particular "retreat" to a contradictory NEP order would revitalize the revolutionary imagination.

One Step Backward, Imagination Forward: Hotheads, Specialists, and NEP

The phrase "transition to NEP" (*perekhod k nepu*) referred to after late 1921 deliberately suggested a disciplined progression and therefore masked conflicting trends and impulses. In this epochal shift, pursuit of immediate socialism gave way to a lengthening of the millenarian time line and the notion of forced compromise with key social groups (peasants, specialists); at the very same time, the ebb of civil war precipitated a shift toward a new advance on the "cultural front," itself offering possibilities of transcending retreat almost as soon as it was begun. The turn to NEP also accompanied a drive to take control of the old universities that culminated in 1922, a campaign against idealism in higher learning, and the intensive building of a system of party education after 1921. Finally, despite such anomalies as an April 1921 report from an Agitprop worker and Cheka consultant advocating the legalization of other socialist parties, the economic plan was decidedly not matched by a "political NEP."[49]

The creation of a party educational system and the articulation of a full-fledged communist educational-cultural mission—both hallmarks of the 1920s order—thus predated the introduction of NEP in 1921. As we have seen, they were more connected to the eclipse of Proletkul't and the ebb of civil war. But the New Economic Policy also had far-reaching effects on both these earlier developments. At the heart of NEP was an endorsement of differentiated economic sectors (state, cooperative, rural); notions of differentiation, parallel systems, distinctions between party and state policy, and even compartmentalization took hold in spheres well beyond the economic. In the arts, Clark even refers to an "increasing apartheid" between high, popular, and proletarian culture

---

ganizatsiia partprosveshcheniia (Moscow: Izdatel'stvo Kommunisticheskogo universiteta im. Sverdlova, 1926), 52–54.

49. E. G. Gimpel'son, "Politicheskaia sistema i NEP: Neadekvatnost' reform," *Otechestvennaia istoriia*, no. 2 (March–April 1993): 29–43.

overtaking the war communist dream of an integral revolutionary culture.[50] While a similar division into separate spheres came to structure the world of higher education, the boundaries of the division (like those of the dualistic party-state itself) were permeable. "Reform" was pursued in the state higher educational institutions even as the very growth of party education threatened gradual reformist approaches. Party education was stimulated to groom itself to replace bourgeois higher education precisely because the "transition period" was to now be lengthy and old institutions were to be tolerated. These central contradictions of the 1920s order grew out of the tensions between the construction of the new and forced toleration of the old and as such were typical of the epoch.

The campaign for the "winning of the higher school" launched at the end of the civil war reflected party priorities and strategies in policy toward higher education. Primacy was given to wresting administrative and hence political control from a professoriat bent on maintaining autonomy. To compound the challenge for the Bolsheviks, the *studenchestvo* in the early years of Soviet power was overwhelmingly non-Bolshevik and contained sizable contingents of activists from other political parties. Mensheviks, SRs, and anarchists, driven underground in the early 1920s, focused attention and hope on the students, their traditional supply of activists.[51]

This situation led the Bolshevik leadership in the early 1920s to rely heavily on the party cells in higher educational institutions, and on militant communist students who led them. The cells gained enormous political and administrative power in the universities, as did, to a lesser extent, the rabfaks. Many communist student politicians thus came to view themselves as leaders on the front lines of a class struggle to transform higher education. The communist student movement straddled the new party institutions and the old universities, and destruction of the old prompted if anything as much enthusiasm as the creation of the new. Although rabfaks, which numbered 64 with 25,000 students in 1922, were not administered by the Party but by Narkompros, politically they were also centers of the communist student movement. A rabfak student in 1923 voiced this perceived mission in the language of ideological warfare that became connected to the communist student

50. Clark, *Petersburg*, 143–47.

51. The literature on student politics outside the Communist Party is sparse. A valuable source is the memoirs of the anti-Bolshevik activist Sergei Zhaba, *Petrogradskoe studenchestvo v bor'be za svobodnuiu vysshuiu shkolu* (Paris: J. Povolozky, 1922).

movement's generational ethos: "The rabfak students, fulfilling their historical role in higher education in their capacity as a proletarian avant-garde, must destroy the higher school as a nest of counterrevolutionaries (and this includes white, pink, three-colored, and all other kinds of counterrevolutionaries) who are among the students and the white-Kadet professoriat."[52]

The "hotheads" who saw their task as the total destruction of bourgeois higher education—and this may well have been the bulk of the communist student *aktiv*—often ignored pressing considerations incumbent upon even the most "anti-specialist" figures in the Bolshevik leadership. Overly precipitous action quite simply threatened the continued functioning of higher educational institutions. Even Narkompros' most influential policymaker on higher education, Pokrovskii, deliberately cast aside his persona of crusading commissar when addressing the Congress of Communist Students in 1920. "We must put off until better days," he enjoined, "all *that is not absolutely necessary.*" Pokrovskii singled out reform of social science and humanities curricula as among the most urgent tasks, but opposed hothead demands to shut down social science and philological departments as a "tactical stupidity."[53]

From the point of view of the communist students, however, it must have been difficult indeed to understand why some repressive measures were necessary and others were blunders. Indeed, the difficulty of fomenting and then reigning in revolutionary sentiment was a perennial result of the militarized party chain of command in the young revolutionary state. To the chagrin of many revolutionaries, the attack on "intelligentsia" and institutional resistance—the two were typically conflated in this struggle—proceeded only in fits and starts. When decisive action finally came in 1922, it produced a higher educational order utterly different than anticipated.

The weakness of the Bolsheviks' hand and their investment in Marxism dictated that attention be focused on the social sciences, and in fact natural science programs such as the Physical-Mathematical Faculty of

52. D. Rozit, "Rabfaki i vysshaia shkola," *Rabfakovets* 1 (June 1923): 9. In contrast to the party schools, devoted above all to the Marxist social sciences, the rabfaks in the 1920s were quickly oriented less toward socioeconomic and pedagogical concentrations and far more toward the training of industrial and technical workers, although the only academic admission requirements in 1922 were reading, writing, and "knowledge of the four rules of arithmetic in whole numbers." See report on rabfaks considered by the Politburo on 22 March, RTsKhIDNI f. 17, op. 3, ed. khr. 284, l. 7–8; Frederika Tandler, "The Workers' Faculty (Rabfak) System in the USSR" (Ph.D. diss., Columbia University, 1955).

53. M. N. Pokrovskii, "Zadachi vysshei shkoly v nastoiashchii moment," *Narodnoe prosveshchenie*, no. 18–20 (January–March 1920): 3–9.

Moscow University were least touched of all departments.[54] In 1920 Sovnarkom appointed a special commission to review social science programs, inviting leading Bolshevik intellectuals such as Bukharin, Volgin, Pokrovskii, Rotshtein, Svortsov-Stepanov, and Friche to take part. This was soon dubbed the Rotshtein commission, after its chair, Socialist Academy member Fedor A. Rotshtein. The commission recommended creating the Party's own red specialists in the Marxist social sciences in a special graduate school, the Institute of Red Professors. By February 1921 the Rotshtein commission had also put together a "program of political literacy for higher educational institutions." Sovnarkom proceeded to ratify this proposal, changing the name to the more advanced-sounding term "social minimum," a group of mandatory courses to be taught in all higher schools. These courses included historical materialism, the proletarian revolution, and the political structure of the RSFSR. For years, however, the social minimum remained a marginalized part of curricula in the universities and VUZy. In the mid-1920s the minimum was designed to take up ten percent of all study hours, but widespread textbook shortages were still reported.[55]

In 1922 the scientific-political section of the State Academic Council (*Gosudarstvennyi Uchennyi Sovet*, or GUS), which assumed the power to ratify academic appointments, began a "verification" of teaching personnel in the social sciences and humanities. In line with the current campaign against "idealist" tendencies in scholarship and publications, the goal was to weed out "theologians, mystics, and representatives of extreme idealism," to reduce the number of philologists and archaeologists in favor of disciplines "comparatively more useful to the state," and to ensure that younger teachers knew the basics of Marxism.[56] Both the social minimum and such open attempts to reconfigure the professoriat, while apparently having little effect in the short term, added fuel to the fire in the mounting struggle over political command in higher education.

The long-awaited confrontation came to a head in 1921–22 over the

54. V. Stratonov, "Poteria Moskovskim Universitetom svobody," in V. B. El'iashevich et al., eds., *Moskovskii Universitet, 1755–1930: Iubileinnyi sbornik* (Paris: Sovremennye zapiski, 1930), 198.

55. "Protokol No. 22 zasedaniia GPP ot 12-go fevralia 1921 g.," GARF f. A-2313, op. 1, d. 18, l. 70; "Postanovlenie Sovnarkom. Upravlenie delami soveta narodnykh komissarov 18/XI 1920," ARAN f. 1759, op. 2, d. 5, l. 313–14; M. N. Pokrovskii, "Postanovka obshchestvovedeniia v komvuzakh, Vuzakh i dr. shkolakh vsroslykh," no exact date, 1926, ibid., op. 1, d. 186, l. 8–13.

56. "Protokol No. 30 Zasedaniia Nauchno-Politicheskoi Sektsii G.U.S. 8-go avgusta 1922 g.," ARAN f. 1759, op. 2, d. 5, l. 19.

new university charter. The result, however, was an ambiguous Bolshevik victory rather than apocalyptic destruction of the bourgeois system of higher education. In 1921, a university statute (*polozhenie*) was ratified as a stepping-stone to a new charter. The obvious aim of the measure was to establish party-state appointment of university rectors and administrations and thus formally abolish university autonomy. A 1921 Central Committee directive to Narkompros, approved with corrections by the Politburo on 10 May, gave party regional committees veto power over Narkompros appointments of rectors and insisted on the "one-person" (*edinolichnyi*) decision-making powers of rectors and deans over collegial organizations.[57] The Party's strategy proved an explosive issue. The decades-long struggle against the 1884 tsarist charter, which had limited university authority over academic and administrative appointments, had been a cause célèbre until its repeal after the February Revolution. Now the Bolsheviks planned to assume even more direct control over university administrations and to ban independent "social organizations" at the universities as well. Communist students and staff had already been brought into the Moscow University administration in 1920, but the permanent subordination implied in the 1921 statute prompted the rector, former Kadet Mikhail M. Novikov, to resign—after a stormy confrontation at Narkompros where he likened Pokrovskii and Lunacharskii to the symbols of tsarist reaction, Pobedenotsev and Kasso.[58]

The communist student leaders reacted with jubilation; this seemed to be the moment for which they had been waiting. An All-Moscow Conference of Komsomol Cells in March 1921 vowed to defeat the "Kadet–black hundred professoriat." The same month, leaders of the "red" group in higher education, 46 communist professors and scholars, called for an end to negotiations, full Soviet control over admissions to higher education, and debate on the higher school to be put on the agenda of the next party congress. Pokrovskii brought this last proposal before the Politburo, which, no doubt wishing to avoid the likely result, considered it "not expedient." But in 1922, Moscow VUZ cells continued to pressure Narkompros to enforce the new charter. The Central

57. "Direktivy TsK," no later than 10 May 1921, RTsKhIDNI f. 17, op. 3, ed. khr. 161, l. 1–7.

58. "Polozhenie ob Upravlenii VUZ RSFSR (priniato v zasedanii kollegii NKProsa 4 marta 1921 g.)," ARAN f. 496, op. 2, d. 119, l. 3; M. Novikov, "Moskovskii Universitet v pervom periode bol'shevistskogo rezhima," in El'iashevich et al., *Moskovskii Universitet*, 191; M. M. Novikov, *Ot Moskvy do N'iu Iorka. Moia zhizn' v nauke i politike* (New York: Izdatel'stvo imeni Chekhova, 1952).

Bureau of Communist Students also lobbied the Central Committee to wield student stipends as "the sharpest weapon of class power politics in the higher school."[59]

At the All-Union Conference of Communist Cells of VUZy, Rabfaks, and Higher Party Schools in April 1922, activist students were told by the head of the Moscow Bureau of the Communist Students that they were witnessing a time "of the most cruel class struggle" in higher education over "the question who will be master." Reflecting the confidence of the cells, the conference resolution boasted that current events proved the communist student body was the only base on which the state could rely in restructuring the higher school. The student cells demanded the right to help determine all party policies affecting "school construction."[60]

With their autonomy threatened and chaotic funding problems resulting from the introduction of NEP, faculty members of the Moscow Higher Technical School went on strike in the spring of 1921. In early 1922, in connection with the new university charter, (but gaining momentum not least because of irregularly paid and meager professorial salaries) "professors' strikes" broke out in Moscow, Petrograd, and Kazan'.[61] A dejected Lunacharskii asked the Central Committee to take him off the faculty of Moscow University and to transfer him to Sverdlov Communist University, because the students had organized "something like a boycott" of his classes and only the rabfak students had appeared. The Politburo—consistently less inclined to embrace a revolutionary offensive that might wreck nonparty higher education than many Narkompros officials, "red" scholars, and communist students—ordered an "immediate" and "peaceful" liquidation of the strike on 6 February. Three more Poliburo resolutions followed concerning immediate amelioration of the "material condition" in higher education, and Preobrazhenskii and Pokrovskii were given reprimands for not ful-

59. "Protokol obshchegorodskoi konferentsii iacheek RKSM gor. Moskvy ot 12 marta 1921," RTsKhIDNI f. 17, op. 60, d. 76, l. 1–2; "Protokol No. 113 Zasedaniia Politbiuro TsK ot 16 marta 1922 goda," ibid., op. 3, ed. khr. 282, l. 1–5; "Tsentral'noe Biuro Kommunisticheskogo Studenchestva. V TsK RKP. Dokladnaia zapiska," no date, 1922, ibid., op. 60, d. 205, l. 92, see also l. 93; "Vypiska iz protokola Konferentsii Sekretarei iacheek Moskovskikh VUZ ot 21 fevralia 1922 g.," ibid., d. 199, l. 11; "Moskovskoe biuro Kom"iacheek Vysshikh Uchebnykh Zavedenii. V prezidium Glavprofobra t. Iakovlevoi," no date, 1922, ibid., d. 75, l. 103.

60. "Otchet zasedaniia Vserossiiskoi konferentsii kom"iacheek VUZ, [Rabfakov i vysshikh partshkol] 26-go aprelia 1922," RTsKhIDNI f. 17, op. 60, d. 224, l. 2, 135 ob.

61. "Protokol Zasedaniia Ob"ed. Biuro iacheek Universiteta Sverdlova ot 12/IV-22 g.," RGAODgM f. 459, op. 1, d. 15, l. 14; "Protokol Zasedaniia Moskovskogo Biuro studencheskoi fraktsii RKP ot 17 fevralia 1922 g.," RTsKhIDNI f. 17, op. 60, d. 216, l. 10; Stratonov, "Poteria," 222–41; Emmons, *Time of Troubles*, 444–45.

filling directives on ending the strike. On 13 February Preobrazhenskii, a leader of the Socialist Academy whose hard-line stance was conditioned by his championship of the new party institutions, resigned from the Politburo special "commission on higher eduction." But the Politburo was not all conciliation; it improved material conditions, but also decreed a reduction in the number of higher schools and professors.[62]

There were still some grounds to believe that an assault on "bourgeois" higher education was imminent. Toward the end of 1922, Central Committee secretary Valerian V. Kuibyshev and Agitprop chief Andrei S. Bubnov instructed regional party committees to take an active part in implementing the new charter, and on its basis to participate in the selection of VUZ administrators and leading professors, to organize citywide networks of communist students, and to monitor curricula so that "proletarian" university students would not undergo a "bourgeois work-over." Typically, these measures were proclaimed the "next step in the winning of the higher school, in which until now bourgeois scholars and bourgeois ideology have ruled."[63]

Such calls to arms, moreover, were buttressed by widespread fears within the Party that the NEP retreat had created a crisis of revolutionary purity and the imminent reassertion of alien socio-ideological influences. The moves to establish control over higher education were closely connected to the August 1922 arrest and subsequent deportation of leading "professors and litterateurs," a group of about 200 people (including families) that cut across the elite of the nonparty intelligentsia in Moscow and Petrograd. The deportees, who were given seven days to prepare for departure or face a trial, included some of the most authoritative scholars at Moscow University, those who had opposed the trial of the SRs that had begun in June, or who were identified with a "renaissance of bourgeois ideology" in a handful of newly viable nonparty publications. In the summer of 1922, lists of "anti-Soviet intelligentsia" were bandied back and forth among Lenin, Stalin, and top GPU officials. Deportees eventually included former rectors of

62. A. V. Lunacharskii, "V TsK RKP v uchetno-raspredelitel'nyi otdel, t. Syrtsovu. 7/III-22 g.," RTsKhIDNI f. 142, op. 1, d. 455, l. 5; Politburo resolutions and addenda from 6, 11, 13 February 1922, ibid., f. 17, op. 3, d. 260, l. 1; d. 261, l. 2, 8; ed. khr. 263, l. 2; ed. khr. 265, l. 3, 10. Lenin at this time reportedly instructed the Old Bolshevik intellectual Ivan I. Skvortsov-Stepanov to give Stalin periodic updates on the activities of academic circles. Skvortsov-Stepanov to Iaroslavskii, 24 February 1927, ibid., f. 150, op. 1, d. 74, l. 34.

63. "Vsem oblbiuro TsK, TsK Natsional'nye Kom. Partii, obkomam i gubkomam RKP. Tsirkuliarno," 14 December 1922, RTsKhIDNI f. 17, op. 60, d. 200, l. 1.

Moscow and Petrograd universities; the historians Aleksandr A. Kizevetter and Anatolii A. Florovskii; and the philosophers Nikolai A. Berdiaev, Semen L. Frank, Sergei N. Bulgakov, and Aleksandr S. Izgoev. Also deported were prominent agronomists, scientists, professionals, and other "thinkers." Coincidentally echoing his famous phrase about NEP lasting "in earnest and for a long time" (*nadolgo*), Lenin told Stalin: "We will clean out Russia for a long time."[64]

The initial Menshevik report of the event perceptively discerned that the arrests were connected with the struggle for control of higher education. Indeed, the laconic announcement of the deportations in *Pravda* on 31 August suggested the principal activity of the anti-Soviet intellectuals was in higher education, and that they had turned public opinion against higher educational reform.[65] The deportations were thus a cleansing, a banishment of anti-Soviet elements to non-Soviet space. All this was complemented by another rationale: the measure was a "crack of the whip" against intelligentsia society (*obshchestvennost'*) as a force capable of aspiring to leadership and influence in the postrevolutionary order.

The earliest plans for the expulsions perhaps lie in a letter from Lenin to Dzerzhinskii on 19 May 1922, which proposed the GPU collaborate with Politburo members in identifying leading anti-Soviet professors and writers. A letter from Trotskii to Kamenev on 9 August 1922 indicates that such a discussion among Politburo members on this subject took place. This fragmentary piece of evidence shows Trotskii providing a polemical profile of a proposed deportee, a well-known literary critic: "Is Nestor Kotliarevskii included on the list? His speech 'Pushkin and Russia,' published by the Academy of Sciences (by the permission of academician Ol'denburg) is saturated through and through with reactionary-serfholding idealism."[66]

The deportations were not the only measures taken in this period by the top leadership to counter the supposed resurgence of bourgeois ide-

64. Volkogonov, *Lenin*, 2:179–86, citing Arkhiv Prezidenta Rossiiskoi Federatsii (APRF) f. 3, op. 58, d. 175, l. 35–36, 72. The most comprehensive single account of the deportations remains Michel Heller, "Premier avertissement: Un coup de fouet. L'histoire de l'expulsion des personnalités culturelles hors de l'Union Soviétique en 1922," *Cahiers du monde russe et soviétique* 20 (April 1979): 131–72. See also "Razgrom intelligentsii," *Sotsialisticheskii vestnik*, 21 September 1922, 10; Gimpel'son, "Politicheskaia sistema," 39; Novikov, *Ot Moskvy*, 324–27; Stratonov, "Poteria," 238–41.

65. "Aresty sredi intelligentsii," *Sotsialisticheskii vestnik*, 8 September 1922, 12; Heller, "Premier avertissement," 160.

66. L. D. Trotskii to L. B. Kamenev, 8 August 1922, RTsKhIDNI f. 323, op. 1, d. 140, l. 5; Heller, "Premier avertissement," 155.

ology. Scarce resources were diverted to found a series of new scholarly and literary "thick journals" designed to bolster Marxist hegemony and mitigate, as one historian has put it, the "corrosive economic and social climate of NEP."[67]

The shift to the 1920s academic order, then, predated and was broader than the New Economic Policy. But the introduction of NEP also had particular ramifications in higher learning, above all the well-known conciliation intended to stabilize the regime's relations with so-called bourgeois specialists. Bolshevik policy clearly carried a carrot along with the stick.

The universities were linked to the new line on the so-called bourgeois specialists (*spetsy*), a term which included state bureaucrats and technical workers as well as scholars. A new wage scale was introduced, paving the way for nonmanual workers to receive significantly higher salaries. Lenin's victorious platform in the trade-union controversy rejected compulsory membership of specialists in mass unions and permitted continued existence of professional organizations. Above all, attacks on specialist-baiting (*spetseedstvo*) and a new stress on "winning over" specialists to Soviet power gave the specialists a place of respect if only a quasi-legitimized identity in the Soviet order—no matter how hostile or divided the impulses of many (arguably all) Communists remained on the question of old elites.[68] It was in 1921–22 that the Central Commission for Improving the Life of Scholars, the "expert commission" of which was headed by party scholars Pokrovskii and Otto Iu. Shmidt but included several academicians and nonparty figures, founded eighteen local sections and widely increased its activities in providing special privileges such as sanatoria for scholars. The economic specialist in VSNKh, Valentinov-Vol'skii, underlined in his well-known memoirs the psychological shift in specialist circles in 1921–22: many "saw in NEP not only the 'repeal' of the hated ration system, but the repeal of a system of ideas which were fettering and destroying life."[69]

67. Roger Pethybridge, "Concern for Bolshevik Ideological Predominance at the Start of NEP," *Russian Review* 41 (October 1982): 445–46.

68. Ronald G. Charbonneau, "Non-Communist Hands: Bourgeois Specialists in Soviet Russia, 1917–1927" (Ph.D. diss., Concordia University, Montreal, 1981), 251, 279–80, 289–300, 350, 461–62; Ettore Cinella, "État 'prolétarien' et science 'bourgeoise': Les *specy* pendant les premières années du pouvoir soviétique," *Cahiers du monde russe et soviétique* 32 (October–December 1991), 469–500.

69. *Piat' let raboty Tsentral'noi komissii po uluchsheniiu byta uchenykh pri Sovete narodnykh komissarov RSFSR (TsEKUBU), 1921–1926* (Moscow: Izdanie TsEKUBU, 1927), 3–16; N. Valentinov [N. Vol'skii], *Novaia ekonomicheskaia politika i krizis partii posle smerti Lenina. Gody raboty v VSNKh vo vremia NEP. Vospominaniia* (Moscow: Sovremennik, 1991), 60.

The Politburo also maneuvered to strengthen an unofficial rapprochement between the specialists and the regime through its partly surreptitious support for the "changing landmarks" movement (*smenovekhovstvo*) of émigré intellectuals. In 1921 a group in Prague had published the namesake collection with the message that the intelligentsia should "go to Canossa" for its fruitless hostility to the Bolshevik regime, which was recreating a Russian great power and unitary state. The idea was found to have resonance among the nonparty specialists in the state bureaucracy (and was first dubbed the "ideology of the specialists" by the sociologist Pitrim Sorokin in December 1921, before he himself was deported as an anti-Soviet intellectual the next year). While many Bolsheviks were immediately hostile to any assumption that the revolution had compromised with Russian national tradition, the dominant response in the Soviet press was triumphalism. The response of Lenin and the leadership was to seize the opportunity: in 1922 the Politburo supported the group's publications financially and demonstrated that Soviet ambassadors abroad had entered into an intricate involvement with the movement's leaders. Still, the flirtation was symptomatic of the intractable ambivalence toward even a compromise with the "bourgeois intelligentsia" deemed highly useful. Even Bolshevik "supporters" of the movement issued dualistic blends of praise and denunciation; and no doubt emboldened by the deportations of intellectuals the same month, Agitprop arranged a campaign against "changing landmarks" in August 1922.[70]

In the end, however, the coincidence of the establishment of a new position for the specialists and the rockiest period in the struggle for political command of higher education undercut the plans of those who wished to immediately and irrevocably transform the existing system. The battle had to be "won" without threatening the edifice on which the new reconciliation with the specialists was built. Lenin publicly rebuked the VUZ communist cells and rabfaks for their overzealous attacks on bourgeois professors, and the thrust of much party policy toward the universities willy-nilly became reining in the powers acquired by the cells and local student "commissars" in previous years, some of whom had seized administrative and even financial control in some in-

70. "Protokol Zasedaniia TsK RKP ot 9/II-1922," RTsKhIDNI f. 17, op. 3, d. 261, l. 3–4; "Protokol No. 27 Zasedaniia Politbiuro TsK RKP ot 21/IX.22 g.," ibid., ed. khr. 313, l. 5. The phrase is from S. S. Chakhotin, "V Kanossu!" in *Smena Vekh* (Prague: Politika, 1921), 150–66. See especially Hilde Hardeman, *Coming to Terms with the Soviet Regime: The "Changing Signposts" Movement among Russian Émigrés in the Early 1920s* (DeKalb: Northern Illinois University Press, 1994), 98–107, 145, 155, 159, 178–79.

stitutions. A main priority now became the consolidation of power in new party-controlled school administrations, which could keep relations with the professoriat under control.[71] In all probability as a result of these policies, the head of the Central Bureau of Communist Students, Zelinskii, appealed to Stalin in 1923 that Politburo decisions tying the hands of the communist student leadership had "made it impossible to work further under such conditions." The 1921–22 battle in higher education therefore cemented Bolshevik administrative control and launched a struggle for Marxism in the social sciences, but muzzled the most ardent revolutionary zeal in the state-run institutions. This resulted in an enduring division of influence within the universities and VUZy and the prospect of further, drawn-out reform between the deportations of 1922 and the Shakhtii affair of 1928.[72]

As with the introduction of NEP itself, Lenin played a large role introducing this tension-riddled compromise in higher education, not just in its political contours but in the direction of higher educational curricula as well. Lenin stepped into a standoff in 1920–21 between Narkompros' advocates of broad-based ("polytechnical") and political education and Glavprofobr's support of an ultra-centralized vocationalism. A compromise solution was dictated: vocationalism would be combined with both general and political education in the VUZy.[73] This did not just affect the shape of the university curriculum, but held important political dimensions as well. The rejection of both radical centralization and a stress on practical educational results had the effect of preserving rather than destroying the influence of the nonparty professoriat within its sphere, as much as this was possible in the conditions of the early 1920s.

The settlement of 1922, fraught with its own tensions in the state

71. "Tsirkuliarnoe pis'mo TsK RKP vsem kom"iacheikam VUZ, Rabfaki i kommunistam, rabotaiushchim v Pravleniiakh VUZ," RTsKhIDNI f. 17, op. 60, d. 205, l. 119; V. I. Lenin, "Iz zakliuchitel'nogo slova po politicheskomu otchetu TsK na XI s"ezda RKP(b) 28 Marta 1922 g.," in *PSS*, 45:121; *O rabote iacheek RKP(b) Vysshikh uchebnykh zavedenii* (Moscow: Izdanie TsK, 1925), 7; Vladimir Iakovlev, "O vzaimotnosheniiakh studorganizatsii s pravleniiami vuzov," *Krasnaia molodezh'*, no. 2 (1925): 77–79.

72. "Otvetstvennyi Sekretar' Ts. B. Komstudenchestva Zelinskii. Sekretariu TsK t. Stalinu," no later than 30 March 1923, RTsKhIDNI f. 17, op. 60, d. 486, l. 75; Fitzpatrick, *Education*, 67.

73. James McClelland, "Bolshevik Approaches to Higher Education, 1917–1921," *Slavic Review* 30 (December 1971): 818–31; V. I. Lenin, "Direktivy TsK Kommunistam-rabotnikam Narkomprosa," in *PSS*, 42:319–21, and "O politekhnicheskom obrazovanii. Zametki na tezisy Nadezhdy Konstantinovny," in *PSS*, 42:228–30; "Massovaia podgotovka spetsialistov i podgotovka nauchnykh Rabotnikov (tipy Vysshei Shkoly). Tezisy O. Iu. Shmidta, odobrennye Narkomprosom," no date, ARAN f. 496, op. 2, d. 109, l. 1.

sector, does not suffice to explain the emergence of an overall 1920s order in higher learning. As we have seen, the transition to NEP not only produced this uneasy alternation between concessions and advance; it accompanied the rise of a new and powerful alternative to all the old institutions.[74]

Efforts to strengthen party education were inititially justified largely in inner-party terms, as a step toward the better socialization of new party members, the creation of a new generation of Bolshevik leaders, and in this period even the solution of the much-publicized internal frictions between leaders and rank and file. The party educational system was plagued by thorny problems when it was launched in the early 1920s. Directives attempted to increase the regulation of student admissions and to initiate the lengthy process of standardizing curricula.[75] It was a time-consuming and often chaotic process to coordinate curricula and textbooks. Problems with finding qualified communist teachers and students were severe. "We are forced to depend on the old party and Marxist cadres," Pokrovskii wryly remarked in 1924, "who are spread so thinly that they are turning into invalids or are setting off directly for the next world."[76]

Yet contrasts between the party and nonparty systems were equally striking. The central party organs had little trouble establishing the principle of direct party control over the burgeoning party educational system; indeed, the new party institutions, unlike the universities, were eager to respond to new curricular and pedagogical initiatives. The higher educational struggle culminating in 1922 affected interpretations of this situation: the party schools became "ours," while the universities were still "theirs"; the universities were lagging behind while the party schools were forging ahead. "The whole system of party schools," Lunacharskii put it in 1921, "is, as it were, a forward march of the avant-garde, a cavalry raid of enlightenment."[77]

74. Party directives of 1920–21 behind the rise of the new system are enumerated in A. Fil'shtinskii, "Sovetskie partiinye shkoly i kommunisticheskie vysshie uchebnye zavedeniia," in *Pedagogicheskaia entsiklopediia*, 3:434–35.

75. "Proekt tezisov k X s"ezdu partii. Glavpolitprosvet i agitatsionno-propagandistskie zadachi partii," GARF f. A-2313, op. 1, d. 92, l. 4; "Sekretar' TsK E. Iaroslavskii. Poriadok komplektovaniia partiino-sovetskikh shkol," no date, 1921, ibid., op. 4, d. 25, l. 1–8; "Predmetnaia skhema obshchei programmy kommunisticheskogo universiteta," no date, ibid., op. 1, d. 1, l. 56–57.

76. "Soveshchanie Narkomprosov Soiuznykh i Avtonomnykh Respublik. I-e zasedanie—27 oktiabria 1924," ARAN f. 1759, op. 2, d. 5, l. 59.

77. A. V. Lunacharskii, "Znachenie sovpartshkol i ikh mesto v sisteme narodnogo obra-

The self-evident contrasts between the new and old systems of education perceptibly drew the participants in the system of party education toward a new pretension, one which appeared to mitigate the compromises the Party had struck with the specialists and the professoriat. The radical transformation of all of higher learning would still take place; only now this would be accomplished first and foremost in new communist institutions. The party institutions could become the basis for an ideological victory over all bourgeois science. One Glavpolitprosvet report, treating the ostensibly dry subject of the academic goals of the party schools, claimed (not entirely logically) that because communist universities had the highest concentration of party members and were focused on the social sciences where Marxism was most developed, "it is possible to create conditions that will guarantee our ideological [*ideinuiu*] hegemony in all areas of knowledge, both methodologically and organizationally."[78] A step backward toward NEP compromise, it seems, provided the springing ground for a forward leap of institution-building and imagination.[79]

The new system of communist education kept one foot in the vast agitprop network and the other in the more rarified world of Marxist scholarship and theory. Party education, as it expanded and broadened its typology of institutions in the first half of the 1920s, retained the multiplicity of aims that had been present at its prerevolutionary founding; now, however, the new resources of the Party and the state, despite the grim material conditions of the early 1920s, allowed for a much broader differentiation of goals within a new hierarchy of institutions. The range of institutional emphases now included remedial, primary, and secondary-level education, including instruction in party politics and Marxism. It also incorporated the training of cadres for the far-flung regions of the new Soviet state and indeed for the world revolution, as well as the advance of high Marxist theory and scholarship.

Just above the efforts toward the mass "liquidation of illiteracy," ground-level organizations of party political education included schools of political literacy, Marxist study circles, and evening soviet-party

---

zovaniia (Rech′ na s″ezde sovpartshkol)," in *Problemy narodnogo obrazovaniia* (Moscow: Rabotnik prosveshcheniia, 1923), 84.

78. "Glavneishie zadachi Kommunisticheskikh universitetov v oblasti uchebnoi raboty v nastoiashchii moment," no date, GARF f. A-2313, op. 1, d. 1, l. 572.

79. A similar phenomenon was observed by Roger Pethybridge, who wrote: "The introduction of NEP did not lead to an abandonment of long-term planning. Psychologically it tended to have the reverse effect." See Pethybridge, *One Step Backwards, Two Steps Forward: Soviet Society and Politics in the New Economic Policy* (Oxford: Clarendon Press, 1990), 177.

schools. These were designed to spread general education in varying doses along with the rudiments of Marxist ideology and the current political agenda to frequently semiliterate party workers. For example, special short-term schools were organized for the workers brought into the Party as part of the "Lenin Levy" in 1924.[80] These kinds of low-level party institutions overlapped with "polit-circles" and courses organized at enterprises, factories, workers' clubs, and party cells, which exploded in number after 1924. A step higher on the "ladder," soviet-party schools of the first and second levels were, in the early 1920s, oriented toward basic training for provincial agitators and propagandists; after 1922, they increasingly turned into schools for rural and regional party and Komsomol workers.[81]

A new array of "higher" party institutions now developed differentiated functions. Since many of these trained semiliterate or poorly educated cadres, academically most cannot be considered more than remedial secondary institutions. Of the institutions that targeted specific groups of cadres, one can count the Central Committee's special training courses for future heads of *uezd* party committees (*Kursy sekretarei Ukomov*), administrated by Agitprop's Kirsanova, who in 1925 was appointed to head the Comintern's newly founded Lenin School.[82] The Communist Academy's Courses in Marxism, initiated in 1922, were geared toward increasing the theoretical knowledge of both up-and-coming party politicians and potential Marxist scholars.

The special tasks inherent in training non-Russians, political émigrés, and foreign Communists were addressed in two special party universities: the Communist University of the National Minorities of the West (KUNMZ), and the Communist University of the Toilers of the East (KUTV). In addition to rehearsing the standard Marxist social science courses (political economy, historical and dialectical materialism, the history of the Party and socialism), all these schools strove to provide

80. *Massovoe partprosveshchenie* (Moscow-Leningrad: Gosizdat, 1926); "Ob uchete raboty sokrashchennykh shkol politgramoty 'Leninskogo nabora,'" no later than spring of 1924, GARF f. A-2313, op. 1, d. 87, l. 89–91. For a standard political literacy curriculum, see M. B. Vol'fson's *Politgramota* (Moscow: Rabotnik prosveshcheniia, 1929).

81. Gabrielle Gorzka, *Arbeiterkultur in der Sowjetunion. Industriearbeiterklubs, 1917–1929. Ein Beitrag zur sowjetischen Kulturgeschichte* (Berlin: Verlag Arno Spitz, 1990), 426; "Sotsial'nyi sostav kursantov obshcheobrazovatel'nykh shkol vzroslykh povyshennogo tipa i sovpartshkol, 9/V-28," RTsKhIDNI f. 12, op. 1, d. 613, l. 5–6. A Soviet work with better than usual archival and bibliographical foundations is Lira Stepanova Leonova's *Iz istorii podgotovki partiinykh kadrov v sovetsko-partiinykh shkolakh i kommunisticheskikh universitetakh (1921–25)* (Moscow: Izdatel'stvo Moskovskogo universiteta, 1972).

82. Piatnitskii to Bubnov, 30 May 1925, RTsKhIDNI f. 531, op. 1, d. 1, l. 11.

political and practical training for communist movements in the students' homelands. The clandestine skills of the underground were emphasized most at the Lenin School, the most important training ground for foreign communists. Students there were trained in techniques of strikes, military insurrection, and espionage; they learned practical skills, such as conduct under interrogation, and were considered potential candidates for the Soviet and Comintern secret services.[83]

On the other end of the spectrum of party education, the more academically oriented party institutions held up as their most important goals the advancement of Marxist theory, scholarship (at first almost solely in the social sciences), and pedagogy. As communist universities were expanded at the outset of NEP to three- and four-year programs, they began to act as alternative universities. They specialized in the social sciences, but included large doses of general education, including language, mathematics, and natural sciences.[84]

At the summit of the academic hierarchy, the Institute of Red Professors and the Communist Academy aspired to produce Marxist researchers and professors, as well as a new generation of party theorists. Two other key institutions, which have yet to find their historian, came to be mentioned in the 1920s together with the Communist Academy as the Party's leading "scientific-research" organizations—the Lenin Institute and the Marx-Engels Institute. In fact, they can be taken as representing two poles in the world of party scholarship.

The Lenin Institute was created along with the incipient Lenin cult in 1924 and put in charge of publications, documents, and an archive on Lenin and Leninism. Because of the centrality of party history for the inner-party struggles, and the place Leninism immediately assumed at the heart of party ideology, the work of the Lenin Institute immediately became a linchpin in high-level political-historical battles as well as in the construction of Leninism. Kamenev was put in charge in 1924, but

83. These schools were joined by the Sun Yat-sen University for Chinese cadres, founded in the autumn of 1925. On the founding of KUNMZ and KUTV, see GARF f. A-2313, op. 1, d. 1, l. 244; d. 69, l. 46–50; and d. 1, l. 442; and Branko Lazitch, "Les écoles de cadres du Comintern: Contribution à leur histoire," in Jacques Freymond, ed., *Contributions à l'histoire du Comintern* (Geneva: Librairie Droz, 1965), 231–55. A few works containing archival research on these institutions have begun to appear: Woodford McClellan, "The Comintern Schools" (forthcoming in a collection edited by Jürgen Rojahn) and "Africans and Black Americans in the Comintern Schools, 1925–1934," *International Journal of African Historical Studies* 26:2 (1993): 371–90; Miin-ling Yu, "Sun Yat-sen University in Moscow, 1925–1930" (Ph.D. diss., New York University, 1995).

84. "Predmetnaia skhema programmy Kommunisticheskogo universiteta," no date, GARF f. A-2313, op. 1, d. 1, l. 5756.

proved unable to spend much time directing institute affairs, so a key figure became the deputy director I. P. Tovstukha—Stalin's *pomoshchnik* from his personal secretariat, two-time head of the Central Committee's Secret Section (repository for classified documents), and author of the first Stalin biography in 1927.[85]

The Marx-Engels Institute (IME), in contrast, was firmly under the hand of the internationally distinguished Marx scholar David Riazanov and had originated before 1921 as a section of the Socialist Academy. Riazanov secured an Orgburo decision in that year to control the staff of the IME and specifically to include nonparty Marxists; in the 1920s he was given the resources to create the largest library in the world on Marxism. With documents purchased in Western and Central Europe, IME also created a preeminent archive on Marx and the history of socialism. In the ten years of its existence, before the institute was merged with the Lenin Institute in 1931 upon Riazanov's arrest, it published not only the largest extant scholarly edition of Marx and Engels but Russian editions ranging from the works of Hobbs, Diderot, Hegel, Ricardo, and Kautsky to those of Adam Smith.[86]

In sum, the commitment made to the expansion of both party education and research after the introduction of NEP reflected a series of priorities high on the agenda of the new regime—from "enlightenment" to high Marxist scholarship, from differing combinations of remedial, general, specialized, and revolutionary instruction to elite theory and formulation of party ideology. The rapid expansion on all levels in the first half of the 1920s was all the more striking considering the financial problems of the revolutionary state.[87] Konstantin Popov, who headed Agitprop's subsection on propaganda which oversaw the party schools, estimated that at the beginning of NEP the entire party instructional system included several tens of thousands of people, while in 1925 the

85. Niels Erik Rosenfeldt, *Knowledge and Power: The Role of Stalin's Secret Chancellery in the Soviet System of Government* (Copenhagen: Rosenkilde & Bagger, 1978), 50, 151–52, 171–73, and passim; Larry Holmes and William Burgess, "Scholarly Voice or Political Echo? Soviet Party History in the 1920s," *Russian History/Histoire Russe* 9:2–3 (1982): 378–98; T. Khorkhordina, *Istoriia otechestva i arkhivy 1917–1980-e gg.* (Moscow: RGGU, 1994), 99–102, 140 n. 18.

86. On the Orgburo decision, Khorkhordina, *Istoriia otechestva*, 96; on IME and 1931, Ia. G. Rokitianskii, "Tragicheskaia sud'ba akademika D. B. Riazanova," *Novaia i noveishaia istoriia*, no. 2 (March–April 1992): 118–20, 130–33.

87. The harsh material conditions of party schools in the early 1920s, in fact, were exacerbated because this system, as opposed to the state sector, was expanded in spite of the financial austerity of NEP. See "Otchet p/o Sovpartshkol Glavpolitprosveta za 1922 g.," GARF f. A-2313, op. 1, d. 83, l. 102–23.

number had swelled to 750,000–800,000. The Tenth Party Congress in 1921 made some kind of party schooling, if only at the level of "political literacy," obligatory for new members of the Communist Party.[88]

At the outset of the new era in the Party's cultural mission, however, an outstanding political question regarding party education remained unsolved. It was not certain which party or state organization would win control over the new educational system and grasp the power to influence its direction.

The Politics of Culture and the Party-State: Formative Struggles on the Third Front

The rise of a system of party education paralleling the old and nonparty institutions overseen by the state might be seen as a reflection of the dualistic party-state itself, in which the Communist Party paralleled all state structures (including commissariat bureaucracies in this period staffed by large numbers of former tsarist officials and nonparty specialists). Yet the theory and practice of this dualism has been understood by historians in different ways. Fitzpatrick, in a seminal article on cultural policy in the 1920s, emphasized the barriers set up in the partition: "In the 1920s official cultural policies were carried out as a rule by government agencies, not by the party." This pointed to a heavy focus on Narkompros and underscored the official nature of the "soft line on culture" it represented.[89] More recently, Kotkin has explained the persistence of the party-state dualism, despite early proposals to abolish parallel party institutions as unnecessary, through the Party's discovery of a postrevolutionary raison d'etre: the conspiratorial shadowing of the state and the pursuit of ideological purity. Kotkin interprets the lasting party-state dualism as creating a structural division between the spheres

88. K. Popov, "Partprosveshchenie v nachale nepa i teper'," *Kommunisticheskaia revoliutsiia*, no. 24 (December 1925): 3–11; also, M. P. Fil'chenikov, "Iz istorii partiinykh uchebnykh zavedenii," *Voprosy istorii KPSS*, no. 1 (1958): 112. The 1925 figure did not include Komsomol political education, rabfaks, or party members studying in state-administered higher educational institutions.

89. Fitzpatrick therefore minimized the role of the Central Committee's Agitprop, maintaining that its role was limited largely to the party schools and to nominating party members for higher education; the "enemies" of the soft line, by implication, were the relatively marginal militants in the proletarian culture organizations (not agencies like Agitprop and Glavlit that were also major players in official policy on the third front). See Sheila Fitzpatrick, "The 'Soft' Line on Culture and Its Enemies: Soviet Cultural Policy, 1922–1927," *Slavic Review* 33 (June 1974): 267–87.

of expertise and economic-technical administration (the state) and ideological and political oversight (the Party).[90]

Both insights—the ratification of spheres of influence along the fault lines of the party-state divide, and the rationale for the enduring division in terms of ideology versus expertise—reveal crucial aspects of the Soviet polity. But both obscure as much as they explain, as can be seen in the story of a formative struggle over the continuation of party-state dualism in the cultural and educational sphere, the emergence of the Main Committee on Political Enlightenment (Glavpolitprosvet, or GPP). An agency under Narkompros, in 1920–21 it attempted with top-level backing to consolidate "party" functions of agitation and propaganda and party education under state control and thus step toward abolition of party-state division of spheres on the third front. It did not succeed, but the struggles surrounding the attempt reveal much broader features of the emerging apparatus of cultural regulation and the place of party education in it.

First and foremost, it became impossible for the Bolsheviks to fully distinguish "ideology" from expertise, propaganda from culture. This can be attributed, first, to the basic fact that party positions and doctrine (the traditional focus of agitation-propaganda) were disseminated using media that were by no means solely reserved for agitprop: when, for example, was a poster cultural but not agitational, or a curriculum educational but not propagandistic? It was partly because the newly established party educational network could be considered part of both the network of agitation and propaganda (as disseminator of the party program) and the world of higher education (as an alternative higher school) that it was not obvious at the outset of NEP which agency would take charge.

Fundamental conceptual ambiguities were complemented by political and institutional ones. Although GPP was defeated, it was not destroyed, and it was succeeded by other state agencies on the third front administration that remained deeply involved in "ideological" affairs, just as party organs like Agitprop became enmeshed in the "cultural" and specialized ones. In practice, the overarching dualism accompanied a crazy-quilt of overlapping competencies and byzantine rivalries in the emergent third front apparat.[91] The bureaucratic infighting of NEP accompany-

90. Consequently, Kotkin attributes the Party's "self-immolation" in the Great Purges in part to the systemic bureaucratic rivalries and quasi-religious revolutionary revivalism that resulted. *Magnetic Mountain*, 282–98.

91. Explored in greater length in my article "Glavlit, Censorship and the Problem of Party Policy in Cultural Affairs, 1922–1928," *Soviet Studies* 44 (November 1992): 1045–68.

ing the triumph of party-state dualism was ideally suited to amplify the contradictions and ambiguities inherent in the division of spheres.

The concepts and terms "political enlightenment," "agitprop," and "culture" tended to merge and expand, given the organicist ethos at the heart of the consciousness-raising revolutionary state. A strict division among them was untenable not least because the regulatory organs had strong political incentives to broaden their jurisdictions, not to confine them.

The transition to peacetime and then to NEP coincided roughly with a series of formative power struggles over the shape of administration on the entire third front. During the civil war the political administration of the Red Army (PUR) played a leading role in propaganda, political art, literacy campaigns, and political instruction; each army and division had a political section (*politotdel*) responsible for newspapers, recruiting party members, and organizing political meetings. Narkompros had assumed the role of most important agency in the arts, the school system, and scholarship. The end of civil war produced a volatile new situation for both of these organizations. The future of the Red Army itself in peacetime was in doubt.[92] While PUR had sent out a barrage of almost 20,000 Communists to the armies and fronts between December 1918 and July 1920, a recent work has argued that its political education efforts were a disaster rather than a success. It does so, however, on the basis of only one case study, by pointing to the chasm separating the urban Communists sent from the center from the pillaging, rural, often anti-Semitic troops of the famed "red cavalry" (*Konarmiia*) in 1920.[93] It is possible that the party leadership's perception of failures in PUR's work in that year may have undercut the agency and spurred recognition of the need for a large-scale commitment to longer-term educational endeavors. What is certain is that Narkompros found itself in 1920–21 under severe pressure from many quarters. Lunacharskii's commissariat was attacked for being too conciliatory toward the intelligentsia, and for ceding virtual monopoly powers to certain avant-garde groups such as the futurists. Finally, the number of party and state agencies taking part in the revolutionary explosion of the most wide-

92. Mark von Hagen, *Soldiers in the Proletarian Dictatorship: The Red Army and the Soviet Socialist State, 1917–1930* (Ithaca: Cornell University Press, 1990), 132.

93. Stephen Brown, "Communists and the Red Cavalry: The Political Education of the *Konarmiia* in the Russian Civil War, 1918–1920," *Slavonic and East European Review* 73 (January 1995): 82–89. This article is vague on the educational efforts carried out, and it is unclear how representative the *Konarmiia* was in terms of political education.

spread activities gathered under the rubric of "political enlightenment" —such as theater and political instruction—had reached what some considered absurd proportions. In 1921 Iaroslavskii justified the need for a new centralizing agency, GPP, by noting that even the Commissariat of Food Supply had a theatrical section and conducted political-enlightenment work.[94]

The push for centralization may have somewhat reduced the proliferation, but it never eliminated the bureaucratic cacophony. Nevertheless, the embattled Narkompros leadership and other enemies of PUR recognized in the high-level support for centralization their chance to reap political gains by centralizing control of political enlightenment. It is emblematic of the endemic conceptual ambiguity that the new agency's very competency depended on how this term would be defined. In 1920 the plans to give Glavpolitprosvet sweeping powers bolstered an expansive definition of political enlightenment, and it became a possibility that the new agency would succeed in acquiring the powers of a dominant agency at the nexus of the entire apparat overseeing the third front. For example, it was set up to include a division of agitation and propaganda, an artistic section, and the committee on the liquidation of illiteracy. At the outset of 1921 GPP claimed 475,000 *politprosvet* personnel under its jurisdiction, a figure that shrank to a mere 10,000 when GPP lost virtually all power a year later.[95]

As PUR's protest in 1920 indicates, the charter of Glavpolitprosvet was drafted by Narkompros, while the Red Army organization was excluded from participation.[96] Glavpolitprosvet was to be under Narkompros and therefore a state agency, but would have direct channels to higher party organs and thus acquire a quasi-party status. Krupskaia, a high Narkompros official and Lenin's wife, was to be the central figure. The Politburo resolution of 28 October 1920 on Glavpolitprosvet, which first advanced the formula that the new organ would "unite all political-enlightenment work," is attributed to Lenin, and the agency

94. Sheila Fitzpatrick, "The Emergence of Glaviskusstvo: Class War on the Cultural Front, Moscow 1928–29," *Soviet Studies* 23 (October 1971): 236–53; Fitzpatrick, *Commissariat*, 242; *Desiatyi s"ezd Rossiiskoi kommunisticheskoi partii. Stenograficheskii otchet (8–16 marta 1921g)* (Moscow: Gosizdat, 1921), 87.

95. "Dekret Sovnarkoma o Glavpolitprosvete," 23 November 1921, GARF f. A-2313, op. 1, d. 1, l. 1; von Hagen, *Soldiers*, 152 n. 56; Robert H. McNeal, *Bride of the Revolution: Krupskaia and Lenin* (Ann Arbor: University of Michigan Press, 1973), 196, 198.

96. "Vypiska iz protokola Orgbiuro Ts.K. ot 25/X-20 g. No. 64," RTsKhIDNI f. 17, op. 60, d. 1, l. 34.

was later designated the "direct apparat of the Party in the system of state institutions." Preobrazhenskii declared: "What we are witnessing is the process of communization of the state apparatus."[97]

As Krupskaia revealed in a letter to the Politburo in 1921, as her organization was rapidly losing power to what became its major rival, the Central Committee's Agitprop department, "the Politburo discussed and appointed [GPP's] committee, and it was ordered that it would include a sufficiently authoritative member of the Central Committee. At first comrade Preobrazhenskii came in to the committee, then comrade Iaroslavskii."[98]

But at the time of the Tenth Party Congress in the spring of 1921 the outstanding issue of the relationship between GPP and the Party remained unresolved. Chances for a takeover of party functions in agitation and propaganda seemed increasingly remote. Debate nonetheless revealed widely differing agendas even among GPP's backers. Lunacharskii, with the most to gain, made the incendiary proposal that all cultural and propaganda tasks not "purely party" be taken away and given to GPP. To justify such a power play, the former "god-builder" attempted to undermine a literal or strict interpretation of party-state dualism, which he claimed was commonly misunderstood. Giving the state more functions would not deprive the Party, but the opposite, since "the Party must be everywhere like the biblical spirit of God." Krupskaia held out the possibility that GPP might someday become a party organ. Preobrazhenskii adopted a middle position, calling for GPP to take priority in uniting political-enlightenment work, but maintaining it should assume only some functions claimed by party organs. Finally, a certain Ivanov arose to have the last word. Announcing that he spoke on behalf of local agitators and propagandists in regional party committees, he denounced Narkompros as an art-obsessed, power-hungry appropriator of the rightful powers of the Party. Ivanov called for the party committees themselves to control political enlightenment, since "only the devil" could make sense of the futurist posters now put

97. "Protokol No. 54 zasedaniia Politbiuro Ts.K. ot 28 oktiabria 1920 goda," RTsKhIDNI f. 17, op. 3, d. 118, l. 1–2; V. I. Lenin, "Proekt postanovleniia Politbiuro TsK RKP(b) o Glavpolitprosvete," in *PSS*, 41:397; M. S. Andreeva, "Glavpolitprosvet—organ gosudarstvennoi propagandy kommunizma," in V. G. Chufarov, ed., *Kul'turnaia revoliutsiia v SSSR* (Sverdlovsk: Ural'skii gosudarstvennyi universitet, 1974), 485–93; McNeal, *Bride*, 195–97.

98. N. K. Krupskaia, "V Politbiuro TsK RKP," 28 November 1921, RTsKhIDNI f. 12, op. 1, d. 458, l. 3–4. Handwritten top center: "t. Leninu." The first GPP meetings in 1920 were attended not only by the top Narkompros leadership, including Krupskaia, Lunacharskii, and Evgraf A. Litkens, but by Preobrazhenskii as well. The 1920 meetings of GPP are in GARF, f. A-2313, op. 1, d. 1, l. 16, 17–18, 24, 25–26.

out by Narkompros, which "already has art, already has science, and now they want to add agitation and propaganda to that."[99]

In 1920–21 GPP and its supporters at times seemed to be winning a two-front battle against PUR and Agitprop. The congress and its aftermath made it possible for GPP to attempt to assume control over PUR's activities in the Red Army, a process which produced fierce resistance in the fall of 1921.[100] The Tenth Congress resolution noted that GPP did have the task of raising the consciousness of party members, and it would carry this out through control of the party schools.[101] Party education initially appeared to be one of Glavpolitprosvet's greatest prizes.

Agitprop, until 1920 simply a coordinating committee of representives from myriad agencies involved in disseminating the Party's message, which had lacked strong leadership and a clear-cut mandate from the Central Committee, emerged the next year as Glavpolitprosvet's major competitor. The agency's powers and aspirations swelled almost immediately, and its status was increased by the fact that the strengthening of the Central Committee apparat was a key factor in an entire complex shift in party-state relations in this period to the side of the Party. It was aided by those agencies, including PUR and the regional party committees, which saw their interests threatened by GPP. The first head of Agitprop in 1920, Ruben P. Katanian, was succeeded at his post by a more energetic young militant, Bubnov. Agitprop's 1921 charter gave the agency four divisions: agitation (with subsections of political campaigns, industrial or "production" agitation, and agitational technology), propaganda (with subsections for internal-party propaganda and the school section), and the press. The school section in 1921 was authorized to participate with GPP in formulating the programs of the party schools and the "social minimum" courses in the VUZy.[102]

As Krupskaia's letter to the Politburo also makes clear, the key moment in Agitprop's victory over GPP came in late 1921, when Ag-

99. *Desiatyi s"ezd*, 74–98; "Tezisy t. Preobrazhenskogo o GPP i agitproprabote partii," 2 February 1921, RTsKhIDNI f. 17, op. 3, d. 128, l. 1–6. On early debates and institutional shifts affecting party-state relations, see Walter Pietsch, *Revolution und Staat: Institutionen als Träger der Macht in Sowjetrußland, 1917–1922* (Cologne: Verlag Wissenschaft und Politik, 1969), 140–56.

100. Von Hagen, *Soldiers*, 137–52.

101. "O rabote Glavpolitprosveta. X s"ezd RKP(b)," March 1921, in *Direktivy VKP(b) po voprosam prosveshcheniia* (Moscow: Gosizdat, 1929), 10–11.

102. "K organizatsii otdela agitatsii i propagandy pri TsK," *Izvestiia TsK RKP(b)*, 18 September 1920, 16; *Deviataia konferentsiia RKP(b). Sentiabr' 1920 goda. Protokoly* (Moscow: Politizdat, 1972), 91, 106, 110, 126–37; "Polozhenie ob Agitatsionno-Propagandistskom otdele TsK RKP (utverzhdeno Orgbiuro TsK RKP 27 noiabria 1921 g.)," RTsKhIDNI f. 17, op. 60, d. 33, l. 1.

itprop's dominance was cemented by the influx of large group of high-ranking party members, some of them transferred directly from GPP. Agitprop's trump card in the struggle against GPP was its status as a "party" institution. Krupskaia protested:

> Is the proposed organization of Agitprop correct? . . . In composition the Agitprop department is no more of the Party than Glavpolitprosvet. Why was Solov'ev, when he was at Glavpolitprosvet, less a party member than when he was transferred to the Agit department . . . ? In my view, we should leave things as they were, and propose that Stalin control the work of Glavpolitprosvet directly, and not through Solov'ev, Vardin, and the 87 comrades who are now going to work at Agitprop . . . the workers who are now being picked for the Agit department should be given to Glavpolitprosvet.[103]

Stalin's association with Agitprop thus seems to have provided a critical boost for the party organization. In April 1921 the Politburo instructed Stalin to spend three-quarters of his time on "party" (as opposed to state) work, including "no less than one-and-one-half hours" with Agitprop.[104]

As the political contest between Agitprop and GPP heated up, an ideological basis for the conflict developed that gave the events of 1921, and GPP's subsequent reduction of power, a lasting significance. Agitprop and the Red Army political workers indicted GPP for the old populist sins of a *Kulturträger* or "non-class" approach, for working for "general enlightenment" rather than political propaganda. In von Hagen's words, "*Kul'turtregerstvo*, and its more Russified variant *kul'turnichestvo*, was a clearly pejorative term from the pre-1917 vocabulary of the revolutionary parties. . . . For the working-class militant, *kul'turnichestvo* was associated with the bourgeois intelligentsia, who endeavored to replace genuine class struggle with the palliative of 'abstract enlightenment activity.'" Glavpolitprosvet workers, as von Hagen points out, certainly did not consider their approach any less political than that of their critics; rather, they prided themselves on integrating cultural and political approaches and on using participatory methods of instruction.[105]

103. Krupskaia, "V Politbiuro TsK RKP," 28 November 1921, RTsKhIDNI f. 12, op. 1, d. 458, l. 3. V. Solov'ev became the deputy director of Agitprop in 1921.

104. It seems most likely those hours were calculated on a weekly basis. Of the "remainder" of his time he was to spend the bulk on the Worker-Peasant Inspectorate. RTsKhIDNI f. 17, op. 3, ed. khr. 199, l. 5.

105. Von Hagen, *Soldiers*, 153, 156.

The lasting resonance of these disputes over the relationship between culture and propaganda can be discerned in the 1928 theses of an Agitprop official called Chistov, whose views could have easily been advanced six or seven years earlier. Chistov attacked GPP's work throughout the 1920s as an example of enlightenment "for its own sake." Both Krupskaia and her GPP deputy Meshcheriakov, in responding to Chistov, cited GPP excesses in politicizing reading materials in the illiteracy campaigns as evidence that they were not guilty of *kul'turnichestvo*, but it is likely that even these protestations would have only confirmed Chistov's suspicions. "On the contrary," Krupskaia noted acerbically, "excesses were always on the side of agitation. Even grammar and literacy were transformed into agit-babble [*agitboltovniu*]."[106]

Krupskaia's 1921 letter to the Politburo suggests how she portrayed the differences between GPP and Agitprop at the height of their political rivalry. There, she asserted that "pure agitation" could never be effective and must always be combined with "enlightenment work." Only the lure of general educational opportunities could make the inculcation of party doctrine and policies palatable to the masses in the long run and at the same time raise their consciousness. Agitprop, she charged, "looks down on enlightenment work, disdainfully calling it 'cultural' in quotation marks; at the same time Agitprop is making this criticism come true by separating out the political work from the enlightenment, which GPP has always tried to combine in its work with the masses." In short, Agitprop professed little interest in the general education work that GPP and Narkompros leaders viewed as an essential component of their approach; rather, it stood for the development of a "pure" party propaganda.[107]

In the course of 1922 the true dimensions of Agitprop's victory over Glavpolitprosvet became apparent. GPP lost control of its massive apparat, was allowed to run out of funds in the often chaotic fiscal austerity of NEP, and was even forced to justify its continued existence.[108] A kind of contract was drawn up to clarify the relationship between GPP

106. Krupskaia to Chistov, no earlier than 12 February 1928, RTsKhIDNI f. 12, op. 1, d. 458, l. 22–24; "Zampred. GPP Meshcheriakov. V Agitotdel TsK tov. Chistovu," 12 February 1928, RTsKhIDNI f. 12, op. 1, d. 458, l. 25–28.

107. Krupskaia, "V Politbiuro TsK," l. 3; A. V. Lunacharskii, "Kommunisticheskaia propaganda i narodnoe prosveshchenie," in *Problemy narodnogo obrazovaniia: sbornik* (Moscow: Rabotnik prosveshcheniia, 1923), 88–93.

108. On the apparat, "V Politbiuro TsK ot komiteta GPP," 24 November 1922, RTsKhIDNI f. 12, op. 1, d. 458, l. 4–5; on finances, "Protokol zasedaniia GPP," 15 June 1922, GARF f. A-2313, op. 1, d. 69, l. 70; "Protokol soveshchaniia redaktsii zhurnala 'Kommunisticheskoe prosveshchenie' ot 2-go Marta 1922 g.," ibid., d. 72, l. 15.

and Agitprop; this document gave Agitprop resounding priority in all matters having a "party character." The document's language made clear that GPP would now become a subordinate organization. As part of this new agreement, the propaganda subsection of Agitprop was instructed to "control the work of GPP" in the realm of party education.[109]

Glavpolitprosvet documents from the mid-1920s show that the agency became largely concerned with political-enlightenment work in the countryside, administering such initiatives as the local "reading huts" and libraries, and attempting to popularize party positions among the peasantry.[110] GPP remained involved in the system of party education, however, and retained some influence in this area. The main reason for this appears to be that the GPP budget financed the communist universities and *sovpartshkoly*; GPP, as part of Narkompros, was officially a state agency and in this way the party schools could be financed out of the state budget. In 1924, the vast bulk of GPP's monthly budget was devoted to the party schools, while approximately one-eighth of the total went to all its other *politprosvet* work combined.[111] Yet the attempt to create quasi-party outposts within the Soviet state and the spread of "party" functions to the state did not end with the decline of Glavpolitprosvet. In 1922 Glavlit was created under Narkompros to coordinate all censorship activities and achieved the transcendence of party-state dualism on the third front for which the earlier impetus behind Glavpolitprosvet may have paved the way.

The main initiative in party education, however, now passed to Agitprop. True to its position in the 1921–22 conflict with GPP, Agitprop's major achievement between 1923 and 1926 was to orient party school curricula around disciplines closely tied to current party politics, such as the history of the party and, after 1924, Leninism; at the same time, the importance of general education was reduced. Agitprop also championed the idea that the higher party schools should produce "practical" party politicians rather than, as in 1921–23, emphasizing the training of erudite Marxist theoreticians and scholars. Agitprop

109. "Polozhenie o vzaimotnosheniiakh Agitpropotdela TsK RKP(b) s Glavpolitprosvetom," GARF f. A-2313, op. 1, d. 1, l. 461.

110. "Plan doklada Glavpolitprosveta na Orgbiuro TsK. Proekt. XII-14–26," RTsKhIDNI f. 12, op. 1, d. 472, l. 81–83; N. K. Krupskaia, "V Politbiuro TsK RKP(b)," 25 February 1928, RTsKhIDNI f. 12, op. 1, d. 458, l. 31–32. The GPP archive from 1926–29 is considered lost. Andreeva, "Glavpolitprosvet," 493.

111. "Zampredglavpolitprosvet V. Meshcheriakov. V Agitprop TsK, 28/II-24," GARF f. A-2313, op. 1, d. 87, l. 19–20.

used its manpower to centralize and standardize party school curricula and increase regulation of the selection of students, making slow but steady progress toward the goal of further proletarianization and stiffening required party qualifications.[112]

Agitprop's ascendancy in the regulation of party education did not just exaggerate the division between the communist institutions and the VUZy. It paved the way for the agency to influence policy toward the old higher educational institutions as well. In academic as in cultural affairs, the line between the Party and the state remained a kind of semipermeable membrane. As was noted, Agitprop from the outset was authorized to deal with the "social minimum" program in higher schools. Agitprop held influence over nonparty higher education especially through its regulatory control over the powerful student party cells.[113] In 1923 Agitprop, with the help of the head of the communist student bureau, Zelinskii, conducted a special investigation into the party cells in Petrograd VUZy. When Zelinskii found "elements of corruption, revisionism, opportunism, and other deviations within the cells," Agitprop chief Bubnov lobbied the Central Committee Secretariat for permission to conduct similar investigations in VUZy throughout the country. The result was a circular directive to the party gubkoms to set up special investigative commissions headed by a gubkom agitprop representative, a representative from the proletarian students, and a Communist from the local Narkompros division.[114]

Agitprop also assumed an important role in influencing the most im-

112. Popov, "Partprosveshchenie v nachale nepa i teper'," 6–7; GARF f. A-2313, op. 1, d. 87, l. 92. Agitprop was staffed by members of the prestigious *propgruppy TsK*, which in the mid-1920s consisted of about a hundred graduates of central communist universities, chosen from those who were the "most developed theoretically and loyal politically." N. Bogomolov, "K predstoiashchemu vypusku kommunisticheskogo studenchestva," *Kommunisticheskaia revoliutsiia*, no. 9 (May 1926): 22–23; "V Agitprope TsK," *Kommunisticheskaia revoliutsiia*, no. 24 (December 1926): 61–64.

113. "Vvedenie v otchet Ts. B. Komstudenchestva v Agitprop TsK 24/II-23," RTsKhIDNI f. 17, op. 60, d. 489, l. 6–9; "Zav. Agitpropotdel A. Bubnov. V Sekretariat TsK. 8 marta 1923 g.," ibid., d. 220, l. 22; "TsB kommunisticheskogo studenchestva. Sekretar' Zelinskii. V TsK RKP t. Bubnovu. Kopiia t. Stalinu," no date, ibid., d. 205, l. 87; "Protokol soveshchaniia po vysshei shkole pri p/otdele propagandy TsK RKP(b) 9-go ianvaria 1923 g.," ibid., d. 471, l. 1–2.

114. "V Tsentral'nyi Komitet R.K.P. Doklad otvetstvennogo sekretaria Ts. B. o poezdke v Petrograd, soglasno postanovleniia Orgbiuro TsK ot marta 1923," RTsKhIDNI f. 17, op. 60, d. 489, l. 10–11; "Doklad organizatora kollektiva Petrogradskogo Gosudarstvennogo Universiteta t. Zelinskomu, predstaviteliu Ts. B. Kommunisticheskogo Studenchestva, 8/III-1923," ibid., d. 489, l. 14–15 (see also l. 16–18); "—Gubkomu RKP(b)," Agitprop circular, no date, 1923, ibid., d. 471, l. 22–23.

portant policies that applied to both state and party education, to VUZy and Komvuzy. These included admissions quotas and requirements, proletarianization, the training of communist teachers and scholars, and student purges. One of Agitprop's main activities became the reviewing and recommending of literature for political education in all institutions, including the VUZy.[115] In this endeavor, Agitprop established particularly close relations with another quasi-party subdivision of a state agency, the scientific-political section of Narkompros' State Academic Council (GUS). This organization, staffed completely by communist intellectuals and headed by Pokrovskii, might be considered a successful example in the academic realm of what GPP failed to achieve, a "communized" state organ. Narkompros, a divided institution, has far too often been associated solely with the personality of Lunacharskii, whose hands were explicitly tied by the Politburo in 1922.[116] The political section of GUS, in charge of academic appointments and curricula in the social sciences, was deliberately created as a communist stronghold in a large commissariat that in other areas was committed to fostering the participation of nonparty specialists. Pokrovskii noted in 1924 that the political section was revising the "social minimum" in "close contact" with Agitprop's propaganda subsection.[117]

Agitprop and the political section of GUS focused their attention on developing the Marxist disciplines in the VUZy and increasing the importance of the social minimum. The communist institutions and the VUZy, in this case, were treated to the same regulatory initiatives in the social science disciplines. Much of Agitprop's clout was reserved for the most politically sensitive topics. After the condemnation of the Trotskyist opposition at the Thirteenth Party Congress in 1924, for example, the history of the party was rewritten by Agitprop and GUS's political section to include heavy-handed anti-Trotskyist teachings, which in January 1925 were made obligatory for the entire system of party education and the mandatory courses in the VUZy. After Lenin's death in

115. "A. Bubnov. V Politbiuro TsK. Sekretno. 2-IX-22 g.," RTsKhIDNI f. 17, op. 60, d. 274, l. 81–82; "Protokol zasedaniia podkomissii po podgotovke prepodavatelei kommunistov ot 6-go dekabria 1924 g.," ibid., d. 738, l. 49; *K XIV s"ezdu RKP(b)* (Moscow: Gosizdat, 1925), 117; "M. N. Pokrovskii. V Agitprop TsK VKP(b) t. G. Knorinu, 18.IV-27 g.," ARAN f. 1759, op. 4, d. 45, l. 1.

116. In 1922 a so-called "constitution" was worked out by which no decision by Lunacharskii held force unless it was approved by his deputies (who then included Pokrovskii, Khodorovskii, and Iakovleva). "Prilozhenie k p. 18 pr. PB No. 39 ot 7.XII.22," RTsKhIDNI f. 17, op. 3, d. 325, l. 9.

117. "Soveshchanie Narkomprosov Soiuznykh i Avtonomnykh Respublik. I-e zasedanie—27 oktiabria 1924," ARAN f. 1759, op. 2, d. 5, l. 59–61, on the origins of GUS, l. 50–51.

1924, Agitprop's propaganda subsection hosted the multiagency meetings that mobilized party forces to launch the "propaganda and study of Leninism," a key initiative in the incipient cult of Lenin. As a part of this mobilization, Agitprop and the GUS political section began to saturate social science curricula with the new discipline of Leninism. The efforts to develop and regulate the curricula in the system of party education thus had significant ramifications for the study of the social sciences in all higher schools. In the mid-1920s, the political section of GUS collaborated with Agitprop to increase mandatory course requirements in Marxism, and revamp their content. This occurred at the very moment when other parts of Narkompros were attempting to strengthen the post-1922 accommodation with the nonparty and non-Marxist professoriat.[118]

While Narkompros was strengthening the *modus vivendi* with the nonparty professoriat, then, its own political section was working along with Agitprop to undermine the compromise. Such contradictions of NEP-era cultural and higher educational policy flowed inexorably from the unstable regulatory crazy-quilt underneath the party-state duality, and the pervasive ambiguity in the basic concepts that governed Bolshevik administration of the third front. In 1929, the collapse of party-state dualism as it had been known during NEP was personified in the replacement of Lunacharskii, the commissar of enlightenment, by Bubnov, the former chief of Agitprop and PUR.

Models, Institutions, and Systems in the 1920s Academic Order

Party institutions first assumed the status of models in the social sciences, the area of most concern to party and Marxist forces in the 1920s and thus the source of greatest friction in the fragile post-1922 academic settlement. Narkompros had first begun efforts to consolidate

118. "Meropriiatiia po ob"edineniiu rukovodstva prepodavaniem obshchestvennykh distsiplin v shkolakh vsekh tipov (postanovlenie TsK ot 2/VII-26 goda)," in *Direktivy VKP(b) po voprosam prosveshcheniia* (1929), 75; "Vypiska iz protokola No. 9 zasedaniia Podsektsii VUZ Nauchno-Politicheskoi Sektsii GUS-a ot 21-go dekabria 1926 g.," RTsKhIDNI f. 89, op. 1, d. 123, l. 2; "Stenogramma soveshchaniia Nauchno-politicheskoi sektsii GUS-a po politminimumu 30 marta 1926," ARAN f. 1759, op. 2, d. 5, l. 190–205; "Zam. Zav. Agitpropotdel TsK K. Popov M. N. Pokrovskomu, NKPros. 6 fevralia 1924," ibid., d. 33, l. 10–13; "O propagande i izuchenii Leninizma," approved by Agitprop's subsection on propaganda, 9 February 1924, GARF f. A-2313, op. 1, d. 87, l. 57–62; Fitzpatrick, *Education*, 75.

change in the social sciences during the civil war by founding social science schools (*fakul'tety obshchestvennykh nauk*, or FONy) at the universities to replace the old history, law, and philology departments. The original hope that the FONy would become centers for the Marxist social sciences, through both the appointment of party scholars and control over the curricula, had already foundered badly by the end of the civil war. The severe shortage of qualified party scholars and the resistance of the nonparty professoriat seemingly undermined the very purpose of the FONy.[119]

The result was that there were attempts to divide the Marxist social sciences from non-Marxist and nonparty "specialized" and "narrowly practical" areas of the social sciences—just the kind of division later found in the spheres of influence in the party-state and in post-1920 higher education between party and nonparty institutions. Beginning in 1920, Glavprofobr attempted to reorient the FONy around specialist training for future employees of the commissariats, including "economic" and "legal" administrations.[120] It seemed that a new practical orientation might save the FONy and in so doing legitimate the value of non-Marxist expertise in social science education.

As the struggle over the university charter heated up in 1922, however, the weakness of the Party's foothold at the FONy proved a more important consideration than the potential benefits of their new programs. Glavprofobr, according to Volgin, reexamined all the FONy; on the basis that they had few or no Marxist or communist teachers, the Central Committee then shut down the schools in Simbirsk, Samara, Orla, Kostroma, Astrakhan, Krasnodar, and elsewhere. Volgin noted that the weakness of party forces made "reform" of these provincial FONy impossible for a very long time; it was considered more advantageous for the Marxist social sciences simply to close them down. The five remaining social science schools (with the exception of the Moscow University FON, which contained comparatively more communist teachers) were given further instructions to maintain only a "narrow specialist" training. Such orders were easier to issue than to monitor. But for the advocates of the new party schools, in any case,

119. Fitzpatrick, *Education*, 69; Bronislava I. Cherepnina, "Deiatel'nost' Kommunisticheskoi Partii v oblasti podgotovki nauchno-pedagogicheskikh kadrov po obshchestvennym naukam v SSSR za 1918–1962 gg. (na materialakh vysshei shkoly)" (Candidate of Sciences diss., Institut narodnogo khoziaistva im. Plekhanova [Moscow], 1964), 24.

120. "Tezisy k dokladu V. P. Volgina. Reorganizatsii FON-ov Rossiiskikh Universitetov," no date, GARF f. A-2306, op. 1, d. 469, l. 10–11.

the major concern was not the modification of the FON programs, but the fact that they represented an organizational rival to the party schools in the social sciences.

In the spring of 1924 conflicts arose over the fate of the remaining FONy. As Pokrovskii's comments in meetings at GUS in March of 1924 make clear, opponents of the FONy wanted to "create a unified higher social science school on the basis of the communist universities." The patrons of party education were calling for the elimination of the remaining FONy because they represented an enclave for the nonparty professoriat in the social sciences.[121] Pokrovskii, who this time sided with the gradualists, wished to preserve the FONy as valuable institutions and to subject them to a continuing influx of Marxist forces.

The opponents of the FONy gained the upper hand; in March 1924 the scientific-political section of GUS ratified the decision to close the FONy at Irkutsk, Rostov, Saratov, and Leningrad Universities. In each case, the FONy were broken up into their constituent parts and instructed to maintain a "narrow specialist preparation."[122] In late 1924 a special five-man Orgburo commission was set up to decide the fate of the last and most important FON, the one at Moscow University. The two minority members of this commission, Pokrovskii and V. Serezhnikov, tried unsuccessfully to preserve the FON as what they called the only remaining "genuine Higher School in the social sciences in the republic." In this minority opinion they were joined by the collegium of Narkompros. The victorious majority of the special commission was made up of the two top Agitprop officials in charge of the party schools, Bubnov and Popov, joined by Narkompros's Iakovleva. Significantly, the majority resolution judged it "fundamentally desirable to unite the functions of the Moscow FON with those of Sverdlov [Communist] University." As two protest letters from the vanquished minority reveal, the decision in the disputed case of the Moscow FON was the culmination of broader plans underlying the elimination of all the FONy in 1922–24. The nonparty professoriat was to be deprived of an organizational base in the social sciences, and the com-

121. "Protokol No. 79 Zasedaniia Podsektsii VUZ-ov Nauchno-Politicheskoi Sektsii GUS 8-go marta 1924," ARAN f. 1759, op. 2, d. 5, l. 86–87; "Protokol 80 Zasedaniia Nauchno-Politicheskoi Setskii GUS-a 15-go marta 1924," ibid., l. 92–93.

122. "Protokol 81 Zasedaniia Nauchno-Politicheskoi Sektsii (Podsektsii VUZ) GUS-a 22-go marta 1924," ARAN f. 1759, op. 2, d. 5, l. 94–97.

munist institutions were to replace the FONy as social science higher schools.[123]

The FONy were thus liquidated as institutions, but once again the results were different than those intended by the champions of party hegemony. Sometimes under the cloak of new names, the old professors managed to continue teaching their specialties.[124] By the mid-1920s, the demise of the FONy assured there was no single institutional or organizational rival to the party schools in social science higher education; but it also effectively broadened the gulf between the Marxist social sciences in the party schools and the teaching in the universities. Paradoxically, the 1924 attempt to ensure the dominance of the party schools simply made the division of higher educational spheres starker.

After 1924 there were renewed attempts to consolidate a party bulwark in the state institutions. A special Central Committee commission beginning work in December 1924 created new departments (*kafedry*) of Leninism and party history in the VUZy and bolstered the party composition of the social minimum teaching staff. As a GUS report in 1926 shows, however, these efforts changed little in the VUZy as a whole: almost all the communist teachers in the VUZy were concentrated in the social minimum courses. "Thus, the social science department in the higher school, in general, remains as before in the hands of the bourgeois professoriat," the report concluded.[125]

Narkompros data show that of the over 12,500 teaching personnel in 17 universities and 86 VUZy in 1925 in the RSFSR, only 6.1 percent were party members. This figure had barely increased by 1928, and even at that time represented only a few percentage points increase over the number of communist teachers in VUZy in the early 1920s. The figure was virtually identical for researchers and scholars as a whole. According to Central Committee data, of the 1,590 Communists classified as scientific (that is, scholarly) workers in the USSR in 1929 (excluding Uzbekistan and Turkmenistan), 42 percent were in Moscow and 61.4 percent were in the social sciences. Yet party members com-

123. "V Orgbiuro TsK RKP(b). Osoboe mnenie men'shenstva komissii Orgbiuro po preobrazovaniiu FON-ov," no date, late 1924, RTsKhIDNI f. 147, op. 2c, d. 5, l. 22–23; V Serezhnikov to G. Zinov'ev, probably October 1924, ARAN f. 1759, op. 2, d. 5, l. 83–85.

124. Fitzpatrick, *Education*, 72–73.

125. "Protokol Zasedaniia komissii po VUZ-am pri TsK ot 1-go dekabria 1924 goda," RTsKhIDNI f. 17, op. 60, d. 738, l. 6–8; "Vypiska iz protokola No. 16 zasedaniia Orgbiuro ot 18/VII-24 g.," ibid., op. 2c, d. 5, l. 5; "Vypiska iz postanovleniia ob 'Obshchestvennoi minimume i propaganda leninizma v VUZ-akh' priniatogo na zasedanii Sekretariata TsK RKP ot 2/I-25 g.," ibid., l. 13; "Tezisy k dokladu o prepodavanii obshchestvovedeniia v shkolakh RSFSR, 1925–26, s popravkami M. N. Pokrovskogo," ARAN f. 1759, op. 2, d. 5, l. 171–86.

prised a mere 6.3 percent of the country's total of 25,286 scientific workers.[126]

Outside the social sciences, the professoriat, as a speech by Pokrovskii in 1929 underlines, had retained *de facto* control over most faculty appointments and the selection of graduate students for the duration of NEP. The situation was somewhat different in terms of the closely monitored composition of the student body in the non-party institutions. According to Narkompros data, by 1925 the contingent of communist and Komsomol students in 17 universities and 86 VUZy in the RSFSR was 10.3 and 10.0 percent; the number of students classified as proletarian was 21.8 percent.[127]

After several years of relative stability in higher learning, the non-party professoriat made raising academic standards among the student body in the VUZy a top priority. The professors won a significant victory in this area in 1926. After the deliberations of a multiagency commission, admission requirements and examinations were reinstated; the previous quota (*razverstka*) system of nomination by organization was modified, although rabfak graduates and party members retained priority in admissions. While Lunacharskii promised the proletarian students that Narkompros had no intention of allowing the new entrance requirements to lower the proletarian contingent in the VUZy, the measure was a significant blow to communist students; overburdened with party work and political literature, they were often the least academically qualified. The Politburo upheld entrance examinations in 1927, although it ordered they should not take on a "competitive character" and rescinded the reserved spaces for children of specialists and the "working intelligentsia" that had been introduced in 1926.[128]

In sum, the shortage of Marxist forces, the acute need for qualified

126. *Narodnoe obrazovanie v RSFSR* (Moscow: Izdatel'stvo "Doloi negramotnost'," 1925), 185; *Statisticheskii sbornik po narodnomu prosveshcheniiu RSFSR 1926* (Moscow: Narkompros, 1928); Kneen, "Higher Education," 39; "Nauchnye kadry VKP(b)," no exact date, 1929, GARF f. R-3145, op. 2, d. 10, l. 35–61.

127. M. N. Pokrovskii, "O podgotovke nauchnykh rabnotnikov," *Nauchnyi rabotnik*, no. 1 (January 1929): 16–28; Fitzpatrick, *Education*, 81–82; *Narodnoe obrazovanie v RSFSR* (1925), 185.

128. "Protokol No. 1 zasedaniia po voprosu o pravilakh priema v VUZ-y," RTsKhIDNI f. 17, op. 60, d. 752, l. 212; N. S. Derzhavin, "O povyshenii kvalifikatsii okonchivaiushchikh vysshuiu shkolu," *Nauchnyi rabotnik*, no. 9 (September 1926): 63–71; A. Abinder, "K voprosu ob akademicheskoi podgotovke molodezhi," *Nauchnyi rabotnik*, no. 11 (November 1926): 33–49; A. V. Lunacharskii, "Doklad k IV Mezhsoiuznoi Gubernskoi konferentsii proletarskogo studenchestva III/19-25 g.," RTsKhIDNI f. 142, op. 1, d. 197, l. 104–13; "Protokol No. 91 Zakrytogo zasedaniia Politbiuro TsK VKP(b) ot 17-go marta 1927," ibid., f. 17, op. 3, ed. khr. 624, l. 5. On recruitment to VUZy during NEP, see Fitzpatrick, *Education*, 87–110.

graduates, and the policies Narkompros pursued toward the nonparty professoriat in the mid-1920s had slowed "reform" of the state-run institutions. In spite of this conjuncture, there is no sign that the communist transformation of all higher education had become any less of a firmly-fixed, long-term goal for party forces at virtually all levels. As Bukharin remarked in a speech to the Thirteenth Party Congress, which was reprinted in 1926, the higher school "has not been won over by us one whit. I in no way demand the expulsion of all nonproletarian elements, but in front of us lies a very complex and difficult task." The image of an unreconstructed ivory tower virtually untouched by the Revolution did not only result from statistical representations of communist weakness. It reflected values attached to the rival educational systems following the split of higher learning into party and nonparty spheres.[129]

In the mid-1920s concrete plans for "communization" of the social sciences were formulated. Pokrovskii noted in an internal report for the scientific-political section of GUS in 1925 that up to 600 professorial positions in the social sciences would have to be filled by newly minted Marxists from party institutions such as the Institute of Red Professors. From the social sciences the plans spilled over into higher education as a whole: "Thus, under the most favorable conditions we can count on the more or less complete 'communization' of our higher school[s] in no less than six years. . . . [M]ore cautiously one would leave ten years for the completion of this process. This time period is clearly too long."[130]

Communization on the most basic level thus implied the promotion of party scholars, and with them party Marxism. But the notion that inner-party norms could be exported to nonparty institutions accompanied the idea that institutions of party education were models for a new higher learning. This gained the imprimatur of the Politburo in July 1923, when it approved Agitprop's draft resolution for the Twelfth Party Congress which called for "a strengthening of our own forces and positions on the cultural front." Soviet-party schools and communist universities would become "model schools" (*obraztsovye shkoly*) of

129. N. Bukharin, "Rechi na XIII s"ezde RKP (Partiia i vospitanie smeny)" in *Bor'ba za kadry: Rechi i stat'i*, (Moscow-Leningrad: Molodaia gvardiia, 1926), 140; E. M. Iaroslavskii, "Partiia i VUZ-y," not earlier than May 1924, RTsKhIDNI f. 89, op. 8, d. 435, l. 1–3.

130. "Tezisy k dokladu o prepodavanii obshchestvovedeniia v shkolakh RSFSR, 1925–26, s popravkami M. N. Pokrovskogo," ARAN f. 1759, op. 2, d. 5, l. 178.

communist enlightenment. "In all schools" social-economic and political education must draw closer "to their type."[131]

Within the party educational system itself, a widespread notion that there were such things as Bolshevik institutions—and that party educational institutions were not just centers of the Marxist social sciences but also shapers of culture and instruments of socialization—became especially explicit when party education formulated its strategies for foreign Communists. After 1925 the Comintern's courses, and later the Lenin School, were consciously integrated into the system of Bolshevik party education. Agitprop played a leading role in organizing the Comintern institutions and teachers were recruited from the Institute of Red Professors and central communist universities. Significantly, the executive committee of the Comintern (IKKI) had set up the school as one means of "bolshevizing" foreign communist parties. Yet perennial problems resulted from what one 1929 account of the institution's activities termed "an excess of various political traditions and habits." Given these, it continued, "you can fully imagine how difficult the task of reeducating the collective was." The school was threatened by splits as many foreign Communists protested against the methods of "Bolshevist upbringing."[132] The Comintern's higher educational endeavors after 1925 demonstrate that only a few years after the Party had consolidated its own system of education, and certainly before it had achieved the grandiose goals that it embodied, the party model was being exported to fit new situations outside the Bolshevik Party, although as yet within the communist camp.

The rise of Bolshevik education had been from the outset intertwined with the adoption of the Bolshevik third front mission to build a new culture, create a new science, shape a new intelligentsia, and mold a New Man. The crucial development after the creation of a unified system of party education was that for the first time there was a concerted

131. "Protokol No. 19 Zasedaniia Politbiuro TsK ot 27 iiulia 1923 goda," RTsKhIDNI f. 17, op. 3, d. 367, l. 24–28. This notion of "model schools" was invoked by the leading party pedagogue A. F. Ryndich in *Metodika i organizatsiia partprosveshcheniia*, 4.

132. *Piat' let Leninskoi shkoly* (Moscow: Izdatel'stvo Mezhdunarodnoi Leninskoi shkoly, 1930), contained in RTsKhIDNI f. 531, op. 1, d. 258, l. 1–94; "Spravka po uchebno-programmnym voprosam mezhdunarodnykh leninskikh kursov. 13 iiunia 1925," RTsKhIDNI f. 531, op. 1, d. 1, l. 12; "Dokladnaia zapiska po voprosu ob organizatsii Mezhdunarodnogo Kommunisticheskogo Universiteta pri Kominterne," no date, RTsKhIDNI f. 531, op. 1, d. 19, l. 5–8; "Pravlenie leninskoi shkoly. Otchetnyi doklad Ispolkomu Kominterna ob itogakh dvukhletnei raboty mezhdunarodnoi leninskoi shkoly," 15 May 1929, RTsKhIDNI f. 531, op. 1, d. 15, l. 1–27.

attempt to actually implement these visions in an institutional framework. The divided 1920s academic order, surrounded by the imperfectly dualistic party-state, tended to ground these visions and channel revolutionary energy above all in the party educational system. But the possibility persisted that the quest would ultimately remake all of higher learning. As a result, even institutional and systemic structures were endowed with political affiliations. Bolshevik missions—and hence the process of revolutionizing higher learning—were now being filtered through a set of rapidly evolving, rising party institutions which had assumed the status of models and instruments of the regime.

2 / POWER AND EVERYDAY LIFE AT SVERDLOV COMMUNIST UNIVERSITY

The urge not only to transform politics, economics and society but to remold the "whole of human life" struck the cultural critic Fülöp-Miller in 1926 as the distinguishing mark of the Bolshevik Revolution.[1] The insight was inspired by the juncture at which he wrote, for the 1920s witnessed the most intense debate perhaps in Russia's history about human transformation. The culture-building and educational mission of the "transition period" turned the Revolution inward; the entrenchment of the new order spurred an attempt to mark the revolutionary in all spheres. The building of a new culture and a New Man, a defining concern of the 1920s in general and party students in particular, was to begin with the revolutionizing of everyday life.

The most significant exploration of early Soviet experiments in lifestyle since Fülöp-Miller conceptually severed grassroots activity and innovation from the grimly regimented utopianism from above associated with the triumph of Stalin.[2] Yet the explosive expansion of the revolutionary and the political into previously uncharted territories preoccupied the revolutionary project precisely when the entire party disciplinary system was entrenched in the 1920s. Uncovering the links, rather than the disjunction, between the evolving political order and the

1. René Fülöp-Miller, *The Mind and Face of Bolshevism: An Examination of Cultural Life in Soviet Russia* (New York: Alfred A. Knopf, 1928), xii, 264–317.
2. Stites, *Revolutionary Dreams.*

half-imagined, half-apparent "new way of life" can be seen as a central historical problem of the direction of the revolutionary enterprise.

Sverdlov Communist University, the first higher party school created after the Revolution, lies at the epicenter of 1920s experimentation as it intersected with the inner-party regime. Communist student youth, Sverdlovians most active among them, were the single most ardent group behind the search for a new everyday life (*byt*) and at the same time were a focal point for the Party's concern for the outlook of the new generation. As the model communist university, this institution also led such experiments as the adaptation of imported theories of American progressive pedagogy to the needs of the Revolution, with the hope of revising the nature of higher education. Such endeavors occurred under the auspices of a Communist Party institution, racked by constant political battles, and fully embedded in the Party's world of power relations.

Debates about lifestyle and the new learning assumed a central place at Sverdlov Communist University because they revolved directly around both liberation and power. The ambitious plans to alter the pedagogical heart of higher education explicitly aimed at reducing the rigid professorial authority held to be characteristic of the old universities. The elaboration of a new lifestyle, in similar fashion, was to unshackle the communist from the constraints of hypocritical bourgeois morality and indeed the patterns of prerevolutionary civilization. This search for liberation, of course, was made under a collectivist banner. Communist students fought to obliterate the private sphere perceived in the bourgeois past and present. Yet the quest for collective values to replace "individualism" characteristically overlapped with the agendas of party disciplinary organs as they also participated in the first attempts to articulate a communist code of behavior. Emancipatory plans to replace old power hierarchies were implemented within a newly established, communist system of power relationships. The revolutionary innovations of this emancipatory agenda mingled with new patterns of coercion in a manner opposite from all declared intentions.

This postrevolutionary fusion, exemplified with particular starkness in the communist student and youth movement but so typical of the communist project as a whole, holds implications for reinterpreting everyday political life in the 1920s. Politics at Sverdlov University, as at all Soviet institutions, cannot be understood outside the context of party cell politics, and for the first time we can trace the history and evolution of a single party cell. This inquiry not only shows the particular manner in which everyday life at Sverdlov University was politicized, but how party cell politics was pervaded by the debate about everyday life. The activities of the Sverdlov party cell over a decade show a preoccupation with questions of *byt*, ethics, collectivism, and behavior along with opposition and the inner-party regime. The activities of this particular cell, of course, were stamped by the quest for living revolution as it gripped the communist student movement in particular, but they also reveal a key element in the evolution of Bolshevik "party discipline" as a whole. Deviance in "communist morality" and lifestyle became intimately associated with political and ideological deviation, and not just among revolutionary students. The links were institutionalized first and foremost in the Party's highest disciplinary organ, the Central Control Commission (TsKK).

Party cell politics was connected to *byt* in another sense as well. The cell was simultaneously the building block of communist mass organization, the basic unit of the party disciplinary regime, and the bastion of rank and file "everyday" political life. As the Party emerged from its formative civil war–era centralization and militarization of its chain of command, a rift between the "lowers" (*nizy*) and "uppers" (*verkhi*) burst into public view. Along with the top-down power arrangements, it was resentment of party officials' privileges, luxuries, and lifestyles—the same concerns that launched the 1920s search for a new *byt*—that spawned tensions over disjunctions between emancipatory promises and dictatorial practices that festered throughout the decade.[3] Questions of lifestyle were thus not just the preserve of utopian dreamers but at the center of party politics, party discipline, and inner-party reactions to the party dictatorship. Even as the growth of party cells in the 1920s mark one of the fundamental developments of the Soviet era in higher educational institutions, the subordination of the rank and file became at Sverdlov the key to local politics and the symbolic point of departure for discussions of inner-party democracy.

Stalin's Great Break, at Sverdlov University and elsewhere, was launched in the turmoil of a "democratization" campaign within the Party. The birth of the Stalin era cannot be understood outside the context of this central phenomenon, which appears neither as Orwellian double-speak nor as a "genuine" revolt "from below." Set against the background of a decade-long, frustrated search for liberation—inter-

3. Robert Service, *The Bolshevik Party in Revolution: A Study in Organizational Change, 1917–1923* (New York: Harper & Row, 1979), 144 and passim; and on militarization in the Party, von Hagen, *Soldiers*.

twined with the refinement of a communist system of power relations extending into everyday life—it emerges as an epochal shift in the power hierarchy of NEP, one which transformed the resentments of a subordinated rank and file into a potent force to be unleashed and manipulated. But the elusive 1920s search for liberation by this time had endowed the entire disciplinary regime within the Party with an extended field of play.

The Rise of the First Communist University

This new vehicle for party education—the first higher party school—emerged only gradually out of what were seen as the Party's most urgent organizational tasks. Indeed, a new type of university was several years away from the short courses for agitators that were initiated even before the Bolshevik rise to power. Between June 1917 and March 1918 tens of thousands went through rapid training sessions organized by Iakov Sverdlov and the military organization of the Bolshevik Central Committee in Petrograd. "Having heard a couple of lectures, taking along a couple dozen brochures, the soldier, worker, or peasant set out for the countryside."[4] Sverdlov proposed similar courses in Moscow with broader programs, and on 10 June 1918 these were set up by G. I. Teodorovich of the agitation section of the VTsIK as the School of Soviet and Party Work.

From training agitators in the early revolutionary months, these Moscow courses shifted from 1918 to 1920 to preparing officials for specific branches of the commissariats and local party organizations. State institutions and the Red Army shipped off their own candidates to the school, and the students usually returned after study to the organization that had nominated them. Thus students "majored" in the Cheka, the Worker-Peasant Inspectorate, the VSNKh, or other commissariats. Within this framework, the teachers, the bulk of whom were high state or party officials, attempted to impart a general Marxist pool of knowledge. The section for the commissariat of labor in 1920, for example, boasted lectures on the history of the trade union movement by the Profintern leader Lozovskii, but more attention was paid to topics such as new Soviet labor legislation, methods of mobilizing workers, and

4. Vladimir I. Nevskii, "Sverdlovskii universitet i Oktiabr'skaia revoliutsiia," in X *[Desiat']* *let Kommuniversiteta im. Ia. M. Sverdlova* (Moscow: Izdatel'stvo Kommunisticheskogo universiteta im. Sverdlova, 1928), 19.

statistics. By far the most time was spent in "practical study" in the branches of the commissariat itself.[5]

Only slowly did a broader course of study emerge that presaged the creation of a party university. The Ninth Party Congress of March 1919 resolved to turn the courses into a "higher party school," but of the 4,417 students passing through between June 1918 and November 1919, only 263 directly took up party posts: 900 went into the state apparatus and 3,253 were sent to the front. A significant step was taken in the fall of 1919, when the school administration decided to lengthen the course of study to six months, half of which became devoted to a "general-theoretical" section designed in the Central Committee. This section offered instruction in such areas as Russian and Western history, law, political economy, and current politics and was thus reminiscent of the prerevolutionary underground party schools. In 1920 such party leaders as Skvortsov-Stepanov, Lunacharskii, and Bubnov were lecturing as the school moved away from the commissariat-based system. As at the Socialist Academy, a specifically party identity was fully elaborated only in 1920–21; in its charter of 1921 Sverdlov was formally baptized "a Higher Party School under the ideological influence of the Central Committee, the goal of which is to train workers and peasants in the theory and practice of communism."[6]

This evolution from agitator training to state-building to party university between 1917 and 1921 occurred at Sverdlov for several reasons. As early attempts to reform the old universities foundered, the fledgling party school, precisely because it did not at first pretend to university-level training, was able to build up a revolutionary and pro-Bolshevik constituency. In 1919–20, for example, 45.7 percent of the students were listed as workers; 12 percent of all students were former metalworkers. The bulk of students had only a primary education, and in 1919 the vast majority were newly enrolled Communists.[7] It was the hopes invested in this sociopolitical profile, notwithstanding the modest

5. GARF f. 5221, op. 1, d. 14, l. 340; "Programma zaniatii na sektsii po okhrane truda v Kommuniversitete Sverdlova," February–September 1920, ibid., d. 4, l. 3–7; letters from Iakov M. Sverdlov to heads of commissariats, ibid., d. 1, l. 4–10. For other sections' programs, see ibid., d. 3, l. 1, l. 19, and d. 2, l. 5–20.

6. GARF f. 5221, op. 1, d. 9, l. 16–19; "Zasedanie Uchebnogo Otdela Tsentral'noi shkoly partiinoi i sovetskoi raboty. 24 noiabria 1919," GARF f. 5221, op. 1, d. 1, l. 1; *Programmy i uchebnyi plan obshche-teoreticheskogo kratkosrochnogo kursa Raboche-krest'ianskogo Kommunisticheskogo Universiteta im. Sverdlova* (Moscow: Gosizdat, 1921), deposited at GARF f. 5221, op. 3, d. 4, l. 96–142; "Organizatsiia partiinoi shkoly," *Izvestiia TsK RKP(b)*, 7 June 1919; "Ustav Kommunisticheskogo Universiteta im. Sverdlova," GARF f. 5221, op. 3, d. 4, l. 68–72.

7. "Organizatsiia partiinoi shkoly," *Isvestiia TsK RKP(b)*, 7 June 1919; GARF f. 5221, op. 9, d. 48, l. 4, and op. 8, d. 55, l. 158–63.

and utilitarian character of the initial program, that set the new institution apart and seemed to assure the beginning of a grand transformation of all higher learning. One chemistry teacher recalled his first Sverdlov lectures, held in an auditorium of Moscow University: "The chemistry hall greeted students of a kind never seen in the history of Moscow University. It was unbearably cold in that auditorium—four degrees below zero. Hundreds of eyes impatiently and greedily gazed at the lecturer. . . . Workers and peasants came to old Moscow University as the first regiments sent by the proletarian revolution."[8]

The school's central location and sponsorship by the Central Committee made it the logical choice for the creation of the preeminent higher party school. A Central Committee commission was formed in 1920 to plan a three-year university program at Sverdlov; staffed by leading Bolshevik intellectuals, it was headed by the first rector, Vladimir Ivanovich Nevskii, an Old Bolshevik who had studied natural science at Moscow University in the late 1890s and later graduated from Kharkov University in 1911. The reorganized Sverdlov University soon drew up plans for the second communist university in Petrograd (named after Zinov′ev), and by extension for the rising network of higher party schools.[9] Nevskii insisted on the introduction of natural science into the Sverdlov curriculum, a move opposed by Riazanov as extraneous to Marxist social science, but endorsed on appeal by Lenin. The transition to a party university thus encompassed a shift to general education and an incorporation of natural as well as social science, and in the early to mid-1920s the first two elements still roughly balanced Marxist and political education in the standard communist university curriculum. Thus new higher educational concerns were layered onto already well-honed preoccupations with political instruction and the production of serviceable cadres.[10]

This widening focus is significant, because the birth of the communist university simultaneously combined a particularistic identification with the Party and a broadening of curriculum that was associated with a

8. I. Przheborovskii, "Iz vospominanii starogo prepodavatelia," in *X let Kommuniversiteta*, 282–83.

9. "Organizatsiia partiinoi shkoly," *Izvestiia TsK RKP(b)*, 7 June 1919, 1; Nevskii, "Sverdlovskii universitet," 18–28; G. I. Okulova-Teodorovich, "Nachalo: vospominaniia," *Sverdlovets*, no. 7–8 (June–July 1923): 58–61. The other commission members were Pokrovskii, Riazanov, Skvortsov-Stepanov, and Bukharin.

10. Nevskii, "Sverdlovskii universitet," 21–22; A. K. Timiriazev, "Kak voshlo estestvoznanie v prepodavanie Sverdlovskogo Universiteta," in *X let Kommuniversiteta*, 165–69; see, for example, "Predmetnaia skhema obshchei programmy Kommunisticheskogo universiteta," not earlier than 1923, GARF f. A-2313, op. 1, d. 1, l. 5756.

higher school. The consolidation of this new educational form might be compared to the *cours révolutionnaires* of the French Revolution of 1793–94—crash courses set up to train skilled workers loyal to the revolutionary regime. A revolutionized curriculum was equated with everything accelerated and modern. "There were 'revolutionary processes of tanning' and there was 'revolutionary . . . manufacture of gunpowder.' Even books were supposed to be sorted in a 'revolutionary' manner." From this beginning emerged a new type of institution, the École Polytechnique, which then formed the basis for a new system of higher education.[11] In the October Revolution, it was characteristically the training of agitators and functionaries, and the assimilation of social and political knowledge, that formed the basis of the frenetic revolutionary courses; but by 1921 the consolidated new educational system had been embodied in the communist university.

The civil war was not a time for most young Bolsheviks to spend in study. But by 1920–21 a new cadre of revolutionary students had begun to form, the vast majority of whom at Sverdlov were males who had served in the Red Army.[12] This dealt a shattering blow to the already fractured ideal of a unified student movement and its embattled traditions of corporate unity. As old traditions of student activism in the universities were now turned against the Bolsheviks, the new party institution (and the *rabfaks*) held out the possibility for reconstructing the student body and its political affiliation. By the early 1920s, on the heels of the splintering of the old student movement and the targeting of

11. Janis Langins, "Words and Institutions during the French Revolution: The Case of 'Revolutionary' Scientific and Technical Education," in Peter Burke and Roy Porter, eds., *The Social History of Language*, (Cambridge: Cambridge University Press, 1987), 143; Langins, *La république avait besoin de savants. Les débuts de l'École polytechnique: l'École centrale des travaux publiés et les cours révolutionnaires de l'an III* (Paris: Belin, 1987).

12. As late as 1926–27, 80 percent of Sverdlov students had served in the Red Army, and all were party members of enough standing to be nominated by their party organizations. GARF f. 5221, op. 8, d. 55, l. 158–63. Sverdlov always led the communist universities with the highest percentage of students classified as working class. See "Kommunisticheskie Universitety (po dannym statisticheskogo p/otdela Narkomprosa na 1-e ianvaria 1924 g.)," *Kommunisticheskoe prosveshchenie*, no. 3–4 (May–August 1924): 57–63. More detailed information on students in 1923–24 suggests that the student body's formal education was minimal: the vast majority had either attended or finished grammar school, and only 10 percent had attended middle school. Candidates of peasant origin were required to have served in the Red Army. By nationality, over 60 percent of the group were Russians and about 20 percent Jewish; no other nationality comprised over 5 percent. See *Kommunisticheskii Universitet imeni Ia. M. Sverdlova. Sostav studenchestva v 1923–24 uchebnom godu* (Moscow, [1924?]). Of the Sverdlov faculty, as of 1925 there were 103 party and 52 nonparty teachers, but the social sciences were dominated by party members (87.5 percent) while in "general education" subjects, nonparty teachers predominated (76.5 percent). "Svedeniia o sostave sotrudnikov i prepodavatelei Komuniversiteta im. Sverdlova, 1 fev. 1925," GARF f. 5221, op. 6, d. 514, l. 63.

many of its anti-Bolshevik activists, a new student tradition had been reinvented with its center of gravity among the communist students. Sverdlov University played a role in developing a self-consciously distinctive outlook, morals, dress, and élan for the new communist student movement. As a Sverdlov rector noted shortly thereafter, "They say it proudly: 'We are *Sverdlovtsy*.' They have founded certain traditions; they have their own songs." One communist student (and future red professor) even argued that there had emerged a new social type, the proletarian student-scholar *cum* Bolshevik revolutionary. The Sverdlov student, it was approvingly noted, could be easily picked out in a crowd.[13]

The revolutionary student identity, and within it the Sverdlov institutional loyalty, comprised a distinctive subculture within the Party. The emergence of the new communist *studenchestvo* of the 1920s, which recapitulated much of the intense social zeal of its prerevolutionary counterpart, lay at the roots of the party students' intensive engagement with fashioning a revolutionary way of life. The group identity also contributed to Sverdlovians' particular political forcefulness as privileged activists yet, simultaneously, rank and filers, as they openly revolted against and then covertly resisted an institutional power structure that invested supreme power in a rector appointed by the Central Committee.

Permutations of Party Cell Politics: Shifting Resentments of the Rank and File

The Sverdlov party cell was founded in 1920 in the corner of a room containing administrative offices, a table, and a cupboard. From the vantage point of this modest cranny, the cell's bureau was only too aware of the challenges it faced. Its main powers lay in selecting students as factory agitators for the Moscow Party Committee, and in this it was sometimes bypassed by the university administration.[14] In the next several years, however, the bureau of the party cell established

13. "Stenogramma t. Antonova-Saratovskogo," January 1923, RTsKhIDNI f. 17, op. 60, d. 233, l. 128; Aleksandr Aikhenval'd, "Studenchestvo vostavshikh nizov. Sverdlovets, kak sotsial'nyi tip," *Sverdlovets* no. 7–8 (June–July, 1923): 18–25. On the late imperial *studenchestvo* as a social community and its disintegration, see Morrissey, "More Stories," 436–50.

14. "Protokol zasedaniia partorganizatorov 2-x god. kursa Sverdlovskogo Universiteta sovmestno s Biuro iacheiki, 10/VIII-21 g." RGAODgM f. 459, op. 1, d. 13, l. 1; "Protokol No. 12 Obshchego sobraniia Kom. iacheiki Sverdlovskogo Universiteta ot 8 Iiulia 1921 g.," ibid., d. 8, l. 17; Vinokur, "Nash 'ugol,'" *Sverdlovets*, no. 7–8 (June–July 1923): 67–69.

itself as the single most powerful organization at the university with the exception of the rector's office, with which it successfully crossed swords.

The Bolshevik network of cells, which before 1917 were sometimes also known as "groups" or "circles," had frequently expanded into party town committees after October. In 1918 much organization work focused on creating as many new cells as possible. Cell secretaries emerged as a crucial political stratum as the Party pursued the slogan first invented by the Novgorod provincial committee in 1918: "total centralization" of party life. The strong secretary controlling the cell agenda, and the docile cell members willing to ratify the proposals presented by higher authority, became stock figures in party debates over the inner-party regime. Protesting the subordinate status of the cell rank and file became a plank in the platforms of successive inner-party opposition groups.[15]

University cells, however, consolidated a more activist and far more powerful position typical of communist factions in nonparty institutions. In the old universities, where Communists were a small minority of the students and a tiny fraction of the faculty, cells became the beachhead of pro-Bolshevik activity and local executors of party-state strategy toward the higher school. At the communist university, however, the initial position of the cell was more precarious. There was no reason for higher authorities to rely overly on the cell; the bias from the first was in favor of the rector, always a high-ranking Communist appointed by the Central Committee. In the early 1920s the cell built up its position with the Moscow Party Committee by providing badly needed teachers and propagandists, but this gave the cell leadership only a little more leverage.[16]

The Sverdlov cell had to win its position, and thus the cell leadership and the rank and file had a common cause even as the bureau consolidated power over its charges. The cell bureau was charged with organizing the party obligations and political life of its members, which at Sverdlov, of course, meant the entire student body. Its bureau was thus in a good strategic position to increase its power, especially since the

15. Service, *Bolshevik Party*, 50, 98, 117–19, 144, 168–71; *Pervichnaia partiinaia organizatsiia. Dokumenty KPSS. Posleoktiabr'skii period* (Moscow: Izdatel'stvo politicheskoi literatury, 1974).

16. As late as 1925–26, as much as one-fifth of the total number of propagandists used by the MK were students from Sverdlov, the Institute of Red Professors, and Moscow University. Catherine Merridale, *Moscow Politics and the Rise of Stalin: The Communist Party in the Capital, 1925–1932* (London: Macmillan, 1990), 147.

school's soviet, officially authorized to run all university affairs not specifically party-related, in practice dealt with administrative matters of the most innocuous kind. The cell's bureau, in contrast, acquired the power to recommend a student's dismissal from the university or even expulsion from the Party, to promote candidate party members to full members, to run school publications, and organize all the obligatory party meetings, holidays, and information sessions.[17]

The bureau's bid for a dominant role put it on a collision course with the one-man management of the rector. Serious conflicts between the cell bureau and the rector occurred during Nevskii's tenure in 1921. In a report to a Central Committee commission examining the university, the bureau complained of disorganized classes, lack of qualified teachers, and failure on the part of the administration to help the bureau raise students' political consciousness. The bureau tried to enhance the sense of scandal by reporting cases of student *kruzhki* discussing issues of freedom of speech instead of the dictatorship of the proletariat. Nevskii defensively rejected most of the students' complaints, but in front of Udal'tsov, the Central Committee representative on the commission, he announced his resignation.[18]

What reversed the balance of power between rector and bureau—and this phenomenon became inherent in the dynamics of the party hierarchy—was an oppositionist association that suddenly destroyed the rector. According to Nevskii's replacement, Vladimir Petrovich Antonov-Saratovskii, his predecessor had supported the Workers' Opposition along with several senior university administrators. According to Antonov, the Central Committee suggested that Nevskii step down.[19] In this top-heavy yet volatile mass party, if the local potentate fell the whole power structure could be momentarily inverted.

Antonov's new administration, however, coming in on the heels of Nevskii's collapse, was regarded with great suspicion during the fol-

17. On the soviet, see *Kommunisticheskii Universitet imeni Ia. M. Sverdlova: X-mu Vserossiiskomu S"ezdu Sovetov* (Moscow: Izdatel'stvo Kommunisticheskogo universiteta im. Sverdlova, 1922), 5–6; "Protokoly zasedaniia Prezidiuma Soveta Komuniversiteta Sverdlova," 1921, GARF f. 5221, op. 2, d. 9, l. 1–35. The bureau's most influential branches were the organizational and agitprop departments. RGAODgM f. 459, op. 1, d. 8, l. 36–45; d. 15, l. 44; d. 27, l. 9–13; d. 31, l. 46, 57.

18. "Doklad Biuro komiacheiki Komuniversiteta im. Ia. M. Sverdlova v komissiiu, naznachennuiu v TsK RKP dlia obsledovaniiu Universiteta," no date, 1921, RTsKhIDNI f. 17, op. 60, d. 66, l. 43–44; "Protokol No. 2 zasedaniia Smeshannoi komissii, ot 11 iiulia 1921 g.," ibid., d. 66, l. 3–4; "Protokol No. 3 zasedaniia Smeshannoi komissii," no earlier than 11 July 1921, ibid., l. 8–9.

19. "Stenogramma t. Antonova-Saratovskogo," January 1923, RTsKhIDNI f. 17, op. 60, d. 233, l. 121, 126.

lowing year. "As soon as I arrived at the University," Antonov recalled, "the students regarded me as a gendarme from the Central Committee." The rise of the Sverdlov cell was decisively furthered in the 1922–23 battle with the new rector Antonov-Saratovskii, who was effectively defeated and dismissed from his post.[20]

The turn to the NEP order had brought the task of training the young generation to the forefront of the party agenda, but simultaneously heightened alarmist warnings that youth would be led astray. Youth, so often the constituency of revolution, became a topic obsessively discussed after 1917. The Bolshevik Party itself had always been primarily "a party of young men."[21] The preoccupation with youth, fueled so much by revolution and Bolshevism, can also be related to such diverse underlying developments as the creation of a period of extended youth as a product of urban social life, the European-wide discovery of adolescence, and the stress on youthful innovation as part of what has been called a "modernizing consciousness." Yet the extraordinary significance youth assumed in the 1920s revolved around two particularly Soviet perceptions: its absolute importance for the future society and its special vulnerability to diversion from the true path. Early Soviet approaches to youth were permeated by the belief in its simultaneous malleability and corruptibility.[22]

The special position of the student as both the promise of the future and the object of special protection reflected these two sides to early Soviet conceptions of youth, and this in turn permeated issues of education. Soon after party students began to devote themselves to long-term higher education, in 1922, the wide-ranging dangers of "academicism" or "scholasticism" were raised in central publications. These terms were centered around condemning bookish, cerebral values that overcame social, political, or revolutionary commitment. Yet the class and anti-

20. Antonov (1884–1965), from Saratov, had been a Social Democrat since 1902; he studied law and history at Moscow University, graduating in 1911, the year he was arrested and exiled. He became a leader of the Saratov Bolsheviks during the war, and from August 1917 to the end of 1918 he was chairman of the Saratov soviet. He later served as a judge in the Shakhtii and Promparty show trials of 1928 and 1930. V. I. Nevskii, ed., *Deiateli revoliutsionnogo dvizheniia v Rossii: Bio-bibliograficheskii slovar'* (Moscow: OGIZ, 1931), 5:114.

21. T. H. Rigby, "A Dictatorship for Communism," in *The Changing Soviet System: Mono-organizational Socialism from Its Origins to Gorbachev's Restructuring* (Aldershot, U.K.: Edward Elgar, 1990), 39, and 51.

22. Anne Gorsuch, "Enthusiasts, Bohemians, and Delinquents: Soviet Youth Cultures, 1921–1928" (Ph.D. diss., University of Michigan, 1992), 25–27; Hilary Pilkington, *Russia's Youth and Its Culture* (London: Routledge, 1994), 43–60. Pilkington perceives parallels between youth and women in the communist state: both were seen as having special revolutionary potential, yet also comprising vulnerable segments of the proletariat requiring separate organizations.

intellectual connotations linked them to broader fears about the potential de-classing of proletarian youth. The specter of deproletarianization was a kind of Pandora's Box: it was as if the party member who discarded the hammer to open a book released a swarm of nonproletarian ills. As it most directly affected Sverdlov University, this discussion underlined the dangers for party students and raised sweeping allegations of loose sexual morals, "scholasticism," and ideological deviations. Since these charges threatened their party and class credentials, however, Sverdlovians hotly denied them.[23] At this sensitive moment, the rector, instead of defending the students, responded by giving the allegations more credence. Antonov, after secretly investigating reports of prostitution in the dormitories, unexpectedly issued a draconian ordinance (the infamous Decree No. 253) governing the behavior of the communist students, ostensibly to shield them against drunkenness, card games, and prostitutes. The incident at once raised issues of the rector's power, the students' class purity, and sensational allegations about students' degenerate lifestyle. A political firestorm was unleashed.[24]

"Mentioning such phenomena in the rector's decree discredits the title of student at a communist university," the cell bureau raged. "It is a bureaucratic, officious production by people who are not acquainted with the everyday life of the students." Student after student attacked the fact that Antonov had bypassed the party cell and treated the Sverdlovians not as seasoned revolutionaries but as schoolchildren. The rector, the bureau concluded, retained no authority among students: "He is permanently discredited in their eyes." Five weeks after the bureau petitioned the Central Committee for Antonov's resignation, Glavpolitprosvet issued the order for the rector to step down.[25]

The high-level commission set up in late December 1922 to investigate the incident, which included top Agitprop and TsKK officials Bubnov and Sol′ts, identified the political dimension behind the student indignation. Antonov spent most of his deposition criticizing a group of "power-seekers" (*vlastniki*) among the party cell leaders, many of whom had held party posts during the civil war. The ex-rector charged

23. Ivan Struev, "Itogi diskussii ob akademizme," *Sverdlovets*, no. 2 (March 1922): 4.

24. "Pravila vnutrennogo rasporiadka v domakh, obshchezhitiiakh i stoloviiakh Universiteta im. Ia. M. Sverdlova, vvodimye v deistvie s 1-go noiabria s/g.," RTsKhIDNI f. 17, op. 60, d. 501, l. 56–61.

25. "Protokol zasedaniia Biuro ot 3/XII-22 g.," RGAODgM f. 459, op. 1, d. 14, l. 3–4; "Telefonogramma No. 421 iz Glavpolitprosveta Komm. Universitetu Sverdlova t. Antonovu, 14/I-23 g.," GARF f. 5221, op. 5, d. 38, l. 7; N. Rusunov, "10 let Sverdlovii," in *X let Komuniversiteta*, 88–89.

that these power-seekers viewed the cell's relation to the administration as analogous to a party committee's command over a soviet. These students, Antonov stated earlier in a separate report to the Central Committee, had connections in the local raikom and Moscow Party Committee, so the cell "line" was always approved. At his deposition, Antonov claimed this very report had been known only to three people in the Central Committee, but had been immediately leaked to the cell bureau.[26]

In the heat of political controversy, it was typical that the dismissed rector raised all the possible sins, from political oppositionism to sexual libertinism, that could discredit the students' position. He pointed to a group of followers of Bogdanov in the academically advanced "lecturer group" and mentioned theft of lightbulbs and other state property. The rector portrayed the threat of sexual promiscuity as so serious that he had had to hire elderly cleaning women for the dormitories. The cell leaders responded by depicting Antonov as high-handed dictator, and they played down his charges as a few unfortunate incidents.[27]

The student leader Struev raised the issue of inner-party democracy—the theme that resurfaces in all discussions of party cell relations between rector, bureau, and rank and file—by charging that Antonov feared democratic input from his subordinates. Every Sverdlov student interviewed by the commission denied the existence of so-called power-seekers. "There are several comrades who believe the presidium of the university must reckon with the decisions of the bureau of the cell on certain questions," one student put it, "and in fact such an opinion is virtually universal."[28] The clash over power and *byt* had altered the political order at the university: the bureau had helped depose a rector who had bypassed the party cell.

The dispute over the rector's dominance carried over into the codification of new charters for communist universities, which were pre-

26. "Doklad t. Antonova," no date, 1923, RTsKhIDNI f. 17, op. 60, d. 501, l. 3–7; "Stenogramma t. Antonova-Saratovskogo," January 1923, ibid., d. 233. In fact, the Krasno-Presnenskii Raikom reported to the commission that the Sverdlov cell was the best and most active of all VUZ cells. "V TsK RKP. Tov. Liadovoi," late 1922, ibid., d. 499, l. 2.

27. "Doklad t. Antonova," cited in full at note 26; "Stenogramma t. Antonova-Saratovskogo," cited in full at note 19, l. 129–31; "Zaved. P-otdelom propagandy K. Popov. V komissiiu po proverke Kommunisticheskogo Universiteta im. Ia. M. Sverdlova," 16 January 1923, RTsKhIDNI f. 17, op. 60, d. 233, l. 119–20.

28. "Tov. Struev—2-aia lektorskaia gruppa," no date, prob. January 1923, RTsKhIDNI f. 17, op. 60, d. 500, l. 32–49; "Zasedanie 26/I-23 goda. Agit-prop. Otdel TsK RKP," ibid., l. 44–58, l. 45; "Protokoly komissii po obsledovaniiu Sverdlovskogo Universiteta ot 6/IV-23 g.," ibid., l. 10–11.

pared in 1922 after the first Soviet-era charters were imposed on the old universities. Antonov put out a draft for Sverdlov University, but Agitprop's Popov rejected it on the grounds that it placed too little power in the hands of top university administrators. It was typical that Popov capitalized on the struggle with the nonparty professoriat to affect inner-party policies; he decried any decentralization of power as a heretical endorsement of liberal "academic freedom." The Sverdlov cell bureau, however, protested even Antonov's draft as an attempt to permanently subordinate the cell to the administration. Despite the discontent, a new charter for communist universities was approved in 1923 which gave the rector the final say on all major questions. Student protests took on overtones of a general inner-party critique.[29] Echoing earlier opposition groups, like the Democratic Centralists, which had most consistently opposed "military methods" in the Party toward the end of the civil war, a lead editorial in the journal *Sverdlovets* sharply noted that in the new charter the rector stood above the cell like military committees in the civil war stood over Red Army cells: "The Soviet plays the role of the Bulygin Duma. The rector is everything. What reigns is not the principle of party dictatorship, but one-man dictatorship. In our opinion, what is good for the Red Army or industrial enterprises is dangerous for an organization like a communist university."[30]

The "party discussion" that brought the supporters of Trotskii into open confrontation with the party majority at the end of 1923 brought out several planks in the new opposition's platforms that directly concerned the position of the rank and file. Although Trotskii had been among the most militant centralizers but a short while before, Trotskyist platforms now called for regular elections to high-level posts and more powers to party cells. The oppositionist majority in the Sverdlov party organization, a rarity in the Party which led to major institutional restructuring in 1924, was linked to the broad political struggle the cell had been waging. Sverdlovians found it eminently possible to believe that more power to lower-level party organizations—that is, to the

29. "Zav. P/Otdel propagandy K. Popov Zav. Agitpropotdelom tov. Bubnovu. 29/IX-1922," RTsKhIDNI f. 17, op. 60, d. 236, l. 101; "Tezisy o normal'nom ustave dlia kommuniversitetov priniatye Ob"ed. Biuro Kommuniversiteta im. Sverdlova," no date, ibid., d. 218, l. 34; "Normal'nyi ustav Kommuniversitetov. Utverzhden Orgbiuro TsK 23/VII-23 protokol No. 23," GARF f. A-2313, op. 4, d. 69, l. 16–24; "Osnovnoe polozhenie Ustava Kommunisticheskogo Universiteta im. Ia. M. Sverdlova," no date, RTsKhIDNI f. 17, op. 60, d. 33, l. 16–18; V. Veger, "Akademicheskaia zhizn' v Kommunisticheskom universitete," *Sverdlovets*, no. 5–6 (March–April 1923): 20–21.

30. "Kommunisticheskie universitety ili kadestkie korpusa," *Sverdlovets*, no. 4 (January 1923): 3, and on the militarization debate, von Hagen, *Soldiers*, 137–52 and passim.

Sverdlov cell—was the main prerequisite for "internal-party democracy." In December of 1923 virtually all the Sverdlov student *kruzhki* were, judging by bureau reports, in some way critical of the official Central Committee positions on internal party matters; virtually all demanded reelections of the party apparatus "from top to bottom."[31]

The new rector, Martyn Nikolaevich Liadov (1872–1947), had been a founding member of Left Bolshevism around the time of the Capri School and had been associated with Georgian Menshevism during the civil war. Perhaps in part because of his own "deviationist" past, as rector and prominent historian of the Party Liadov maintained a vociferously orthodox stance throughout the inner-party struggles until the late 1920s. He conceived his major goals, aside from the liquidation of all deviations, as proletarianizing the student body and restructuring the curriculum of the communist university to make it more useful to the Party.[32]

Liadov's total support for the Central Committee majority and attempts to shut off further discussion at the university in 1923–24 led to even more tensions with student leaders. He was denounced in the cell for "factionalism" when he gathered Central Committee supporters from the students in his office to plan strategy. At the height of the opposition's success at the university—when students denied the Party's top leader Zinov'ev the floor at a cell assembly until Preobrazhenskii could be summoned for a rebuttal—Liadov attempted to exploit this "demonstration against the Central Committee" to prevent further discussion of party "disagreements." This time he was simply disregarded by the cell.[33] Throughout, the cell rank and file and bureau members had united in a struggle against the rector and had equated improvement of the inner-party regime with acquisition of more power by the party cell.

31. "Protokol No. 72 zasedaniia Plenuma Ob"biuro iacheek, kursovykh iacheek i partorganizatorov ot 15/XII-23 g.," RGAODgM f. 459, op. 1, d. 18, l. 14–15; "Protokol No. 1 zasedaniia Ispolbiuro sovmestno s partorganizatorami i otvetrukoviditeliami partkruzhkov," 9 January 1924, ibid., d. 23, l. 1; E. H. Carr, *The Interregnum, 1923–1924* (London: Macmillan, 1960), 312.

32. See M. N. Liadov, "O zadachakh i perspektivakh Kommunisticheskogo universiteta im. Ia. M. Sverdlova (Doklad na studencheskom sobranii)," in *Chem dolzhen byt' Kommuniversitet* (Moscow: Izdatel'stvo Kommunisticheskogo universiteta im. Sverdlova, 1924), 3–12; for a biography of limited utility, see S. V. Deviatov, *M. N. Liadov. Zabytaia biografiia* (Moscow: Izdatel'stvo VZPI, 1992).

33. RGAODgM f. 459, op. 1, d. 18, l. 14; "Protokol No. 64 zasedaniia Plenuma Ob"biuro iacheek RKP(b) universiteta Sverdlova ot 29-go noiabria 1923 g.: ob intsidente na partsobranii," ibid., l. 10–11; Mnukhin, "Beglye vospominaniia," in *X let Kommuniversiteta*, 320–21.

In 1924, however, the back of the university opposition was broken. The 1924 purge decimated the ranks of the Sverdlov students; party cell politics was put on a new footing. Liadov helped found a new power structure in which he himself entered a newly created presidium of the bureau.[34] With the rector now personally leading the cell as a bastion of party orthodoxy, and student politicians now anxious to erase the stigma of the university's oppositionist reputation, student resentment was redirected. Rank-and-file students now protested against the heavy-handed methods of the bureau and invoked the ideal of inner-party democracy against the student leaders. Protests at a party meeting in 1926 exemplified the reorientation: "The atmosphere in our cell is stifling and unhealthy. Onotskii [the cell secretary] brings in command methods [*elementy komandovanii*] to the concept of internal party democracy. . . . Onotskii looks for enemies of the party where they don't exist." Another added: "He who criticizes the work of the cell bureau is now an oppositionist." A third opined that it was necessary to be "critical" within the allowences of the Party, and that Marx himself said one must be critical. Liadov dismissed them all as "political youngsters." "Six years ago," he said, "anyone who wanted could come to the university and open up a discussion. This will happen no more . . . now we have the cell bureau."[35]

The bureau, as the rector implied, had now become the administrative center of political power at the university. In September 1925 the rector and vice-rector (*prorektor*) were brought in as members to the presidium of the bureau and supported the reelection of the same cell secretary who had presided over the repressions of 1924. Critics among the older students wanted to replace this candidate, as he himself acknowledged; he characterized their "discontent" as the desire for "broad democracy" (*shirokaia demokratiia*). A second-year student explained: "The question is not in the [party] line but in methods." Uglanov, the head of the Moscow party organization and a pillar of the entrenched hierarchical order that prevailed in the most important party

34. One of the many transformations occurring in 1924, this was part of a broader plan to increase the power of the rectors of communist universities in the wake of the strong support for the opposition among student cells. "Postanovleniia i rezoliutsiia II-i konferentsii Kommuniversitetov, 1924," GARF f. 5221, op. 5, d. 89, l. 15; see also GARF f. A-2313, op. 1, d. 87, l. 93. The presidium of the Sverdlov bureau was eliminated in 1926. "Tezisy otcheta o rabote Biuro iacheiki, 2 marta po 28-e sentiabria 1926 g.," RGAODgM f. 459, op. 1, d. 27, l. 19–23.

35. "Protokol No. 1 obshche-partiinogo sobraniia Kommuniversiteta Sverdlova ot 28/IX-1926," RGAODgM f. 459, op. 1, d. 27, l. 14–18; "Kratkie svedeniia o rabote iacheiki RKP(b) Komuniversiteta Sverdlova za period s 1/X-24 g. po 1/IV-25 g.," ibid., d. 25, l. 69–74.

committee during NEP, made a personal appearance at the university to propound a kind of managerial definition of "Bolshevik democracy": "People spoke here about democracy, but what is the essence of Bolshevik democracy? To pose political questions at the right time. To correctly choose workers to enact the political line; to collectively enact the general line . . . this is democracy. . . . It is important to us [the MK] that comrades come out of the university with a correct idea about democracy."[36]

The thrust of party cell politics had changed dramatically between the early and mid-1920s. The realignment after the suppression of the opposition in 1924 had polarized the students into a cell leadership and a rank and file. The participatory ideal raised by Sverdlovians now centered, not on greater power for the cell as a whole, but greater power for the communist students against a repressive cell leadership in alliance with the rector.

In this realignment the bureau profited from an institutionalized position of control over the lifestyle of its wards, the rank and file. This position grew out of the hierarchical inner-party regime that by the end of the civil war had placed a premium on cell secretaries guarranteeing ratification of a predetermined agenda at cell meetings; the power of the cell leadership was enhanced by its function of monitoring and evaluating all cell members. At Sverdlov, a network of cell organizers presented the bureau with reports on student groups and individuals. With disciplinary functions in the hands of the cell leadership, the bureau helped identify punishable behavior. Reports from 1922, for example, criticized students suffering from "academicism." Another report indicted a comrade Erman for uncomradely relations with female students: epitomizing the single most widespread complaint among female Communists about their male comrades, he saw in them "only a woman, in the oldest sense of the word." A third referred to "abnormalities" in student ethics, including possessiveness towards property and theft.[37]

The cell bureau in its evaluations strove to label the sociopolitical essence of the person. Mentality was explained by class affiliation; or, as in the case of purveyors of "intelligentsia psychology" or "petty-

36. "Protokol zasedaniia Plenuma Biuro iacheiki RKP(b) Kommuniversiteta im Sverdlova. IX/29 [1925]," RGAODgM f. 459, op. 1, d. 25, l. 8–10; "Protokol zasedaniia Biuro iacheiki Kommuniversiteta Sverdlova ot 16–go sentiabria 1925 g.," ibid., l. 40–43. Uglanov's views on inner-party democracy were influenced by his personal belief in tight discipline, support for managers, and distrust of rank-and-file participation. See Merridale, *Moscow Politics*, 51 n. 25.

37. Service, *Bolshevik Party*, 168; "Protokol ob"edinennogo zasedaniia mestnykh biuro Universiteta Sverdlova ot 2/I-22," RGAODgM f. 459, op. 1, ed. khr. 15, l. 1.

bourgeois individualism," was it the other way around? What made the new classification schemes impossible to dismiss was their power to exclude students from the university.[38]

The formal disciplinary powers of the bureau, spanning political activity and everyday life, were codified in the party court the bureau ran. In the 1921 charter of what is called the "disciplinary court," this body was authorized to judge violations in the dorms, academic infractions, and actions unbecoming a student at a communist university. This court, later referred to as the "comrades" or "party court," was a party organization not formally bound by Soviet jurisprudence (although the format of testimony and calling witnesses was observed). One of the five members of the court, elected by a student meeting, acted as prosecutor in each case and was responsible for gathering evidence.[39] The comrades courts of trade unions were designed, with dubious success, to bolster work discipline, but were phased out in 1922 after administrative personnel began to be "indicted" as well. Higher educational tribunals persisted, however, as forums for evaluation of student lifestyle.[40] At Sverdlov the court bridged the realms of politics and behavior with a rough and ready justice. In 1922 Sverdlov party organizer Gurnov was suspended from the Communist Party for a year for the theft of butter from the university kitchen after a fellow *kruzhok* member informed on him; but the court also considered a case against students who defended freedoms of speech and press in a university discussion.[41] The power invested in the cell leadership to judge and discipline its members made the evaluation of everyday life a form of combined political and social control. Yet the politics of lifestyle became something broader than the prerogatives of the local leadership. Just as censorship inspires but often becomes less pervasive than self-censorship, the effort to elaborate revolutionary and communist standards of behavior blossomed into a vast party project of self-regulation and self-control.

38. GARF f. 5221, op. 4, d. 21, l. 55–56, and l. 84; RGAODgM f. 459, op. 1, d. 15, l. 1.

39. "Ustav distsiplinarnogo suda studentov Komm. Universiteta Sverdlova s vnesennymi izmeneniiami zasedaniia Biuro [iacheiki] ot 13 oktiabria 1921 g.," GARF f. 5221, op. 3, d. 40, l. 26.

40. Lewis H. Siegelbaum, "Defining and Ignoring Labor Discipline in the Early Soviet Period: The Comrades-Disciplinary Courts, 1918–1922," *Slavic Review* 51 (Winter 1992): 705–30; on VUZ comrades courts, Peter Konecny, "Library Hooligans and Others: Law, Order, and Campus Culture in Leningrad, 1924–1938," *Journal of Social History* (forthcoming); on comrades courts in Komsomol clubs and youth communes, Gorsuch, "Enthusiasts," 119.

41. "Protokol zasedaniia Prezidiuma Biuro iacheek Universiteta Sverdlova ot 10-go maia 1922," RGAODgM f. 459, op. 1, d. 15, l. 55; "Partiinomu Sudu pri Kommunisticheskom Universitete. Zaiavlenie. 27/IV-21 g.," RTsKhIDNI f. 17, op. 60, d. 66, l. 53–54.

Byt: Ethics, Behavior, Deviation

Byt, which moved to the center of the Bolshevik movement in the 1920s, can only somewhat inadequately be translated as everyday life or lifestyle. It also carried the connotation of way of life, mores, and existence. Intense concern with conduct and behavior, often combined with explicit moralism about issues like sobriety and punctuality, had from the first been part both of student corporatism and the workers' movement.[42] But the central place *byt* assumed in Bolshevism, and in the communist student movement in particular in the 1920s, can be attributed to a number of new developments. A preoccupation with the "revolutionary everyday" came to the fore as a way of transforming the NEP "retreat" into a cultural advance, as the opening manifesto of a major youth journal declared.[43] Most important, creating a new *byt* for the first time became intimately associated with seemingly realizable potentialities of forging a new order on a society-wide scale. *Byt* came to be seen as the stuff of which the New Soviet Man would be made.

This was therefore the realm in which abstract party and revolutionary values—whether collectivism, revolutionary engagement, or political loyalty—could be identified in the here and now. Lifestyle and habits marked one's relationship to the revolution. After Nevskii was transferred from the rectorship of Sverdlov to run the Lenin Library, Communists there railed to him against the "old professor" employees who kissed women's hands and eschewed the word "comrade." Such "abnormal" old habits, not corresponding with "Soviet *byt*," were used as arguments for their dismissal.[44] *Byt* served as a badge of political affiliation, staking out the boundaries of revolutionary and reactionary.

The agony of the 1920s debate about the proper communist way of life, however, was that the revolutionary camp, which had embraced in a Manichaean way the motto *tertium non datur*, remained intractably divided when it came to fully mapping out those boundaries. This was sensed by the conservative professor Got′e, who in his diary referred to the Bolsheviks as gorillas and dogs, when he exclaimed with a mixture of sarcasm and astonishment: "'They' are full of bourgeois prejudices. . . . Pokrovskii is celebrating his twenty-fifth scholarly jubilee.

42. P. Ivanov, *Studenty v Moskve. Byt. Nravy. Tipy* (Moscow: Tip. obshchestva rasprostraneniia poleznykh knig, 1903). See especially Mark D. Steinberg, "Vanguard Workers and the Morality of Class," in Lewis Siegelbaum and Ronald Grigor Suny, eds., *Making Workers Soviet: Power, Class, and Identity* (Ithaca: Cornell University Press, 1994), 66–84.

43. "Molodoi rabochei gvardii," *Molodaia gvardiia*, no. 1–2 (April–May 1922): 3–5.

44. RGAODgM f. 474, op. 1, ed. khr. 6, l. 69.

This alone is a bourgeois prejudice!"[45] From the Left, even more condemnation was heaped on the party leadership by militant iconoclasts for concessions to old ways. A manifesto of a "group for communist *byt*" which circulated in the universities in the mid-1920s declared the Soviet order the product of its intelligentsia party rulers, who had ceased to be revolutionaries. The only remedy was to rear true and uncontaminated communists from childhood.[46]

A primary realm of contestation within the party camp in the early 1920s over the communist way of life revolved around the development of a Bolshevik ethics and morality. On the one hand, the radical student rejection of the very concept of morality, drawing on materialist philosophical currents, was well known and, indeed, often exaggerated. Aikhenval'd noted: "Try telling a Sverdlov student that he is a type of moral person. After a humorous and disdainful look you will be bombarded with the most serious proof that morality is withering away, that one must discard the term, that under communism there will be no morality, that Marx said this in one place, Kautsky that in another, and Darwin this in a third."[47]

It would have been more difficult, on the other hand, for such a student to invoke an even more relevant authority: Lenin. In his most famous pronouncement on issues of *byt* at the Third Komsomol Congress of 1920, cited constantly in the decade that followed, Lenin explicitly opposed any youthful repudiation of the concept of communist ethics. Lenin never doubted the necessity of morality for Communists; it was simply defined in terms of class and party. Morality was simply that which served to destroy the exploitative society and to aid the proletariat in building a new society of communists.[48] Lenin's acceptance of the concept of communist morality opened the door to further efforts to develop it in a Bolshevik framework.

But who would determine what served the interests of the new society? Lenin's formulation, it could hardly fail to be observed, privileged

45. Emmons, *Time of Troubles*, 388.

46. Quoted extensively in A. Gorlov, "Bogdanovsko-messianskie otkroveniia k molodezhi," in *Komsomol'skii byt* (Moscow-Leningrad: Molodaia gvardiia, 1927), 226–48.

47. Aikhenval'd, "Sverdlovets, kak sotsial'nyi tip," 24–25.

48. "V. I. Lenin o sushchnosti kommunisticheskoi partiinoi etiki (morali, nravstvennosti)," in M. A. Makarevich, ed., *Partiinaia etika: Dokumenty i materialy diskussii 20-x godov* (Moscow: Politizdat, 1989), 220–22. One of the most forceful arguments ever made for the Bolshevik class-based conception of morality is Trotskii's "Ikh moral' i nasha," *Biulleten' oppozitsii*, no. 68–69 (August–September 1938).

the Party in determining what was moral. Others left this central issue further in the background. Yet all new Bolshevik formulations of morality involved placing the interests of collectivities—class, party, revolution, regime—over the individual, and most revolved around determining rules of conduct. The Bolshevik feminist and Workers' Opposition leader Aleksandra Kollontai, far from subverting the dominant definitions, defined morality as "rules by which to live." Their final form would simply emerge with the new social order; yet communist morality was nonetheless those rules cemented by the "working class collective," not the individual. And the "basic rule of life for the Communist," she concluded, is that "private life" (*lichnaia zhizn'*) cannot be separated from the collective.[49]

A major impetus behind the articulation of a communist lifestyle in the early Soviet period was thus concern with the principles that were to govern a behavioral code for party members. Even if the notion of morality itself was divisive, therefore, implicitly moralistic injunction was ubiquitous.[50] The urge to prescribe an official code of revolutionary behavior can be traced to a party consideration of ethics during a time of civil war scarcity, state allocation of resources, and hunger. A. A. Sol'ts, a high figure in the TsKK, noted that discussions of revolutionary ethics were characteristic of the other socialist parties, but "in the course of all its struggle, [the Bolshevik Party] never discussed this." Sol'ts called the 1921 Party Conference the first official forum in which ethics as a topic was discussed.[51] This recognition came out of the civil war experience, when questions of *byt* were inflammatory: some local party committees on their own initiative attempted to form "ethical commissions" that would determine such questions as how much food each party member should take. Party leaders, not surprisingly, preferred a more amorphous set of guidelines rather than a constricting code that might be

49. A. Kollontai, "Pis'ma k trudiasheisia molodezhi. Kakim dolzhen byt' kommunist?" *Molodaia gvardiia*, no. 1–2 (April–May 1922): 136–44.

50. A critique of Trotskii's writings on bureaucratization, for example, argues that at their root lay hidden moral criteria about proper standards of behavior for Communists. David W. Lovell, *Trotsky's Analysis of Soviet Bureaucratization: A Critical Essay* (London: Croom Helm, 1985). In fact, the discussion of bureaucratization was a subset of the debate about *byt*, and Trotskii was a leading participant in both. To act bureaucratically was thus as much a deviation from proper behavior as drunkenness. How else can one explain the seemingly bizarre concern with the "bad manners" of party secretaries in a leading theoretical discussion of state bureaucratization? (4).

51. A. A. Sol'ts, "Iz otcheta Tsentral'noi Kontrol'noi Komissii na XI s"ezde RKP(b), 28 marta 1922 g.," in Makarevich, *Partiinaia etika*, 141–45.

turned against the leadership itself. "We said, down with all sorts of ethical commissions, what is needed is an active proletarian sense."[52]

Efforts to define revolutionary conduct in the name of collectivism and proletarian values in a time of near starvation helps explain how the emerging discussion of *byt* revolved around revolutionary asceticism, fears of "social corruption," and an obsession with purity and self-denial.[53] Such core concerns were accentuated with the mass influx of new members into the Party and the vices, luxuries, and temptations perceived in the shift to the NEP economy. New demands from within the TsKK itself surfaced in the early 1920s to ratify a "code of communist behavior," and a commission including Iaroslavskii, Krupskaia and Sol'ts was actually formed to consider the question.[54] Since conflicting currents of iconoclasm and anti-iconoclasm rendered a positive definition of revolutionary lifestyle elusive, the association of NEP with a crisis of corrupting influences helped to further constitute communist behavior in terms of rejection of dangerous or stigmatized social phenonomena. The term "Nepification" (*onepivanie*) was commonly used in discussions of *byt* to refer not only to the influence of Nepmen, the former exploiting classes, kulaks, and even noncommunist wives of party members, but to moral degeneration resulting from the restaurants and cabarets that flourished with NEP. The phrase "NEP in the state university" was coined by one activist to refer to the balls, dances, and other entertainment that became possible in the more prosperous 1920s; he called for the liquidation of such "disgusting offspring of NEP" and the establishment of "control of proletarian organizations over all concerts and events."[55]

This Bolshevik puritanism was not simply the affair of student militants and party moralists. The concern with the appearance of prole-

52. A. A. Sol'ts, "Iz zakliuchitel'nogo slova na XI s"ezde RKP(b)," in Makarevich, *Partiinaia etika*, 146.

53. Eric Naiman has discussed gastronomic and sexual implications of this revolutionary asceticism in "Revolutionary Anorexia (NEP as Female Complaint)," *Slavic and East European Journal* 37 (Fall 1993): 305–25.

54. It rejected a "detailed code" in favor of general principles, but the movement to ratify "norms of behavior" and ethical "laws" (*zakony*) continued into the mid-1920s. Some local Komsomol organizations passed such behavioral codes, in one instance at the provincial level with the approval of the Gubkom agitprop. The central Komsomol leadership criticized these codes for attempting to decree what could only be the product of long-term "political-enlightenment work." See *Politicheskoe vospitanie Komsomola* (Moscow-Leningrad: Gosizdat, 1925), 18–20.

55. On Nepification, "O partetike. Proekt predlozhenii prezidiuma TsKK II Plenumu TsKK RKP(b)," in Makarevich, *Partiinaia etika*, 151–70, and S. L'vov, "'Nep' v Gosudarstvennom Universitete," *Krasnyi student*, no. 1 (1924): 36–37.

tarian purity determined even the face the new regime revealed to the outside world. In 1926 the Worker-Peasant Inspectorate drafted rules approved by the Politburo that forbade Soviet diplomats in bourgeois countries to don "special clothing," display expensive dishware, or exhibit more than "maximal modesty" at receptions. Typical was not just the implied connection between asceticism and class purity but the open threat of disciplinary reprisal: violators would be held "strictly accountable."[56]

The intimate identification of NEP with moral and class degeneracy in *byt* was paralleled by warnings, to which Nevskii joined his voice, that NEP opened the door to bourgeois restoration in all other parts of the societal "superstructure" from science to art to ideology. Far more than the well-ordered policy shift pictured in political commentary, "NEP" in the party imagination thus became a complex of insidious threats from class aliens and a barrage of images of moral corruption. As Selishchev's sociolinguistic study of revolutionary terminology laconically notes in a section on word changes, the term NEP lost its primary meaning of New Economic Policy and became semantically synonymous with "new bourgeois strata," speculation, and Nepmanism. This explains Zinov'ev's extraordinary plea in his report of the Central Committee to the Twelfth Party Congress in April 1923: "We have to separate the terms "NEP" and the "New Economic Policy." You undoubtedly catch yourselves, when you say NEP, painting a picture of the Nepman and his unpleasant traits. We often use the phrase 'a victory over NEP.' . . . This happens because we mix up NEP with the Nepman."[57]

The NEP economy and the party hierarchy, however, only increased blatant disparities in standards of living and the potential for officials to acquire privileges. The Bolsheviks were charged with betrayal of the revolution by a wide array of critics and faced the fear of corruption within.[58] The pervasive concern with purity in a time of retreat from

56. "Prilozhenie NKRKI SSSR o banketakh (utverzhdeno Politbiuro TsK VKP(b) 30.XII.26 g.)," RTsKhIDNI f. 17, op. 3, ed. khr. 608, l. 17–18.

57. V. Nevskii, "Restavratsiia idealizma i bor'ba s 'novoi' burzhuaziei," *PZM*, no. 7–8 (June–August, 1922): 113–31; A. M. Selishchev, *Iazyk revoliutsionnoi epokhi: Iz nabliudenii nad russkim iazykom poslednykh let (1917–1926)* (Moscow: Rabotnik prosveshcheniia, 1928), 196; *Dvenadtsatyi S"ezd Rossiiskii kommunisticheskoi partii (bol'shevikov). Stenograficheskii otchet. 17–25 aprelia 1923 g.* (Moscow: Krasnaia nov', 1923), 33. For a suggestive discussion of the "obsession of NEP's transitional mentality with purity and corruption on all levels," see Eric Naiman, "The Case of Chubarov Alley: Collective Rape, Utopian Desire, and the Mentality of NEP," *Russian History/Histoire Russe* 17 (Spring 1990): 1–30.

58. Mervyn Mathews, *Privilege in the Soviet Union: A Study of Elite Life-Styles under Com-*

egalitarianism made *byt* into an explosive political weapon; it became imperative for party organs to assert primacy over the evaluation of communist conduct. Newly created party control commissions recast the discussion of ethics to propagate the axiom, so ubiquitous in official pronouncements about *byt* in the 1920s, that "the interests of party, of class stand above everything." The groping to codify correct communist behavior was in this way transmuted into a demand for obedience sanctioned in the name of morality.[59] This, as the party disciplinarians would have readily recognized, was a fundamentally political act.

The discussion of morality and behavior within the context of NEP comprised just one facet of the broader enterprise of conceiving a new *byt*. A modernizing notion of a more advanced way of life also became part and parcel of the concept of cultural revolution; the introduction of better habits, according to many party intellectuals, carried the connotation of remolding "backward" cultural norms. "What does cultural revolution mean?" Bukharin, for example, expressed it. "It means change in the characteristics of people, in their habits, in their feelings and desires, their manner of life, their *byt*." Trotskii's immensely popular 1923 *Questions of Byt* linked high standards of personal behavior with the acquisition of culture and equated this with the most significant revolutionary tasks. "We need to learn how to work well: precisely, cleanly, economically," Trotskii enjoined. "We need culture in work, culture in life, culture in *byt*." For Trotskii, and for many other Communists, proper hygiene, the vodka question, and the "struggle for cultured speech" were transformed in this period, at least rhetorically, into the paramount tasks of the Revolution.[60]

The striving for a communist uniformity in the realm of *byt* splintered, however, in part along the lines of many of its subcultures. To a significant wing of the Party, less vocal in published discussions about *byt* and disdainful of the theoreticians and intellectuals, the stress on "culture in *byt*" and the respectability implied in the official moralism

---

munism (London: George Allen & Unwin, 1978), 59–90. For a contemporary analysis of the "restoration of the social pyramid" by the sociologist Pitrim Sorokin, see V. V. Sapov, ed., "Zabytaia stat'ia Pitrima Sorokina," *Vestnik Rossiiskoi akademii nauk* 62, no. 2 (1992): 125–29. For the Politburo special commission report on "Kremlin privileges"—compiled during the 1920 discussion of the rift between party "uppers" and "lowers," but stopped from dissemination—see "Kak zhili v Kremle v 1920 godu. Materialy Kremlevskoi komissii TsK RKP(b)," *Neizvestnaia Rossiia XX Vek* (Moscow: Istoricheskoe nasledie, 1992), 2:261–81.

59. E. M. Iaroslavskii, "O partetike. Doklad na II Plenume TsKK RKP(b) 5 Oktiabria 1924," in Makarevich, *Partiinaia etika*, 170–96; Fülöp-Miller, *Mind and Face*, 394–99.

60. N. Bukharin, "Za uporiadochenie byta molodezhi," in *Komsomol'skii byt*, 99; Lev Davydovich Trotskii, "Voprosy byta," in *Sochineniia* (Moscow: Gosizdat, 1927), 21:3–58.

contradicted the Party's proletarian character. The term *zaezzhatel'stvo* (roughly meaning "going overboard") was coined to describe Bolsheviks who reveled in vulgar, tough speech and stereotypically proletarian behavior. Stalin's 1925 deflection of Lenin's damaging testament—"Stalin is too crude"—referred to these values and might be taken as a sign of their potency. "Yes, comrades, I am a direct and crude person, that is true, I do not reject it."[61]

Even as the notion of a uniform communist *byt* remained a ideal construct as elusive as party monolithism itself, the debate helped expand the conception of the cultural realm to encompass manners, dress, language, sexuality, and indeed all aspects of behavior. Instead of comprising a private or traditional realm—now linked either to bourgeois individualism or to backwardness—all these areas merged into the broader political and revolutionary agenda. The long-term effect was to justify an attempt at wholesale reconstruction of traditional cultures, especially by 1928 when cultural revolution was increasingly recast as armed assault. For example, in that year a lead editorial in the journal *Revoliutsiia i kul'tura* made the claim: "The militant socialist reeducation of the consciousness and work habits and *byt* of the masses represents one of the forms of class struggle." In a discussion the same year linking bohemianism among students to sexual deviance, gypsies, and decadence, the Old Bolshevik scholar of religion and psychology, Mikhail Reisner—himself the son of a Baltic nobleman who as a young man had immersed himself in Tolstoyan philosophy—remarked that the easiest way to deal with the idle intelligentsia might be to put them in "concentration camps."[62]

While control commissions and party leaders emphasized loyalty to the Party in discussion of *byt*, debates in communist student publications revolved more around the proper understanding of collectivism. The interests of the Party and those of the collective, however, could hardly be disengaged. As it had been for decades within the radical intelligentsia, collectivism was understood in its most general sense as devotion to the common interest above the personal, almost always to the point of self-denial. In the 1920s, however, collectivism also acquired a series of more immediate connotations and even obligations

61. Boris Volin, "Bol'sheviki-zaezzhateli," *Na postu*, no. 4 (November 1923): 11–28; Selishchev, *Iazyk*, 68–69, 83. Stalin repeated a similar statement in 1927 in "Trotskistskaia oppozitsiia prezhde i teper'," in *Sochineniia* (Moscow: OGIZ, 1946–51), 10:175.

62. "Za leninskoe ponimanie voprosov kul'turnoi revoliutsii," lead editorial, *Revoliutsiia i kul'tura* 15 June 1928, 5–7; M. A. Reisner, "Bogema i kul'turnaia revoliutsiia," *Pechat' i revoliutsiia*, no. 5 (July–August 1928): 95.

for party students. It implied certain living arrangements, social or educational work (most often carried out through the party cell), and commitment to current affairs above one's studies or career.[63]

It was possible, to be sure, to question whether the mere fulfillment of quasi-official obligations represented true collectivism. A storm of letters was provoked when a student's missive published in a Leningrad student newspaper decried precisely the lack of civic values (*obshchestvennost'*) in the "useless meetings, uncounted hours of gabbing, mechanical ticking off of various obligations, registrations and reregistrations." A central publication soon found an explanation for such sweeping criticisms of Soviet life: the student, Iurov, had consorted with prostitutes and contemplated suicide. But what the commentator found even more insidious was a pervasive party attitude about prostitutes and drunkenness: "There's no big sin here; the main thing is not to make noise." The debate about *byt*, it can be inferred from such exposés, had became simultaneously a part of political life, an attempt to overcome resistance to model codes of behavior, yet also an effort at self-regulation of conduct.[64]

A feuilleton in the newspaper *Sverdloviia* demonstrates the attempt to impart social and political obligations through a stereotypical portrait of a collectivist and an individualist. It contrasts two Sverdlov students, comrade "Partiitsev" (party member) and comrade "Knizhnikov" (bookworm), one who conscientiously fulfills his social work outside the university, the other who talks over the heads of the sailors he is assigned to teach. The party-minded one is neat, precise, busy; he uses his time on the tram to compose an article on the peasant question; the bookworm cares only about his studies and is a deviationist (an Enchmenist) to boot. The piece closes as the individualist curses the bureau of the Sverdlov party cell.[65]

In the day-to-day political affairs of Sverdlov University, the necessity of representing everyday behavior in sweeping socio-ideological terms was obligatory. Petty-bourgeois individualism, for example, was a common and sufficient ground for purge. In the political rough-and-tumble one person's proletarian collectivist could very well become another's

63. See the discussion in E. Troshchenko, "Vuzovskaia molodezh'," *Molodaia gvardiia*, no. 4 (April 1927): 129–43, esp. 132–33.

64. M. Rafail, "'Iurovshchina' i ee korni," *Revoliutsiia i kul'tura*, no. 12 (30 June 1928), 21–26. The work of both Konecny, "Library Hooligans," and Gorsuch, "Enthusiasts," focuses on recalcitrant student subcultures, such as "bohemians," which reflected the failure of the dominant culture fully to reshape attitudes.

65. B. Krasnyi, "Tipy prikreplennykh," *Sverdloviia*, 31 May 1923, 2.

pernicious individualist; yet this only served to make evaluations of *byt* even more integral to the everyday political struggle. A purged Sverdlov student petitioned: "In the decision [of the purge commission] the manifestation of 'individualism' on my part is discussed. I have not displayed such traits and in the decision not one concrete anticommunist act is brought to bear."[66] Especially interesting here is the interchangeability of individualism and anticommunism. A disciplinary system in which individualist traits could be equated with political treason created a powerful mechanism for the punishment of nonconformity.

In early Soviet visions of the path to the collectivist future, to be sure, the ultimate place of the individual remained under dispute. The Taylorist techno-utopia of Gastev, for example, seemed to welcome the advent of anonymous, standardized, machine-like "proletarian units"; Bogdanov replied that comradely cooperation really meant elimination of all subordination and for the first time realization of full individuality. Some literary voices openly defended the personal from politics; the cost of attacking the private realm in the name of the collective forms the subject of a 1927 short story by Panteleimon Romanov, "Trial of a Pioneer." The young pioneer Andrei Chuganov is followed and caught by his comrades reading poetry to a girlfriend, tried and convicted for subverting the collective, disrupting the training of "soldiers of the revolution," and refusing to reveal the contents of the poems.[67]

An anti-private egalitarianism was at the heart of one of the most ambitious postrevolutionary attempts to put into practice new principles of *byt*: the organization of communes. Here, students also led the way. Communalism, of course, often made a virtue of necessity, since it reduced food costs, shared insufficient housing, and facilitated cultural activities. But a passionate faith in the promise of collectivism pervaded the commune movement, to the point where some communes insisted on sharing of all space and possessions, including underwear. Disagreements flared over how far to restrict "personal life," whether familial or sexual ties were permissible within the communes and whether children should belong to parents. The strains this put on communes could become overwhelming, and many of the experiments were short-lived.[68]

66. "V Prezidium Komuniversiteta im. Sverdlova ot studenta 3-kursa 9 kruzhka S. M. Krianga. 5–IX-22 g.," GARF f. 5221, op. 4, d. 25, l. 49, and a similar case on l. 52.

67. Kendall E. Bailes, "Alexei Gastev and the Soviet Controversy over Taylorism," *Soviet Studies* 29 (July 1977): 378–80; P. Romanov, "Sud nad pionerom," *Molodaia gvardiia*, no. 1 (January 1927): 86–91.

68. Ibeen-Shtrait, "Studencheskie kommuny," *Krasnyi student*, no. 8–9 (August–September 1924): 44–45; Stites, *Revolutionary Dreams*, 205–22; Gorsuch, "Enthusiasts," 124–28.

The model of the *kommuna*, which in varying degrees eliminated all personal property and possessions, to many became associated with communism itself. The commune movement in early Soviet society could not but intersect with the regime's own claims on collectivism. Local Narkompros branches, for example, supervised a network of communes, and each was attached to a "Soviet institution" where many commune members found work. Each commune member had to pledge a kind of oath upon entrance. An example of this pledge affirmed that communards could express their opinions before a collective decision, but afterward must subordinate themselves to that decision—a formula based on the Party's doctrine of democratic centralism. The pledge closed with the statement: "I recognize that to build a [new] life through communes is possible only under the Soviet political system." When urban Communists were unleashed on the countryside in the 1929–30 collectivization drive, the *kommuna* model provided widespread justification for seizure of peasant possessions, from pigs and chickens to the clothes off kolkhozniks' backs.[69]

Sverdlov students initially were scattered in housing around Moscow, and lack of dormitory space was so acute that many camped in groups of ten to fifteen in the university's larger classrooms. But the acquisition of dormitory space by the mid-1920s also resulted in the establishment of the Sverdlov University commune, which as a student commune attached to an educational institution was hardly unique. The M. N. Liadov commune—named after the rector who took such a strong interest in *byt*—was dedicated, according to its charter, to "raising its members in a collectivist spirit" and prosecuting the struggle against "all petty-bourgeois, philistine-individualist holdovers." Living arrangements were tied to political life through an extension of the party cell bureau's lines of authority. The commune's elected president sat on the cell bureau, which closely observed the affairs of the commune. In the dormitories that housed the commune, student leaders (*starosti*) monitored the activities, conflicts, and infractions of student members and reported to the party cell.[70]

69. "Nekotorye stat'i ustava 'kommun trudovoi molodezhi' (proekt)," no date, GARF f. A-2313, op. 1, d. 57, l. 138; "Zaiavlelenie pri vystuplenii v kommuny trudovoi molodezhi Vasmannogo Raiona," no date, ibid., l. 143; Sheila Fitzpatrick, *Stalin's Peasants: Resistance and Survival in the Russian Village after Collectivization* (New York: Oxford University Press, 1994), 50.

70. "Dokladnaia zapiska (po zhilishchnomu voprosu Universiteta)," no date, 1923, GARF f. 5221, op. 6, d. 81, l. 15; "Ustav kommuny im. M. N. Liadov," 4 October 1926, RGAODgM f. 459, op. 1, d. 27, l. 87–96, and d. 31, l. 46.

An overriding concern united all these areas in the search for a new communist way of life, from the elaboration of communist ethics, to the grappling with the corruption of NEP, to the regulation of values through collectivism. Discussion in all these realms was drawn toward condemning deviance. The most far-reaching significance of what one might call the politics of everyday life—and the area in which the search for a new *byt* was integrated into the Bolshevik polity most profoundly—is that the most petty infraction could be linked to deviation in a political culture that set Manichaean distinctions between correct and incorrect, healthy and degenerate, orthodox and deviationist. The lengthy list of deviations of student *byt*—bohemianism, hooliganism, sexual libertinism, philistinism, individualism, Enchmenism, Mininism, Eseninshchina, etc.[71]—were all precisely "-isms," deviations from an imagined norm. The entire rogue's gallery was united under the overarching term "degenerate" (*upadochnyi*, which can also be translated as "decadent" or "defeatist").[72] Degeneracy in its early Soviet usages had connotations embracing all behavior associated with individualism and alien classes. As in political or ideological deviation, one false move carried with it the danger of "infection" from the entire "disease." One prominent discussion of petty-bourgeois influences among youth cast the oft-discussed "epidemic" of youth suicide as pure degeneracy, the highest stage into which all its manifestations could grow.[73]

71. Emmanuel Enchmen was a former SR and sometime worker in Ivan P. Pavlov's laboratory on conditioned reflexes, whose 1920 *Eighteen Theses Concerning the Theory of the New Biology* took an extreme materialist view rejecting all causality outside physiological reflex; S. Minin propounded an extreme positivism repudiating abstract thought as tools of the exploiters. Both counted virtually their only supporters among the communist students of the early 1920s, and Minin apparently propagandized sympathetic students at Sverdlov University in 1920–21. David Joravsky, *Soviet Marxism and Natural Science, 1917–1932* (London: Routledge & Kegan Paul, 1961), 93–97. These two "deviations" expressed in exaggerated form what the dialecticians came to call "philosophobia," scientistic and mechanistic trends common in early Soviet Marxism. See, for example, A. Troitskii, "Filosofiia na sluzhbe revoliutsii," *PZM*, no. 4–5 (April–May 1924): 12–19. When Enchmenism and Mininism were condemned, they were associated with the rejection of the concept of morality on the part of communist students.

72. By comparison, German nationalist and Nazi usages defined degeneracy as a fusion of political and aesthetic qualities indicating "inferior racial, sexual, and moral types." See Stephanie Barron, "Modern Art and Politics in Prewar Germany," in Barron et al., eds., *"Degenerate Art": The Fate of the Avant-Garde in Nazi Germany* (Los Angeles: County Museum of Art, 1991), 11–13.

73. I. Bobryshev, *Melkoburzhuaznye vliianiia sredi molodezhi*, 2d rev. ed. (Moscow-Leningrad: Molodaia gvardiia, 1928), 98, 101. According to Kennth M. Pinnow, suicide in Bolshevik discourse represented an antithesis of the championed values of strength, optimism, and submersion of the ego in the collective. Pinnow, "Out of the Morgue and into Society: Suicide Statistics and the Creation of a 'Soviet' Forensic Medicine in Russia, 1920–1929" (paper presented at the fifth World Congress for Central and East European Studies, 1995).

The "sexual question" (*polovoi vopros*) was couched in shocking metaphors of purity and depravity and clearly attracted the most intense interest in the student discussion of *byt*. Malashkin's *Luna s pravoi storony*—one of the major literary works that became a focus of the debate on youth morals, and one set at Sverdlov University—adroitly inserted vivid depictions of sexual promiscuity by using it as a metaphor for ideological deviation. The Komsomol member Tania Aristarkhovaia, whose poor peasant background is of course a symbol of sexual innocence, comes to Sverdlov University and falls under the influence of Trotskyist deviationists. The leading Trotskyist, the free-love advocate Isaika Chuzhachok (a name derived from *chuzhoi*, or alien) is depicted as a degenerate Jewish dandy from Poltava. Tania inevitably is infected by the degeneracy of her milieu: she takes twenty-two lovers and becomes a frequent user of alcohol, hashish, and other narcotics, as well as a participant in the "Athenian nights," or orgies, that were supposedly common among the amoral students.[74] In this fictional Sverdlov University, sexual and ideological deviance were one.

For all the lurid images of a degenerate *studenchestvo*, both high-ranking party moralists, party students, and experts participating in the debate shared a prurient stress on sexual sublimation and denial.[75] While the scientism and materialism of the age on the one hand opened up the discussion, too great a preoccupation with sexual matters was painted among all three groups as the inward-looking individualism of a "parasitic element." The perpetuation of the professionals' theory that sex wasted energy at expense of the nation, advanced in the social criti-

74. S. I. Malashkin, *Luna s pravoi storony, ili neobyknovennaia liubov'* (Moscow: Molodaia gvardiia, 1927). Malashkin began his literary activities as a proletarian poet and worker from Sormovskii zavod. A. O. [Pavel Ivanovich Lebedev-Polianskii], review of S. Malashkin, *Muskuly. Poemy* (Moscow: Krasnyi Dom, 1918), in *Proletarskaia kul'tura*, no. 6 (February 1919): 41–42. The interesting debate around his novel *Luna* is largely reprinted in S. Gusev, ed., *Kakova zhe nasha molodezh'? Sbornik statei* (Moscow-Leningrad: Gosizdat, 1927), but see also the 1926 Communist Academy discussion, "Lebedev-Polianskii, P. I. O povesti Malashkina 'Luna s pravoi storony.' Stenogramma doklada i preniia po dokladu na zasedanii sektsii po literature i iskusstvu, 13 dekabria 1926," ARAN f. 350, op. 2, d. 86, l. 1–85. For a review of the most frequently discussed literary works on the topic of "degeneracy" and student sexual mores by a participant in the antidegeneracy campaign, see Bobryshev, *Melkoburzhuaznye vliianiia sredi molodezhi*, 114–27.

75. According to Francis Bernstein, "sexual enlightenment," as propounded especially by venereologists, neuropsychiatrists, and social hygenists in the Commissariat of Public Health, was conceived as a major part of the "struggle for a new *byt*." Physicians played a prominent role in conceptualizing sexual normality and abnormality, until more punitive methods of control emerged in the late 1920s and sexual matters disappeared from public discussions after 1932. Bernstein is completing a Columbia University Ph.D. dissertation, "'What Everyone Should Know about Sex': Narkomzdrav and Sexual Enlightenment, 1918–1932."

cism of physicians after 1905, was now, *mutatis mutandis*, upheld to conserve collectivist energy for the good of socialism. Typically, Iaroslavskii cast the very act of paying too much attention to the sexual question as a sign of degeneracy.[76] A chorus of voices thus cast self-abnegation as the most positive of social and political acts.

Student sex surveys in prewar Russia had provided a scientific justification for theories positing that the revolutionary sublimation of sexual energy during the Revolution of 1905 had given way to post-1907 decadent introspection. Now, Sverdlov University provided a focal point for the statistical representation of postrevolutionary student mores. The 1923 Sverdlov survey, drawing on data from 1,615 students, provided grist for the conflicting fears and hopes invested in the new student body. On the one hand, indications that 45 percent of students practiced masturbation fueled the identification of students with degeneracy. Yet 85.7 percent of the Sverdlovians, when asked, came out for monogamous relationships. Some commentators used this to justify a proletarian patriotism that declared the new students more moral than their vanquished bourgeois predecessors. It was in this context, as well, that a Sverdlovian echoing the broader party antipromiscuity campaign made the attempt to collectivize the sexual question by casting it as part of the class struggle: "It is imperative to liquidate that conception of the sexual question that views it as the personal affair of each person," an interpretation of the survey results in the Sverdlov journal exhorted. One must adhere to the morals of one's class—or else one becomes an "enemy of one's own class."[77]

A key figure linking the professional and party world in the discussion about communist students, morality, and sexuality was Aron Borisovich Zalkind. A Moscow psychoanalyst adhering to the Adlerian school before the Revolution, Zalkind's speciality was listed in a direc-

76. See N. Kazanskii, "Kollektivisticheskoe tuskneet, kogda slishkom raspukhaet liubov'," *Krasnyi student*, no. 4–5 (1924): 41–42; and advice from the experts: Professors Ivan Ariamov, "Znachenie sokhraneniia polovoi energii dlia molodezhi," and B. Gorinevskii, "Polovoi vopros," both in *Komsomol'skii byt*, 287–90 and 283–86, and E. Iaroslavskii, "Neskol'ko slov o byte," 30 March 1926, RTsKhIDNI f. 89, op. 9, d. 53, l. 3. On social and political themes in scientists' post-1905 discussion of sexuality, see Laura Engelstein, *The Keys to Happiness: Sex and the Search for Modernity in Fin-de-Siècle Russia* (Ithaca: Cornell University Press, 1992), 243–45.

77. F. W., "Voprosy vospitatel'noi raboty," *Sverdlovets*, no. 5–6 (March-April 1923): 38–44; "Anketa o polovoi zhizni studentov Kommunisticheskogo Universiteta," *Zapiski Kommunisticheskogo universiteta imeni Ia. M. Sverdlova* (henceforth cited at *ZKS*) 1 (January 1923): 370–409; Sheila Fitzpatrick, "Sex and Revolution: An Examination of Literary and Statistical Data on the Mores of Soviet Students in the 1920s," *Journal of Modern History* 50 (June 1978): 252–78; Engelstein, *Keys*, 248–53; Morrissey, "More Stories," 256–57, 378.

tory of physicians in 1925 as psychopathology; he became a leading figure in the early Soviet study of children (the discipline of pedology) and among "Marxist pedagogues." The communist *studenchestvo* became a special object of study; his conclusions in key ways reinforced party moralists and the party disciplinary regime. For example, Zalkind diagnosed higher incidences of psychological neuroses among party oppositionists, whom he alleged suffered from an excess of emotionalism (an association with hysteria and femininity). His recommended cure was "a strengthening of party reeducation." His findings also fitted squarely into the chorus of professional and party voices calling for sexual sublimation for the good of the Revolution; his maxim was that "sexuality [*polovoe*] must be subordinated to class [*klassovomu*]."[78]

Yet the moralist in the party context in the 1920s who perhaps most vociferously linked political and personal deviations was none other than rector Liadov. His argumentation is significant on several counts. Liadov, again, traced the roots of all current ills to the "period of reaction" between 1907 and 1910, vividly contrasting the intelligentsia's unnatural perversion with collectivist proletarian purity.[79] This longstanding association of degeneracy with an epochal turn away from revolution by contrast equated revolutionary offensive with purification, a sweeping away of all the sickly contamination of NEP. Liadov also treated degeneracy as a master deviation that spanned withdrawal from social problems, cult of the ego, Nietzschean hero-worship, pornography, and hooliganism. He lumped these together as the ideology of the wavering, petty-bourgeois intelligentsia. At the start of NEP, this same intelligentsia, desiring money and material comforts, wormed its way into Soviet institutions, supported the changing landmarks movement (*smenovekhovstvo*), and Trotskii in 1923. Regardless of the period in which it appeared or its particular incarnation, then, degeneracy represented a devious infiltration of the enemy. Every step toward socialism, Liadov theorized, brings out a new form of degeneracy among this segment of the intelligentsia, which then infects the less firm. The resemblance of this argument to Stalin's 1929 theoretical innovation famously justifying the Great Break—that the closer socialism approaches the more the class struggle is exacerbated—seems coincidental, as Lia-

78. The above is drawn from Aleksandr Etkind, *Eros nevozmozhnogo: Istoriia psikhoanaliza v Rossii* (Moscow: Gnosis, 1994), 260–64, and the many books published by Zalkind in the 1920s.

79. Liadov's own statements in fact display a distinct continuity with social-democratic responses to the "sexual question" in the post-1907 discussion. See Engelstein, *Keys*, 377–79.

dov, as we shall see, himself ended up as associated with the "Right Deviation."[80] Yet the striking similarity reveals how closely the discussion of degeneracy was intimately related to that of political opposition.

If the imagery of sick deviance and healthy orthodoxy spanned the realms of politics and *byt*, the connections between political and lifestyle deviance were firmly anchored in the party-wide disciplinary regime that emerged after 1920. The party disciplinary organs, the control commissions set up in that year, were created to monitor both political deviations and infractions of communist *byt*; these functions were irrevocably intertwined in their activities. While the Cheka perhaps set the precedent with its mission to uncover crimes not only of counterrevolution but of speculation, the Ninth Party Conference of September 1920 marked a new phase in the organization of party discipline.

At this time the Central Control Commission (TsKK) was formed; and the Tenth Congress, in March 1921, established rules governing election of local control commissions, giving them powers to respond to complaints and initiate investigations. The Tenth Congress, as is well known, also passed two other resolutions on discipline, "On the Unity of the Party" and "On the Syndicalist and Anarchist Deviation in Our Party." These documents authorized expulsion from the Party for factional activity. The TsKK, in 1920 headed by Dzerzhinskii, who was soon replaced by Iaroslavskii, was thus set up as part of the original mechanism designed to enforce the ban on factions. But one of the main rationales for its existence was the investigation and prosecution of all crimes "and other deeds" violating "communist ethics." Sol'ts reported in 1921 that the new control commissions were attempting to try ethical infractions, such as acquisition of "personal comforts," without excess legal formality.[81]

The TsKK in the 1920s emerged as a kind of inner-party political police, the main prosecutor of measures against the successive political oppositions. While at the Twelfth Party Congress the TsKK had nine

80. M. N. Liadov, "Blizhaishie zadachi v bor'be s upadochnymi nastroeniiami i, v chastnosti, s 'eseninizmom,'" *K leninskoi uchebe*, no. 6 (October–November 1926): 9–18, and "The Functions of a Communist University," *Labour Monthly* 8 (July 1926): 435–40; and I. V. Stalin, "O pravom uklone v VKP(b)," in *Sochineniia* 12:31–39.

81. *TsKK-RKI v osnovnykh postanovleniiakh partii* (Moscow-Leningrad: Gosizdat, 1927), 3–22; "Iz polozhenii o kontrol'nykh komissiiakh vsem partiinym organizatsiiam RKP," *Izvestiia TsK RKP(b)*, 20 December 1920, reprinted in Makarevich, *Partiinaia etika*, 127–28; *Desiatyi s"ezd Rossiiskoi kommunisticheskoi partii. Stenograficheskii otchet (8–16 marta 1921 g.)* (Moscow: Gosizdat, 1921), 33–36.

members and a staff of 50, in 1923 it was combined with the Worker-Peasant Inspectorate (RKI) to yield a staff of 150. Iaroslavskii, as head of the TsKK, assumed the role not only of chief ideologist against the oppositions, but enforcer of all the party rules and regulations against them. This role was so notorious that an inflammatory poster at the United Opposition's 1927 demonstrations on the tenth anniversary of October pictured Stalin as a gendarme holding an attack dog named Iaroslavskii by a leash. In 1926 the Mensheviks' political commentator in Moscow charged: "Already there aren't two Bolsheviks who will speak openly, tell one another about their doubts and so on. They fear the . . . TsKK, which has its eyes and ears everywhere." In an implicit defense of the private sphere that drew applause from the Leningrad opposition, the oppositionist member of the TsKK, Bakaev, condemned the "unhealthy" growth of denunciations (*donositel'stvo*) to the organ that prevented "a friend from telling his friend a sincere thought." Typically, Bakaev called for strict discipline and harsh punishment of this new sin—only now the deviation was denunciation itself.[82]

Local party committees organized their own control commissions, which were subordinated to the TsKK. All indications are that the bulk of these commissions' work was related to issues of *byt*—drunkenness, petty corruption, and the like—which, in addition to other reasons, were considered political matters because they undermined the prestige and power of the Party. Infractions of "party discipline" were not only a standard topic in debates on party ethics, but were prosecutable by the control commissions as ethical violations. Discipline was thus cast as an ethical issue, *byt* as a political one. Sol'ts, in a report on party ethics at Sverdlov University, acknowledged that many control commission informants were motivated by political rivalries, although he made light of the often petty circumstances involved: "With us it is like this—you all, most likely, are aware of this—some comrades gather, get drunk together, and then one after the other go to complain at the c[ontrol] c[ommission]. They argue about who drank more, who drank less. . . . This can only happen because they want to put one another

82. *TsKK-RKI*, 90; E. M. Iaroslavskii, "Vystuplenie o vnutripartiinom polozhenii. Stenogramma," probably November or December 1927, RTsKhIDNI f. 89, op. 8, d. 513, l. 5; I., "Vokrug s"ezda RKP (pis'mo iz Moskvy)," *Sotsialisticheskii vestnik*, 16 January 1926, 16, and "Po Rossii," *Sotsialisticheskii vestnik*, 1 November 1926; *XIV S"ezd Vsesoiuznoi Kommunisticheskoi partii (b). 18–31 dekabria 1925 g. Stenograficheskii otchet* (Moscow: Gosizdat, 1926), 566, 595–96.

away." The Old Bolshevik shrewdly concluded: "This has its source in a struggle for power."[83]

The links between political and lifestyle deviation were not restricted to the discussions of *byt*; they were built into the structure of the party disciplinary regime. This explains how the language, concepts, and even specific transgressions that animated the discussion of degeneracy were mirrored in the struggle against political oppositions. Trotskii complained privately to Bukharin in 1926 that cell secretaries of the Moscow organization, in the midst of Uglanov's fight against the opposition, spread the information that Trotskii only gave speeches for the bourgeoisie and reaped a profit from the ticket sales. The polemic against Trotskyism perhaps most widely distributed after 1924 was Semen Kanatchikov's *History of One Deviation*, which by 1925 had gone through five editions. This work portrayed Trotskii in terms identical to those in the discussions about *byt*. Trotskii is described as an individualist, isolated from the masses, a carrier of "intelligentsia traits." He rejects discipline, gathering around him loners (*odinochki*) prone to hysterical panic.[84] Just as Trotskii's criticisms of the party leadership in 1923 were attributed to pessimistic hysteria, so "degenerate moods" among youth were described as panicked pessimism. Such descriptions of deviance acquired force precisely because they functioned in both politics and everyday life, bringing out the despicable opposites of officially encouraged values such as optimism, loyalty, discipline, commitment, and, ultimately, conformity and obedience.

The circle between politics and *byt* is closed when it is recalled that the Trotskyist opposition received its main support from student youth; that for years students and intellectuals were stereotyped as carriers of all kinds of moral and political deviations; and that students were in fact removed from production, thus "declassed" and linked to the intelligentsia.[85] The power of this cluster of ideas and images, grounded as they were in the emergent disciplinary regime, helped divert the search for liberation into a hunt for deviance.

83. A. A. Sol'ts, "O partetike. Doklad, chitannyi v Kommunisticheskom Universitete im. Ia. M. Sverdlova," in Makarevich, *Partiinaia etika*, 278.

84. Trotskii to Bukharin, 4 March 1926, Trotsky Archive, bMS Russ 13T-868; S. Kanatchikov, *Istoriia odnogo uklona*, 5th ed. (Leningrad: "Priboi," 1925), 3–7.

85. For a protest against the view of students as "third-class party members," see S. B-ich, "Bol'noe v vuzovskoi deistvitel'nosti," *Krasnoe studenchestvo*, no. 5 (May 1926): 76–78.

Education and Authority: Ironies of Pedagogical Reform

The civil war period placed heavy emphasis on short-term training revolving around the commissariats, but some compromise, as we have seen, was already made with general education and Marxist theory. In the years after the shift to the three-year program in 1920, two successive educational approaches at the party school came to define communist university education for the duration of the decade. As a reaction to the war communist effort, another major approach took shape: the dominant goals of the early 1920s became raising the general educational level and training "red scholars" with disciplinary specializations. As before, virtually every major party intellectual and politician taught or made an appearance at the university, not to mention nonparty guests such as the agronomist Chaianov.[86]

In 1924, after Lenin's death and the university purge, Liadov and his administration mounted a concerted attack against the curriculum of 1921–23 as a part of the broader campaign against "scholasticism." What emerged in 1924 was a general redefinition of the tasks of the higher party school. The dominant goal was no longer, as in 1921–23, to educate scholarly Marxists and specialists, but to produce well-rounded, politically literate party leaders. One result was that general education lost priority; for example, Russian language was taken off the study plans in 1924–25. Practical tasks were reemphasized, and partially as an antidote against future oppositions the new disciplines of Leninism and party history saturated the curriculum.[87]

Liadov articulated a well-defined agenda. He expressly rejected the ambition of making Sverdlov into a center of Marxist scholarship and called for the university to become more practical, more proletarian, and more useful to the Party. Yet Liadov and his ally Konstantin Popov of Agitprop both championed a definition of "practical" in education that

86. Vladimir Petrovich Antonov-Saratovskii, "Universitet imeni Sverdlova v 1921–22 g.," *ZKS* 1 (January 1923): 247–303; "Protokol zasedaniia Metodicheskoi komissii pri kafedre Istorii," 4 May 1923, GARF f. 5221, op. 4, d. 29, l. 13; "Otchet Rektora o rabote Kommunisticheskogo Universiteta im. Sverdlova za 21–22 uchebnyi god," no date, 1922, RTsKhIDNI f. 17, op. 60, d. 233, l. 6–26. For example, Lunacharskii lectured on Russian literature, Kritsman taught economic history, Stalin gave his 1924 lectures on Leninism. On Chaianov's teaching at Sverdlov, see "Otvet klevetnikam," *Sverdlovets*, no. 2 (March 1922): 15.

87. S. Muraveiskii, "Voprosy uchebnoi raboty Komm. Universitetov (Iz doklada na zasedaniia Uchebnogo Soveta 14 aprelia 1924 g.)," in *Chem dolzhen byt' Kommuniversitet*, 15–26; Simonov, "Uchebnaia rabota v Sverdlovii za 1927–28 uchebnom godu," in *X let Kommuniversiteta*, 52–79.

was not transparent. On one level, they understood practical to mean a reworking of academic programs to give them a less abstract character and to ensure that courses in theory revolved around concrete and contemporary examples. But they also understood "practical" to mean standardizing the social sciences around core methodologies as expressed in two master disciplines, historical materialism and, after 1924, Leninism.[88]

Liadov's new "practicality" thus still emphasized theory—it was just a simplified and more regimented theory. Instead of the emphasis on specialized scholarship supported by other Old Bolshevik intellectuals, which was most frequently tied to their own areas of expertise, Liadov wanted to codify the teaching into more easily absorbed postulates and make it relevant to party *praktiki*, not future Marxist scholars. Liadov, the champion of practicality, himself taught historical materialism.

The Second Conference of Communist Universities, following on the heels of the Thirteenth Party Congress in 1924, passed a range of measures to futher proletarianize party institutions. Three years of "production" and party experience could be waived only by party committees nominating the candidate or for workers from the bench. Students should be older, more "proletarian" in terms of work experience, and higher in the party ranks.[89] The 1924 shift in educational policy affected the composition of the Sverdlov student body.[90] Liadov mounted an effort to influence the occupational background of working-class students as well. Before 1924, students classified as workers clearly included children of workers. In 1924, Liadov resolved that the university would become working-class "not in words, but in fact." This increased the average age of the Sverdlovian: in 1922–23 68 percent were under twenty-five, but in 1927–28 this fell to 21 percent. An effort was

88. "Tezisy k dokladu Liadova o reorganizatsii Komvuzov. (Materialy k s″ezdu rektorov Komvuzov)," no date, 1923, GARF f. 5221, op. 5, d. 89, l. 1; "Otvetnye tezisy t. Popova K. A. O tezisakh Sverdlovskogo Komm. Universiteta," no date, 1923, ibid., l. 5–6; "Soveshchanie prepodavatelei Universiteta im. Sverdlova 8/X-23. Doklad t. Liadova 'Zadachi Universiteta i metody prepodavaniia,'" ibid., d. 71, l. 1–2 ob.

89. "Postanovleniia i rezoliutsiia II-i konferentsii Kommuniversitetov 1924," GARF f. 5221, op. 5, d. 89, l. 8–19.

90. After the introduction of the three-year course, enrollment had declined from 1,910 in 1921–22 to 1,073 in 1923–24. With the purge of 1924, the student body was slashed to 530 for 1924–25. Enrollment climbed back to 717 by 1927–28; a fourth year of study was added in 1925–26. In contrast to this decline, one notes a sharp rise in the percentage of students coming from the working class, from 45.7 percent in 1919–20, to nearly 70 percent in 1922–24. After new proletarianization policies were set by the party in 1924, this figure jumped to over 80 percent from 1924–25 through 1927–28. GARF f. 5221, op. 9, d. 48, l. 4. Slightly different numbers are cited in ibid., op. 8, d. 55, l. 158–63.

launched to recruit "genuine industrial workers" from the metal, textile, and railroad industries.[91] These priorities prevented Sverdlov University from achieving any significant increase in the number of female students, which fluctuated between 10 and 20 percent of the student body in the 1920s—somewhat higher than in the Party as a whole, but roughly half that of higher education.[92]

As opposed to his recruitment policies, the "new practicality" Liadov succeeded in imposing after 1924 had important opponents. For one thing, Liadov was challenged by many of the Sverdlov teachers who were committed to a more traditional brand of theoretical Marxism, who believed, for example, in a focus on the political economy of capitalism rather than beginning with the study of Soviet conditions. Some party administrators also disagreed with Liadov's views; foremost among them Pokrovskii, who derided Liadov's opposition to an academic focus. What occurred in the 1924 shift at Sverdlov, therefore, was that priorities were once again reshuffled—hardly in a neat or decisive manner—between general education, theory, and practical party training.[93]

In light of these 1924 changes geared at making Sverdlov more useful to the Party, it may seem paradoxical that this was also the year the boldest experiment of the 1920s in transforming pedagogy in higher education, the Dalton Plan, was officially adopted. Moreover, this plan was not put forward by Agitprop, the party leadership, or Liadov, but represented the pet project of the progressive party educators, among whom virtually the only politically important personage was Krupskaia.[94]

91. M. N. Liadov, "Dostizheniia Sverdlovii (Doklad na plenume MK VKP(b) 1928 g.)," in *X let Kommuniversiteta*, 45–46. Of the approximately 70 percent workers at Sverdlov in 1923–24, 34 percent were classified as industrial workers. B. M. Gessen, "Zadachi Universiteta i uroven' prepodavaniia," *ZKS* 2 (1924): 295–303.

92. The majority of these women achieved the necessary party experience in the Central Committee's Zhenotdel, from which they were nominated. See GARF f. 5221, op. 8, d. 55, l. 158–63; "Protokol soveshchaniia studentok Sverdlovskogo Komuniversiteta," 1929, no exact date, RGAODgM f. 459, op. 1, d. 33, l. 74. In January 1922 women comprised 7.8 percent of the Party's membership, 13.7 in October 1929. On the Party's gender structure, see Rigby, *Communist Party Membership*, 360–63.

93. "Stenogramma zasedaniia ekonomicheskoi kafedry 24 sentiabria 1923 g.," in *Sbornik po voprosam partprosveshcheniia* (Moscow: Izdatel'stvo Kommunisticheskogo universiteta im. Sverdlova, 1924), 164–69; "Diskussiia o programme po politekonomii v Kommvuze: zasedanie ot 15 marta 1924 g.," *ZKS* 2 (1924): 326–70; Pokrovskii's remarks in "Stenogramma zasedanii Nauchno-Politicheskoi Sektsii GUS-a, 20 marta 1925g," ARAN f. 1759, op. 2, d. 5, l. 142–48; "Protokol zasedaniia Pravleniia Komuniversiteta im. Sverdlova ot 24/VIII-24," GARF f. 5221, op. 6, d. 54, l. 11.

94. On the Narkompros educators and postrevolutionary pedagogy, see Oskar Anweiler, *Geschichte der Schule und Pädagogik in Rußland vom Ende des Zarenreiches bis zum Beginn*

Yet the other great changes in the watershed of 1924 opened the door to this experiment as well.

The Dalton Plan, also known as the Laboratory Plan, originated in the enthusiasm for John Dewey's pedagogical maxim of "learning by doing." A follower of Dewey, Helen Parkhurst, developed the method in Dalton, Massachusetts. Originally designed for children under nine, the method called for each student to work out a "contract," an educational program tailored to the needs of the individual. Regimented class hours were abolished and students were free to roam and fraternize with fellows of all ages; work took place in various "laboratories" with teachers trained in each subject. Between 1922 and 1933 Parkhurst's book, *Education on the Dalton Plan*, was published in nineteen languages.[95]

In late 1922 Krupskaia, prompted by several considerations, gave highly favorable reviews of Parkhurst's book. The "planned" nature of study was appealing, as was the emphasis on practical work and learning by doing. In addition, the plan would allow teachers to work with greater numbers of students and economize on textbooks. In 1923 the editorial board of Krupskaia's pedagogical journal, *Na putiakh k novoi shkole*, championed the plan against its critics.[96]

As this method was being promoted in pedagogical circles, educators in the party schools were searching for new methods in higher education. The prerevolutionary universities were portrayed in the years after 1917 as bastions of professorial elitism, where students passively gazed at the podium and memorized abstruse lectures. Bolstering student "independence" and linking teaching to praxis were almost universally championed by educators after the Revolution. From 1921 to 1924 lectures were increasingly abandoned at Sverdlov in favor of seminars, known by the more revolutionary term *kruzhki* (study circles). In this period as well lectures were widely "discredited" among the communist

---

der Stalin-Ära (Berlin: Quelle & Meyer Verlag, 1964), 155–77, and Larry E. Holmes, *The Kremlin and the Schoolhouse: Reforming Education in Soviet Russia, 1917–1931* (Bloomington: Indiana University Press, 1991), 27–36.

95. Helen Parkhurst, *Education on the Dalton Plan* (New York: E. P. Dutton, 1922); Evelyn Dewey, *The Dalton Laboratory Plan* (New York: E. P. Dutton, 1922); C. W. Kimmins and Belle Rennie, *The Triumph of the Dalton Plan* (London: I. Nicholson & Watson, 1932).

96. N. Krupskaia, review of Parkhurst and Dewey, *Na putiakh k novoi shkole*, no. 3 (November 1922): 164–68; "Primechanie redaktsii," *Na putiakh k novoi shkole*, no. 3 (May 1923), 254–55. On Krupskaia's views of Dewey from 1916 until his visit to the USSR in 1928, see John T. Zepper, "Krupskaya on Dewey's Educational Thought," *School and Society* 100 (January 1972): 19–21, and Anweiler, *Geschichte*, 159–62.

students as authoritarian holdovers from bourgeois *byt*, and the party schools became the most eager advocates of pedagogical reform.[97]

At the same time, the mechanisms for curricular centralization were firmly put in place in party higher education. This can be attributed most of all to the activities of Agitprop and Glavpolitprosvet, successive congresses of soviet-party schools and communist universities, Central Committee directives, and distribution of standardized reading lists and study plans. By 1924 enough centralization had occurred that if a new methodology was endorsed, it could (at least on paper) be almost universally adopted in the party schools. The Third Congress of Soviet-Party Schools on 7–10 June 1924, again following the Thirteenth Party Congress, gave a detailed resolution supporting the Dalton Plan for the higher schools. In 1924–25 the Dalton Plan was introduced in almost all soviet-party schools and communist universities.[98]

Under the Dalton Plan as it was implemented at Sverdlov and elsewhere, the teacher led introductory lessons and helped formulate individual or group research assignments (often containing interdisciplinary "complexes" of themes). Then, the *kruzhki* met independently and with the teacher for the duration of the course. Paralleling the debates about "democracy" in the party cell, the method was designed to increase the activity (*aktivnost'*), independence (*samodeiatel'nost'*), and power of the students; paralleling the debates on *byt*, the method was proclaimed to promote collectivism and ties to production. "The role of the teacher changes dramatically," one pedagogue wrote in a typical passage. "He no longer 'teaches.' . . . He is no longer a dictator. . . . Now he is simply an experienced person, a consultant, who helps the student in his independent work." Education would no longer hand down received formulas; it would be a process of discovery. The classroom would be turned into a laboratory.[99]

As in the realm of *byt*, however, changes after 1924 were hardly the

97. A. F. Ryndich, "Ocherk razvitiia metodiki sovpartshkol i komvuzov," in Ryndich, *Metodika*, 7–48.

98. A. F. Ryndich, ed., *Laboratornyi plan i ego znachenie v metodike kommunisticheskogo vospitaniia* (Moscow: Izdatel'stvo Kommunisticheskogo universiteta im. Sverdlova, 1926); "Ocherk razvitiia"; "Dal'tonskii laboratornyi plan v sovpartshkolakh (po dokladu tt. Krupskoi i Briunelli)," in Ryndich, *Metodika*, 164–68; and A. Fil'shtinskii, "Blizhaishie zadachi metodiki," *Leninskaia ucheba*, no. 1 (January 1926): 14–18.

99. Evgenii Briunelli, "K voprosu o primenenii Dal'tonovskogo laboratornogo plana v sovpartshkolakh," *Kommunisticheskoe prosveshchenie*, no. 4–5 (June–October 1923): 65–68; A. Fil'shtinskii, "Dalton-plan i issledovatel'skii metod," in A. F. Ryndich, ed., *Sovpartshkoly i komvuzy* (Moscow: Gosizdat, 1926), 132; Anweiler, *Geschichte*, 260–85; John T. Zepper, "N. K. Krupskaya on Complex Themes in Soviet Education," *Comparative Educational Review* 9 (February 1965): 33–37.

ones of which the party pedagogues dreamed. As one Dalton proponent lamented in 1926, "However strange it may seem, it is all the same certain that the highly energetic implementation of the Dalton Plan in all schools has not corresponded with movement forward in the application of contemporary and progressive teaching methods."[100]

The new pedagogy, like communist standards of conduct, became a means of marking the revolutionary and reactionary—and loyalty and resistance to the Party. Just as *byt* was integrated into the Party's disciplinary system, the regime's surveillance organs used the new pedagogy as a benchmark in evaluating the professoriat. GPU reports, repeatedly expressing deep hostility toward the intelligentsia, noted opposition to the Dalton Plan in profiles of individual professors. A 1924 social evaluation (*svodka*) of the professoriat cited resistance to the new pedagogy as a clearly "counterrevolutionary phenomenon." Standard secret police forms sent to the localities in this period often included sections for reports on the professoriat's outlook on new methods of teaching.[101]

Indeed, by aiming at a replacement of the lecture system the Dalton Plan threatened professorial authority, and the new "active" methods provoked widespread opposition in the universities.[102] For supporters among the pedagogues and in the communist universities, however, there were fundamental principles at stake: the ideal of student group initiative was one goal common to all the new methods and was eagerly embraced by Sverdlov students.[103] Yet the end result, according to Ryndich, was only that students "are afraid of independence, they fear to make the slightest movement independently."[104]

It was perfectly clear to leading party intellectuals that the principle of independent interpretation embodied in progressive teaching methods contradicted many aspects of Leninist theory and practice. Liadov, at

100. Fil'shtinskii, "Dalton-plan," 132.

101. V. S. Izmozik, *Glaza i ushi rezhima: Gosudarstvennyi politicheskii kontrol' za naseleniem Sovetskoi Rossii v 1918–1928 godakh* (St. Petersburg: Izdatel'stvo Sankt-Peterburgskogo Universiteta Ekonomiki i Finansov, 1995), 123, 133.

102. Even 1926 official plans for the universities still allocated half the time for lectures. P. Valeskaln, "Ugroza novym metodam prepodavaniia," *Krasnoe studenchestvo*, no. 9 (November 1926), 11–12; A. I. Dzens-Litovskii, "K voprosu o Dal'ton-laboratornom plane i lektsionnom metode v vysshei i povyshennogo tipa shkolakh," *Nauchnyi rabotnik*, no. 9 (September 1926): 59–62. Even the rector of Leningrad University, the philologist N. S. Derzhavin, subjected the new pedagogy to a blistering attack in "K voprosu o metodakh prepodavaniia v vysshei shkole," *Nauchnyi rabotnik*, no. 5–6 (May–June 1926): 37–50.

103. For example, "Zadachi 'Leninskoi Ucheby,'" *Leninskaia ucheba*, no. 1 (January 1926): 3, and I. Petin, "Nuzhna li kollektivnaia konsul'tatsiia v laboratornom plane," ibid., 32.

104. A. F. Ryndich, "Laboratornyi plan na konferentsii Komvuzov (3–5 fev. 1926 g.)," in Ryndich, *Sovpartshkoly i komvuzy*, 121; and Ryndich, "Ocherk razvitiia," 39.

one Sverdlov cell bureau meeting, openly announced that he had "always been very wary of the Dalton plan."[105] In a discussion of pedagogy in 1923 Pokrovskii told the Socialist Academy it was unfortunate that only American "bourgeois pedagogical literature" was so popular in Soviet Russia: "American methods consist of teaching everyone to pose questions and develop them independently. But I can imagine what would happen to our party discipline when every Komsomol member poses and solves these questions. . . . It is at variance with our praxis."[106] However, one reason the plan could be integrated into the communist university—and indeed, a primary reason it did not live up to its promises—was that it reinforced one of the basic political and organizational practices of the university, the division of the student body into circles or *kruzhki*.

The origins of *kruzhki* at Sverdlov can be traced to 1919. When lectures were predominant in the years after the party school's founding, students were forced to sit through eight to ten hours of back-to-back two-hour lectures. In 1919 this was already recognized as a failure, and the first attempts to form *kruzhki* soon followed. "Collective discussions" were organized around set themes, such as "What is the grain monopoly," or "What has soviet power given to workers and peasants?" The groups had about twenty-five students at first, later thirty-five to forty, and were divided by academic qualifications. But the *kruzhki* were not only organized for academic purposes; by 1923 they were considered the building block of party work within the cell system. The fundamental importance that the circles assumed in the 1920s becomes clear when it is discovered that the academic *kruzhki* were in fact identical to those which the party cell used to subdivide the students for political work.[107]

In other words, the very groups elevated to academic predominance under the Dalton Plan carried on the primary political discussions organized by the party cell.[108] In the first semester of 1925–26, for example,

105. "Protokol No. 17 zakrytogo zasedaniia Biuro iacheiki Komuniversiteta Sverdlova ot 17/III-1927 g.," RGAODgM f. 459, op. 1, d. 29, l. 16.

106. "Stenogramma plenuma chlenov Sotsialisticheskoi Akademii. 11.10.1923 g.," ARAN f. 350, op. 1, d. 19, l. 37–38.

107. "Metody raboty v Komm. universitet im. Ia. M. Sverdlova," no date, GARF f. A-2313, op. 4, d. 35, l. 4–6; V. Riabokon', "Ocherednye zadachi partraboty," *Sverdloviia*, 31 May 1923, 1; I. Onotskii, "Nekotorye itogi i perspektivy raboty iacheiki VKP(b) Sverdlovskogo Universiteta," *Leninskaia ucheba*, no. 2–3 (March-April 1926): 57–58.

108. The connection between the Dalton Plan and the *kruzhki* seems confirmed by the passage by the Third Conference of Soviet-Party Schools, the very body that recommended adoption of the Dalton Plan in 1924, of a resolution calling for special attention to be focused on the

these groups discussed the plenum of the Moscow party committee, the Central Committee's October plenum, the Locarno treaty, and other topics connected to current political affairs. Rapid adjustments in the curriculum, if necessary, could also be implemented through the *kruzhki*. After Lenin's death, for example, when a flurry of measures was taken in the middle of the year to "saturate" the curriculum with Leninism, it was the *kruzhki* organizers who met with Agitprop's Popov and the academic departments to implement the changes.[109]

The *kruzhki* thus became the basic unit of both academic and party work. In the period after the purge of 1924 the cell bureau targeted oppositionists in the *kruzhki* not only during cell events but in academic discussions.[110] But intervention was only one factor affecting the work of the *kruzhki*. If education was organized in the very same groups that debated the party resolutions, who could even attempt to say when an academic discussion began and a political struggle ended? The Dalton Plan helped turn the classroom less into a laboratory than into a literal extension of the party cell's political arena.

Implementation of both party and academic purges was closely tied to the *kruzhki*. The general party purge of 1921 was conducted for Sverdlov students (those who had not already passed through purge commissions in their own localities) at open meetings of the *kruzhki*, with representatives from the Moscow raikom. Each *kruzhok* was charged with organizing the questionnaires and other necessary material for the purge commissions. In 1922 and 1923 regulations for annual end-of-year academic purges were finalized. According to these regulations, these purges were defined by "the general communist principles of a party review [*proverka*]" combined with the academic criteria appropriate for safeguarding higher Marxist education. In other words, the regulations for academic purges authorized from the start party-political considerations, the standards of communist *byt*, and academic-ideological criteria. In the 1923 purge of one of the more academically advanced "lecturer groups," when one-fourth of the ninety-seven students were purged, seven were removed for insufficient practical party experience, five for academic insufficiencies, and five for unfavorable

---

formation of party *kruzhki* within the party cells of all the schools. GARF f. A-2313, op. 1, d. 115, l. 88.

109. Onotskii, "Nekotorye itogi," 58; "Protokol No. 6 ot 16/II-24 g. Zasedaniia Partkafedry sovmestno s kruzhkovodami," GARF f. 5221, op. 5, d. 124, l. 5–6.

110. "Vypiska iz otcheta Biuro iacheiki VKP(b)," no exact date, 1924, RGAODgM f. 459, op. 1, d. 23, l. 16.

Liadov's *kruzhok* (circle) at Sverdlov Communist University in 1923–24. Martyn Nikolaevich Liadov, rector of the university, is in the second row, fifth from the left. Reprinted by permission of the Museum of the Revolution, Moscow, Russia.

evaluations. At the height of the campaign against scholasticism, these students' "manner of thinking [*myshlenie*]" was rated as either "abstract," "concrete," or "mixed."[111]

In a rare published criticism of this system of evaluation, an article in the Sverdlov newspaper titled "Is this necessary?" the author described the heights of tension the purges provoked: "In the preliminary purges and repeat purges [*perechistki*] there were real battles [*srazheniia*], and if as a result there were no physical cripples, then there was no mean

111. "Protokol ot 9 oktiabria 1921 g. zasedaniia Biuro sovmestno s partorganizatorami dvukhgodichnogo kursa," RGAODgM f. 459, op. 1, d. 13, l. 11; "Polozhenie o proverke osnovnogo kursa," 1922–23, no exact date, GARF f. 5221, op. 4, d. 71, l. 17; "Chistka lektortsev," *Sverdloviia*, 28 June 1923, 3. This prompted the author of this article to query: why not half-mixed or a quarter-mixed?

number of moral sufferers." After all this many excluded students managed to be reinstated through political connections, the author claimed. "Cannot selection [of students] be limited by other means, but not by purges?" An answer was soon forthcoming: "Is control necessary?"[112]

One fact not recalled was that the academic purges had in fact replaced a traditional system of trimesterly examinations (*zachety*) used in 1921. The system of academic purges did include evaluations (*spravki*) on performance in each of the trimesters, but clearly the new system of evaluation gave much more of an opportunity to introduce questions relating to party work and standards of conduct. According to one 1923 report, for example, the group evaluations measured abilities, development, classwork, and party-mindedness (*partiinost'*). The latter category embraced such areas as party work, theoretical and practical abilities, and deviations, examples of which were individualism, petty-bourgeois philistinism (*meshchanstvo*), and inclinations toward private property (*sobstvennichestvo*). Other areas evaluated were activism (*aktivnost'*), relations with comrades, and opinions on important questions of sociopolitical life.[113] The replacement of examinations with the purges therefore also increased the importance of the *kruzhki*. One account even boasted that these were no purges from above, but self-purges (*samochistki*).[114]

The Laboratory Plan, the system of purges, and the organization of party cell political life all worked together by 1924 to merge political, lifestyle, and academic evaluations of the rank and file into the single forum of the *kruzhki*. The combination must have produced an intensity in their functioning that is difficult to imagine. The *kruzhki* represented nothing less than the organizational fusion of the realms of politics, education, and *byt*.

Origins of the Great Break: Self-Criticism and Power Relations

The top-down power structure at Sverdlov University had become an entrenched hierarchy typical of the party organization during NEP. The broadening of the communist disciplinary field affected everybody, to

112. I. S., "Nuzhno li eto?" *Sverdloviia*, 31 May 1923, 1; V. I. V., "Nuzhen li kontrol'?" ibid., 18 June 1923, 3.

113. V. Veger, "Prezhde i teper' (piatiletie universiteta Sverdlova)," *Kommunisticheskoe prosveshchenie*, no. 3 (May-June 1923): 50–52.

114. F. I. Shablonskii, "Chistka v vysshei partshkole (Iz opyta Universiteta Sverdlova)," *Sverdlovets*, no. 4 (January 1923): 8.

be sure, but superordinate authority remained far less vulnerable to it. That suddenly changed with the introduction of the criticism/self-criticism campaign of 1928. On the eve of the industrialization drive, the attack on specialists and right deviationists, and the purge of the party and state apparat, the war on bureaucracy legitimized and encouraged attacks on mid-level functionaries (and those loyal to Stalin's rivals) throughout the system. The self-criticism campaign provided a fundamental tool in the Stalin faction's consolidation of power and the launching of the Great Break.[115]

The entrenched power structure of NEP buckled under an upheaval of the rank and file, which was both encouraged and constrained at the top. Uglanov's Moscow party organization, where discipline had been most tight, was affected with special force, as the entire Moscow leadership became associated with the "Right Deviation" in the leadership in the fall of 1928. In October, the turning-point in Uglanov's ouster, the lists prearranged for low-level elections to *raions* and cells were abolished in the name of "broad democracy," a temporary device to break the hold of local leaders that was repeated in the prewar period only on the eve of the Great Purge of 1937.[116]

At the same time, the nature of acceptible criticism was quickly constricted and superordinate authority maintained: *Pravda* articles and party directives made it abundantly clear that genuine "proletarian" criticism was supposed to be constructive, not turned on the foundations of the socialist state. Criticism could be dialectically transformed into self-criticism and forced upon anyone in a weakened position, again broadening the disciplinary regime. The campaign publicized a spate of *byt* scandals such as drunkenness, corruption, and rape, prompting Trotskyist oppositionists to accuse the Stalinists of boosting levels of degeneracy.[117]

The most important historical moment for the *kruzhki* at Sverdlov University came in 1928. The cell bureau was suddenly put in the same precarious position as local political powers throughout the country. It

115. The fact that many arrests resulted from critical articles in the "wall papers," often handwritten newspapers put out with input from the rank and file, shows that the announcement of the self-criticism campaign produced genuine upheaval. For example, "Razve stengazeta vinovata? Stengazeta pod arestom," *Stennaia gazeta*, 17 February 1929, 1. Moscow Trotskyists, however, immediately perceived the campaign's political uses and interpreted the introduction of "self-criticism" as a Stalinist tool to engineer a "palace coup." See Trotsky Archive, bMS Russ 13T-1392.

116. Merridale, *Moscow Politics*, 211, 302 n. 130. I am also indebted to her discussion of the self-criticism campaign, 211–15 and passim.

117. Moscow (?) Trotskyists, "O Samokritike," 2 June 1928, Trotsky Archive, bMS Russ 13T-1612.

responded as countless other authorities did, by attempting to stifle unwanted criticism. In September and October 1928, stormy meetings at Sverdlov of a kind not seen since 1923–24 raised criticisms of the entire state of affairs at the university. Two issues—control of the cell bureau by the rector and administration, and the subordination of the *kruzhki* to the bureau—led to disruptive arguments in cell gatherings. During the assault on Uglanov's Moscow party leadership in October, Liadov stormed out of one meeting, after which all the "faults" of the university were discussed.[118]

Pent-up frustrations of the rank and file were vented. One student demanded at a general party meeting, "The bureau must react on time to the decisions of the *kruzhki* . . . the [political] meetings of the *kruzhki* have been dead, since the speakers [*dokladchiki* assigned by the bureau] only paraphrase what is written in 'Pravda.'" Another added that the main "line" of the university had been the "strangling of the activism of the student body." A third chimed in that the party organizers in the circles frequently disrupted self-criticism and took no part in it. The response from the bureau, in the person of its secretary Volkov, was conciliatory. "In regard to freedom of speech [*o svobode slova*] and repression [*zazhim*], the meeting of the fourth-year class already noted that democracy has been significantly expanded in the past year. . . . Recently the bureau has attempted to guarantee a maximum of democracy."[119]

The outpouring was extraordinary and connected with the ouster of Uglanov's Moscow machine. Both Liadov and the Sverdlov bureau were compromisingly tied to the long-time head of the Moscow party organization; Uglanov was welcomed to Sverdlov even after the October 1928 Moscow Committee plenum, when Stalin and Molotov personally intervened in order to destablize his grip on the MK. Uglanov survived until November. At that time he was linked to the "Right," and the entire Moscow organization was compromised. As 1928 drew to a close, the Sverdlov bureau was left scrambling to reverse itself, weed out rightists, and prove its orthodoxy anew. The rank and file blamed the cell bureau for not reacting to political signals in time, but the bureau leadership claimed the "whole university" was at fault.[120]

118. "Protokol obshchego partsobraniia studentov II kursa Universiteta im. Sverdlova ot 8/X-1928 g.," RGAODgM f. 459, op. 1, d. 30, l. 33.

119. "Protokol No. 1 obshchego sobraniia iacheiki VKP(b) Komuniversiteta Sverdlova ot 25/IX-28 g.," RGAODgM f. 459, op. 1, d. 30, l. 7–8.

120. Merridale, *Moscow Politics*, 46–67; "Protokol No. 3 obshcheuniversitetskogo sobraniia

The bureau attempted to regain its balance, characteristically, by linking criticism of the bureau on the part of the *kruzhki* to oppositionism or deviationism. One student fought this at a party meeting in February 1929:

> It is implied that all the criticism that has been turned directly against the bureau of the cell . . . has been criticism against the Central Committee. . . . This is, of course, a complete perversion of self-criticism. One might ask how will it be possible after this to speak out and criticize the cell bureau? . . . After all, how is it possible to speak and criticize, when any criticism against the bureau will be looked on as criticism against the TsK?[121]

In the discussions of the *kruzhki* themselves, where the self-criticism campaign was carried out, the rank and filer continued to complain that the students were constantly on the receiving end of criticism, but "organizers" were immune. Bureau attempts to bring the *kruzhki* under much tighter control were also discernible. This occurred, in part, through careful monitoring of statements made in the circles and an aggressive effort to criticize "mistakes" made in circle discussions.[122] The effect of the bureau-*kruzhki* conflicts of 1928–29 was that the cell bureau began to document statements by rank-and-file students to a qualitatively higher degree than it had throughout the 1920s.

At the same time, the university as a whole was made more vulnerable because Liadov and the bureau were linked to the ousted Uglanov leadership. Political vulnerability thus increased everywhere: the rank and file were monitored more by the bureau, and the bureau was forced to prove the orthodoxy of the university as a whole when it faced the outside.[123] Liadov appeared disoriented, first supporting the Uglanov leadership, then repenting after the tide turned. The most ferocious unmasker of deviations and degeneracy was now infected by the Right

---

iacheiki VKP(b) Komuniversiteta Sverdlova ot 20/X-1928," RGAODgM f. 459, op. 1, d. 30, l. 38–41.

121. "Protokol obshchego sobraniia iacheiki Komuniversiteta Sverdlova ot 5/II-29 g.," RGAODgM f. 459, op. 1, d. 32, l. 2.

122. For example, "V pravlenie Universiteta i Biuro iacheiki [ot] Studenta 7 kruzhka IV kursa Osipova O. M.," no date, RGAODgM f. 459, op. 1, d. 33, l. 94; "Rezoliutsiia biuro iacheiki po itogam prorabotki partkruzhkami reshenii Moskovskoi XVII-i Gubpartkonferentsii priniataia edinoglasno ot 3-go Marta 1929," ibid., l. 54–55.

123. "Tezisy k otchetu Biuro Iacheiki," covering October 1928–October 1929, RGAODgM f. 459. op. 1, d. 32, l. 30; "Otchet 1-go kursa za 1928–1929 Uchebnyi god," GARF f. 5221, op. 11, d. 31, l. 26–34; "Protokol No. 7 obshchego sobraniia iacheiki Komuniversiteta Sverdlova ot 29/1–1929," RGAODgM f. 459, op. 1, d. 32, l. 1.

Deviation, and there was no cure. "When I meet close comrades, they turn away from me as from a betrayer of the party line, they try not to notice, they cross to the other side of the street," he said pathetically. After having insisted for years that no deviation was accidental, that they were all symptoms of the same disease, he seemed to realize the hopelessness of his defense as he uttered it: "It is impossible to insist that for me this was not some kind of accidental mistake, that it was in the nature of my way of thinking."[124] Within the university, even as the cell bureau regained its dominance, Liadov was open to attack along with other top university administrators.[125] The inversion of the power structure thus served to increase vulnerability all the way down the line, with the exception of the ascendent Stalin leadership. The rank and file, and the university as a whole, were now subject to abrupt mobilization. The Central Committee ordered Sverdlov and other party schools to carry out special early graduations in 1929 and again in 1930, in order to send upper-level students to the countryside during the drive for collectivization.[126] At Sverdlov Communist University, the Great Break had begun.

The pseudo-populism of the self-criticism campaign, combined with the buckling of the party power hierarchy, had unleashed the pent-up pressures that had been building on the rank and file in previous years. The self-criticism session, emerging out of the campaign of 1928, became the institutionalized ritual by which the rank and file were not only invited but required to attack their immediate superiors.[127] At the same time, the disciplinary regime, which encompassed an aspect of communist self-regulation, was expanded as the party watchword became struggle against deviations on both Left and Right. Only the idea of the single, monolithic center emerged unscathed. Having formed the paradigm for Stalin's defeat of all oppositions, the dynamics of the

124. "Mandelshtam (Liadov). VI Plenum MK i MKK VKP(b) . . . Preniia," no date, Trotsky Archive, bMS Russ T-2798.

125. See clippings from newspaper *Sverdloviia* in RGAODgM, f. 459, op. 1, d. 33, l. 25; "Protokol No. 18 zasedaniia Biuro iacheiki Sverdlova ot 15–II-29," ibid., l. 22; "Zaiavlenie [v Pravlenie i Biuro iacheiki]," no date, 1929, ibid., l. 27.

126. "O rabote sovpartshkol v 1929–30 uchebnom godu," GARF f. A-2313, op. 5, d. 150, l. 3, and "Zasedanie po chistke Glavpolitprosveta, 2-go ianvaria 1930 g.," RTsKhIDNI f. 12, op. 1, d. 509, l. 16. In 1932 Sverdlov University's academic character and political prestige were drastically altered, as communist universities were turned into "higher communist agricultural schools" by Central Committee decree. See Leonova, *Iz istorii*, 37, 53.

127. Self-criticism as a Stalinist ritual which could temporarily invert the power hierarchy is discussed by Alexei Kojevnikov in "Games of Soviet Democracy: Ideological Discussions in Science Around 1948" (paper presented to the Midwest Russian History Workshop, Indiana University, 1995).

Great Break were mythologized in the Party. As both model and tactic, they achieved the profound function of periodically venting the frustrations of the rank and file, of revitalizing the search for liberation and deviance, and reinforcing the center. The cycle of pseudo-democratic revivalism, temporary inversion of the power hierarchy, and purification-upheaval was reenacted in the Great Terror and again in the late 1940s.[128]

128. Kotkin, *Magnetic Mountain*, 293–97; Yoram Gorlizki, "Party Revivalism and the Death of Stalin," *Slavic Review* 54 (Spring 1995): 1–22; on Stalin's defeat of his rivals and mythopoesis in party history, George Enteen, "Soviet Historiography and the Problem of Myth" (forthcoming).

3 /

POLITICAL CULTURE AT THE INSTITUTE OF RED PROFESSORS

The problem-ridden endeavor of creating red experts, communist scholars, and proletarian intellectuals was endowed with an institutional base with the founding of the Institute of Red Professors (IKP) in 1921. The immediate justification for establishing the Party's only graduate-level institution of higher learning was the need for university scholars in the Marxist social sciences. But during NEP IKP actually sent only 25 percent of its graduates into academic careers. As "one of the weapons of our party on the ideological front," its mission quickly broadened to encompass the training of the cream of the new party intelligentsia and a political "changing of the guard" (*smena*).[1] This link between the attempt to forge a political elite and the Party's own most advanced educational endeavor turned IKP into the most important center of party-Marxist training for rising party politicians, publicists, and scholars in the 1920s.

IKP's special mission and identity, therefore, was of all the party institutions most closely bound up with the great revolutionary theme of

1. "Ustav Instituta krasnoi professury," no date, 1921, GARF f. 5284, op. 1, d. 2, l. 79; the quotation is from "Tezisy M. N. Pokrovskogo k voprosu o programmakh i metodakh prepodavaniia IKP," ratified by the IKP academic council 9 October 1923, ibid., d. 100, l. 6; the figure is from Valerii D. Solovei, "Rol' Instituta krasnoi professury v stanovlenii sovetskoi istoricheskoi nauki" (Candidate of Sciences diss., Moscow State University, 1987), 37. See also his "Institut krasnoi professury: Podgotovka kadrov istorikov partii v 20–30-e gody," *Voprosy istorii KPSS*, no. 12 (1990): 87–98.

the red expert—two words which, by the entire situation the Party found itself after 1917, were invariably placed in stark opposition to one another, but whose coupling encompassed the scope of the institute's task in a nutshell. The graduates expected from the new institutions would be both revolutionaries and scholars, Bolsheviks and intellectuals, reds and experts. The combination would address one of the acute dilemmas of the early Soviet period, the forced reliance on the bourgeois specialist, who could not be of the Revolution even if he were learned and loyal. The red professor would acquire and then impart knowledge as a learned Bolshevik revolutionary, ultimately obviating the reliance on old elites and ensuring victory on the third front. In a landmark speech in 1924 on the young generation of "red specialists" and "our own professors," Nikolai Ivanovich Bukharin, the Politburo member and party theorist closely associated with IKP, affirmed that the type of people trained would answer "the question 'Who Will Beat Whom' [*Kto Kogo*]."[2]

Such was the context of aspirations in which the Institute of Red Professors came into being, which inclined this pathbreaking center of Bolshevik thought to develop the project of creating the red expert as much in terms of party, state, and society as academia, education, and scholarship. What was at stake in training red professors—and this informed the history of the institution in concrete ways ranging from the prosecution of purges to the production of red scholarship—was the necessity of raising up an ideal new group, a squared circle of an intelligentsia with all the positive attributes of the steely-eyed proletariat and none of the negative ones of the quavering bourgeois intellectual.

The prospect of raising up a new stratum of intellectuals in an officially egalitarian "dictatorship of the proletariat" confronted the Bolsheviks with many of their thorniest dilemmas and unspoken taboos. Education of a new intelligentsia might be construed to mean that the society which, according to Lenin's dictum, "any cook" could govern was creating a closed, elite caste; that intellectual activity and specialized knowledge might take precedence over physical labor; and that "scholastic" higher learning had triumphed over revolutionary praxis. IKP's evolution, therefore, reflected all the tensions and conflicts growing out of its contradictory attempt to raise up an anti-elitist elite. Its very name, the Institute of Red Professors, embodied these tensions.

2. *Trinadtsatyi s"ezd Rossiiskoi kommunisticheskoi partii (bol'shevikov). Stenograficheskii otchet. 23–31 maia 1924 g.* (Moscow: Krasnaia nov', 1924), 539.

As a crucible of politics and culture for a younger generation of party intellectuals in the 1920s, IKP was able to cultivate a distinctively combative variety of Bolshevik political culture. This put red professors at the forefront in elaborating a ritualistic system, rooted in that culture, for identifying political and ideological deviance. Indeed, IKP's political culture, reflecting the ethos of the rising party intelligentsia, influenced the direction of Marxist thought at the institute; further, the party style in intellectual life epitomized by IKP began to spread to the broader academic world.

The history of political-ideological struggle in the 1920s within the context of communist political culture at IKP suggests the much broader necessity of rethinking the nature of inner-party opposition. In this area, as elsewhere, party politics has been approached in far too narrow a fashion. In light of a richly expressive political culture spurring the development of powerful rites and ideological constructs centrally concerned with prosecuting or deflecting charges of deviationism, it becomes impossible to interpret political struggles as a straightforward confrontation of forces. In fact, by the time of what will be called the invention of a "Right Opposition" in 1928–29, allegedly finding a bastion of support at IKP, the development of communist political culture often precluded clear-cut alignments of political forces or declarations of allegiance. Rather, the political culture, which will be explored through the vehicle of IKP, had become so centered around hiding potential opposition and revealing deviation that the political process itself had acquired the stylized character of drama and had assimilated the Marxist-Leninist methodology of "unmasking" what was to a significant degree a fictitious, ubiquitous, and necessary opponent.

In Search of the Red Specialist: Qualifications versus "Scholasticism"

Institut krasnoi professury was founded on 20 March 1921 by a Sovnarkom decree signed by Lenin as a three-year graduate school with departments of history, economics, and philosophy.[3] Pokrovskii and a core group of party scholars such as Viacheslav P. Volgin, Nikolai M. Lukin, Vladimir V. Adoratskii, and Abram M. Deborin, as well as top

3. "Institut krasnoi professury," 13 April 1921, RTsKhIDNI f. 17, op. 60, d. 64, l. 34; GARF f. 5284, op. 1, d. 2, l. 1; S. M. Dubrovskii, "K istorii Instituta krasnoi professury," *Istoricheskii arkhiv*, no. 6 (1958): 76.

Bolshevik leaders like Preobrazhenskii, Radek, and Bukharin, oversaw a significant expansion during the mid-1920s. In 1924 a fourth year of study was added for advanced students, a two-year "preparatory section" was established to promote students of proletarian and peasant origin, and in following years departments of law, natural science, literature, and party history were added. In 1921, 93 students entered the institute; by 1928 this figure had increased to 483.[4] With most of the stars among Bolshevik scholars and theorists at some point connected to the institute, it developed an intensive and rigorous academic program in the early 1920s not only focusing on Marxist classics but also including immersion in "pre-Marxist" philosophers and non-Marxist political economists and historians.[5] Many early graduates became leading party scholars themselves or prominent party litterateurs.[6] But it was one of the fundamental paradoxes of IKP's pathbreaking attempt to create the red expert that this academic rigor, while cementing the nascent institution's reputation, was a dubious success; it raised fundamental fears that the new intellectual would be more professorial than red.

Such fears became overriding concerns grounded in the scope of the ambitions the Party held for a new party intelligentsia; they were exacerbated by continuous innovations of the early 1920s that strove to

4. Dubrovskii, "K istorii Instituta," 87. Deborin, a Menshevik from 1907 to 1917 and the leading Marxist philosopher of the 1920s, was an unusual case among those I have classified as party scholars, since he did not formally join the Party until 1928; but as editor of the leading philosophical journal *Pod znamenem marksizma* from 1922 to 1930, he was a party member in all but name. On his life and fate, see Ia. G. Rokitianskii, "Nesostoiavsheesia samoubiistvo," *Vestnik Rossiiskoi akademii nauk* 63, no. 5 (1993): 458–62.

5. Initially, the most important text in the first year of study was Marx's *Kapital*; for each seminar the student's research paper had to be based on "primary sources." See M. N. Pokrovskii, ed., *Trudy Instituta krasnoi professury. Raboty seminariev, filosofskogo, ekonomicheskogo i istoricheskogo za 1921–1922 gg.* (henceforth cited as *Trudy IKP*) (Moscow: Gosizdat, 1923), 7, 8, 14, 99. Deborin's philosophy seminars sought in the Plekhanovian tradition to interpret the history of philosophy as culminating in the rise of Marxian materialism, but in contrast to trends which "contemporized" philosophy at IKP after 1924, the early work of his students treated the works of Descartes, Spinoza, Hume, and Rousseau. See A. M. Deborin, ed. *Istoriko-Filosofskii sbornik—IKP sektsiia filosofiia* (Moscow: Izdatel'stvo Kommunisticheskoi Akademii, 1925).

6. In the former category, among those who survived the purges of the 1930s, one could include the prominent historians Isaak I. Mints, Anna M. Pankratova, the agrarian historian Sergei M. Dubrovskii, and the historian of the Decembrists, Militsa V. Nechkina; in the latter category, among those who did not, the entire "Bukharin school" of publicists, including Aleksandr N. Slepkov, an editor of the party theoretical organ *Bol'shevik*. For a listing of the graduates of the first class (selected in part by their future political fortunes) see O. D. Sokolov, *M. N. Pokrovskii i sovetskaia istoricheskaia nauka* (Moscow: Mysl', 1970), 245.

create, even as the Party's scholarly forces were weak, a more perfect identification between Marxism as an intellectual system and Bolshevism as a political movement. By this I mean to raise the most basic problem that surfaced soon after the institute's founding: its identity as a specifically communist school. "Our task is, above all, to prepare good Marxists," Pokrovskii declared in the first publication of the red professors' work; yet in the next breath he stressed the students "are not only future professors, but party workers as well."[7] There was no clear precedent to determine the concrete implications of this determination to train both scholars and Communists. Was it not sufficient to accept Marxist methodology (and at least not be anti-Soviet), or did all red professors have to be party members? If so, how would newcomers and converts from other socialist parties be accepted into the fold?

Because the commission of party intellectuals that founded the institute believed it would be lucky to find 25 young Communists to join IKP, according to Pokrovskii, non–party members were allowed to apply for IKP's first class in 1921. Instead they were flooded with 289 applications, including a large response from party members who wished to resume their educations after the interruption of the civil war. After 192 were invited for testing, 93 were accepted, among them a small group of only about 10 non–party members.[8] While their numbers were hardly overwhelming, the very presence of non-Communists threatened the nature of IKP as a party school; this proved an issue of importance through the end of 1922. Virtually from the opening of classes, on 1 September 1921, the administration took measures to drive out some of these few nonparty students. The IKP party cell repeatedly debated the issue with the administration and Pokrovskii over the course of the year. In a formal protest to the bureau of the party cell, the nonparty students claimed they were being excluded from student meetings in which institute affairs were discussed. Finally, the Orgburo reexamined

7. Pokrovskii, introduction to *Trudy IKP*, 7–8.

8. According to Pokrovskii, of the ninety-three students accepted to the first class in 1921, only eighty-one remained after the general party purge of 1921 and some dismissals on academic grounds; six of these were not party members. *Trudy IKP*, 6, 10; GARF f. 5284, op. 1, d. 135, l. 13. Another document, however, put the number of nonparty students at over ten, even after the dismissals. RTsKhIDNI f. 17, op. 60, d. 64, l. 36. IKP's elite status and location in Moscow thus made it less accommodating to sympathizing nonparty students than other party institutions; in the communist universities and soviet-party schools across the country, larger numbers of nonparty students were forced out only in the purges of 1923 and 1924, and some stayed on even longer. Leonova, *Iz istorii*, 44, 48.

the student body toward the end of 1922 and finalized a rule to exclude non–party members.[9]

A troika of Old Bolsheviks on the purge commission for IKP organized as part of the 1921 all-party purge, in a confidential report to Agitprop, give a clearer indication why the handful of nonparty students seemed to pose a threat greater than their numbers would imply. Of the more than eighty students in the first class at IKP, the report warned, only about ten were Bolsheviks with pre-October 1917 party rank. The rest, aside from the non-Communists, were either young Communists who had joined the Party in recent years, or former Mensheviks, Bundists, SRs, and Poale-Zionists. In other words, recent party recruits, especially former members of other socialist parties, dominated IKP's first class and were clearly suspect. The report proposed a number of measures to combat the "accidental" and "variegated" composition of the institute. Chief among the recommendations was to form a standing IKP admissions committee, to reevaluate the student body periodically, and to admit only Communists with at least three years of party experience.[10]

This recommendation on the admissions committee was adopted, and the institute's identity as a Bolshevik higher school was reinforced in 1922–23 through such measures as the imposition of an entrance requirement of two-year party membership, which was quickly upped to three years, then five years in 1924, and up to eight and ten years in certain departments by 1929. Agitprop also restricted the number of students who had been members of other parties, since "in the experience of the institute, we can report that former members of other parties . . . offer less security in terms of political and ideological reliability."[11]

The severe shortage of qualified Bolshevik scholars, however, made it impossible at first to find enough teachers within the ranks of the Party, despite Pokrovskii's lobbying efforts in the Central Committee to recruit overworked party leaders.[12] The only alternative was to recruit

9. "Protokol zasedaniia Pravleniia IKP," 15 December 1921, GARF f. 5284, op. 1, d. 2, l. 22; "Obshchee sobranie [kommunistov IKP]," 21 June 1922, RGAODgM f. 474, op. 1, d. 2, l. 16–17; "Zasedanie biuro iacheiki IKP," no date, 1922, ibid., l. 29–30; "V biuro kommunistov," 29 September 1922, ibid., d. 3, l. 46.

10. K. Zavialova, I. Al'ter, Beloderkovskii, "V Agit-Propagandistskii otdel TsK," no date, 1921, RTsKhIDNI f. 17, op. 60, d. 64, l. 36. The authors noted that they had joined the Party in 1906, 1909, and 1909 respectively.

11. "Zav. Agitpropom TsK Knorin. V Ts.K.K. 16 noiabria 1926," RTsKhIDNI f. 17, op. 60, d. 800, l. 46.

12. M. N. Pokrovskii, "V sekretariat TsK RKP. Dokladnaia zapiska," no date, RTsKhIDNI f.

nonparty teachers. Yet the party leadership at first viewed this solution with such trepidation that Lenin had to make the decision. In 1921 the question of allowing Marxists associated with the Mensheviks to teach was debated several times in the highest echelons of the Party, first in connection with Moscow University, then Sverdlov Communist University, and finally IKP.

In the spring of 1921 Pokrovskii wrote to Lenin about the department of social sciences (FON) at Moscow University. All the communist teachers they could find had already been enlisted. Would it be acceptable to recruit Mensheviks such as G. A. Groman, O. A. Ermanskii, N. I. Sukhanov, and Iu. O. Martov? Lenin responded: "I doubt it very much, better to hand the question over to the Politburo TsK."[13] While coming out against the widespread employment of Mensheviks in this way, Lenin took a different stance in relation to certain other individuals. In early 1921 the Orgburo ruled that the ex-Menshevik Liubov' Aksel'rod-Ortodoks, a prominent Marxist philosopher and student of Plekhanov, could not teach at Sverdlov University. Under pressure from that school, Emel'ian Iaroslavskii, on behalf of the Orgburo, wrote to Lenin asking if Aksel'rod and the other prominent former Menshevik philosopher, Deborin, should be allowed to teach. Now Lenin wrote: "In my opinion *definitely* both. It will be useful, because they will support Marxism (if they start to agitate for Menshevism, we will catch them: OBSERVATION IMPERATIVE)." When IKP opened in September 1921, a separate decision came from the Politburo to allow the two philosophers to teach there.[14] In this way some nonparty scholars were tolerated at the party schools. Pokrovskii bitterly complained that in the first few years not only nonparty Marxists but actual bourgeois professors had to be relied on to teach their "own grave-diggers," the young red professors. In later years, however, nonparty teachers were still a noticeable presence; in 1929 they comprised seven out of sixty-nine teachers, or almost 10 percent of the faculty. It was characteristic

---

147, op. 1, d. 35, l. 11; "Vypiski iz protokola zasedaniia Orgbiuro TsK," 13 October 1922 and 29 April 1923, ibid., l. 4, 9.

13. Lenin to Pokrovskii, no earlier than 4 March 1921, in *Leninskii sbornik* (Moscow: OGIZ, 1945), 35:231.

14. Iaroslavskii to Lenin, 20 April 1921, and Lenin to Iaroslavskii, undated, RTsKhIDNI f. 89, op. 1, d. 82, l. 1. Lenin's response is written in pencil on the same sheet. The letters were published in *Leninskii sbornik* (Moscow: Partiinoe izdatel'stvo, 1932), 20:323. A third figure, the old "godbuilder" Vladimir A. Bazarov, who had been associated with the Mensheviks as recently as the civil war, was prohibited, however, from teaching a course on Marx's *Kapital*. "Vypiska iz protokola No. 59 zasedaniia Politbiuro TsK RKP," 13 September 1921, RTsKhIDNI f. 147, op. 1, d. 35, l. 2.

of the period that beneath the loud hostility to non-Bolshevik Marxism and "bourgeois science" alike such compromises were made. It could not have been without Pokrovskii's approval that even such decidedly non-Marxist figures like the historian of France, academician Evgenii V. Tarle, continued to make teaching appearances at party schools until anti-intelligentsia reprisals began with the Great Break.[15]

An equally enduring set of ambiguities, which would continue to prove divisive as the decade progressed, involved the selection of students. Who should be given entrée into the upper reaches of the Party? What should prove more important, scholarly capabilities, social origin, or party service? The higher party schools of NEP used a quota system (*razverstka*) in which places were reserved for candidates nominated by Central Committee departments and the regional party committees. In contrast to other party schools, however, this system was modified at IKP so that candidates also had to pass an academic examination, displaying their familiarity with reading lists of Marxist and Bolshevik classics and submitting written work. At the same time, the files of the IKP admissions committee (*mandatnaia komissiia*) show that party rank and record, not to mention recommendations and connections, often assumed greater importance than academic qualifications.[16]

There were a large number of examples of intervention to admit individual students—as on 12 September 1922 when Valentin N. Astrov, a future member of Bukharin's entourage and later head of the "history of the Party" department, was admitted through the "intercession" of Agitprop. In September 1921 the administration, headed by Pokrovskii, took the decision to allow "highly qualified old party comrades to enter IKP as students outside the required norms." Corruption of the system, in which well-connected students were admitted without testing, seems to have been an endemic problem. Although all higher education after the Revolution faced an endemic crisis of standards due to new access policies and low literacy levels of workers and party members, it is

15. See 1929 list of faculty, GARF f. 5284, op. 1, d. 336, l. 42–44, and d. 100, l. 17. Nonparty teachers at IKP in the 1920s included A. N. Savin, S. N. Valk, P. I. Liashchenko, and B. D. Grekov. GARF f. 5284, op. 1, d. 336, l. 42–44; L. V. Ivanova, *U istokov sovetskoi istoricheskoi nauki: Podgotovka kadrov istorikov-marksistov v 1917–1929 gg.* (Moscow: Mysl', 1968), 126–27. In 1928 Tarle attempted to use his teaching experience at party institutions as a form of political protection; see "Pis'mo v redaktsiiu zhurnala 'Bol'shevik'" and "Otvet akademiku E. Tarle," *Bol'shevik*, 15 March 1928, 95–96.

16. Minutes of the admissions committee from the early 1920s are contained in GARF f. 5284, op. 1, d. 5.

nonetheless startling that in this "postgraduate" center of advanced theory there were cases similar to the 1923 incident when three students were rejected because of "low level of literacy" (*malogramotnost'*), and "lack of data on ability to do scholarly work"; yet because of "party considerations" the final decision on two of the students was left up to the Central Committee.[17] Even the seemingly axiomatic requirement of basic education could be overruled in the ongoing search for a truly red expert.

Party-political considerations in admissions became more formally represented in February 1923, when a Central Committee functionary received a permanent place on the admissions committee. Final decisions on all admissions were ratified by the Orgburo. By the second half of the 1920s, the Central Committee Secretariat was setting yearly admission policies on the number of students and their class backgrounds in advance; projections were then approved by the Orgburo. Agitprop almost certainly had a role in these decisions, since it was responsible for vetting nominees for admission from central party organizations.[18]

Within the space of a few years, then, IKP had moved from its 1921 call for applications—in which a majority of Communists had materialized seemingly only by sheer chance—to a complex system of cadre selection which involved the Central Committee departments, the IKP admission committee, and regulations and target figures attempting to govern the political and social profile of the student body. This shift in the early 1920s, in fact, comprised one part of a far broader phenomenon, the origin of the *nomenklatura* system of appointments that came to structure the entire Soviet political system.

The term *nomenklatura* was initially used to refer to three master lists of positions, which took shape between 1923 and 1925; each list specified appointments that were to be approved, according to their importance, by different echelons of the Central Committee from the Politburo down. As we have seen, the Orgburo approved IKP admissions. In addition, as part of this emerging centralized method of allocating appointments, all communist students at universities and party schools were "distributed" to positions upon graduation. What was distinctive about this development was not the central party organs' deep involve-

17. GARF f. 5284, op. 1, d. 2, l. 63, l. 11, and ed. khr. 5, l. 19.

18. "Instruktsiia dlia Mandatnoi komissii IKP," 26 February 1923, RGAODgM f. 474, op. 1, d. 4, l. 3; "Vypiska iz protokola No. 89 zasedaniia Orgbiuro TsK VKP(b)," 28 December 1928, RTsKhIDNI f. 147, op. 1, d. 35, l. 39.

ment in the minutiae of personnel decisions; the Politburo had revealed its concern for this in its very first meeting in 1919.[19] Rather, what emerged by the mid-1920s was the systematic codification of the prerogatives of the central party organs. Yet the evolution of admissions and appointments at IKP reveals that the integration of the red professoriat into this system was not a simple imposition. Rather, IKP as an institution needed to coordinate its actions with those organs in its admissions committee and many other ways.

Indeed, the reliance on centralized vetting of cadres must have seemed compelling to the IKP administration and admissions committee. The great hopes invested in the red expert, the sweep of political, social, and ideological attributes expected from the red professor, were blatantly at odds with the suspicions expressed about the first entering class. The same discrepancy between far-reaching expectations and what was frequently termed the "human material" at hand can be seen as a prime characteristic of the Party as a whole. This dissonance, above all, ensured that after 1921 IKP itself was as busy devising safeguards to improve its own composition as the top party organs were in regularizing their prerogatives of ratification.

Anti-Intellectual Intellectuals and Anti-Professorial Professors

The work of the IKP admissions committee and the party organs produced a group of red professors that was increasingly elite in terms of its rank, connections, and prospects. This, coupled with the teaching appearances at the institute of party leaders such as Preobrazhenskii, Bukharin, Radek, Zinov'ev, and Iaroslavskii, not to mention foreign revolutionaries like the Hungarian Comintern official Bela Kun, quickly made the original intention of training university social scientists something of an anachronism. As Pokrovskii later put it to his seminar, "The Institute of Red Professors long ago outgrew the modest task of preparing professors of social sciences. . . . [It] prepares the political *smena*, a

19. For example, "Nomenklatura 1" was a list of all major party and state posts filled by the Central Committee (many through the Politburo); it included first secretaries of republics, obkoms, kraikoms, people's commissars, and "ambassadors to large countries." See T. P. Korzhikhina and Iu. Iu. Figatner, "Sovetskaia nomenklatura: stanovlenie, mekhanizmy deistviia," *Voprosy istorii*, no. 7 (1993): 25–38; and Volkogonov, *Lenin: Politicheskii portret* 2:102, citing a 1925 Politburo decree on the nomenklatura lists in RTsKhIDNI f. 80, op. 19, d. 1, l. 6–14. For the first Politburo meeting, see RTsKhIDNI f. 17, op. 3, ed. khr. 1.

new ruling political generation for our party and for the proletariat in general." The institute's rising political importance took place in a context where party leaders warned repeatedly that the new cadres sent to higher education could lose their party and proletarian attributes, turn into a careerist caste of privileged specialists, and acquire all the old flaws of the prerevolutionary intelligentsia.[20]

It was perhaps inevitable that the character of IKP education would come to seem inadequate and smacking of an "intelligentsia approach," even to some of the Old Bolshevik founders. The early curriculum was notable for its highly theoretical bent and a reliance on a small group of Marxist classics. When a department of "soviet construction" (*sovetskoe stroitel'stvo*) was proposed in 1921, only three or four students were interested, and the idea was rejected. Early reading lists and study plans attest to the almost exclusive focus on academic high Marxism. The economics section, for example, would have been more accurately designated a department of political economy; courses on theory, historical materialism, and the history of capitalism were the backbone of the program, and a lone course on economic policy was offered in the third year.[21]

Not only could IKP be charged with favoring "theory" at the expense of "practice," but it was all too easy to correlate this with a compromising social composition. In a "proletarian" party which during NEP included less than one percent of members with a higher education,[22] the institute's approximately 90 percent intelligentsia membership in 1921–24 was another indicator of a Bolshevik bastion of the elite, in a movement and regime that closely bound its self-image and legitimacy with its ostensibly proletarian and egalitarian nature. What is most interesting about the resulting charges of scholasticism, which became a leitmotif in IKP's history, was that they seem to have come most persistently from the party scholars, students, and intellectuals themselves.

Anti-intellectualism had deep roots in Russian Social-Democracy, a movement in which intellectuals tried to spread a "proletarian" ideology to workers. The central Leninist notion of "professional revolutionary" opened the way for both groups to assume a new identity within the Party, yet still accorded a glorified role to those intellectuals who

20. "Seminarii T. Pokrovskogo II-kursa 5 marta 1928," ARAN f. 1759, op. 2, d. 20, l. 102; for example, "Budushchee intelligentsii," in V. N. Soskin, ed., *Sud'by russkoi intelligentsii. Materialy diskussii, 1923–25* (Novosibirsk: Nauka, sibirskoe otdelenie, 1991), 16.

21. GARF f. 5284, op. 1, d. 2, l. 10; "Programma ekonomicheskogo otdeleniia," no exact date, 1922, ibid., l. 45.

22. Rigby, *Communist Party Membership*, 401.

had joined the proletarian cause. By doing so, however, they broke with the "bourgeois intelligentsia" and all the values it was held to represent, making any new embrace of intellectual identity problematic. Thus a deep-seated current of anti-intellectualism flowed not only from Marxist heroicization of the proletarian, or from all the currents in the workers' movement that revolted against intelligentsia tutelage, but also from the intellectuals' own "hatred of the intellectual, curious, and cerebral side of themselves."[23] After 1917, the most ardent embrace of the anti-intellectual tradition within the Party came from "ultra-left" inner-party opposition groups, which bitterly indicted the party intelligentsia for bureaucratism and pro-specialist policies. At the heyday of party factionalism, the most important group involved in "intelligentsia-baiting" was the Workers' Opposition in 1920–21. But oppositional groups before (such as the Military Opposition) and after (like the Workers' Group of 1923) sounded interconnected anti-specialist, anti-bureaucratic, and anti-intelligentsia themes.[24]

After the suppression of the Workers' Opposition, any critique implicating the party intelligentsia along with the bureaucracy as a new form of exploitation risked crossing the line into oppositionism. This situation held several consequences for IKP. It rendered an institution of party intellectuals particularly vulnerable, because it (as opposed to the social basis of the regime) could be safely criticized. It made it all the more incumbent on party intellectuals to prove they were not "torn from the working masses." It was against this backdrop that deep currents of anti-intellectualism continued to well up from within the party intelligentsia itself. In short, the critique of "scholasticism" in the early 1920s in party academia might be seen as a distillation, typically put under a single deviationist rubric, of traits the party intelligentsia hated in itself. It stood for arid hair-splitting and impracticality, theory without practice, science without politics, cerebral erudition without action and commitment.

Red professors were an especially easy target within the Party for accusations of having a scholastic, academic, or intelligentsia approach. For example, when a group of IKP students defended the traditional

23. Stites, *Revolutionary Dreams*, 73; on anti-intellectualism, 72–76. An extreme hostility toward the intelligentsia in the socialist movement became known as the deviation of "Makhaevshchina," a pejorative derived from the writings at the turn of the twentieth century by the Polish socialist Machajski. The most complete account of the trend is in Marshall Shatz, *Jan Wacław Machajski* (Pittsburgh: University of Pittsburgh Press, 1989).

24. Fitzpatrick, "Bolsheviks' Dilemma," 25–30; the classic work on the programs of the successive oppositions remains Robert Vincent Daniels, *The Conscience of the Revolution: Communist Opposition in Soviet Russia* (Cambridge: Harvard University Press, 1960).

organization of academic disciplines in higher party education against importing the interdisciplinary "complex method" that Narkompros pedagogues championed for the lower grades, Lenin's wife Krupskaia, the chief proponent of the method, openly derided them in *Pravda* as "Marxist-Talmudists" and "Marxist professors, ignoring reality." When even the word "professor" was derogatory, the red professors could only retort that vulgarizers underestimated the abilities of the working class, and this itself was an intelligentsia approach.[25]

Deep-seated goals of creating a new intelligentsia organically attached to the proletariat thus helped foster an identity crisis among party intellectuals, who found a way to bolster their revolutionary image by deriding values associated with intellectual work. Even top party theorists such as Bukharin and Preobrazhenskii found it necessary or expedient to criticize the "scholasticism" of the early IKP.[26] If IKP's own leading theoreticians would not defend the institute from charges of scholasticism, who would?

It was in the heat of polemics that the anti-intellectualism of the intellectuals became ingrained. In the Party's leading theoretical journal, *Bol'shevik*, the IKP graduate Ionov, a powerful figure in the publishing world who had become an impediment to the ambitious activists of the proletarian culture camp, bristled when accused of having spent revolutionary years in study. His accuser, the young leader of the Russian Association of Proletarian Writers (RAPP), Averbakh, was of course implying that rejection of a militant class definition of culture must be attributable to an intelligentsia background. "For the information of comrade Averbakh," the insulted IKP graduate replied, "[I] count in my party experience, in addition to study at IKP, the underground, prison, the death sentence, and work in the Red Army and Navy."[27]

If as revolutionaries IKP intellectuals hastened to indict one another for possessing intelligentsia traits, as scholars they felt an equally pressing need to disassociate themselves from the "apolitical" neutrality associated with the nonparty professoriat. On this issue, rector Pokrovskii

25. Valentin Astrov et al., "'Ukomplektovannyi marksizm,'" *Pravda*, 21 November 1923, 1; Nadezhda Krupskaia, "Soedinenie marksistskoi teorii s praktikoi kommunizma," *Pravda*, 25 November 1923, 1. The originals, with Krupskaia's handwritten corrections, are in the Krupskaia *fond*, RTsKhIDNI f. 12, op. 1, d. 611, l. 2–3, and d. 854, l. 4–5.

26. See "Diskussiia o programme po politekonomike v komvuze (predsedatel'stvuet E. Preobrazhenskii)," in *ZKS* 2:343; N. I. Bukharin, "Lenin kak Marksist: Doklad na torzhestvennom zasedanii Kommunisticheskoi akademii," 17 February 1924, in *Izbrannye proizvedeniia* (Moscow: Izdatel'stvo politicheskoi literatury, 1988), 58.

27. Leopol'd Averbakh, "Eshche o klassovoi bor'be i voprosakh kul'tury," *Bol'shevik*, 31 December 1926, 87–104, and I. Ionov, "Pis'mo v redaktsiiu," ibid., 105–6. I am indebted to Katerina Clark for suggesting this characterization of Ionov.

was in a unique position to influence the institute's mission; of all the Old Bolshevik scholars he had the closest connection to prerevolutionary academia, having written his master's dissertation at Moscow University under the famous historians Kliuchevskii and Vinogradov. His transition from the world of scholarship to the revolutionary movement and back may account both for his defense of academic rigor in the 1920s and for his particularly virulent rejection of the impartiality of bourgeois scholarship and a professorial identity. In one of the first, mild critiques of Pokrovskii's historical schema, which dominated Marxist historiography in the 1920s and was pervaded by a reductive economic determinism, first-year IKP historian Nikolai L. Rubinshtein hesitantly rebuked his master for insufficient exploration of "ideology." Pokrovskii retorted that if he were "only a professor" such criticism might be "devastating," but "in my perhaps very humble way I am also a participant of the revolution."[28]

Pokrovskii's elevation of a revolutionary identity over the scholarly was at the crux of his "quarter century struggle with academic science" and his famous maxim that history is "politics projected onto the past." In an extraordinary lecture on Lenin's death in 1924 delivered at the Central Committee's school for secretaries of *uezd* party committees, Pokrovskii interpreted the entire Bolshevik-Menshevik split as a dispute over Menshevik leader Martov's desire to include "all professors and students," in other words "the intelligentsia," into the Party. If not for Lenin's understanding of "the meaning of professors," the Party would have turned into a "decrepit intelligentsia organization" that "would have never produced any kind of revolution."[29]

Anti-intellectualism has been been embraced by intellectuals themselves in various times and places, but in this instance comprised an essential and strikingly overt part of the "proletarian" Party's intellectual environment. This could not but deeply influence the red professors. In order to keep the students "close to the masses" the IKP administration and party cell overloaded them with agitation work in the factories, teaching work around Moscow, and a full schedule of party meetings. In 1926 Pokrovskii referred to four to seven hours per day being spent by red professors on non-IKP work.[30]

28. M. N. Pokrovskii, "Po povodu stat'i tov. Rubinshteina," *PZM*, no. 10–11 (October-November 1924): 210–12.

29. Ts. S. Fridliand, "Voinstvuiushchii istorik-marksist (k shestidesiatiletiiu so dnia rozhdeniia M. N. Pokrovskogo)," *PZM*, no. 9–10 (September-October 1928): 5, 14; M. N. Pokrovskii, "Lenin, kak tip revoliutsionnogo vozhdia (Iz lektsii na kursakh sekretarei ukomov)," ibid., no. 2 (February 1924): 69.

30. "Zadachi i plan partiinoi raboty slushatelei IKP v 1922–23 Uchebnom godu (s oseni

The taint of scholasticism rendered the institute in its first years not simply vulnerable but also unstable. The question of student admissions was linked to criticisms of "academicism," since a proletarianized student body would doubtless be less academic; the curriculum was open to revision on the grounds that it was too removed from "reality." Calls for a "struggle with the scholasticism that exists in communist universities" were among the resolutions passed at the Thirteenth Party Congress in 1924.[31]

As far as the reform of the curriculum was concerned, however, there were two distinguishable sides to the struggle against scholasticism. One was a vocationalist impulse to train more practically oriented specialists, not abstract theorists; the other was a desire to force academic work into channels more immediately relevant to current politics. Although the program in political economy was criticized in 1924 for its "scholastic" lack of concern with contemporary Soviet economy, curriculum reforms during NEP never succeeded in making the institute more vocationalist, considering that as late as 1930 IKP graduated only twelve economists, all of them versed primarily in theory.[32] Even as the theoretical orientation was never abandoned, it was constantly criticized as a scholastic escape from "socialist construction." This curious phenomenon thus seems more connected to the internalized streak of anti-intellectualism of the Bolshevik theorists themselves than from either a homespun or technocratic vocationalism hostile to all abstraction. The bogey of scholasticism, with all its class connotations, provided a powerful incentive to forge an institutional mission and identity for the red expert that would wash away its stain.

Verification of the Red Expert: Purges and Promotion Policies

IKP opened in September 1921 in the midst of a "re-registration" and "verification" of all party members; this was the first all-party purge, approved by the Politburo on June 21 and scheduled to begin August 1. The timing of the two events in 1921 is not entirely accidental. IKP's

1922 goda)," no date, fall 1922, RGAODgM f. 474, op. 1, d. 2, l. 37; GARF f. 5284, op. 1, d. 2, l. 74, 89; M. N. Pokrovskii, "Postanovka obshchestvovedeniia v komvuzakh, Vuzakh i dr. shkolakh vzroslykh," no date, 1926, ARAN f. 1759, op. 1, d. 186, l. 10.

31. *KPSS v rezoliutsiiakh i resheniiakh*, 9th ed. (Moscow: Politizdat, 1984), 3:282.

32. "Diskussiia o programme po politekonomike v Komvuze," in *ZKS* 2:343; Evgenii B. Pashukanis, "Reorganizatsiia Instituta krasnoi professury," *Za leninskie kadry* (Organ partkollektiva IKP) 1 (March 1930): 1.

opening, the result of a planning process begun by top Bolshevik intellectuals in the Rotshtein commission in 1920, represented a fruition of the post–civil war opportunities to shift the Party's focus to the third front; yet the shift to "peaceful reconstruction" also stimulated a post-victory decision to weed out careerists or aliens who had supposedly insinuated themselves into the Bolshevik side. The Politburo thus accepted Lenin's proposal that purge commissions consist only of Old Bolsheviks of working class origin and adopted a recipe for a massive reduction of membership. Anyone "at all doubtful" should be purged; mistakes could be rectified by reinstatement later. In fact, a later TsKK report gave the results of the 1921 general purge as an enormous reduction of 30.3 percent of party members and candidates. The precarious nature of intelligentsia status within the Party is also indicated in the Politburo's directives for the operation: workers in factories and demobilized Red Army soldiers in the countryside should be subjected to a "minimum of formalities"; but anyone with access to "privileges," white-collar personnel (*sluzhashchie*), and all those who had belonged to other parties any time after October 1917 should be given special attention.[33]

IKP, a party institution born in the midst of this radical all-party prophylaxis, adopted the purge as its own basic tool for regulating the social, political, and intellectual activities within its walls. On 22 December 1921, Pokrovskii announced the formation of a Central Committee commission to review the composition of the institute; a representative of the bureau of IKP's party cell was to join it. Models taken from the Party's political life also became the regular method of academic evaluation. At IKP the administration in 1922–23 introduced an "academic purge" (*akademicheskaia chistka*) at the end of the school year. But because deficiencies in Marxist ideology were of course academic deficiencies, such purges were never solely or even primarily concerned with issues of academic ability and preparedness. In fact, there was never any pretense of limiting the academic purge to academics: instructions on the goals of these purges at IKP and other party schools consistently underlined that "party" and "social" considerations were as important as academic ones. The administration could also dismiss individual students outside the annual academic purge. In practice,

33. "Protokol No. 41 Zasedaniia Politbiuro Ts.K. RKP ot 21.VI.21 goda," RTsKhIDNI f. 17, op. 3, d. 17, l. 1–2; Emel'ian Iaroslavskii, "V Politbiuro TsK VKP (b)," no date, 1929, RTsKhIDNI f. 613, op. 3, d. 17, l. 29–30. This top secret report evaluates the results of all major purges from the 1920s. On the 1921 purge see Rigby, *Communist Party Membership*, 96–100.

it justified explusion with reference to both academic and political faults—or a marvelously laconic conflation of the two, "He will never make a red professor."[34]

As a few high-profile student scandals preoccupied the institute in the first years, it also became established practice to resort to a kind of extraordinary purge to expel unwanted individuals above and beyond the general purges. In 1923, the last of the nonparty students, S. S. Ainzaft, a prolific author on pre-1905 Russian labor, was purged after the bureau of the party cell condemned him for "specifically expressed Menshevik tendencies." After the bureau revealed that Ainzaft had been "registered" as a suspect at the GPU, this decision was then ratified by the admissions committee and the administration. In similar actions, some others were expelled for being associated with the social-democratic Zionist party Poale-Zion.[35] These individual cases were not officially called purges (*chistki*, *proverki*); the purge itself proved simply the most elaborate measure in an entire system of academic and political evaluation.

As the institute grew and the party cell bureau, the academic departments, and even student seminars played greater roles in these decisions, the purge itself became almost less significant than the constant process of evaluation. Advancing from the first class to the second, for example, was by no means automatic; it became the occasion for evaluation, promotion, or expulsion. Student groups from seminars and departments began to try to influence these decisions. Each group interested in making recommendations to the administration introduced evaluation procedures, to the point that vote-taking—carrying with it the threat of a mark on one's record or the recommendation of expulsion—was extended to each seminar, and even beyond that, to each major research paper (*doklad*) presented.[36] In this way the threat of expulsion was built into the very fabric of life at the institute.

34. "Polozhenie o proverke osnovnogo kursa [komuniversiteta im. Sverdlova]," no date, 1922 or 1923, GARF f. 5221, op. 4, d. 71, l. 17; "Rezoliutsiia biuro iacheiki ob akademicheskoi proverke [IKP]," 15 May 1928, ARAN f. 1759, op. 2, d. 21, l. 56–57; GARF f. 5284, op. 1, d. 2, l. 101, and op. 1, d. 260, l. 2.

35. "Protokol zasedaniia Biuro kommunistov IKP," 13 March 1923, RGAODgM f. 474, op. 1, d. 5, l. 3; GARF f. 5284, op. 1, d. 5, l. 12. On the expulsion of Poale-Zionists, see "Iz protokola Biuro iacheiki IKP," 18 January 1926, GARF f. 5284, op. 1, ed. khr. 170, l. 17. Nevertheless, Ainzaft's 1922 book on the police-sponsored trade-unions of Zubatov and Gapon before 1905 went through four editions between 1922 and 1925.

36. See, for example, the files entitled "Protokoly zasedanii i sobranii seminarov," GARF f. 5284, op. 1, d. 192, and "Protokoly starost osnovnykh otdel i sobranii seminarov," ibid., d. 338.

The "academic purge" of June 1923 marked a shift from a participatory to a "conspiratorial" method of organization. Cell leaders and the administration were determined not to repeat the experience of the previous year, in which all the students met in a kind of mass meeting to discuss the purge and wrangle over the results. An administrator told students gathered at a party meeting on 26 June: "Insofar as last year's 'democratic' manner of conducting [the purge] discredited itself, we recognized the necessity of giving the purge a 'non-democratic' and conspiratorial character." Opponents of the new methods—in which the purge commission alone gathered information from individuals, reached a decision and reported it to the bureau of the cell—charged that the commission was guilty of factionalism. But an attempt in the cell to put the new methods to a vote was itself voted down.[37] With this anticlimax the academic purge lost the participatory character it originally possessed. The ordinary student would now take part only by denouncing another or defending himself.

In the resulting lists of purged students ratified by the IKP administration, with one-sentence justifications beside the names, we encounter the wide net of categories typically used to explain purges. Many were purged for various academic reasons; others were expelled as "passives," insufficiently active in party or pedagogical work. There were also many political-ideological justifications—students purged for "non-Marxist tendencies" or being "politically alien to our party."[38] There is every reason, as we shall see in the cases of Trotskyists purged on various grounds, not to accept such categories as transparent. What they do show is how the red expert—not just in the abstract but in institutional practice—was open to evaluation on a gamut of academic, political, and ideological grounds. The 1923 purge also highlights the involvement of top party leaders in validating such evaluations, since in the wrangling that customarily followed the IKP bureau sent emissaries to Zinov'ev, Trotskii, Bukharin, Kuibyshev, and Molotov.[39] The precedent of "conspiratorial" practices in 1923 would prove decisive the

37. "Vypiska iz protokola obshchego sobraniia kom"iacheiki IKP," 18 February 1922, RGAODgM f. 474, op. 1, d. 2, l. 2; "Protokol obshchego sobraniia slushatelei-kommunistov IKP," 26 June 1923, ibid., d. 4. l. 5–10.

38. "Protokol zasedaniia komissii po chistke," 20 June 1923, GARF f. 5284, op. 1, d. 2, l. 101–4. There is particularly complete information on the 1923 purge, in which 67 of the 409 students at IKP in the classes of 1921–1923 were expelled. On 23 May 1923 the bureau of the party cell formed a purge commission of seven members, all of them prominent students in the party organization, and delegated the secretary of the bureau to represent the commission at the Central Committee. "Protokol zasedaniia Biuro kommunistov [IKP]," 23 May 1923, RGAODgM f. 474, op. 1, d. 5. l. 9.

39. GARF f. 5284, op. 1, d. 2, l. 107; RGAODgM f. 474, op. 1, d. 5, l. 15, 16; "Kossior

next year, when the institute was thrown into the limelight for its support for the Trotskyist opposition.

The Trotskyist Imagination and the Watershed of 1924

An opposition centered around Lev Davydovich Trotskii, in leadership consisting of his own loyalists and former left oppositionists of various stripes, coalesced during the leadership power struggles of the interregnum after Lenin's second stroke of March 1923 and began to make hesitant steps to garner broader support in the Party. The Trotskyist opposition has most frequently been analyzed in terms of its left program: rapid industrialization and economic planning, internationalism, anti-NEP themes. But the most explosive issue it raised, which subsumed even the largest policy stance, was the notion of the degeneration and "bureaucratization" of the Party's "old guard."[40] This notion went to the heart of the Trotskyist opposition's sociopolitical explanation of where the Party had gone astray, which the "ultra-left" tended to put in more radical terms of exploitation and a new bourgeoisie. But by throwing down a symbolic gauntlet to the "old guard," the party leadership, Trotskii and his opposition momentarily inverted the far-reaching demands that Bolshevism's high ideal of the professional revolutionary had placed on its followers—with a particular resonance for party students and red professors.

With his 1923 appeal to youth as the "barometer of the Party," Trotskii gave permanent revolution, as it were, a generational twist. In this formulation, which became infamous in the Party, it was above all bureaucratization (which could corrupt even the "old guard") that endangered revolutionary purity. The call for revolutionary renewal over bureaucratism was central to the Trotskyist imagination and was certainly more inspiring than the opposition's political operations, which were rather easily outmaneuvered in 1923–24 by Stalin's political machine.[41]

(VTsSPS) Komissii po peresmotru slushatelei Instituta krasnoi professury," no date, 1923, RTsKhIDNI f. 17, op. 60, d. 503, l. 34, 34 ob.

40. For an interesting discussion, see Lovell, *Trotsky's Analysis of Soviet Bureaucratization: A Critical Essay*; see also Baruch Knei-Paz, *The Social and Political Thought of Leon Trotsky* (Oxford: Oxford University Press, 1978), 367–441.

41. The classic account remains E. H. Carr, *The Interregnum* (London: Macmillan, 1960), 257–366.

The appeal to youth suggested a more unabashedly affirmative image of communist students, red professors among them; instead of the *smena* being "declassed" by study, the leadership had been corrupted by power! This forbidden logic seems to have been what electrified many student supporters of the opposition at the universities and party schools. Party cells there became among the few politically important party organizations to openly vote for opposition platforms. *Pravda* reported in January 1924 that the opposition was supported by forty Moscow student cells, the Central Committee by thirty-two; but in fact the opposition may have claimed up to two-thirds of the student cells.[42] At IKP in particular, Trotskii's support may also have been due to the influence of leading oppositionists (Preobrazhenskii at the time taught the seminar on theoretical economics, and Radek a course on the history of German social democracy), and the fact that many IKP students were civil war veterans, to whom the organizer of the Red Army held a strong appeal.

As the "party discussion" got into full swing at the end of 1923, IKP and other party schools found themselves at the center of the storm of meetings and resolutions. On 16 December 1923 the triumvir Kamenev and the oppositionist Radek faced off at the institute, and in a highly charged meeting that lasted until 6 a.m. the next day, the students voted for the opposition's resolution 83–47. "We consider extremely dangerous the full-fledged persecution of the 'opposition,'" the resolution, proposed by Radek, declared, "and the tendentious character of the information in 'Pravda' on the course of the discussion." A separate resolution specifically condemning Stalin for his articles in *Pravda* was passed 90 to 40.[43]

IKP's condemnation of Stalin and *Pravda* assumes significance in light of the formal protest to the Politburo from Trotskii, Piatakov, and Radek claiming that Stalin's proxy Nazaretian had been specially assigned to the Party's main newspaper not just to slant coverage in the "party discussion" but to falsify published documents. In response, the Politburo majority opened a TsKK investigation, at the same time charging the opposition with distribution of secret documents such as the Declaration of the 46 to party cells and Red Army personnel.[44]

To many communist students, already sympathetic to the opposi-

42. Darron Hincks, "Support for the Opposition in Moscow in the Party Discussion of 1923–1924," *Soviet Studies* 44:1 (1992): 141.

43. "Protokol obshchego sobraniia kommunistov IKP," 16 December 1923, RGAODgM f. 474, op. 1, d. 4., l. 22–25.

44. "Protokol No. 59 Zasedaniia Politbiuro TsK RKP ot 2-go ianvaria 1924 g.," RTsKhIDNI f. 17, op. 3, d. 407, l. 7–9.

tion's program, the triumvirate's methods of attack and denunciation had themselves become a major issue. At IKP on 2 December, Preobrazhenskii critiqued the internal party regime and sparked an earnest student discussion on the values of inner-party democracy (*demokratizm*), which could be easily contrasted to the "conspiratorial" dominance of the party cell bureau in local institutional affairs.[45]

The defeat of the opposition in spring of 1924 opened the door for the party majority drastically to change the order at the party schools and universities, which had proven such fertile ground for opposition support. This was done on several levels, which taken together would consitute a watershed in the history of party education and IKP, especially since the struggle had brought political tensions to new heights. "Supporters of the opposition and supporters of the TsK lived, studied, and worked completely separately," one student recalled a few years later. "Former friends became enemies."[46] Soon after the "discussion" was ended, the Orgburo proposed and the Politburo approved on March 20 a purge (*proverka*) of the "nonproletarian" membership of the Party, to be carried out in "Soviet" (state) and VUZ (student) cells. This was to be designed as a "cleansing" (*ochistki*) of the Party of "elements socially alien, corrupted [*razlozhivshikhsia*] and estranged [*otorvavshikhsia*] from it."[47]

The Politburo ratification of the 1924 purge reflected alarm at high levels for the broad support for the opposition at party schools and student cells. Stalin himself did not forget the votes of the party schools.[48] Moreover, communist students, because they were widely seen as the backbone of the future party leadership and because they were believed to hold influence over worker opinion through their positions as agitators and instructors in workers' cells and factories, were a political force more important than their already significant numbers; as a Politburo resolution noted on completion of the purge, they were "the future organizers and leaders of the party and the state."[49]

45. "Protokol obshchego sobraniia slushatelei-kommunistov IKP," 2 December 1923, RGAODgM f. 474, op. 1, d. 4, l. 17–18.

46. Mnukhin, "Beglye vospominaniia," in *X let Kommuniversiteta*, 320–21; RGAODgM f. 459, op. 1, d. 18, l. 10–11.

47. "Protokol No. 80 Zasedaniia Politbiuro TsK RKP ot 20/III-1924 g.," RTsKhIDNI f. 17, op. 3, ed. khr. 428, l. 5.

48. "O pis'me Trotskogo i zaiavlenii 46-ti (Iz zakliuchitel'nogo slova t. I. Stalina na XIII partkonferentsii)," in K. A. Popov, ed., *Diskussiia 1923 goda: Materialy i dokumenty* (Moscow-Leningrad: Gosizdat, 1927), 8.

49. "Prilozhenie k prot. PB No. 27 p. 13 ot 19/X-1924. O rezul'tatakh proverki (v okonchatel'noi redaktsii)," RTsKhIDNI f. 17, op. 3, ed. khr. 467, l. 11. According to evidence cited by Fitzpatrick, in 1924 a tenth of all party members were students of some kind, half of them in

Plans for the purge quickly followed the Politburo ruling. On 29 March 1924 a major meeting on the party schools was held at Agitprop's subsection on propaganda, which directly oversaw the party schools and was headed by IKP teacher Konstantin A. Popov. With administrators from most of the major communist universities present, Agitprop planned in advance huge target numbers for each institution in the upcoming cell purges (to be carried out in conjunction with spring "academic" purges) as well as reduced 1924 admissions projections, in order drastically to cut the number of students at the schools. In the case of IKP, Pokrovskii and Agitprop's Sergei I. Syrtsov were summoned on to the Central Committee Secretariat to discuss student cuts.[50]

The second measure to follow the defeat of the Trotskyist opposition was the ratification of a drastic reduction in higher education as a whole, which had been on the agenda since the introduction of so-called cost-accounting (*khozraschet*) in VUZy in 1922.[51] The timing of these cuts in 1924, as well as Agitprop's simultaneous planning of the purge and reduced admissions for party schools, indicates that the action ordered from the top was part of a restructuring of higher education in the wake of student support for the opposition.

Consider the plans for the universities, which were run by Narkompros. On 26 March 1924 Zinov'ev himself, senior member of the ruling triumvirate, made a highly unusual appearance at the Narkompros collegium, which then determined to cut the number of university students to prewar levels. On 10 April an order from the Politburo signed by Stalin gave concrete numbers: the contingent of students at RSFSR VUZy would be cut by 30,000, with an equivalent number in the union republics. A special commission chaired by Pokrovskii was ordered to discuss the plans for carrying this out at one of the next meetings of the Politburo.[52] The report of this commission was approved by the Politburo on 24 April; it affirmed a cut of no less than 30,000 VUZ students "by means of the purge" (*po chistke*). The purge itself should be consid-

---

VUZy and Komvuzy; a fourth of the Moscow party organization was made up of students. Fitzpatrick, *Education*, 95.

50. "Protokol soveshchaniia komuniversitetov pri P-otdel Propagandy Agitpropa TsK," 20 March 1924, GARF f. 5221, op. 5, d. 89, l. 21; "Vypiska iz protokola No. 80 zasedaniia Orgbiuro TsK," 14 March 1924, RTsKhIDNI f. 147, op. 1, d. 35, l. 17.

51. Peter Konecny, "Chaos on Campus: The 1924 Student *Proverka* in Leningrad," *Europe-Asia Studies* 46:4 (1994): 618–19.

52. "Protokol No. 84 Zasedaniia Politbiuro Tseka RKP ot 10-go aprelia 1924 goda," RTsKhIDNI f. 17, op. 3, ed. khr. 432, l. 5; Fitpatrick, *Education*, 98.

ered a test of "academic capability," yet at the same time give "maximum advantage" to proletarian students. White-collar Soviet employees (*sovsluzhashchie*) and "offspring of the bourgeoisie" should be treated "especially harshly."[53] Here was a mandate to purge both "social aliens" and academic incompetents, with a tacit emphasis on student supporters of Trotskii. The typical necessity of balancing social, political, and other criteria, combined with the need felt even by communist administrators to protect their home institutions from decimation by purge commissions; it is hardly a surprise that the resulting purges of the party cells and student bodies of higher schools carried out from May to the fall of 1924 were highly chaotic.[54]

Chaotic implementation, however, does not capture the full meaning of the 1924 purge for party students. "Noise, cries and wails were completely inevitable," TsKK chief Kuibyshev noted in his report to the Thirteenth Congress. He was not just putting on a brave face. If the purge was perceived as a reliable way to regulate party composition so that it was free of social aliens, then the resulting chaos was an unmitigated disaster; no wonder some Narkompros officials rebelliously opposed the purge, particularly because it turned their own domain upside down. But if it was intended or perceived as a draconian collective reprisal against the *studenchestvo*, then chaos was a byproduct of success, and never again did higher schools display the political "disloyalty" they had in 1923–24. Indeed, the final report accepted by the Politburo in October 1924 praised the great "instructive" character of the purge.[55] Even the purge had come to be considered a didactic instrument.

Such target quotas set at the top were not unique to the 1924 purge; they were at least discussed during the planning of the next major purge in 1929. In that year, Iaroslavskii in top secret correspondence with the Politburo referred to advance guidelines that aimed for a reduction of less than 10 percent of party membership in general. On one occasion

53. "Prilozhenie" to "Protokol No. 86 Zasedaniia Politbiuro TsK RKP ot 24.IV.1924 goda," RTsKhIDNI f. 17, op. 3, ed. khr. 434, l. 11–13. However, "nonproletarian" medical, agricultural, and technical VUZy were to be treated "cautiously."

54. Fitzpatrick, *Education*, 98, 100; Konecny, "Chaos," 563–78; "V Tsentral'nuiu komissiiu po akademicheskoi proverke VUZ-ov RSFSR. Otchet o rabote komissii po akademicheskoi proverke FON-a pri MGU," no earlier than 27 May 1924, RTsKhIDNI f. 17, op. 60, d. 755, l. 142–43; "V vysshikh uchebnykh zavedeniiakh," *Sotsialisticheskii vestnik*, 10 May 1924, 13–14.

55. *Trinadtsatyi s"ezd*, 284; Fitzpatrick, *Education*, 100; "O rezul'tatakh proverki," cited in full at note 49, l. 9–11. The official Narkompros report criticized the purge as an extraordinary measure with "negative effects," but praised positive improvements in the composition of the student body, academic motivation, and relations to Soviet power. "Itogi akademicheskoi proverki sostava studenchestva vysshikh uchebnykh zavedenii," 25 July 1924, RTsKhIDNI f. 17, op. 60, d. 755, l. 125–29.

he also requested "orientation" figures for leading organizations in particular. By then, the purge was even more explicitly justified as an edifying process that would make the Party "harder" and more "monolithic."[56]

A key legacy of the 1924 purge, therefore, was that it targeted certain groups but also acquired a deliberately indiscriminate character. At the IKP purge, conducted in June 1924 by an MKK commission, this was certainly the case.[57] Pokrovksii, whom we have seen as an architect of the nationwide student purge in his role as Narkompros's "point man" on higher education, found himself scrambling to protect certain students, protesting to the TsKK that IKP students were summarily dismissed and "the worth of a given comrade as a future professor was completely ignored." Indeed, IKP students found themselves in a particularly vulnerable position. Since almost all the students were of intelligentsia background, almost anyone could be purged for social origin. "For the time being we can prepare professors only from *intelligenty*, and from workers we can only prepare students," Pokrovskii maintained. His letter of protest indicates that 34 percent of IKP's student population was purged, although the rector later recalled that as a personal favor Iaroslavskii, head of the TsKK, helped him reinstate several students.[58] Students not dismissed from the Party were exiled to "mass" or "low-level" party work in the provinces. As Popov's letter to the TsKK a year later shows, IKP's admission committee would not readmit some of these students without proof in the form of recommendations from local party organs that they had indeed outlived their oppositionist tendencies. Toward the end of the MKK purge commission's activities in June 1924, the Moscow party committee instructed the Khamovnicheskii Raikom, which had the institute in its jurisdiction, to

56. E. Iaroslavskii, "V Politbiuro TsK VKP (b)," no date, 1929, RTsKhIDNI f. 613, op. 3, d. 17, l. 29–30; RTsKhIDNI f. 613, op. 2, d. 65, l. 24–25; "O predstoiashchei chistke partii," *Bol'shevik*, no. 4 (28 February 1929), 3. Official 1930 data reported 8.9 percent of party members and 12 percent of candidates were purged. A. Kh. Mitrofanov, *Itogi chistki partii* (Moscow-Leningrad: Gosizdat, 1930), 57.

57. "Protokol No. 145 zasedaniia Tsentral'noi proverochnoi komissii pri partkollegii TsKK RKP(b) ot 31-X-24 g.," RTsKhIDNI f. 613, op. 2, d. 7, l. 64–67; "Protokol No. 105 Zasedaniia Parttroiki Tsentral'noi Proverochnoi Komissii pri Partkollegii TsKK RKP ot 9-IX-24 g.," ibid., d. 6, l. 23–25.

58. "V Tsentral'nuiu kontrol'nuiu komissiiu," no date, ARAN f. 1759, op. 2, ed. khr. 22, l. 240; M. N. Pokrovskii, "Vsem sekretariam TsK VKP(b) i tov. Molotovu," 5 February 1931, RTsKhIDNI f. 147, op. 1, d. 33, l. 45; "Tov. Syrtsov (Agitprop) Tov. Bazanovu, Sekretariu MKK," no date, 1924, ibid., op. 60, d. 772, l. 4–5. Pokrovskii soon became an advocate of proletarianization.

observe the IKP cell more closely and to oversee reelections to the institute's cell bureau.[59]

Finally, it can be established that Trotskii's supporters were indeed targeted in the 1924 purge, although oppositionist tendencies were openly discussed as grounds for purge only in high-level Agitprop and Central Control Commission meetings. The oppositionist activities of purged IKP students, for example, were noted when considering their readmission to the institute a year later. To cite only one case, a student whom Popov in 1925 identified as an oppositionist (B. S. Borilin) had been officially purged in 1924 not as a Trotskii supporter but as "an alien element having nothing in common with the revolution."[60]

The language of purge strove to be curt and businesslike, but it was also flexible and ambiguous. The records of the Central Control Commission troika set up to hear appeals from the purges of VUZ and soviet party cells contains documentation on the thousands of cases the troika reconsidered, all giving a brief biography and the original purge decision. To be sure, sometimes there were highly specific justifications for purge offered, such as those connected with violations of the norms of communist *byt*: "sexual relations with women of loose morals in the restaurant 'Bar' in January 1923."[61] But rationales tended toward vagueness, in keeping with the official silence on targeting Trotskii supporters. In the cells of higher educational institutions, students were purged as "ballast," as "accidental elements" or simply as "alien." One of the most ubiquitous categories, that of "alien element," did not simply refer to ascribed class position, but was used interchangeably with "ideologically alien."[62]

59. RTsKhIDNI f. 17, op. 60, d. 755, l. 81, 81 ob; "Vypiska iz protokola No. 5 zasedaniia Sekretariata [Moskovskogo komiteta RKP] ot 24/VI-24," ibid., d. 772, l. 1.

60. "Vypiska iz protokola No. 174 zasedaniia Partkollegii MKK ot 7, 8, 9, 14 i 15 iiunia 1924 goda," RTsKhIDNI f. 17, op. 60, d. 755, l. 83; "Agitprop Zam. Zav. K. Popov. V Sekretariat TsKK," 4 June 1925, ibid., l. 81, 81 ob. Other documents suggesting Trotskyists were targeted include Lunacharskii to Krupskaia, 14 May 1924, GARF f. A-2306, op. 1, d. 3397, l. 242–43; "Protokol obshchego sobraniia kommunistov IKP," 6 June 1924, ARAN f. 1759, op. 2, d. 21, l. 2; and even *K XIV s"ezdu RKP(b)* (Moscow-Leningrad: Gosizdat, 1925), 98.

61. "Protokol zasedaniia Parttroiki partkollegii TsKK RKP ot 10-go marta 1924 g.," RTsKhIDNI f. 17, op. 1, d. 19, l. 4–8.

62. "Protokol No. 118 zasedaniia parttroiki Tsentral'noi proverochnoi komissii pri partkollegii TsKK ot 25/IV-24," RTsKhIDNI f. 613, op. 2, d. 6, l. 75, 83, 91, 117. For more such lists, see op. 1, d. 20, and d. 19, l. 1–164. The TsKK eventually reversed decisions on over one half of all dismissed party members in the 1924–25 purges of "nonproduction cells." Iaroslavskii's 1929 report to the Politburo indicated 5.9 percent of the members of those cells were purged in 1924–25, a figure which was reduced to 2.7 percent after the TsKK had heard all

The setting of advanced quotas at the top, combined with the necessity to camouflage the charge of Trotskyism, held significant ramifications that went far beyond the immediate effects of the purge. Both these hallmarks of the purge process heightened the interchangeability of the social, ideological, political, and academic justifications for the purge itself.[63] The red expert had been viewed from the start as a model in all, not just the last, of these realms; now, in the trauma of purge, the organicist inclination to fuse categories was given free reign in a major party-political operation.

This institutionalized fusion of categories held important implications for Soviet political culture and also comprised another legacy of the 1924 watershed for IKP. The party majority conjured up a potent brew of social, political, ideological, and academic deviations to account for the disloyalty of the students. The anti-Trotskii campaign had consistently portrayed the opposition as petty-bourgeois, so the time-honored connection between social origin and political deviation was the easiest link to make. Although Trotskii had made an appeal to students along generational lines, oppositionism was now painted as a clear-cut class issue; Trotskyism in the schools was due to their petty-bourgeois social composition.[64] Petty-bourgeois Trotskyists were now tied to all the ideological faults of "scholasticism." This provided further impetus for a modification of the curriculum. To put the icing on the cake, the students supposedly guilty of scholasticism were then portrayed as academically incompetent. Iaroslavskii began to tell stories of how the purge had revealed IKP students' gross unfamiliarity with elementary Marxism. This entire amalgam—symbolically lumping social, political, ideological, and academic deficiencies—was welded together in a campaign conducted through the party cells and written into the party platform at the Thirteenth Party Congress.[65] The "barometer of the party"

---

appeals. Iaroslavskii, "V Politbiuro TsK VKP(b)," no date, 1929, RTsKhIDNI f. 613, op. 3, d. 17, l. 29–30.

63. Unfortunately, the literature on purges in the 1930s has rarely been concerned with the experiences of the 1920s and has sometimes treated purge categories in a literal-minded way. For example, see Roberta T. Manning, "The Great Purges in a Rural District," in J. Arch Getty and Manning, eds., *Stalinist Terror: New Perspectives* (Cambridge: Cambridge University Press, 1993), 194–96.

64. One activist objected that many working-class rabfaks had strongly supported the opposition. *O rabote iacheek RKP(b) Vysshikh uchebnykh zavedenii* (Moscow: Izdanie TsK, 1925), 32.

65. "Rasshirennoe sobranie Krasno-Presnenskogo komiteta partii s aktivnymi rabotnikami iacheek," 27 November 1924, RTsKhIDNI f. 89, op. 8, d. 442, l. 15; Iaroslavskii, "Partiia i VUZ-y," no earlier than May 1924, RTsKhIDNI f. 89, op. 8, d. 435, l. 2–3; "Po povodu

Group photograph of students and teachers of the Institute of Red Professors in 1925. Reprinted by permission of the Museum of the Revolution, Moscow, Russia.

was in disgrace. For participants in this political culture, 1924 drove in the message as never before: a politically loyal communist student was, or at least by all official party logic should also be, an orthodox Marxist, a pure proletarian, and even a good student.

Ambiguities of Social Engineering: Dilemmas of the Proletarianization Drive, 1924–28

The doubts cast on IKP's political loyalty and social composition in 1923–24 jolted the institution and provided the impetus for a far-reaching experiment in restructuring its social composition. This drive to modify the class background of the red expert at IKP was not unexpected; soon after the institute's founding Pokrovskii had termed increased proletarian presence a long-term goal, and Narkompros's rabfak administration had lobbied for it in 1923.[66] But IKP took concrete action only in 1924, in tandem with a party-wide campaign. Proletarianization in this elite center of party higher education would compound the identity crisis of the party intellectuals.

The fetish with fixing in place reductive class categories, which became an organizational and theoretical enterprise of giant proportions in the 1920s, was part of the regime's project of "classing" in Marxist terms an elusively shifting, layered postrevolutionary society.[67] NEP was thus the great age of Marxist classification and record-keeping. But as the consequences of this enterprise noticeably shifted in 1924 to involve large-scale refabrication of the Party's own social composition, nowhere were the dilemmas more acute than at IKP, the Party's intelligentsia-dominated center for training the red expert. The upward march of percentages of workers became firmly entrenched at IKP between 1924–

---

vystuplenii tov. Trotskogo," *Pravda*, 28 December 1924, 4; "Materialy zasedanii sektsii XIII s"ezda RKP(b) o rabote sredi molodezhi pod predsedatel'stvom N. I. Bukharina," in N. I. Bukharin, *K novomu pokoleniiu: Doklady, vystupleniia i stat'i, posviashchennye problemam molodezhi* (Moscow: Progress, 1990), 184–206.

66. See *Trudy IKP*, 7; GARF f. 5284, op. 1, d. 2, l. 92.

67. For an incisive interpretation of the construction of "estate-like" Marxist classes from the 1920s to the 1930s, see Fitzpatrick, "Ascribing Class." On the complexities of determining proletarian status, see Sheila Fitzpatrick, "The Problem of Class Identity in NEP Society," in Fitzpatrick et al., eds., *Russia in the Era of NEP: Explorations in Soviet Society and Culture* (Bloomington: Indiana University Press, 1991), 15–18. On class-discriminatory legislation, see Elise Kimerling, "Civil Rights and Social Policy in Soviet Russia, 1918–1936," *Russian Review* 41 (January 1982): 24–46.

28 and could not be directly challenged in IKP debates; yet the very nature of IKP as a special center for high Marxism seemed to be put in jeopardy. No consensus was reached on how to square this next circle in the institute's path; contradictory information was gathered and opposite recommendations pursued in a debate over recruitment and educational mission.

In announcing proletarianization, IKP once again followed the Party's lead. At the Thirteenth Party Congress, a large-scale worker recruitment drive into the Party was approved, which upon Lenin's death in January 1924 became known as the Lenin Levy. Between 1924 and 1926 this effectively doubled the Party's membership with the admission of one-half million "production-line workers." By the end of 1924, there were in Moscow alone 1,000 political literacy schools to train recruits for party membership. IKP itself founded a two-year preparatory section to train students classified as workers to move up to the regular departments; in admissions, the necessary party membership of three years was waived for new worker applicants, while it was raised to five years for all others. Before 1924, the student body at IKP had contained fewer than eight percent workers.[68]

The results of proletarianization at IKP ostensibly seemed clear: an upward curve in the number of working-class red professors. IKP statistics showed overall worker presence increasing to 21 percent in 1924, a little over 30 percent from 1925 to 1927, and up to 39.75 percent in 1928. The percentage of "white-collar" students declined in the same period from about 90 percent in 1921–23 to 55.38 percent in 1928. The old universities, under the influence of a professoriat much opposed to proletarianization, showed a more gradual rise from 17.8 percent workers in 1924–25 to 30.3 percent in 1928–29. Thus global statistics for higher education should not disguise that specifically party institutions like IKP, and certainly communist universities where the question of standards was not as sensitive, went much farther in carrying out proletarianization.[69] When all higher education was set on breakneck

68. John B. Hatch, "The 'Lenin Levy' and the Social Origins of Stalinism: Workers and the Communist Party in Moscow, 1921–28," *Slavic Review* 48 (Winter 1989): 568; GARF f. 5284, op. 1, d. 98, l. 12; ARAN f. 1759, op. 2, d. 24, l. 4.

69. "V Sekretariat TsK—dokladnaia zapiska. K voprosu ob IKP," no date, 1929, GARF f. 5284, op. 1, d. 135, l. 13; James McClelland, "Proletarianizing the Student Body: The Soviet Experience During the New Economic Policy," *Past and Present* 80 (August 1978): 124. According to Narkompros data from 1 January 1924, the ten *komvuzy* then in existence were made up of 47 percent workers and children of workers, 33.5 percent peasants and children of peasants, 12 percent *sluzhashchie*, 0.3 percent Red Army soldiers, and 7.2 percent "others." Cited in Leonova, *Iz istorii*, 44.

proletarianization between 1928 and 1932, the precedent of five years of experience made it possible to argue that IKP was simply strengthening existing policies that had not yet been fully implemented.[70]

The triumphal upward march of percentages, however, disguised many ambiguities. IKP statistics did not indicate if these were "workers" by social origin or "class position," meaning their occupation in 1917, or upon enrollment in the Party. But certainly they were not "from the bench," since the IKP debate centered around what kind of workers should be admitted—those from the party apparat or from other educational institutions. Moreover, the malleability of the categories was underlined when the "intelligentsia" contingent referred to before 1924 was simply replaced retroactively with another term more standard in party statistics, white-collar employees.

The dilemmas of attempting to reconstruct the student body were dramatized after internal IKP studies revealed proletarian students (as well as those few of peasant background) received significantly worse grades than those classified as white-collar.[71] A wide range of documents show that the decline from the elite academic ethos of 1921–24 had become a major issue at IKP by the mid-1920s. On 8 March 1926 the administration resolved to "consider it impossible to admit to the departments . . . persons who do not know literary Russian sufficiently."[72] Pokrovskii bluntly told his seminar: "I have to say, you do not know how to write Russian. After all, there have been a whole series of scandals." Especially at the preparatory section, a number of internal reports attest to an educational crisis resulting from "a low level of literacy among a number of students." By 1929, however, 48 percent of all IKP students in the institute itself had moved up from the preparatory section.[73]

70. IKP's percentage of "workers" reached 50 percent in 1930–31 and peaked at 64 percent in 1931–32, again significantly higher than statistics for higher education as a whole. See the article signed Dubynia and [Anna M.] Pankratova, "Desiat' let Instituta krasnoi professury," *Bor'ba klassov*, no. 8–9 (1931): 24; McClelland, "Proletarianizing the Student Body," 124.

71. "Tezisy i predlozheniia uchebnoi komissii po voprosam ob itogakh priema 1927," GARF f. 5284, op. 1, ed. khr. 134, l. 21.

72. GARF f. 5284, op. 1, d. 260, l. 10. The importance proletarianization assumed at IKP is underlined in a 1926 letter from Bukharin to Pokrovskii claiming a student from one of the "oldest Bolshevik families" had been rejected from IKP because his father was an engineer. It took a letter from Bukharin, at the height of his power, to admit the student. "Don't be angry at such 'interference' [*penetration pacifique*] in the internal affairs of the institute," Bukharin joked. "You, after all, are not an English trade-unionist." Bukharin to Pokrovskii, 21 September 1926, ARAN f. 1759, op. 4, d. 418, l. 1.

73. Pokrovskii's remark is contained in ARAN f. 1759, op. 2, d. 20, l. 106; on the preparatory section, see "O perestroike raboty podgotovitel'nogo otdeleniia," no date, GARF f. 5284,

The crisis of standards in party academia was compounded by the fact that the first students in the early 1920s had usually completed middle school or some higher education before the Revolution. At IKP, by the mid-1920s this reserve had run out. Moreover, other data the institute collected showed thirty nationalities at IKP in 1928. The four largest national groups were Russians (56.65 percent), Jews (19.19 percent), Latvians (5 percent), and Ukrainians (4.1 percent). Although one report made much of the "high level of preparation of Jews" for academic work, there was no attempt to correlate class and nationality with academic performance.[74]

Nonetheless, by the time two groups of students had entered the main institute from the preparatory section, in 1927–28, a major debate had erupted over the direction and purpose of the institute as a whole. Entrance examinations had been reinstated in higher education, so a discussion of standards was legitimized. This discussion revealed a preoccupation with allocating places among the four major sources of IKP recruitment: party politicians from party committees and the apparat (the so-called *aktiv*), rabfaks, communist universities, and "other" (nonparty) institutions. All but the last would have significant numbers of working-class party members; the issue of debate was therefore not proletarianization *per se*, but which group the institute should favor.

Agitprop's Popov, an IKP teacher whose word in this debate obviously carried much weight, made no secret of his preference; he pressed for higher recruitment from party committees. He claimed this would not damage IKP's scholarly mission: "It is completely false to say an orientation toward the party *aktiv* would require a lowering of standards for those matriculating: one must recognize that the *partaktiv* is already not so illiterate." In other debates in 1927, some students seconded Popov's championship of party officialdom, fearing that strict academic testing and requirements "would in fact close the door of IKP to workers and comrades in practical party work."[75]

On the other side of the dispute, other teachers and students pleaded in the interests of IKP's scholarly mission not to reject recruitment from

---

op. 1, d. 336, l. 128; "Protokol obshchego sobraniia pervoi gruppy vtorogo kursa podgotovitel'nogo otdeleniia," 19 April 1927, ibid., d. 193, l. 21; *Biulleten' zaochnoi konsul'tatsii IKP*, no. 1 (1931): 4.

74. "Tezisy i predlozheniia," l. 21 (cited in full at note 71).

75. "Protokol sobraniia slushatelei II-gruppy II-kursa," 22 April 1927, GARF f. 5284, op. 1, d. 193, l. 32; "Protokol zasedaniia prepodavatelei i starostata Podgotovitel'nogo otdeleniia IKP," no date, 1927, ibid., ed. khr. 134, l. 25–28.

the state sector "social-economic VUZy" altogether. But that impinged on the two other established constituencies, party students graduating from communist universities and from *rabfaks*. As opposing groups pushed their own agendas, the supporting data seemed contradictory at best. One internal study declared *rabfak* graduates did the worst academically, another declared communist university graduates were the least literate. The issues were further obscured through the use of a "masked" category of "other types of schools," which apparently referred to nonparty institutions. In sum, no one openly questioned proletarianization, and even the results of discussion, seemingly a compromise, held an unmentioned ramification: it was resolved to increase allotments to party committees and communist universities, without weakening the commitment to the *rabfaks*. But this would seemingly come at the expense of the unmentioned "other" category, the graduates of nonparty institutions.[76]

IKP thus muddled through the crisis of standards that came in the wake of proletarianization. At the same time, the institution, and it seems above all the red professors themselves, were unwilling to reformulate IKP's mission and to set their sights on anything less than their elite status as future leaders in the scholarly and theoretical world. At one point in 1927 the administration—perhaps recognizing that the preoccupation with advanced scholarship begun in 1921–24 was unrealistic in light of proletarianization and orientation toward the party *aktiv*—voted to change IKP's name to "Higher School of Social Sciences." This move, denoting a clear diminution of status for what had become much more than an ordinary higher school, was made without consulting students or the academic collegium. A storm of criticism apparently torpedoed the change: the philosophy department, for example, called the name change a capitulation to the bourgeois professoriat and a disarmament on the ideological front. In a flash, the pride of a self-conscious elite broke through: the philosophers warned about caving in to certain unnamed "workers in our party, who are enemies of training the professoriat through IKP."[77] The red professors would have their proletarian credentials, affiliations with the party *aktiv*, and their rightful place at the summit of Marxist scholarship too.

76. "Tezisy i predlozheniia," l. 20 (cited in full at note 71); "Protokol zasedaniia prepodovatelei i starostata," l. 25 (cited in full at note 75). For more debates on IKP's purpose and raising standards, see GARF f. 5284, op. 1, d. 338, l. 18, and d. 134, l. 127.

77. "V Pravlenie IKP, 17.III.27," GARF f. 5284, op. 1, d. 338, l. 17; see also another student protest on the name change in the same file, unnumbered page between l. 17 and l. 18.

Social Science in a Different Key: Curricular Reform and Red Scholarship

Who were these students who defended the claims of the red professoriat? A profile of IKP graduates and students gives some indication of the place of "red scholarship" in the Marxist social sciences of the 1920s. The total number of students accepted for study at IKP between 1921 and 1928 was 1,966; of these, 194 red professors were graduated between 1924 and 1928, in economics or political economy (88 graduates), philosophy (42), Russian history (32), history of the West (18), natural science (9), and law (5). The majority, over 58 percent, were listed as Communists who joined the Party between 1918 and 1920; another 35 percent joined the Party in 1917 or before. Like the vast majority of intellectuals of all kinds during NEP, most lived after graduation in Moscow or Leningrad. The administration's report highlighted two main channels of employment after IKP: into party journals and newspapers (*Pravda*, *Bol'shevik*, and *Proletarskaia revoliutsiia* were the ones named first) and "party-pedagogical work," including at IKP itself, since in 1928 over half IKP's faculty were graduates of the institute.[78]

A bibliography in Pokrovskii's archive listing all the published works by IKP history students and graduates through 1928 gives some insights into "red scholarship." IKP's administration, following the institutional and conceptual practice of the Marxist social sciences in general in the 1920s, made a firm distinction between "science" (*nauka*) on the one hand, and the lower forms of popularized, instructional, disseminated Marxism—"political enlightenment" and writing on current political and ideological themes (referred to as "publicistics") on the other. This is shown in the adminstration's own scientific calculation that red professors by 1928 had published 559 "scientific articles" and 1468 "popular-publicistic" pieces, not counting newspaper articles and reviews.[79]

The bibliography shows that the two genres of publications were combined in the output of virtually every red professor. To take an example, Aron I. Gaister, student from 1922 to 1925, wrote one book for party propagandists on class differentiation in the countryside and another on "agriculture in capitalist Russia, 1861–1905." In 1923 David A. Baevskii published a history of the workers' press from 1878 to 1907, but he also wrote guides for party agitators. Some, like the

78. "V Sekretariat TsK," l. 11–17 (cited in full at note 69); list of early graduates, GARF f. 5284, op. 1, d. 98, l. 69.

79. "V Sekretariat TsK," l. 13 (cited in full at note 69).

Bukharinist Astrov, were much more heavily involved in publicistics, writing dozens of articles on Leninism and inner-party opposition; but Astrov also maintained a "scientific" research interest in German and Austrian Social-Democracy.[80] The trend suggests that red professors in the 1920s cannot be understood outside their simultaneous roles as publicists and scholars, even though Marxist social science continued to conceptually demarcate scholarship and publicistics as separate genres of writing for certain types of journals and publications.

In the early IKP, this distinction was replicated in the realm of attitudes toward social science as well. For example, comments by teachers, faculty discussions, and grading of student work all emphasize the widespread conviction that true Marxist science, as opposed to mere political enlightenment, demanded a "critical approach to the material" and "an independence and originality of thought."[81] Red professors, however, were expected to shift effortlessly between both worlds, to be both students of social science and teachers of political enlightenment, scholars and popularizers. At the same time, IKP was subject to curriculum reform that attempted to contemporize study and fight scholasticism. This affected the boundaries, conceptual and institutional, between high Marxism, *nauka*, and the disseminated or publicistic forms of mass Marxism.

As early as 1923, Agitprop, with approval from the bureau of the IKP party cell, put together a blueprint to bring the institute closer to "the tasks of the present." Every problem of political economy should, if possible, be "connected to the conditions of the epoch of proletarian dictatorship and capitalist encirclement." The history department would study more contemporary topics, such as the civil war and the current situation. Philosophy would be less concerned with the history of philosophy and more engaged with "the struggle with idealism and deviations in Marxism."[82] Agitprop's plan, which was originally put forward during the discussion of "scholasticism" by Konstantin Popov with the

80. "Rabota slushatelei istoricheskogo otdeleniia," no date, 1928, ARAN f. 1759, op. 2, d. 20, l. 175–219.

81. GARF f. 5284, op. 1, d. 2, l. 25; see also d. 170, l. 1.

82. "Tezisy Agit-propa TsK VKP s popravkami, vnosimymi Biuro kommunistov IKP," no date, 1923, GARF f. 5284, op. 1, d. 100, l. 10; "O napravlenii uchebnoi i nauchnoi raboty IKP (postanovlenie soveshchaniia pri Agit-prope TsK)," no month or day given, 1923, GARF f. A-2313, op. 4, d. 69, l. 44; "Tezisy t. Popova," no date, 1923, GARF f. 5284, op. 1, d. 100, l. 9; "Soveshchanie pri Podotdele propagandy TsK RKP po uchebnomu planu i programmam IKP," 27 October 1923, RTsKhIDNI f. 147, op. 1, d. 35, l. 12–13.

ardent support of Sverdlov University rector M. N. Liadov, undermined IKP's earlier distinctions between high Marxism, *nauka*, and the more "mass" forms of disseminated social and political knowledge.[83]

In two meetings on IKP at Agitprop's subsection on propaganda in October and November 1923, Pokrovskii and Preobrazhenskii turned out to be the most energetic critics of Popov and Liadov. When the Sverdlov University rector remarked that IKP was training "narrow specialists" and that all study must be based on "concrete reality," Preobrazhenskii retorted that Liadov's approach might be satisfactory for a school of political literacy, but for the institute it would be a "waste of time." Pokrovskii's defense of a historical approach and broad general preparation resulted in some compromise phrases on "deep theoretical knowledge" in the final Agitprop document.[84] Nevertheless, the 1923 discussion launched a lengthy process of reform of the IKP academic program.

In this process Pokrovskii played a complex and often contradictory role in relation to scholarship at the institute. In his 1923 "theses," Pokrovskii emphasized that the red professor must be versed in both Marx and his "critics," but in the next breath railed against false objectivity divorced from the goals of the Party. By 1928 the former student of Kliuchevskii was complaining that his seminar alone at the institute made the attempt to impart familiarity with non-Marxist literature.[85] As rector, however, Pokrovskii was not loathe to modify his convictions when political considerations intruded. Pokrovskii at first defended the intelligentsia composition of the early IKP, noting that "a microscope is a microscope, whether a proletarian or a bourgeois looks into it, and what they will find there depends on who knows how to look better." But after 1924, the rector quickly shed his reluctance to proletarianize the institute; he also became a promoter of the extension of Marxism into natural science when this moved up on the agenda of party scholarship, and IKP students began to write dissertations on topics such as

83. Popov's 1923 plan, untitled with handwritten corrections, is in RTsKhIDNI f. 17, op. 60, d. 466, l. 44. Popov pointedly singled out the philosophy program for "fundamental revision" because of the stress on "pre-Marxian" philosophy established by Aksel'rod and Deborin.

84. "Protokol soveshchaniia po uchebnomu planu i programmam Instituta krasnoi professury pri P-otdel propagandy Agitpropa TsK RKP," 20 October 1923, RTsKhIDNI f. 17, op. 60, d. 466, l. 38–39, and 10 November 1923, ibid., l. 45–46; "O napravlenii uchebnoi i nauchnoi raboty Instituta krasnoi professury (Postanovlenie soveshchaniia pri Agitprope TsK, v redaktsii soglasovana s I.K.P.)," no date, 1923, ibid., l. 52.

85. "Tezisy M. N. Pokrovskogo," l. 21–22 (cited in full at note 1); "Seminarii t. Pokrovskogo II-Kursa, 5 marta 1928," ARAN f. 1759, op. 2, d. 20, l. 106, 138.

"Materialism and Idealism in Theoretical Chemistry."[86] A microscope, apparently, was no longer just a microscope.

Curriculum reform after 1923 attempted to make the "scientific" work more contemporary and more engaged with the Party's "current tasks." Red historiography, for example, treats no topic before the Decembrist revolt of 1825; and the vast bulk of history-writing concerns a small cluster of "revolutionary" subjects (history of socialism, the workers' movement, and the Revolution itself) in the two decades before 1917.[87] In 1926 Pokrovskii noted statements at a conference of university rectors "that IKP produces incompetent professors, and therefore the Institute of Red Professors is totally unneeded." While strongly defending IKP's record, the historian nevertheless could not help remarking that the red professors were "undereducated" (*nedouchkami*), and came out with the extraordinary statement: "If you ask me whether one could appoint one of my students [from IKP] to a *kafedra* of Russian history, then I will say—no, impossible, because they do not know Russian history as a whole. . . . [When they arrive at IKP] they do not know a single foreign language."[88] This remark, it needs to be recalled, came from the driving force fighting for the "communization" of all social science teaching in higher education.

More relevant did not necessarily mean more practical; it meant demands on academic work were directed at tying it, like publicistics naturally were, to the "current situation" and party tasks articulated outside the institute. Several broad trends facilitated this attempt. The most important was the inauguration at IKP of new disciplines—Leninism in 1925 and the history of the Party in 1927—that were themselves prominent fronts in ongoing party struggles. Especially influential in "contemporizing" the curriculum was the advent of Leninism as a discipline. High-level intra-agency commissions formed after Lenin's death met in the attempt systematically to inject Leninism into the academic programs of all higher educational institutions. The subject of Leninism, an elastic field memorializing Lenin's contribution to Marxism, the Party,

86. Pokrovskii, *Trudy IKP*, 5. A list of natural science department dissertations can be found in "Protokol zasedaniia Uchebnoi Kollegii IKP, 28/XI-28," GARF f. 5284, op. 1, d. 336, l. 14. The most substantial historical treatment of Pokrovskii remains George Enteen's *The Soviet Scholar-Bureaucrat: M. N. Pokrovskii and the Society of Marxist Historians* (University Park: Pennsylvania State University Press, 1978).

87. See "Rabota slushatelei." A discussion of "contemporary" and "revolutionary" themes in Marxist historiography is contained in Iu. V. Krivosheev and A. Iu. Dvornichenko, "Izgnanie nauki: Rossiiskaia istoriografiia v 20-x-nachale 30-x godov XX veka," *Otechestvennaia istoriia*, no. 3 (May-June 1994): 143–58.

88. Pokrovskii, "Postanovka obshchestvovedeniia," 1. 10 (cited in full at note 30).

and the Revolution, therefore saturated curricula at a time when virtually every intellectual and political tendency in the party vied with its opponents by claiming the mantle of orthodox Leninism. It reached the point that the dean of the preparatory section complained in 1927 that the very same material was being repeated in political economy, Marxist philosophy, and Leninism.[89]

Both curriculum reform and the red professors' own deep involvement in publicistics and political enlightenment, which offered political relevance and ties to the masses, formed the background against which social science at IKP was instrumentalized (to use an expression common at the time) as a weapon of struggle. The activity of the red professors became a many-fronted struggle that was theorized in journals and books and acted out in seminars and meetings; occasionally it even bordered on a physical brawl. The confrontation with the United Opposition in 1927 was played out at IKP, according to one witness, when oppositionist Karl Radek tried to speak at an IKP forum and was literally dragged away from the podium.[90]

On Agit-trials and Theory Seminars: Drama and Ritual in Unmasking Deviance

"The *kruzhok* is an arena—in which [students] comport themselves sometimes like gladiators, sometimes like young cocks," a Sverdlov University student wrote in 1924. "The *kruzhok* is an arena—where you study the use of weapons to repel attack at every crossroad of life."[91] We have already seen the pivotal importance of the *kruzhok* at Sverdlov University. At IKP, the counterpart to the Sverdlovian *kruzhok* was the seminar, but images of spectacles and sports of combat, of cockfights and gladiators apply equally well to it. IKP's theory seminars did not occur in a splendid Marxist-Leninist isolation, but formed a distinctive part of broader Bolshevik and early Soviet political culture. By mimicking in seminar the conventions of the Party, which itself was at the same time deeply enmeshed in developing forums in politics and culture for

89. "O propagande i izuchenii Leninizma," 9 February 1924, GARF f. A-2313, op. 1, d. 87, l. 57–62. Commissions included Agitprop, Glavpolitprosvet, GUS, the Komsomol, VTsSPS, the Red Army's PUR, and the Lenin Institute. See "Vypiska iz postanovleniia ob obshchestvennom minimume i propagande leninizma v VUZ-akh priniatogo na zasedanii Sekretariata TsK RKP," 2 January 1925, RTsKhIDNI f. 147, op. 2c, d. 5, l. 13; GARF f. 5284, op. 1, d. 193, l. 21.

90. Esfir' B. Genkina, "Vospominaniia ob IKP," in *Istoriia i istoriki: istoriograficheskii ezhegodnik, 1981* (Moscow: Nauka, 1985), 268–69.

91. Mikhail Rogov, "Ocherki Sverdlovii," *Molodaia gvardiia*, no. 5 (1924): 200–201.

influencing and styling group behavior, the young red professors affirmed their party and revolutionary (rather than scholastic) commitment.

The seminars' activity was not explicitly conceived as ritual, insofar as that implies high degree of established ceremony and comprehension of the rite by initiates; nor was it a spectacle that dramatized material for the stage (*intsenirovka*), which implies a script. Nevertheless, elements of both ritual and drama made their way into what were after all public performances, whose actors had grown up in a revolutionary culture in which the need to devise distinct social practices, rites, and novel methods of instruction had assumed singular importance. The new cultural practices of the October Revolution, after having developed in an exuberant, often chaotic and heterodox environment exemplified by the mass festivals of the civil war period, had given way to the increasingly scripted methods and canons of NEP. Nothing indicates the Bolshevik struggle to master spontaneity and yet preserve revolutionary values in the new culture more than what became the standard practice of planting the crowds at public celebrations with "cells of fomenters" whose "premeditated enthusiasm would inspire spontaneous emotion."[92] As this suggests, one of the most relevant axes around which the emerging Soviet political culture can be analyzed is the interplay between two of its major values, revolutionary enthusiasm and scripted Bolshevik discipline. Sometimes the two clashed, at others they reinforced one another. IKP, as a self-consciously revolutionary and Bolshevik institution, incorporated this basic tension.

The conventions of "political enlightenment work," which IKP students were as party instructors expected to have assimilated, thus helped shape the character of academic seminars, which turned into performances that were transcribed and recorded for the higher authorities; and in this way IKP's cognitive activity, in ways perhaps only sensed by its participants as they learned their lessons, comprised a vital part of the broader revolutionary political culture, blending revolutionary activism with increasingly organized ritual. These assertions will be brought out through a substantial historical detour into the evolution of a surprisingly related form of revolutionary culture, the agitational trial. The links with the Bolshevik political culture of the red professors will presently become apparent.

Theater was, in Clark's memorable phrase, the "cradle of Soviet cul-

92. Von Geldern, *Bolshevik Festivals*, 146; also Stites, *Revolutionary Dreams*.

ture." Avant-garde theater activists, in her words, were before 1917 developing theater as a "construct for a totalizing experience" to overcome alienation and transform humanity. When these currents meshed in revolution with a Bolshevik embrace of theater as an educational and propagandistic device, theater became the queen of the revolutionary arts.[93] It might be added: as Bolshevik politics itself acquired an increasingly didactic function and scripted character the revolutionary polity itself became more theatrical. One of the least known genres in the flowering of propaganda theater after October, agit-trials were mass spectacles, amateur theatricals, realist revolutionary drama, and Soviet rituals. They were variously referred to as agit-trials, model trials, sanitation trials, polit-trials (*politsudy*), and show trials (*pokazatel'nye sudy*). The practice of staging mock trials with political or instructional themes arose during the civil war in the Red Army. With possible roots as diverse as mock trials used for decades in the Russian bar, prerevolutionary popular cultural preoccupation with courtroom disputations, and peasant popular justice (*samosud*), the agit-trial is one of the best illustrations of how an indigenous, popular revolutionary practice coexisted with increasingly organized attempts to standardize it in the 1920s. It marks the space in which forms of Soviet popular culture with diverse Russian roots overlapped with Bolshevik political enlightenment in a concern with revealed guilt.[94]

Early agit-trials placed great emphasis on improvisation, so much so that we have little documentation on the genre's early days during the civil war. Even so, the setting was so realistic and the tensions so intense that those acting out roles (often of a counterrevolutionary or class enemy) at times became alarmed for their own safety.[95] Early mass spectacles, such as the 1920 trial of Baron Vrangel' in which 10,000 Red Army soldiers participated, gave way to what one scholar calls the "scripted" mock trial of NEP. Theorists of propaganda theater championed the "illusion of reality" created by replication of the courtroom and juridical procedure. Stereotypical characters were easily recogniz-

93. Clark, *Petersburg*, 74–104.

94. In what follows I am indebted above all to what are, to my knowledge, the only two sustained analyses of agit-trials: Julie Anne Cassiday, "The Theater of the World and the Theater of the State: Drama and the Show Trial in Early Soviet Russia" (Ph.D. diss., Stanford University, 1995), and Elizabeth A. Wood's unpublished paper, "Agitation Trials: Theater and State Power in Post-Revolutionary Russia."

95. Cassiday, "Theater," 54. See a description of the "new method" during the civil war, as enacted in the School of Infantry Officers of the Red Army, in Alexander Barmine, *One Who Survived: The Life Story of a Russian Under the Soviets* (New York: G. P. Putnam's Sons, 1945), 65.

able by their emblematic names and essentialized class behavior. In these dramas, the kulak was always greedy and the proletarian hungry for enlightenment.[96]

By the 1920s, then, the agit-trial, from its roots in the rough-and-ready mass meetings of red partisans, became an official Soviet ritual of the "political enlightenment" repertoire in such settings as workers' clubs, people's courts, the Red Army, and the Cheka. From a popular "new method," able to adapt well to political themes because it had elements both of spontaneous game and scripted theater, the balance tilted increasingly toward the latter, as attempts at standardization such as publishing model trials proliferated.[97] Like other forms of propagandistic dramatization such as the "living newspaper," the agit-trial also became a regular feature of revolutionary theater, as drama groups, including those in universities and party schools around the country, used the trials as vehicles for didactic plays with political themes. Along with mass holidays, meetings, lectures, and spectacles, Glavpolitprosvet recommended agit-trials in 1921 as a standard activity for clubs in higher educational institutions for the benefit of those institutions seeking funding.[98]

Here was drama as revolutionary ritual par exellence. The nature of the political and the revolutionary proved elastic, as the trials were adapted for different audiences and purposes. In the 1920s, major types of trials concerned counterrevolutionaries and party-political themes; public health and sanitary knowledge; antireligous propaganda; and production and lifestyle issues in factory and countryside. Even concepts like pornography or policies like NEP could be put on trial. The "old ways" were judged, as was a peasant *krasnoarmeets* accused of infecting his wife with gonorrhea. The fact that specialists such as public health officials and agronomists wrote many of the agit-trials may help explain the genre's self-conscious anti-aestheticism, but the point

96. "Vidy massovykh postanovok," in Ryndich, *Partiino-sovetskie shkoly*, 124; Cassiday, "Theater," 56, 61.

97. Gorzka, *Arbeiterkultur*, 348; Eugene Huskey, *Lawyers and the Soviet State: The Origins and Development of the Soviet Bar, 1917–1939* (Princeton: Princeton University Press, 1986), 137; von Geldern, *Bolshevik Festivals*, 109–10; "Rabota v Krasnoi Armii, Militsii i voiskakh VChK," prob. December 1921, GARF f. A-2313, op. 1, d. 1, l. 450–51.

98. S. Kotliarenko, "Iz opyta klubnoi raboty v sovpartshkole," *Kommunisticheskoe prosveshchenie*, no. 6 (November-December 1926): 161–63; V. Pletnev, "Massovaia propaganda cherez iskusstva," *Kommunisticheskaia revoliutsiia*, no. 4 (February 1927): 51–60; "Polozhenie o studencheskikh klubakh pri V.U.Z. Respubliki, 23/VII-21 g.," GARF f. A-2313, op. 3, ed. khr. 29, l. 9; "Polozhenie o edinoi seti i tipakh klubov R.S.F.S.R., 28/IX-21 g.," RTsKhIDNI f. 17, op. 60, d. 54, l. 1.

of this propaganda realism was to depict *idealized* political behavior, that is, behavior not as it was, but as it should be.[99] The agit-trial showed its connections to the avant-garde and early revolutionary theater through its primary insistance on audience participation. The agit-trial on the one hand forced that much-anticipated leap past the proscenium arch by electing audience members to the jury and asking the entire audience to render its verdict. Yet the scripted Soviet culture cultivated convention to the degree that the trials' outcome and participants' roles were "overdetermined." Witnesses were planted in the audience, the equivalents of cells of fomenters in a sea of threatening spontaneity.[100]

Students were initiated into the "theatricalized life" of Soviet political culture not only through their contact with political enlightenment work and clubs.[101] At the "real" show trial of the SR Party in 1922, Sverdlov students and young Communists reportedly rehearsed for four hours before they rallied at the train station against foreign socialist dignitaries, allowed in to the country as defense representatives for the accused SRs; in front of the courthouse, the students were mobilized to chant "death to the SRs!" As elements of ritualistic theater in the trial of the SRs were immediately obvious to the well-informed, Menshevik commentators at the time referred to a "ritual affair" and a "scripted" or "staged" trial.[102] Life imitated art; political life in these years was linked to the cultural forms and rituals of political enlightenment by many threads.

The connection between the agit-trial and IKP seminars is not remote. One of the most striking of the red professors' conventions in theoretical and political discussions was the practice known as "working [somebody] over" (*prorabatyvat'*)—to bombard someone with intensive criticism from many sides, not unlike the "relentless questioning" of prosecutor and judge in the agit-trial.[103] Such interrogation was also connected to the unwritten rules governing denunciation, which frequently took the form of presenting evidence, above all compromising information from the biography of the accused: "I have knowledge that Torner wavered for a long time after the Fourteenth Party Congress . . .

99. Wood, "Agitation Trials," 4, 7–8; Cassiday, "Theater," 56–57, 61.

100. Clark, *Petersburg*, 111–12; Cassiday, 65–66 and passim.

101. The phrase comes from the title of chapter 7 of Fülöp-Miller, *Mind and Face*.

102. S. Dvinov, "K protsessu SR (pis'mo iz Moskvy)," *Sotsialisticheskii vestnik*, 2 August 1922, 5–6; "Komu eto nuzhno," ibid., 21 March 1922, 1–3; L. Martov, "Krovavyi fars," ibid., 18 June 1922, 3–5; "K protsessu S.R.," ibid., 20 June 1922, 10–11.

103. Wood, "Agitation Trials," 13.

We all know how he approached the question of the dictatorship of the party and evaluated the social forces of the Chinese revolution. It is said that Torner spoke out previously against Lenin's brochure 'An Infantile Disorder,' and recently asserted that if Lenin were alive, he would still reject it."[104] In academic debates, criticisms centered on "methodology," but this, like categories used in the purges, was an umbrella term under which political, academic, and ideological faults could be found. In the group dynamics of the seminar or meeting, it was not uncommon for the seminar leader (*starosta*) to take charge of exposing others' methodological mistakes. In essence, he acted as prosecutor and judge. In the department of natural science in 1926 and 1927, for example, Vasilii N. Slepkov, the brother of the historian Aleksandr Nikolaevich, played such a role. During this period he introduced a barrage of motions labeling fellow students "methodologically unsatisfactory," "disloyal" to the seminar, "methodologically incorrect," and perpetrators of "blunders from a methodological point of view." That this did not destroy the work of the seminar, but rather was seen as a legitimate function, is suggested by the fact that the watchdog was unanimously elected dean (*dekan*) of the natural science department in 1927.[105]

The distinctiveness of the political culture did not merely lie in the attack on ideological and political deviation—this had been part of Bolshevism long before. But the elevation of a process of struggle to make revelation of guilt the defining element of group relations even among comrades was indeed an innovation; the "working over," while practiced among party scholars elsewhere, was far more distinctive of the younger generation, and was linked to the ethos of IKP in particular. For example, Pokrovskii later claimed he had been "worked over" at IKP several times since 1924, and by temperament he was inclined to welcome the process; also, he was too powerful to be really stung at IKP during the 1920s. Pokrovskii noted that other intellectuals from the older generation, however, took a less favorable attitude to the custom: "How dare some illiterate whipper-snappers [*mal'chishki*] criticize me, an Old Bolshevik?"[106]

Working somebody over was not a staged performance in the same way as a scripted or theatrically staged agit-trial: its outcome was not

104. GARF f. 5284, op. 1, d. 193, l. 52.

105. Ibid., d. 192, l. 45, 46, 48–49, 561, and d. 338, l. 29.

106. M. N. Pokrovskii to E. M. Iaroslavskii, 27 February 1930, RTsKhIDNI f. 89, op. 8, d. 39, l. 3.

always predictable. Nonetheless, "scripted" elements could be easily incorporated, from campaigns, texts, or the Party's current arsenal of deviations. Trotskii, the object of organized attack in 1927 on the intensely factional topic of the Chinese Revolution, likened the discussion in the IKP cell to a pelting with chunks of garbage.[107] It is possible the deliberately coarse heckling style favored by the Stalin faction in confrontations with the opposition after the mid-1920s served as a model. Like the purge, another political ritual, "working over" assumed stature as process rather than for the particular accusations employed.

The culture of combat led to something seemingly nonexistent in the first few years of the institute—denunciations and ideological evaluations of the faculty. But such risky attacks were unlikely to be random; they provided opportunity for high-level machinations on the part of prominent party theorists. IKP students became embroiled in the classic political maneuver of creating a groundswell of criticism "from below" against one's enemies. For example, the Hungarian émigré Aleksandr I. Var'iash, who taught in the natural science department, was a prominent "mechanist" philosopher who opposed the primacy the Deborin school accorded Hegelian dialectics. In 1926, as the debate between mechanists and Deborin's dialecticians heated up, Deborin moved to consolidate control at IKP and on the editorial boards of key journals. At the same time, the natural science students unanimously denounced Var'iash for combining "Marxism with a range of bourgeois theories"; the teacher was removed.[108]

But revolutionary zeal, that other axis of the political culture, was also clearly expressed in the seminars. The genuine explosiveness of student criticism itself is suggested by the fact that, like the agit-trial before it, there were attempts to standardize and control the IKP seminars. The administration, not formally bound to accept the votes of student groups, attempted to regulate the format of the student discussions by introducing standard categories for student evaluations, such as "activism" and "ability to do scientific work." There is also evidence that

107. L. Trotskii, "Ne nado musoru! V Tsentral'nyi komitet VKP(b). V biuro iacheiki Instituta krasnoi professury. 22/IV.27," Trotsky Archive, T-3052.

108. GARF f. 5284, op. 1, d. 192, l. 20, 33, 56, and d. 338, l. 21. For an attack on Deborin's attempts to consolidate institutional control at this time, see Ivan I. Skvortsov-Stepanov to Molotov, handwritten, undated letter marked "Sekretno. Lichno," RTsKhIDNI f. 150, op. 1, d. 82, l. 15. Var'iash, who also used his Hungarian name Sandor Varjas, had served under Bela Kun and came to Moscow in 1922. On his place in the mechanist faction and his disputes with the Deborinites, see Joravsky, *Soviet Marxism and Natural Science*, 143–45.

members of the administration at times tried to curtail the increasing power of the student meetings.[109] But could revolutionary zeal and calculated discipline really be distinguished? A purged Trotskyist in 1927, charging that his expulsion for academic incompetence was politically motivated, taunted his colleagues: "You seem to be pursuing a revolutionary cause, but in actual fact you are only fulfilling the directives of the higher organs."[110]

Working over, denunciation, and attack were among the most stylized elements of interaction in a complex field of play. Far more common than the extraordinary measure of working over was alliance-building and minor sniping; in case of a deadlocked seminar, a party cell bureau representative could be brought in. Two other hallmarks of the seminars stand out: the constancy of evaluation and the adversarial nature of the process. The seminar votes in fact were passed on to the administration, which could decide to purge a student, and this explains the air of grave ceremony involved in the seminar gathering. Constant evaluation led to an extraordinarily high degree of mutual scrutiny, and everyone seemed to keep track of the precise wording of the negative evaluations from the previous year. The seminars' collective evaluations, the original purpose for recording the meetings, grew out of the ubiquity of evaluation established to monitor the red expert; in this sense the political culture adapted to institutional structures and practices of purge and promotion.[111]

The constant evaluation contributed to the second aspect, the intensity and pervasiveness of struggle. Consider this excerpt, by no means atypical, from the record of a 1925 meeting of philosophy students:

> Considered: A statement on the necessity of presenting the administration with an evaluation of the report of comrade Sokolov (on Kant). Proposal of Stoliarov: "To consider that Sokolov worked through a great deal of material in the report, but that from the perspective of the methodological basis of the report it does not entirely answer the demands of the Marxist method." First amendment of comrade Dmitriev: cross out the word "entirely." Additional amendment of comrade Dmi-

109. GARF f. 5284, op. 1, d. 192, l. 26, and d. 338, l. 12.

110. "Protokol sobraniia slushatelei II gr. II kursa P/otdel 31/v/27," GARF f. 5284, op. 1, ed. khr. 193, l. 44.

111. "Protokol obshchego sobraniia seminarov russkikh istorikov 2-ogo kursa," GARF f. 5284, op. 1, d. 192, l. 22, and l. 8–9.

triev: Taking into account the entire past work of comrade Sokolov at IKP, consider it expedient to *expel him from the Institute*.[112]

It is obvious that the form, purpose, and language of this gathering of philosophers was adopted directly from the model of the party cell meeting in political life. Just as the agit-trial ended with the indictment and reading of the sentence, so the seminars ended in the passing of the resolution.

It has been argued that "culture and, in the case in point, scholarly or academic culture, is a common code enabling all those possessing that code to . . . express the same meaningful intention through the same words, the same behaviour patterns and the same works."[113] The most striking aspect of IKP's academic culture as reflected in the seminars is that it cannot be separated from its political culture. In the most immediate sense of its practices and distinctive customs, IKP's seminars, like Sverdlov's *kruzhki*, were literally an extension of party politics.

It is fascinating to note that in the course of the 1920s as IKP was developing its combative ethos in its seminars, the Moscow party schools for Chinese cadres, KUTV and Sun-Yat Sen University, were also refining their own "struggle-criticism" and "study-criticism sessions," which like the IKP seminars bore a distinct resemblance to party cell meetings. Responding to the particular cultural heritage of the Chinese Communists, they were designed to break down traditions of saving face, group harmony, and exaggerated respect for authority; they prefigured what later became principal Chinese communist techniques for influencing group behavior.[114] In Soviet Russia, the early forms of revolutionary political culture were also being codified into official, country-wide methods as well. "Working over" in the IKP style was followed by the "criticism/self-criticism" campaign of 1928 and consolidated into an official Stalin-era form. Agit-trials were complemented and later supplanted by the "real-life drama" of "genuine" show trials:

112. "Protokol zasedaniia slushatelei II i I kursa filosofskogo otdeleniia, 3/III/25," GARF f. 5284, op. 1, d. 192, l. 1.

113. Pierre Bourdieu, "Systems of Education and Systems of Thought," *International Social Science Journal* 19:3 (1967): 339.

114. Jane L. Price, *Cadres, Commanders, and Commissars: The Training of the Chinese Communist Leadership, 1920–45* (Boulder, Colo.: Westview Press, 1976), 36, 96. Price cites a Chinese source indicating that Sun-Yat-Sen University's famous "28 Bolsheviks," later leaders of the Stalinist faction in the CPC, attended IKP classes (101 n. 17). See also Yueh Sheng, *Sun Yat-sen University in Moscow and the Chinese Revolution: A Personal Account* (Lawrence: University of Kansas, Center for East Asian Studies, 1971), 81.

didactic and educational, displaying markedly more scripted qualities by the end of the 1920s, featuring obligatory mass participation and audience plants, and sharing with agit-trials "a fluid boundary between stage and life."[115]

As one link in the evolution of IKP's own criticism techniques, and indeed a moment of triumph for them, we can note a pivotal episode when Stalin personally authorized perhaps the most far-reaching "working over" by IKP militants of the Great Break generation. On 9 December 1930 Stalin personally met with the party cell of IKP Philosophy. The Deborin School, vying with the mechanists for most of the 1920s, had in 1929–30 emerged victorious; but now Stalin urged the IKP philosophers "to beat [the Deborin school] in all directions, to beat [them] in places where they have not been beaten before." The result was that Deborinism was targeted as "Menshevizing idealism," which in several accounts ultimately paved the way for the young IKP philosophers to themselves become academicians, help crown Stalin as Lenin's heir in philosophy, and contribute to the transformation of Marxist-Leninist philosophy into a kind of watchdog metadiscipline.[116] The political authorization in this case, the organized or scripted element, actually comprised a directive to foment revolutionary zeal.

My concern in relaying this episode is not to indulge the oversimplified conclusion that IKP's pre-1929 culture of attack was exclusively Stalinist. Stalin in 1930, no less than Deborin in 1926, found it expedient to manipulate conventions already prevalent in party academic life, even if his manipulations by that time had the power to affect those conventions. IKP in the 1920s entrenched a kind of political-academic combat that was not unique to this institution, but which in the scholarly world was most developed there because of a distinctively militant, red professor ethos. This ethos was rooted in the group dynamics of its seminars, which centered around a process of exposing deviance, the conventions of which bore striking resemblance to other revolutionary rituals and Bolshevik cultural forms. Two major ways in which these conventions spread can be suggested: outward, to the nonparty academic community, and inward, to affect Marxism-Leninism itself.

115. I am summarizing Cassiday's illuminating and original discussion of "theatrical paradigm" in early Soviet show trials, which concentrates on the trial of SRs in 1922 and the Shakhtii trial of 1928. Cassiday, "Theater," 82–118.

116. The notes of a participant, the future academician Mitin, are cited by Rokitianskii, "Nesostoiavsheesia samoubiistvo," 459–60; see also V. V. Umshikhin, "'Nachalo kontsa' povedencheskoi psikhologii v SSSR," in M. G. Iaroshevskii, ed., *Repressirovannaia nauka* (Leningrad: Nauka, 1991), 137.

Krementsov's important discussion of rhetoric and rituals of Soviet science identifies a number of adaptations that the nonparty scholarly community made to imitate "Bolshevik lexicon and style" as well as specific political group activities. Focusing on the behavioral sciences, but allowing that he could be writing about any discipline, he traces the rise from the 1920s to the 1930s of a style of "ideological" criticism in professional critical literature, filled with martial rhetoric and primarily concerned with exposing dissent in a scholarly enemy. He also shows how certain kinds of ritualistic party activities—from criticism/self-criticism to jubilee meetings—took hold as a symbolic vehicle for scholars to demonstrate devotion.[117] As Krementsov implicitly recognizes, as these practices were incorporated into academia, they represented the norms not simply of the Party per se, but of party scholarship, developed in communist academic institutions.

Marxist social science itself, or more precisely Soviet Marxism as an intellectual system, evolved in tandem with the political culture and ingrained rituals of group behavior. After all, cognitive activity could not be kept discrete from the broader culture in which it was created, especially since that culture, as suggested most strongly in the case of IKP's mission to create the red expert, was explicitly concerned with breaking down barriers among the political, the social, and the academic.

In classical Marxist analysis, stripping away ideology to reveal underlying class interest was a central methodological device; yet the situation of the Bolshevik Party in the 1920s dictated a more pervasive and consequential urge to unmask. Soviet Marxism developed in a social order in which the imposition of "proletarian" or "class alien" affiliations onto a shifting, ambiguous social structure led to constant masking and unmasking of social identity.[118] In political life, especially in the cases of the Trotskyist and United Oppositions, the Party faced a struggle not just to condemn oppositionists declaring themselves to be the true orthodox Leninists but to reveal hidden oppositionists driven underground. Even more ominous, to escape reprisals oppositionists acted to all outward appearances the parts of loyal party members.[119]

Against this broader background, and in the context of an academic

117. Nikolai Krementsov, "Rhetoric and Rituals of Soviet Science," unpublished paper, 1–40, and his *Stalinist Science* (in press, Princeton University Press).

118. Daniel Orlovsky produces some interesting material suggesting the "masked quality of Soviet society" in "The Hidden Class: White-Collar Workers in the Soviet 1920s," in Siegelbaum and Suny, *Making Workers Soviet*, 220.

119. "Direktiva TsK ob otnosheniiakh k byvshym oppozitsioneram (utverzhdena Politbiuro TsK VKP(b) 18.X.1929)," RTsKhIDNI f. 17, op. 3, ed. khr. 763, l. 6.

culture rooted in the party struggle, scholarly and theoretical writings adopted specific methodologies of attack analogous to the methods deployed in the group dynamics of the seminar. For example, in January 1928 Bukharin's right-hand man, the IKP graduate and teacher Aleksandr Slepkov, wrote an article in the Party's theoretical journal called "Weapons of Victory." Ostensibly an essay on the history of the Cheka/GPU, arguing that the secret police was justified in preserving "extraordinary measures" during NEP, the centerpiece of the article was a denunciation of academician Tarle. Following the same conventions of attack we have seen in the seminars, the article unveiled compromising evidence from Tarle's past: the historian's 1918 collection of documents on French revolutionary terror was designed to prove the dangers of violence to revolution and thus, it was implied, discredit the secret police.[120] If Slepkov's technique was standard, the potential repercussions were unusually grave.

It was not just the particular methods of the political culture, however, that were homologous in the group seminars and the theoretical journals; so was the very centrality of the process of struggle and revealing disguised deviation. A paper from an IKP philosophy student written in the 1927–28 academic year, to cite but one example from a mode of thought, argued that "contemporary revisionism is marked by the fact that it calls itself orthodox, even more than that, *the most* orthodox Marxism."[121] The two organizing principles of this crystallizing intellectual style, struggle and the revelation of deviation, could at some point crowd out all other substance. The reponse of one psychologist, V. M. Borovskii, to a red professor describes this phenomenon best:

> Maliarov is trying to undertake the "pepper" style that Marx, Engels, and Lenin used in their polemical writings. But . . . their "pepper" was a tasty addition to a substantial meal. It is said that in bad cafes pepper is used to flavor rotten meat. Maliarov did an even simpler thing: he feeds you with pepper alone, without any meat or other food . . . It is not criticism, it is a fireworks show.[122]

120. A. Slepkov, "Orudie pobedy (k istoricheskoi roli chrezvychainykh organov po bor'be s kontrrevoliutsiei), *Bol'shevik*, no. 1 (15 January 1928), 46–55; the book cited is E. V. Tarle, *Revoliutsionnyi tribunal v epokhu Velikoi frantsuzskoi revoliutsii* (Moscow: "Byloe," 1918).

121. L. Man'kovskii, "Marksizm Georga Lukacha," in I. Luppol, ed., *Protiv noveishei kritiki marksizma. Sbornik kriticheskikh ocherkov* (Moscow-Leningrad: Gosizdat, 1929), 1.

122. Quoted in Krementsov, "Rhetoric and Rituals," 24.

The closing reference to a public display or performance also provides a telling clue to the tight links between political culture and intellectual style.

Party political commentary, as well, became a showcase for techniques of unmasking the "true" nature of the enemy, usually the opposite of what it declared itself to be. Movements disguising themselves as leftist were in reality rightist: Slepkov, a member of Bukharin's entourage and the IKP graduate who became the most prominent polemicist against the Trotskii and United Oppositions in the central party press, argued in 1924 that the Trotskyist opposition may have started out as "left," but soon found an ideological fusion with "right opportunist" tendencies.[123] In early 1928, he developed a similar argument to show that the Left Opposition had been transmuted into left Social-Democracy; therefore, Trotskyists masquerading as Bolsheviks were really ex-communist renegades even more dangerous than old, open opportunists.[124] At about the same time, another author in the same journal attempted to describe contemporary political analysis: "Rightists call leftists right, and leftists call rightists left in quotation marks; 'rightist rights' and 'leftist lefts,' 'rightist lefts' and 'leftist rights'—in truth, where is the line?" In this article, published months before the first hint of the Stalin-Bukharin conflict that unmasked the "Right Opposition" within the Party, and in fact printed in the theoretical journal dominated by Bukharin and his entourage of red professors, the author employed the convention of "dialectically" inventing a deviation. Since right deviation was objectively more dangerous at the given moment, he concluded, the left deviation "inevitably is transformed into the right deviation" and becomes "a singular expression of the right danger."[125] Unmasking had become an intellectual game; soon it would become high political drama.

123. A. Slepkov, "Ob 'uklonakh' i vozmozhnykh putiakh vozmozhnogo pererozhdeniia," *Bol'shevik*, no. 3–4 (20 May 1924), 23.

124. A. Slepkov, "Kak reagirovala oppozitsiia na resheniia XV s"ezda," *Bol'shevik*, no. 3–4 (29 February 1928), 19–31.

125. M. Brudnyi, "O pravoi i levoi opasnosti," *Bol'shevik*, no. 1 (15 January 1928), 26–34; in a similar vein, "Pravaia, levaia, gde storona," *Za leninskie kadry* 1 (March, 1930): 2. Suggestive insights into such relativistic pairings at the heart of Soviet "ideolanguage"—and their manipulation in the "inventions" of rightist and leftist deviations—are contained in Mikhail Epstein, "Relativistic Patterns in Totalitarian Thinking: The Linguistic Games of Soviet Ideology," in *After the Future: The Paradoxes of Postmodernism and Contemporary Russian Culture*, trans. Anesa Miller-Pogacar (Amherst: University of Massachusetts Press, 1995), esp. 128–29.

The Invented Opposition: IKP and the Revelation of the "Right Danger"

Because of its association with Bukharin when he was condemned as the head of a "right deviation," IKP in virtually all Western accounts has been characterized as a bastion of the Right in 1928–29.[126] But this not only misconstrues events at IKP itself, but conflates high-level factional struggle in the leadership with a related but distinct development, the political-ideological creation of a Right Opposition.

The trio of party leaders Bukharin, Rykov, and Tomskii, swiftly outmaneuvered by the Stalin majority in 1928 and branded as ringleaders of a right deviation, obviously conceived of themselves neither as rightists nor as deviationists; they were revealed as such. The political tendency they represented neither acted nor desired to act as an opposition; it was in the process of its defeat unmasked as such.[127] The "right deviation" in 1928–29 thus assumed perhaps its greatest importance, not in the political challenge its reluctant leader-victims made to the Stalin group in the high-level power struggle, but in precipitating a party-wide shift in the political culture. It marked a climax of several trends growing out of party political culture that we have seen affecting intellectual and ideological life as well: the eclipse of "conscious" opposition by the shadow world of masked dissent; the emerging centrality of the unmasking itself as process; and the diffusion of the "omnipresent conspiracy" to the point where hidden rightists were both everywhere and nowhere. Anyone familiar with party writings in 1928–29 will recognize the climate that led to a sharp increase in conspiratorial thinking, one casting suspicions on the ostensibly loyal and orthodox in a variety of

126. The classic account of the Right in 1928–29 is in Stephen F. Cohen, *Bukharin and the Bolshevik Revolution* (Oxford: Oxford University Press, 1980), 270–336. Cohen's most substantial source on IKP (431 n. 31; 296, 450 n. 118) and the most influential "eyewitness" account of the Stalin-Bukharin conflict in general, is Abdurakhman Avtorkhanov's attempt to combine memoirs and Sovietological analysis, *Stalin and the Soviet Communist Party: A Study in the Technology of Power* (New York: Praeger, 1959). Avtorkhanov, however, is not a reliable source. He claims to have been a well-connected IKP student linked to high-level rightists in Moscow in 1928–29, but his personal file from IKP Istorii, where he studied from 1934 to 1937 (GARF f. 5143, op. 1, d. 255), places him as a twenty-year-old rabfak student in Groznyi. In short, his depiction of Bukharinism cannot be separated from his reconstruction of his own past. For a full-length piece of source criticism, see Michael David-Fox, "Memory, Archives, Politics: The Rise of Stalin in Avtorkhanov's *Technology of Power*," *Slavic Review* 54 (Winter 1995): 988–1003.

127. See especially Merridale, *Moscow Politics*, 46 and passim.

contexts too wide to catalog here. Suffice it to say that the preoccupation with "double-dealing" dates to this period.[128]

The invention of opposition was, however, hardly a novel phenomenon in party life. To cite the most relevant precedent, a major preoccupation of the ruling triumvirate in 1924 was to create a doctrine labeled Trotskyism and depict it as utterly divorced from Leninism. When Zinov'ev and Kamenev joined Trotskii in the United Opposition, according to Trotskii's interesting 1927 explanation, Zinov'ev explained to his erstwhile enemy: "There was a struggle for power. The whole art consisted of linking old disagreements with new questions. For this purpose 'Trotskyism' came into being." But the power of endlessly reiterated political myths was such that after several years even some of their inventors began to believe them. At a meeting of Trotskii and Zinov'ev supporters at Kamenev's apartment, two Leningraders began to repeat the standard litany of Trotskyist deviations (underestimation of the peasantry, etc.) reportedly prompting Zinov'ev to exclaim: "What are you doing mixing yourselves up like that! After all we ourselves thought up this 'Trotskyism!'" Although Trotskii himself claimed to have understood long before that the triumvirate had striven deliberately to create Trotskyism, he registered the profound impression the incident had made upon him and his comrades.[129]

The difference between 1924 and 1928, however, was that while the creation of a deviation served as a political weapon in both cases, Trotskii and his followers were nonetheless willing and able to be an opposition; Bukharin and his fellow "rightists" only maneuvered as a group within the ruling leadership. While Trotskii supporters actively distributed platforms and documents in 1924 to student party cells, those branded as "rightists" bent over backward not to break party discipline and never brought the struggle to the rank and file even in Moscow.[130]

The "right danger," as we saw in the rhetoric of the future "rightist"

128. For example, Em. Iaroslavskii, "O dvurushnichestve voobshche i dvurushnikakh-trotskistakh v chastnosti," *Bol'shevik*, no. 4 (28 February 1929), 18–28. The creation of "the image of an organized 'Right Opposition'" is all too briefly invoked as a starting point for Gábor Támas Rittersporn's "The Omnipresent Conspiracy: On Soviet Imagery of Politics and Social Relations in the 1930s," in Getty and Manning, *Stalinist Terror*, 106.

129. "K voprosu o proiskhozhdenii legendy o 'Trotskizme' (Dokumental'naia spravka)," 21 November 1927, Trotsky Archive, bMS Russ 13-T-3122.

130. Catherine Merridale, "The Reluctant Opposition: The Right 'Deviation' in Moscow, 1928," *Soviet Studies* 41 (July 1989): 382–400.

Slepkov, had entered into the party lexicon well before the "right deviation."[131] The "whole art" for Stalin in 1928–29 was to link the diffuse danger most frequently associated with specialists, NEPmen, and bureaucrats with the particular personages of his factional enemies; at the same time, keeping the danger diffuse by stepping up the hunt for still unnamed, hidden rightists surely helped cripple potential inner-party objections to the Great Break.

The significant place IKP assumed in the invention of the right deviation cannot be understood outside the institution's emergence as a distinct symbol in the inner-party struggle in the mid-1920s, when a small but tightly knit group in Bukharin's entourage gained notoriety as the institute's most prominent publicists against inner-party opposition. This group of about fifteen red professors, including the brothers Slepkov, Aikhenval'd, Astrov, David Petrovich Rozit, Aleksei Ivanovich Stetskii, A. N. Zaitsev, and others, gained prominence and a degree of notoriety through their work at *Bol'shevik* and *Pravda*; many also worked in Bukharin's personal secretariat and continued to teach at IKP. As a group, they became known as the "Bukharin School."[132]

In their primary work as party publicists, these red professors produced among the most vociferous attacks on the successive oppositions; some of their number were sent to Leningrad after Zinov'ev's ouster in order to clean house ideologically through regional and local agitprop departments in the oppositionist stronghold. Small wonder it was the Leningrad oppositionists who first attacked this group as a "new school" at IKP, making derogatory references to the red professoriat and associating this prominent yet small circle with the institute as a whole. The Leningrad Opposition thus mobilized the anti-scholastic imagery brought out in 1924 by the party majority against Trotskii. Interestingly enough, two Trotskii supporters also joined in this tradition in 1927; while polemicizing with red professors representing the official line, they depicted the Bukharin School as the Party's "specialists" in discrediting oppositionist platforms; the aim was to associate "professor Slepkov" and his colleagues with bourgeois specialists, and the term

131. See, for example, Trotsky's 1927 identification of "the right danger," which he here associated most closely with Rykov and "Rykovites," as the main threat of Thermidor. "Iul'skii plenum i pravaia opasnost' (Posleslovino k pis'mu 'Chto zhe dal'she')," 22 June 1927, Trotsky Archive, bMS Russ 13-T-3126.

132. For a full-length discussion of the Bukharin School and its members, see C. I. P. Ferdinand, "The Bukharin Group of Political Theoreticians" (Ph.D. diss., Oxford University, 1984); for evidence on work in Bukharin's secretariat, see GARF f. 5284, op. 1, d. 56, l. 6. See also Cohen, *Bukharin*, 217–18.

Bukharin with his students from the Institute of Red Professors (mid-1920s). Sitting in the first row (left to right): Ivan Adamovich Kravaev, Ian Ernestovich Sten, and Vasilii Nikolaevich Slepkov. In the second row (left to right): Dmitrii Petrovich Maretskii, A. N. Zaitsev, Grigorii Petrovich Maretskii, Nikolai Ivanovich Bukharin, David Petrovich Rozit, Aleksei Ivanovich Stetskii, Aleksandr Iakovlevich Troitskii, and Aleksandr Nikolaevich Slepkov. Reprinted by permission of the Museum of the Revolution, Moscow, Russia.

spetsy was repeated several times for emphasis. Now, it was the party orthodox, in the person of Iaroslavskii, who defended the revolutionary credentials of the red professors, praising them as "among the best communist-Leninists."[133]

133. V. Emel'ianov and T. Khorechko, "Nash otvet Slepkovu," in Iu. Fel'shtinskii, ed., *Arkhiv Trotskogo* (Moscow: Terra, 1990), 4: 87–98; and Iaroslavskii's articles "O novoi shkole" (orig. in RTsKhIDNI f. 89, op. 8, d. 452, l. 1–2), *Pravda*, 24 December 1925, 3, and "Novoe i staroe v 'novoi' oppozitsii," *Pravda*, 24 July 1927, 5; Ferdinand, "Bukharin Group," 96. After the experience of reprisals against the opposition in 1924, the United Opposition found little

As Stalin and Bukharin and their allies fell out in the first half of 1928 in part over programmatic differences stemming from the Party's left turn, there is some evidence that factional maneuvering in the Moscow party committee shook the leadership of the IKP party cell. By summer, Stalin used his traditional strength in party appointments to remove members of the Bukharin School from the editorial board of *Pravda*. Around the same time, Bukharin apparently acquiesced to the transfer of about fifteen red professors from his "school" to provincial teaching assignments around the country. The timing is crucial. These factional maneuverings, which organizationally decapitated a potential "right opposition" at IKP, took place during or before the summer months of 1928.[134] Yet the political maelstrom surrounding "rightists," and indeed the entire ideological creation of a right deviation, occurred during and after the fall of 1928, in fact after the Bukharin school at IKP was either absent or defeated.

It is in the revelation of the Right Opposition that Stalin's political theater came into play. A storm of attacks on the "right danger" in the Party was unleashed in the fall of 1928; even Bukharin and his associates took part in denouncing the Right. Stalin's tension-building technique was a six-month-long unmasking of rightists, beginning with small or abstract targets and culminating in the condemnation of "Bukharin and Co." in February 1929.[135] On top of the self-criticism upheaval, the anti-specialist turn, and the campaign against the right danger, the final unmasking of Bukharin, Rykov, and Tomskii as the revealed rightist leaders followed in the best traditions of revolutionary theater—especially the kind, as in the most riveting agit-trials, where the full extent of the guilt of the masked enemy is tantalizingly unclear for a lengthy period.

At the party schools, the shake-up in the Moscow Party Committee in October–November 1928, a key moment in linking the right danger to Bukharin's person, caused vast confusion until political orientation was regained. This itself indicates a degree of distance between the creation of the right deviation and the factional struggles preceeding it. For ex-

---

support at IKP. One report put the number of IKP students supporting the opposition in 1926 at 10 percent of the total. M. Shamberg, "Oppozitsionnyi blok i studenchestvo," *Krasnoe studenchestvo*, no. 8 (1 November 1926), 4–6.

134. See a lengthy Politburo document on struggles at *Pravda*, "Chlenam i kandidatam TsK VKP(b). 6.IX.1929," RTsKhIDNI f. 17, op. 3, ed. khr. 756, l. 16; Ferdinand, "Bukharin Group," 246–47; "Dorogoi tovarishch," Moscow Trotskyist(?) to Trotskii(?), September 1928, Trotsky Archive, T2442.

135. Daniels, *Conscience*, 336–44.

ample, sixty members of the Communist Academy cell on 24 October convened a closed meeting that opened with the declaration that the problem of the "Right Opposition" had arisen in the previous three or four days. A discussion ensued at which the right danger was ritually condemned, but speakers could not bring themselves to believe Bukharin was its personification. According to the speaker Vainshtein, "The right deviation undoubtedly exists and it is necessary to fight it. . . . [But] there are no deviations with Bukharin." Egorov warned: "We begin to break party discipline speaking about deviations in the TsK and Politburo." Faingar came out with the most interesting statement: "The right deviation is much more dangerous (if it exists) than the left. In the matter of party information things are very bad. Sometimes nonparty people know more than we do ourselves. . . . Recently I heard from one bourgeois lady (a masseuse) that Bukharin was removed from the post of editor of 'Pravda.'" Were these communist students closet Bukharinists? It is highly doubtful, since they first unanimously voted to "direct the fire against the right deviation, which represents the main danger in our party" and then plaintively demanded better party information.[136]

At Sverdlov University's cell in November, one activist caused a commotion by dramatically declaring: "Right here at the university there are deviations of a left and right nature (noise). . . . The Bureau together with the party organizers must expose and destroy them." Yet a moment later the same speaker added: "And if they do not exist, then that is good (noise)."[137] Was this activist masking the existence of the right deviation, or were deviationists masking themselves? Even if neither were the case, the process of unmasking would go on.

The very existence of rightists, of course, depended how such deviationists were defined. Reports showing a reluctance to make "struggle with the right deviation" a main priority could be used to demonstrate the existence of such a deviation.[138] A hunt for masked deviationists in late 1928 and 1929 became important for the sake of the hunt itself and branched out from rightists to "conciliationists," waverers, "objective" rightists, and those who underestimated the right danger.

At IKP in the fall of 1928, the situation was somewhat different in that Bukharin and his supporters had personally been present, and three

136. "Protokol No. 7 obshchego sobraniia chlenov i kandidatov VKP(b) iacheiki Kom. Akademii ot 24–go Oktiabria 1928," RGAODgM f. 477, op. 1, ed. khr. 20, l. 102–4.

137. "Protokol No. 5 obshchego sobraniia iacheiki Komuniversiteta Sverdlova ot 29/XI-1928," RGAODgM f. 459, op. 1, d. 30, l. 48–50.

138. See, for example, "Protokol No. 4 zasedaniia Biuro iacheiki Komuniversiteta Sverdlova ot 17–go oktiabria 28 g.," RGAODgM f. 459, op. 1, d. 31, l. 70.

or four members of the cell of about 300 members were stigmatized as associates of the removed members of Bukharin's entourage. Despite months of protestation of their loyalty to the party line and their anti-rightism, much activity in the cell revolved around unmasking their right opportunism. In the course of 1929, they too were purged. By 1929, much IKP theoretical work was directed against the anti-Leninist "mistakes of the right opportunists."[139]

The two factions that vied for control in IKP's party cell in the fall of 1928 may well have been motivated by personal animosities and desire for organizational command. Their concrete political differences became arguments over whether to struggle more to root out left oppositionists or right deviationists. Both groups expressed full support for the general line of the Party; indeed, the cell was later commended in a January Central Committee resolution for having "fulfilled the tasks of struggle with the right deviation." However, spokesmen for the minority "left-wing" group (reportedly twenty percent of cell members) took the position that rightism was still pervasive and that that hidden Slepkovites remained at IKP. They complained the majority was spending as much time fighting them (as leftists) as rooting out rightists. To resolve the intractable conflict that had paralyzed the cell, Pokrovskii and thirty-five red professors were called in to a January 1929 meeting with Stalin and Molotov at the Central Committee Secretariat.

According to the report of a participant who took verbatim notes and sent them to the Moscow party committee, Stalin ordered a compromise in which the cell bureau was reelected and factional struggle renounced. Stalin, clearly not pleased with the leftist minority, remarked pointedly that conciliators of the left opposition were now appearing, and that the struggle against left deviationism was being forgotten; Molotov made clear that the left minority was harder to control from the Central Committee's point of view. Both sides were reprimanded in somewhat different terms for ignoring struggle on two fronts, against both Left and Right. Stalin's decisions were later written up point by point in a resolution on IKP's cell put out in the name of the Central

139. See the letter from one teacher associated with Bukharin: Vladimir Kuz'min, "Pis'mo v redaktsiiu 'Izvestii.' Kopiia v Biuro iacheiki IKP, 5/III-29," RGAODgM f. 474, op. 1, ed. khr. 9, l. 78; "Vyvody po obsledovaniiu iacheiki [IKP] sostavitelei za vremia s 1/1 po 1/X/29," ibid., d. 9, l. 150–73; and, for example, the report for Adoratskii's seminar for third-year students in the "history of the party" department: Ian P. Krastyn', "Lenin o soiuze proletariat s krest'ianstvom i oshibki pravykh opportunistov," no date, 1929, GARF f. 5284, op. 1, ed. khr. 384, l. 50–103.

Committee.[140] Here we observe Stalin dampening revolutionary zeal when it threatened to produce organizational breakdown. But the episode also confirms that IKP politics in the fall and winter of 1928 had elevated the shadow struggle to the point where it had become a liability to the leadership that had encouraged it.

None of this prevented IKP as a whole from being attacked as a stronghold of Bukharinism. Radicals from the institute itself turned on the IKP cell as "an organization of lacquered Communists, Slepkovites and concealed right opportunists." In defense against these and similar accusations, the bureau of the cell several times documented all the measures taken against those few associated with the Right and protested bitterly to the Central Committee that "one cannot fling these accusations at the whole cell simply because there were a few comrades close to Bukharin and Slepkov at IKP."[141] Similarly, IKP also came under fire in the central press in 1929. Long after Bukharin, Rykov and Tomskii had been disgraced, it was felt necessary to prove that "rightists use united tactics in their struggle with the party"—in effect, to establish that the Right was a genuine opposition, like the Left Opposition before it.[142] IKP continued to be a convenient symbol, its members forced to prove their loyalty and revolutionary credentials over and over again.

The making of the right deviation after the fall of 1928, and the association of the "right danger" with inner-party opposition, thus grew out of the high-level leadership skirmishes that preceded it.[143] The distinction, and the elusiveness of the Right itself, is implied in an analysis by Lars Lih: "There is an air of paradox about the right deviation. On the one hand, it was an ephemeral political opposition, quickly called into being by Stalin's change of course in 1928 and as quickly

140. "IKP, po informatsii t. Fin'kovskogo na biuro R[ai] K[oma]," 3 December 1928, RGAODgM f. 474, op. 1, d. 9, l. 50–54; "Rezoliutsiia TsK o polozhenii v iacheike IKP," no later than 18 January 1929, ibid., l. 2–3. Students then wrote letters of self-criticism to renounce their previous positions. See l. 181–83. Other documents from IKP's cell support this reconstruction of events; for example, "Protokol obshchego sobraniia part"iacheiki IKP," 18 January 1929, ibid., l. 1. One memoir identifies Fin'kovskii as an Old Bolshevik, head of the raikom where IKP was located, and a "well-known troubleshooter." Sheng, *Sun Yat-sen University*, 29.

141. "V TsK VKP(b)," no date, 1929, ARAN f. 1759, op. 2, d. 21, l. 168, and 1. 94–100; RGAODgM f. 474, op. 1, d. 9, l. 4, 20–22, 25.

142. "Fraktsionnaia vylazka pravykh v iacheike Instituta krasnoi professury," *Pravda*, 13 November 1929, 3; G. K., "Reshitel'nyi otpor pravym," *Izvestiia*, 28 February 1929.

143. The use of the term "deviation" rather than "opposition" as the standard appellation thereafter is significant because it indicates a reluctance even on the part of the victors to accord the Right the status of a full-fledged opposition.

defeated. On the other hand, it seemed to the Stalinist leadership to be a permanent enemy that could never be entirely rooted out." Lih suggests that rightism in Stalin's mind was connected to the notion of infection from bourgeois specialists that could touch any party member, and thus the right deviation "was defined less by any specific set of beliefs than by the logic of Stalin's attitude."[144] It is interesting that Lih's insight applies not just to Stalin's particular mindset (for even he was in many ways the product of his milieu) but to a political culture revolving around combating infection, even, if necessary, before it appeared. The case of IKP is especially poignant, for in its search for the red expert it had been struggling for the greater part of a decade to immunize itself against the specialist within—the manifestations of "scholasticism" and "academicism," the dangers of divorce from the proletarian masses, that the party scholars and intellectuals perceived in their own midst and which party higher education strove to combat.

The search for the red expert at IKP, the attempt to mold a type of educated and scholarly Bolshevik who would not be contaminated by such qualities, became a prime Bolshevik initiative in the Marxist social sciences during NEP and in the history of the party intelligentsia. The enterprise was born in conflict bequeathed by the identity crisis of party scholars and the anti-intellectualism of the Bolshevik intellectuals. It was shaped by the evolving structure of life in the party institution, marked by constant evaluation, purges that fused wide-ranging categories of evaluation, a curriculum uneasily poised between *nauka* and mass Marxism, and the shocks of the social reconstruction of an elite institution. This environment, combined with the ethos of the young red professors, contributed to a distinctively combative brand of Bolshevik political culture which informed both the party intellectual style at IKP and the practice of politics. This culture's particular techniques of unmasking hidden deviance within the context of an omnipresent struggle extended from the education in the seminars, to the theoretical writing in the social sciences, to the inner-party political process. In this sense, the written word and the group gathering formed part of a continuum, a stage upon which the embattled red expert acted out a drama of revolutionary struggle.

The intricate web of interconnections explored here between culture, politics, and intellectual style point to a kind of Bolshevik ecosystem in

144. Lars Lih, introduction to Lih et al., eds., *Stalin's Letters to Molotov* (New Haven: Yale University Press, 1995), 49.

which the constituent parts evolved in tandem.[145] The analogy is useful, for an ecosystem can undergo shocks: IKP in the 1920s witnessed two such major shifts, the watershed of 1924 and the attack on the Right in 1928–29. In between, we have traced the spread within the ecosystem of a predator, an element of malignant fantasy: the struggle against hidden deviance, the elevation of the process of unmasking over the face of the unmasked. The underlying structures, the cultural predisposition, and the immediate political rationale were all in place so that this predatory component of the system could rage unchecked. For the communist intellectuals—to paraphrase a pertinent observation about revolutions—"Stalinism" was not made; it came.[146]

145. After I had arrived at this metaphor via political culture and institutional environment in the 1920s, I discovered that at the center of Clark's recent work is the notion of an "ecology of revolution," used to describe a cultural system which, rather than developing in a unilinear fashion, was marked by "punctuated evolution." Clark, *Petersburg*, ix–28.

146. Wendall Phillips's aphorism is referred to in Theda Skocpol, *States and Social Revolutions* (Cambridge: Cambridge University Press, 1979), 17.

4 /

SCIENCE, ORTHODOXY, AND THE QUEST FOR HEGEMONY AT THE SOCIALIST (COMMUNIST) ACADEMY

Bolshevik intellectuals presented their cause as a class struggle with bourgeois academia. Their primary field of battle in higher learning, however, was first and foremost institutional. When Evgenii B. Preobrazhenskii insisted in the Socialist Academy's newly founded journal in 1922 that the academy "represents the highest scientific research institute of Marxist thought," the academy leader was linking the Bolshevik declaration of war in organized intellectual life to his own institutional base. It has rarely been considered, but such assertions of primacy implied as many internal ramifications for the Bolsheviks as outward effects for the nonparty intellectual world.

The Socialist Academy—Preobrazhenskii elaborated on his claim to authority—"does not recognize social science not operating on the basis of Marxism. . . . The Academy must turn itself into its own kind of Gosplan in the realm of ideology."[1] In this formulation, the assertion of *orthodoxy*, and the vision of a new kind of planned science, or *nauka*, is intertwined with the claim to *hegemony*—not simply of a doctrine, a party, or a class, but of an institution.[2]

1. E. Preobrazhenskii, "Blizhaishie zadachi Sotsialisticheskoi Akademii," *Vestnik Sotsialisticheskoi Akademii* (henceforth cited as *VSA*), no. 1 (November 1922): 7, 9.

2. "Hegemony" is employed not in the Gramscian sense, but in the blunter meaning most frequently implicit in the Bolshevik use of the word *gegemoniia*, denoting wide-ranging domination, political subordination, and control over activities and resources.

No matter that Gosplan, the central state planning agency, was of negligible importance at the time Preobrazhenskii wrote; no matter, indeed, that the Socialist (after 1924, Communist) Academy never achieved the hegemony in the Soviet scholarly world that its leaders coveted. The fact that the Party's leading theorists at the academy treated issues of orthodoxy and the creation of a new science squarely within the context of monopolistic institutional aspirations had a profound impact on the development of party-Marxist academia in the 1920s. The history of the Communist Academy is the history of a failed quest for institutional hegemony.

"Party scholarship," a term I use to denote a party-Marxist movement in higher learning which made the academy its flagship institution, emerged only at the end of the civil war as a confluence of developments: the suppression of the other socialist parties, the first attempts to establish sanctioned programs in the social sciences, and the foundation of Communist Party academic institutions. Although there were many feuding divisions within it, party scholarship was in its broadest outlines cohesive during NEP: it identified with an official ideology (party Marxism, or, as it was called after Lenin's death, Marxism-Leninism), a political movement in control of the state (the Bolshevik Party), a social group (the party intelligentsia), and an institutional base (the new party institutions of theory and research). Because the Communist Academy emerged in the early 1920s as the most influential bastion of party scholarship, its evolution is a window into the entire relationship between the movement's dreams of monopoly and the life of the mind.

In the changing world of postrevolutionary academia, the representatives of party scholarship were frequently powerful party politicians and state regulators. The academy's presidium—a small group approved by the Orgburo with the mandate to set institutional policy, modeled more on the bureau of a party cell than the bourgeois faculty meeting—was for most of the 1920s headed by the deputy commissar of education Pokrovskii and the influential economic adviser and TsIK official Miliutin.[3] Yet powerful Bolshevik officials and theorists were in the aca-

3. Miliutin superseded Preobrazhenskii as the informally designated second-in-command in the presidium after the latter became a leader of the Trotskyist Opposition in 1923. In 1922 the presidium included a Politburo member (Bukharin), Pokrovskii, Preobrazhenskii, Miliutin, an academy founder and member of the collegium of the commissariat of foreign affairs (Fedor A. Rotshtein), and a leading Bolshevik intellectual and editor of *Izvestiia* (Ivan I. Svortsov-Stepanov). In 1924 it was expanded by adding the head of Agitprop, Bubnov; the historian of the French Revolution, Nikolai M. Lukin; and party scholars Volgin, Timiriazev, and Riazanov. "Vypiska iz protokola zasedaniia Orgbiuro TsK ot 14/VIII-22 g. No. 46," RTsKhIDNI f. 147,

demic realm essentially parvenu competitors against established non-Marxist and nonparty scholars in discipline after discipline. This proved a compelling reason for the communist scholars to assert their own institutional base along with their scholarly authority.

The academy, in consequence, formulated an emerging set of core institutional aspirations. Articulated by academy leaders and running like a red thread through the academy's history, these missions spurred institutional change in the course of the 1920s. They coexisted in several distinct varieties. The oldest, dating from the civil war period, was the ambition of becoming the Party's "theoretical center," which would influence (and, perhaps, regulate) Marxist methodology. In the midst of the rapid expansion of NEP, this overlapped with more concrete plans of establishing the academy as the premier Marxist scientific-research institution, which would (at least in the future) control or approve plans for other party institutions. Finally, hegemonic goals spilled over into higher learning as a whole. In its most grandiose moments, the Communist Academy aspired to become the dominant scholarly institution in the land, or, as Pokrovskii often put it, a party academy of sciences.

The most obsessive, if sometimes camouflaged impulse behind the monopolistic yearnings of the Communist Academy revolved around the nonparty scholars, "bourgeois" professors, and their prominent institutions. Insofar as they were perceived as the main institutional-ideological threat to Bolshevik intellectuals, the nonparty scholars received the full brunt of the Communist Academy's institutionalized *Angst*. The rise of party scholarship thus occurred in a subtle dialogue with nonparty academia, and the Communist Academy's evolution is unintelligible outside this rivalry. The Communist Academy leaders not only scorned their "bourgeois" counterparts; at the same time, they coveted their prestige and the material wealth of their institutions.

The Communist Academy's evolution was also driven by the innovations and organization of party scholarship. To justify its desired position in the new scholarly world, the academy was prompted to transform itself from a "Marxist debating club with a library"[4] in 1918 to a sprawling but centrally run network of research institutes and societies in the 1920s that increasingly defined their aims in terms of service for the Party and the state. In part to reinforce its claims as an emerging

op. 1, ed. khr. 33, l. 2; for other Orgbiuro protocols from August 1922 and October 1924, see l. 4 and 13. For a full listing of presidium members, see Joel Shapiro, "A History of the Communist Academy, 1918–1936" (Ph.D. diss., Columbia University, 1976), 356–59. A bureau of the presidium was created in 1926.

4. The phrase is in Fitzpatrick, *Education*, 68.

"party Academy of Sciences," the academy pressed to the forefront of the effort to put "collective work," academic planning and "practical" tasks at the top of the scholarly agenda. Both developments significantly changed the face of Marxist scholarship in the 1920s.

The development of the Communist Academy is also connected to the problem of orthodoxy. There is an obvious distinction between the orthodoxy of Soviet Marxism of the 1920s—when a major dynamic was a competition for the claim to doctrinal truth—and the *partiinost'* (party-mindedness) of the Stalin period, in which the decisions of the Party and its leadership were enshrined as the highest court. As John Barber has put it, "By the late 1920s this concept [of *partiinost'*] had undergone a major change from its original Leninist form. . . . [T]he principle was firmly established that the worth of intellectual work depended primarily on whether or not it assisted the achievement of the regime's objectives."[5] Yet the key question for the historian—precisely how such a principle was "firmly established"—remains a mystery.

The enforcement and definition of orthodoxy at the Communist Academy was directly shaped by the values and ambitions of party scholarship. Inverting the twin standards of pure science and institutional autonomy associated with liberalism and nonparty academia, the academy reoriented itself more tightly around service to the party-state. In tandem with this, the new *partiinost'* originated as a kind of ideological service function that superseded older Bolshevik conceptions of science.

The Bolshevik intellectuals thus set out to conquer the academic world. In several senses, theirs was a split field of vision. They dreamed about the future, yet maneuvered ceaselessly through the here and now; they tried to harness the sanction of the top party leadership, yet their yardstick of measurement was the "bourgeois" academicians. In all cases, the most striking effect was the drawn-out transformation of their own enterprise.

Three Incarnations of the Socialist Academy

The idea of founding the Socialist Academy of Social Sciences (*Sotsialisticheskaia Akademiia Obshchestvennykh Nauk*, or SAON) reportedly originated in early spring 1918 when Bolshevik jurist Mikhail A.

5. John Barber, "The Establishment of Intellectual Orthodoxy in the U.S.S.R., 1928–1934," *Past and Present* 83 (May 1979): 153–54. On the origins and transformation of the concept of *partiinost'*, see the classic account in "Lenin and the Partyness of Philosophy," chapter 2 of Joravsky, *Soviet Marxism*, 24–44.

Reisner, who had studied law in Warsaw and Heidelberg, complained to Pokrovskii about the poor theoretical knowledge of many comrades. Two further justifications for a new institution became apparent. As Lenin suggested when he heard Pokrovskii's report on SAON on 25 May 1918, the academy could organize a badly needed press to publish Marxist classics and social science research.[6] At the same time, the resistance of the professoriat at Moscow University to the new regime was at its height, and a new academy was attractive as a political counterweight. The provisional budget of 3.5 million rubles in 1918, half of it reserved for 30 full members and 145 staff, indicated the new regime's willingness to support the fledgling institution at a level not radically lower than that of the Academy of Sciences.[7]

Pokrovskii, in his keynote address at the academy's gala jubilee ten years later, divided the academy's history into three stages—1918, 1919–21, and post-1922: "If the Hindu brahmins, as is well known, are born twice, then our Academy has been born at least three times." This periodization is indeed clearly marked by successive academy charters, membership, and missions. It is interesting that the Marxist historian, whose ultra-materialist approach to Russian history was later branded as "vulgar sociologism," emphasized a much more subjective, even elusive factor when contemplating the history of his own institution. The evolution of the early Socialist Academy, he implied, was fueled by its articulation of its mission and its relationship with the Party.[8]

In its first, shortest-lived incarnation, the academy was marked by an eclectic membership and an enthusiasm for socialist unity. The academy's 1918 charter, approved by Sovnarkom on 15 June, called for a free association promoting "scientific advancement of questions of socialism and communism." The original membership list, approved by Sovnarkom ten days later, reads like a who's who of international socialism and includes members (the elitist title "academician" was never used) such as Kautsky, Luxembourg, Longuet, Hilferding and others unlikely to participate in the academy's affairs.[9]

6. "Primechanie M. Pokrovskogo," *VSA*, no. 1 (November 1922): 38–39; V. A. Doroshenko, "Kommunisticheskaia Akademiia i ee rol' v razrabotke voprosov otechestvennoi istorii (1918–1935)" (Candidate of Sciences diss., Moscow State University, 1968, 22).

7. M. N. Pokrovskii, "Kommunisticheskaia Akademiia (kratkii ocherk)," *Informatsionnyi biulleten'* [Kommunisticheskoi Akademii], no. 3–4 (June–December 1926): 1; Shapiro, "Communist Academy," 38–40; Kendall Bailes, "Natural Scientists and the Soviet System," in Koenker et al., *Russian Civil War*, 271.

8. "10 let Kommunisticheskoi Akademii. Vstupitel'noe slovo M. N. Pokrovskogo na iubileinom zasedanii plenuma Kommunisticheskoi akademii 25 maia 1928 g.," *Vestnik Kommunisticheskoi Akademii* (henceforth cited as *VKA*), no. 28, (1928): 8–18.

9. "Polozhenie o Sotsialisticheskoi Akademii Obshchestvennykh Nauk," no date, 1918,

Non-Marxists on the Russian Left such as Belyi, Blok, and Ivanov-Razumnik—literary figures most closely associated with the Left SRs—were also included as members. In fact, Left SRs involved in setting up the academy, including D. A. Cherepanov and D. A. Magerovskii, reportedly insisted on calling the academy "Socialist" rather than "Communist," and this name was already established before the Left SRs were expelled following their break with the Bolsheviks in June 1918. In one of the first meetings of the academy's "Scientific-Academic section" on 14 June a new composition of academy members was ratified by a small core group of academy founders, including Pokrovskii, Reisner, the Marxologist David B. Riazanov, and former Left Bolshevik Aleksandr A. Bogdanov. They supported Riazanov's proposal to remove candidates for membership who belonged to the SR party.[10]

The scholarly mission of the academy in its first incarnation was blurry, since it was not certain whether most energies would be channeled into a socialist higher school or into advanced research. The early academy was preoccupied not with the "scientific-research" section, as the original charter termed it, but above all with the "study-enlightenment" department, consisting of a "free higher school . . . familiarizing the broad masses with the teachings of socialism and communism." Academy members taught their areas of expertise: Skvortsov-Stepanov lectured on political economy, Proletkul't literary critic and future head censor Pavel I. Lebedev-Polianskii on proletarian literature, Lukin on the French Revolution, and so on. But when the academy opened its doors to 1,870 students in October 1918, the toiling masses largely stayed away: almost two-thirds of the students had either completed secondary education or had attended university, and 92.4 percent were listed as engaging in "intellectual labor."[11]

The 1918 charter called for an egalitarian, democratic power struc-

---

ARAN f. 643, op. 1, d. 158, 1. 2–3; Shapiro, "Communist Academy," 20–23, 31–38. The appendixes of this dissertation contain lists of academy members and the composition of its presidium from 1918 to 1930.

10. A. Udal'tsov, "Ocherk istorii Sotsialisticheskoi Akademii (1918–1922 g.g.)," *VSA*, no. 1 (November 1922): 14; "Protokol No. 1 zasedaniia Nauchno-Akademicheskoi sektsii Sotsialisticheskoi Akademii Obshchestvennykh Nauk," 14 June 1918, GARF f. 3415, op. 1, d. 5, l. 1–3; "Protokol No. 2 Soedinennogo obshchego sobraniia Nauchno-Akademicheskoi i Uchebno-Prosvetitel'noi sektsii Sotsialisticheskoi Akademii Obshchestvennykh Nauk," 8 August 1918, ibid., l. 4–6. Early core members also included the Marxist literary critic Vladimir M. Friche, jurist Aleksandr G. Goikhbarg, and several others.

11. "Polozhenie o Sotsialisticheskoi Akademii," 1918 (cited in full at note 9); "Raspisanie lektsii i zaniatii po sotsial'no-istoricheskomu razriadu Sotsialisticheskoi Akademii Obshchestvennykh Nauk na II-i trimestr 1918–1919 uch. g.," ARAN f. 597, op. 3, d. 5, l. 3; "Svedenie o sostave slushatelei Sotsialisticheskoi Akademii k 15 oktiabria 1918 g.," GARF f. 5221, op. 4, d. 103, l. 2–3.

ture capped by a central and a student soviet. But the fifteen places on the student soviet were usurped by the Bolshevik faction in a meeting on 6 October 1918, although only 23.69 percent of the students were listed as Communists, and 55 percent of the students belonged to no party. On 29 October the communist faction passed a new regulation: SAON would accept as students only supporters of soviet power, defined as those who could present two recommendations from proletarian or Soviet organizations, or two well-known party members, confirming that they stood on a "soviet platform."[12] The original conception of a "free school" open to all over age sixteen was soon further undermined. A student meeting in February 1919 voted to accept only students with a "communist worldview," and, in keeping with the practice of party schools, to have the bulk of them nominated directly by party, Red Army and Soviet institutions. This resolution was accepted 49–12.[13] Socialist unity was being replaced by Bolshevik primacy.

In this and one other important respect the early years set the tone for the rest of the academy's history: its leaders were from the outset acutely aware of the institution's great historical purpose. In the fall of 1918, a proclamation written and translated into major foreign languages expressed its grandiose sense of mission. "The peasantry built cathedrals; the aristocracy, castles and palaces; the bourgeoisie created theaters and universities," it read. "The proletariat has founded the Socialist Academy."[14] Although such romantic language went out of style with war communism, the sweep of the academy's ambitions remained.

Another element of continuity with the future was that even the initial flush of socialist solidarity did not forstall action to stake out a position as the new republic's authority in the social sciences. In June 1918 the Academy of Sciences attempted to expand its activities in the social sciences by founding an Institute of Social Sciences in Petrograd, which would, as academicians such as Aleksandr S. Lappo-Danilevskii envisaged it, provide a bulwark against future encroachments by Marxism. The newly founded Socialist Academy, consulted on the advisability of the project, managed to deliver a decisive veto.[15]

The academy's "second birth" in 1919 was decisive in further altering the political and ideological physiognomy of the fledgling institu-

12. Udal'tsov, "Ocherk," 23; "Protokol komiteta po delam slushatelei ot 21-go noiabria 1918," GARF f. 3415, op. 1, d. 36, l. 1; Doroshenko, "Kommunisticheskaia Akademiia," 33.

13. "Protokol obshchego sobraniia slushatelei Sotsialisticheskoi Akademii Obshchestvennykh Nauk" 21 February 1919, GARF f. 3415, op. 1, d. 26, l. 2.

14. Quoted in Udal'tsov, "Ocherk," 17.

15. Vucinich, *Empire of Knowledge*, 97–98; Shapiro, "Communist Academy," 43–45.

tion. In a major overhaul of its membership, nineteen of the thirty-nine academy members were new, and the socialist dignitaries abroad were dropped. In its second incarnation, the academy membership list encompassed prominent Bolshevik theorists. The new equivalents of Kautsky and Hilferding were top Bolsheviks who rarely if ever participated in the academy's work, such as Zinov'ev, Kamenev, Krupskaia, Kollontai, and Trotskii. The list also included prominent party intellectuals who participated as much as time and politics would allow, such as Radek, Bukharin, and Lunacharskii; and the active core participants including Miliutin, Lukin, Skvortsov-Stepanov, Friche, the historian of utopian socialism Viacheslav P. Volgin, and the other founders mentioned earlier. There remained several major exceptions to the new rule: Menshevik leader Iulii Martov was a new member in 1919 and remained in the academy until 1921, along with leftists such as Maxim Gor'kii, Nikolai N. Sukhanov, and Vladimir A. Bazarov, the former Bolshevik "godbuilder" then associated with the Mensheviks.[16]

Documentation on the academy's activities during the civil war is sparse, but a shift in emphasis in the second phase is clearly discernible. The chief goal now was to become a theoretical center. The civil war academy was essentially a forum for papers and a sponsor of a few high-profile publications. The best-known example was Bukharin and Preobrazhenskii's *ABC of Communism*, drafts of which were reviewed in academy sessions.[17]

This move toward a center of theory came about because of the collapse of the enlightenment section. Academy members later referred to the "crisis of 1919," when virtually all the students were sent off to fight at the front. The entrance of at least some top Marxists into the universities and creation of social science faculties (the academy itself helped set up the FON at the new university in Smolensk), depreciated the value of the instution's preoccupation with socialist education. In the laconic second charter, approved by TsIK in April 1919, the new membership was approved and the enlightenment section dropped. The academy's function was now defined in terms of promoting "scientific-research work."[18]

Amid the hardening political battle lines of civil war the academy was

16. Shapiro, "Communist Academy," 352.

17. "Protokol zasedaniia prezidiuma Sotsialisticheskoi Akademii Obshchestvennykh Nauk, 15 oktiabria 1921," GARF f. 3415, op. 1, d. 86, l. 10. Even in 1922, because of "the poor condition of the Academy archive," an academy member could not reconstruct a list of papers given there a few years before. Udal'tsov, "Ocherk," 37.

18. Pokrovskii, "Kommunisticheskaia akademiia (kratkii ocherk)," 1–2; S. Lopatkin, "10 let Kommunisticheskoi akademii," *Revoliutsiia i kul'tura*, no. 21 (15 November 1928), 41; Shapiro, "Communist Academy," 68–73.

drifting toward a full indentification with the Party. There would be no decree, of course, defining the Bolshevik nature of the academy's "scientific" work. The anarcho-communist Grosman-Roshchin, petitioning for membership to the academy in 1920, had been informed of the academy's intention to admit only Communists as members. But he professed confusion about whether this meant only Marxists, since he considered himself a non-Marxist communist.[19] But despite ambiguities, by the introduction of NEP the membership of the academy included a leading cast of the most prominent Bolshevik scholars and politicians of intellectual bent, and this advanced the equation of academy goals with those of a specifically party scholarship.

This equation was also strengthened when the enlightenment section was replaced with a much more selective and party-oriented educational function. The "courses in Marxism," a party school considered higher than Sverdlov University and lower than the Institute of Red Professors, was founded in 1921 to train rising party apparatchiki in Marxist theory.[20] The presence of these important pupils ensured that the academy intellectuals could never fully retreat within the institution into a rarified world of high Marxist theory.

Not only membership and the party school, but also early service functions bolstered the academy's turn toward a party-oriented mission. Efforts were made to better organize the aid the academy, as a body of Marxist experts, could render the Party and the state. This initiative grew naturally out of the academy's high-level membership. Rotshtein, for example, the head of one of the SAON bureaus (*kabinet*) on foreign policy and an official in the commissariat of foreign affairs, asked that institution and the Comintern to send questions requiring analysis to the academy.[21] In addition, the Party began to use the academy for tasks demanding a discerning command of doctrine. Beginning at the end of 1918, for example, the Central Committee called on the academy to compile lecture outlines for inexperienced party workers involved in educational work in the Red Army.[22]

19. I. Grosman-Roshchin to A. V. Lunacharskii, 10 January 1920, GARF f. A-2306, op. 1, d. 429, l. 169.

20. "Protokol No. 5 Komissii po vyiasneniiu nuzhd vysshikh kommunisticheskikh uchebnykh zavedenii," no date, RTsKhIDNI f. 17, op. 60, d. 4, l. 15.

21. D. A. Mikhailov, "Podgotovka rukovodiashchikh i teoreticheskikh kadrov partii v usloviiakh stroitel'stva sotsializma (1918–1932 gg.)" (Candidate of Sciences diss., Akademiia Obshchestvennykh Nauk pri TsK, Moscow, 1968), 121.

22. "Chlen prezidiuma S[otsialisticheskoi] A[kademii] M. Reisner deistvitel'nomu chlenu Akademii N. I. Bukharina," 4 October 1918, GARF f. 3415, op. 1, d. 7, l. 136.

No matter how much the academy's second, civil war phase established the academy's political-ideological identification, the institution still could not articulate a genuine mission either in terms of academia or Marxist science. The reasons for this were obvious; in the midst of war the academy's activities were so modest that plans to augment its role were all but superfluous. Some academy meetings consisted of nothing more than seven or eight shivering people attempting to eat frozen potatoes.[23]

It was thus only in its third incarnation, which coincided with the introduction of the NEP order, that party scholarship's identification with the academy reacted with plans to become the center of Marxist science. The mixture proved volatile. Pokrovskii's formulation captured the thrice-born academy's NEP-era ambitions: "We had the opportunity to turn away from pacifist illusions and become an institution that is, as I have often said, our party Academy or, at least, a very firm basis for a Communist academy of sciences."[24]

Enmity and Emulation: Proletarian versus Bourgeois Science

The cult of *nauka* was embraced by party intellectuals with a particular twist. Science was linked, as in broad segments of the nonparty academic intelligentsia, with progress and better societal organization. But party scholarship invested the authority of *nauka* in revolutionary, "proletarian," collectivist, and politically partisan values (portrayed as diametrically opposed to "bourgeois" institutional autonomy, "pure" science, and nonpartisan neutrality). While Bolshevik attacks on the nonparty academic intelligentsia's ethos of "science for its own sake" were something of a caricature—given that it was precisely a commitment to social reform and opposition to tsarism that had shaped the liberal academic intelligentsia—the communist linkage of pure science with institutional autonomy was substantially accurate and indeed went to the heart of liberal academic ideology well beyond Russia's borders. The concept of "pure science" arose in the 1840s in the German context to distinguish professional scholars from the "learned amateur"

23. "10 let Kommunisticheskoi Akademii. Vstupitel'noe slovo M. N. Pokrovskogo."
24. Ibid.

and historically was closely linked to ideals of academic autonomy informing the Humboldtian university reforms in Berlin.[25]

Inverting these two tenets of liberal academic ideology, the Bolsheviks retained the link between them. For the Bolshevik intellectuals *nauka* was never neutral, above all in the social disciplines, and institutions were always partisan. In his 1922 article in the *Vestnik*, Preobrazhenskii called for a "united front of scientific communism against bourgeois pseudo-science," to be led, of course, by the academy.[26]

Yet for party intellectuals building the new society, one of the main tests of scientific worth (*nauchnost'*) was practical utility; and this put the Marxist theorists at the academy in a painfully awkward situation. By virtue of the name and pretensions of the Socialist Academy, its natural "bourgeois" enemy was the internationally renowned Academy of Sciences, which had quickly demonstrated the enormous practical utility of its bourgeois science to the proletarian state.[27]

In contrast to the stance of the nonparty professoriat, a majority of academicians had expressed their willingness to work with the new regime as early as the general assembly of 24 January 1918. In this they were prompted by deeply felt priorities centered around the preservation of Russian science. Yet it is crucial to recognize they were also motivated by the desire to preserve the Academy of Science's place as Russia's premier scientific institution, which had been partially eroded in relation to the universities in the decades before 1917.[28] The accommodation the Academy of Sciences won from the Soviet government, beginning with the negotiations in the spring of 1918, was based on an explicit agreement to provide help to the state on questions of economic and technical importance. In return, the Academy of Sciences received government funding, protection of its material base and publications, and extensive institutional autonomy. This settlement was supported

25. The University of Berlin then became the undisputed model for university reformers throughout Europe in the late nineteenth century, the formative period in the rise of the modern research university. See especially Björn Wittrock, "The Modern University: The Three Transformations," in Sheldon Rothblatt and Björn Wittrock, eds., *The European and American University since 1800: Historical and Sociological Essays* (Cambridge: Cambridge University Press, 1993), 303–62.

26. Preobrazhenskii, "Blizhaishie zadachi," 6.

27. Vucinich, *Empire of Knowledge*, 91–122; Bailes, "Natural Scientists," 271–80.

28. See Vera Tolz's prosopographical work on the academicians, "Combining Professionalism and Politics: Russian Academicians and the Revolution" (ms. based on Ph.D. diss., University of Birmingham, 1993), chap. 2.

energetically by Lenin, who forbade communist "mischief-making" around the academy.[29]

With growing strength in the natural and applied sciences, the Academy of Sciences, only nominally under the jurisdiction of Narkompros, developed working relationships with Sovnarkom, VSNKh, and other commissariats.[30] The Bolshevik intellectuals most closely associated with the Socialist Academy, with few exceptions, were clearly not representatives of those wings of the Party most inclined to support such a *modus vivendi* with the old Academy of Sciences or reliance on the "bourgeois" specialists. Pokrovskii, who never concealed his sharply honed animosity toward the old academic world, was among the "mischief-makers" responsible for one of the unrealized motions brought to the collegium of Narkompros in 1918 to dissolve the Academy of Sciences as an anachronism and create a state-organized association of Russian science in its place. Others, such as Bogdanov and his collaborators in the movement for proletarian culture, heralded the opening of the Socialist Academy as the signal for the collapse of outmoded bourgeois science and the birth of a new scientific collectivism.[31]

Bogdanov's prediction proved premature. After the introduction of NEP, the Academy of Sciences' relationship with the state was preserved by an influx of funds and commitments to scientists that were approved at the highest levels of the Party.[32] This impeded outright assaults from the party intelligentsia and Bolshevik Left. In 1923, Vladimir I. Vernadskii, the renowned geochemist and one of the Academy of Science's leading representatives in its relations with the government, was able to write Ivan I. Petrunkevich in Paris: "The Russian Academy is the single institution in which *nothing* has been touched. It remains as before, with full internal freedom. Of course, in a police state this free-

29. See especially I. D. Serebriakov, "Nepremennyi sekretar' AN akademik Sergei Fedorovich Ol'denburg," *Novaia i noveishaia istoriia*, no. 1 (January–February 1994): 225, 229; K. V. Ostrovitianov, ed., *Organizatsiia nauki v pervye gody sovetskoi vlasti (1917–1925). Sbornik dokumentov* (Leningrad: Nauka, 1968), 24, 103–5.

30. Robert A. Lewis, "Government and the Technological Sciences in the Soviet Union: The Rise of the Academy of Sciences," *Minerva* 15 (Summer 1977): 779–81.

31. V. P. Leonov et al., eds., *Akademicheskoe delo, 1929–1931*, vol. 1 (St. Petersburg: Biblioteka RAN, 1993), xiii, xiv; Kendall Bailes, *Science and Russian Culture in an Age of Revolutions: V. I. Vernadskii and His Scientific School, 1863–1945* (Bloomington: Indiana University Press, 1990), 153; "Otkrytie Sotsialisticheskoi Akademii," *Izvestiia*, 2 October 1918, 3.

32. L. D. Trotskii to V. I. Lenin, 4 November 1921, in "Chetyre milliarda rublei uchenym Petrograda," *Vestnik Rossiiskoi akademii nauk*, 64, no. 12 (1994): 1100–108.

dom is relative and it is necessary to defend it continually."[33] Before the elections of 1929, there was not a single academician who was a member of the Communist Party.

The postrevolutionary entrenchment of two rival academies led the Communist Academy to find its outlet for competition with the Academy of Sciences primarily in the realm of symbolism and rhetoric. Before 1925, Bolshevik intellectuals complained that the Academy of Sciences' special relationship with Sovnarkom endowed it with *de facto* all-union status, which the Communist Academy lacked. When the Academy of Sciences won formal all-union status in 1925 on its 200th anniversary, the Communist Academy reacted quickly, ensuring that it followed suit with all-union designation in 1926. The Communist Academy was acutely aware of this competition with the Academy of Sciences over status; in this case Pokrovskii enlisted the aid of TsIK secretary and party politician Avel' S. Enukidze to ensure the Communist Academy maintained official parity with its rival.[34]

The phraseology of party resolutions on the Socialist Academy, notably at the Twelfth Party Congress in 1923, were accorded the status of writ there not least because they seemed to bolster the status and prestige of the institution. It seemed the recognition of primacy that the Communist Academy sought could only come from the Party.

As in tsarist times, the Academy of Sciences was recognized as the "highest scientific institution" in the land. Yet it has rarely been observed that this same title was also bestowed upon the Communist Academy in its 1926 VTsIK charter.[35] The situation was not clarified by other contradictory signals coming from the Party and the state. Hoping to garner international prestige for Soviet science, the Politburo ensured the 200th jubilee of the Academy of Sciences in 1925 produced a windfall of official recognition and promises of support for that institution.[36] Yet when Sovnarkom founded the Lenin Prize on 23 June 1925 for a

33. Bailes, *Science and Russian Culture*, 157, citing 10 March 1923 letter in Vernadsky Collection, Bakhmeteff Archive, Columbia University.

34. "Stenogramma zasedaniia Biuro Prezidiuma Kommakademii," 27 February 1926, ARAN f. 350, op. 1, d. 53, l. 2; see also "Protokol No. 1 Zasedaniia Biuro Prezidiuma ot 11/XII 1924 g.," ibid., d. 26, l. 1.

35. The phrase, "vysshee uchenoe uchrezhdenie Soiuza SSR," was actually ambiguous, carrying the meaning "supreme" and "higher" (as in higher education) at the same time. Only in the 1935 charter of the Academy of Sciences is the ambiguity resolved by adding the phrase, "uniting the most outstanding scientists in the country." For successive Academy of Sciences charters, see *Ustavy Akademii Nauk SSSR, 1724–1974* (Moscow: Nauka, 1974).

36. "Protokol No. 70 zasedanii Politbiuro TsK RKP(b) ot 8 iiulia 1925 goda," RTsKhIDNI f. 17, op. 3, ed. khr. 510, l. 6; also ed. khr. 509, l. 1, 3, and ed. khr. 516, l. 1.

scientific work "of great practical significance" in any field, the terms of the award were sent to the Communist Academy presidium for ratification; the committee judging the prize, headed by Pokrovskii, was formed at the Communist Academy, even though the first winners were prominent natural and applied scientists. The question of which institution would ultimately triumph remained unresolved throughout the 1920s: "Would the Academy [of Sciences] become a truly Soviet institution or would it have to be replaced?"[37]

The rivalry with bourgeois academia held concrete financial implications as well. It was a constant complaint at the Communist Academy that the nonparty scholars received large salaries and support from the Soviet government, while Marxist scholars struggled with inadequate means. The relatively low salaries offered to young researchers (*sotrudniki*) at the Communist Academy, indeed, was a frequently mentioned gripe in the broader competition for academic cadres that the academy perceived with its nonparty rivals. As Pokrovskii put it starkly in 1924, if "we do not take and use" the young scholars, they will "go to the [bourgeois] professoriat." This sense of competition explains the academy's policy, maintained until the late 1920s, of allowing many nonparty *sotrudniki* to work at the academy.[38]

The caustic Riazanov thundered against the inferior financial position of Marxist science in the Soviet state, expressing the long-held sentiments of the party intelligentsia in particularly inflammatory terms. Although conditions improved toward the middle of the decade, the complaints continued throughout the 1920s. If a young scholar earned as little as 80 rubles a month, Riazanov charged, why would he want to work in a "pitiful institution" on Marx and Engels, when "working against Marxism, on Soviet money, against the proletariat, he earns 300 rubles (applause). All this is done on our money, our means. . . . [We must make] Marxism, Marxology a privileged discipline, just as others were in the old, prerevolutionary times."[39]

37. Loren Graham, *The Soviet Academy of Sciences and the Communist Party, 1927–1932* (Princeton: Princeton University Press, 1967), 74–77; on the Lenin Prize, A. V. Kol'tsov, *Razvitie Akademii Nauk kak vysshego nauchnogo uchrezhdeniia SSSR, 1926–1932* (Leningrad: Nauka, 1982), 22.

38. "Protokol obshchego sobraniia chlenov Kommunisticheskoi Akademii," 17 April 1924, 385, 390. The policy of accepting nonparty *sotrudniki* was criticized in the mid-1920s; certain parts of the academy (such as the Institute of World Economy) were known for employing more non-party members. A policy was set to reduce the nonparty ranks, and this became a major preoccupation in 1928. See "Protokol zasedaniia Prezidiuma Kom. Akademii ot 28 aprelia 1928 goda," ARAN f. 350, op. 1, d. 190, l. 56–57, and also l. 61, 87.

39. "Pervaia vsesoiuznaia konferentsiia marksistsko-leninskikh nauchno-issledovatel'skikh

Beneath the loud declarations there lurked an exaggerated respect for scientific prestige. Party scholarship's relationship to "bourgeois" science cannot be simplified to differing degrees of animosity, with "hard-line" radicals bent on destruction and moderates ready for greater accommodation. The Socialist Academy leadership clearly hoped to emulate its more established rival. At the end of 1922 Pokrovskii revealed to his academy's general assembly that he frequently met with Academy of Sciences officials in his capacity at deputy commissar of education. Almost wistfully he recalled how such "arch-practical" projects of the rival academy such as earthquake observation centers had aroused the interest of military and transportation officials. "Allow me to inquire," he drily remarked, "how our activity is connected to real life. We imagine that the Academy is a gathering of scholars. That was in the eighteenth century, but we live in the twentieth. . . . [O]ur academy will become like [the Academy of Sciences] only when all our sections find truly practical work for themselves."[40] What he neglected to say was that the ethos of the academicians still favored fundamental research, and that he was comparing apples and oranges by pitting a new "practical" mission for Marxist social science against natural and applied research.

The surest indication of this relationship of simultaneous emulation and enmity with the nonparty rivals is that major organizational changes in the Socialist Academy were always surreptitiously measured against the Academy of Sciences. On 2 November 1919, Riazanov's proposal to organize the academy by "study centers" (*kabinety*) was first acted upon. Each study center was designed to focus on a theme, such as the history of the revolutionary movement in the West. These centers achieved very few results other than some bibliographical compilations. Next, these centers were upgraded to "sections" (*sektsii*), which became the basic units of the academy. When Riazanov proposed transforming these sections into more consolidated, semi-independent institutes run by one prominent director, he drew an explicit comparison to the Academy of Sciences, which had by 1919 begun to realize goals dating back to the early 1910s to create a series of research institutes.[41]

---

uchrezhdenii (22–25 marta 1928 g. Stenograficheskii otchet)," *VKA*, no. 26 (1928): 253. Cited hereafter as "Pervaia konferentsiia."

40. "Obshchee sobranie chlenov Akademii. 19 dekabria 1922," ARAN f. 350, op. 1, d. 8, l. 3.

41. "Protokol obshchego Sobraniia Sotsialisticheskoi Akademii, 2-go noiabria 1919," GARF

It has seemingly gone unnoticed that the resulting reform of the Socialist Academy's structure in the 1920s helped decide the unique solution the Soviet Union eventually adopted toward the macro-organization of science. The "scientific-research institute," championed well before the Revolution by a segment of the scientific intelligentsia, could be seen as an advanced imitation of European networks of research institutes. But because they flourished primarily after 1917, supporters could also claim them as an inherently "revolutionary" structure. Of 88 institutes in the RSFSR in 1925, 73 were founded after the Revolution, most in the natural and applied sciences; only 19 of these focused on the humanities and pedagogy. These institutes were largely autonomous and administered for the most part by Narkompros or the Scientific-Technical Department (NTO) of VSNKh. The idea of research institutes was widely embraced by both the Soviet authorities and the scientific intelligentsia in the 1920s, but the question remained: how much of this new structure would be based on foreign (largely German) borrowing and how much on "revolutionary innovation?"[42]

The key innovation from the Bolshevik point of view was centralization and planning; and this could be achieved under the control of an academy. Riazanov, whose views on the subject turned out to be perhaps the most influential within the *Komakademiia*, by 1924 wished not only to emulate the Academy of Sciences but to surpass it by turning the entire Communist Academy into a network of research institutes.[43]

Riazanov certainly had grounds for viewing a network of institutes as a model more suitable for modern research than the honorary academies. The example Riazanov invoked, as others did, was the Kaiser-Wilhelm-Gesellschaft (KWG), the German organization founded in 1910–11 to coordinate a union of scientific and technical research institutes, in this case sponsored by industry with significant aid from the

---

f. 3415, op. 1, d. 64, l. 5; G. D. Alekseeva, "Kommunisticheskaia akademiia," in M. V. Nechkina et al., eds., *Ocherki istorii istoricheskoi nauki v SSSR* (Moscow: Nauka, 1966), 4:202; V. A. Ul'ianovskaia, *Formirovanie nauchnoi intelligentsii v SSSR, 1917–1937 gg.* (Moscow: Nauka, 1966), 68–69.

42. F. N. Petrov, "Nauchno-issledovatel'skie instituty SSSR," *Molodaia gvardiia*, no. 9–11 (October 1925): 146–49; the quotation is from the most significant piece of research on this topic, Loren R. Graham's, "Formation of Soviet Research Institutes: A Combination of Revolutionary Innovation and International Borrowing," *Social Studies of Science* 5 (August 1975): 317.

43. "Protokol obshchego sobraniia," 17 April 1924, 385 (cited in full at note 38).

state. Riazanov's enthusisasm for adapting the German example to Soviet imperatives of centralization garnered the cachet of progress for party scholarship. It also reflected another sidelong glance at the bourgeois academicians, since Academy of Sciences permanent secretary Sergei F. Ol'denburg maintained close ties with German colleagues in the Gesellschaft. Riazanov's views were in yet another sense representative of Bolshevik thinking in that he ignored altogether the research university. His opinions diverged from those of the nonparty scientific intelligentsia—which in the 1920s often saw in the formation of institutes a chance to protect autonomy and institutionalize specialized fields—in that he envisaged the academy as the "organizing center," with institutes as the building blocks of expansion.[44]

When the Communist Academy, in its impatience to adopt the most advanced structure for twentieth-century research, began the process of transforming its "sections" into institutes in 1924, it marked a de facto ratification of a new ideal in Bolshevik academic organization: a centralized, umbrella academy presiding over an expanding network of semi-autonomous research institutes. In this sense, the changes in the structure of the Communist Academy presaged the organizational model adopted during the bolshevization of the Academy of Sciences in 1929–32. As we shall see, many of the same people, notably Riazanov and other Communists elected to the Academy of Sciences, laid the first plans for that institution's reorganization. The universities, because of the political landscape of postrevolutionary academia and the perception that they posed a continuing threat to party scholarship, were ruled out as the research centers of the future. For a moment in 1928, Riazanov did suggest that the research institutes would eventually become independent and that academies in general would be rendered obsolete. Yet Pokrovskii and others dismissed this on the "political" grounds that it would eliminate central control; Riazanov himself soon reversed his position. What is significant is not Riazanov's short-lived rhetorical rejection of academies (representing a threat to the Academy of Sciences during the bolshevization campaign) but the fact that Bolshevik intellectuals had come to treat an expanding network of research

44. Jürgen Nötzold, "Die deutsch-sowjetischen Wissenschaftsbeziehungen," in Rudolf Vierhaus and Bernhard von Brocke, eds., *Forschung im Spannungsfeld von Politik und Gesellschaft: Geschichte und Struktur der Kaiser-Wilhelm-/Max-Planck-Gesellschaft* (Stuttgart: Deutsche Verlag, 1990), 778–800; "Plenarnoe zasedanie prezidiuma Komm. Akademii, 15-go iiunia 1926 g.," ARAN f. 350, op. 1, d. 45, l. 4.

institutes under the centralized leadership of an academy as a given necessity at the summit of higher learning.[45]

If the Academy of Sciences in the 1920s served as an organizational model partly to be emulated, partly to be overtaken, in terms of values it represented the epitome of what the Bolshevik intellectuals wished to reject. Yet even rejection can imply an important influence, since it helps define what is adopted instead. The Socialist Academy consciously inverted the most cherished ideals of the liberal wing of the academic intelligentsia. Under the last tsar, liberal academia had become convinced that institutional autonomy represented the highest prerequisite for the advancement of *nauka*; this belief was ingrained during the decades spent in opposition to the notorious 1884 university charter, which allocated many administrative functions to the state. The ideals of institutional autonomy and professional rights were given new impetus after the February revolution, only to be assaulted once again after October.[46]

The Bolshevik critique of academic liberalism was advanced by party theorists grouped around the academy as they set about organizing their own institution. The professoriat was portrayed as a closed caste, lecturing on esoteric topics from a high pedestal, avoiding political and social commitment, and displaying the cowardly wavering of the bourgeois *intelligent*. A 1918 advertisement for the Socialist Academy proudly announced that there were no titles, just positions; members were elected for five-year terms, not for life; and there are "no privileged priests or formal authorities, hollow titles or caste powers. All people in the Academy, beginning with the students and ending with the members, are comrades and brothers."[47]

In the struggle over university administration culminating in the imposition of the university charter of 1922, nonparty critics of the Bolsheviks repeatedly protested that only institutional autonomy could guarrantee free thought, scholarly creativity, and "freedom for *nauka*."

45. "Pervaia konferentsiia," 266; Graham, "Formation," 322; Fitzpatrick, *Education*, 231–32.

46. O. N. Znamenskii, *Intelligentsiia nakanune velikogo oktiabria (fevral'-oktiabr' 1917 g.)* (Leningrad: Nauka, 1988), 152–79. The most illuminating discussion of the values of the academic intelligentsia in prerevolutionary Russia is in James C. McClelland, *Autocrats and Academics: Education, Culture, and Society in Tsarist Russia* (Chicago: University of Chicago Press, 1979), 58–94.

47. Quoted in Udal'tsov, "Ocherk," 17. Pokrovskii gives a critique of bourgeois academic conventions in his introduction to *Trudy IKP*, 3–5.

One further result of the heated struggle over party-state involvement in university administration in the half-decade after 1917, therefore, was that a whole complex of "liberal" academic ideals were thoroughly discredited by the Bolsheviks. They were therefore inaccessible in almost any form for the Bolshevik intellectuals as they entered into their formative period of institution-building in the 1920s. The Communist Academy shunned the notion of institutional autonomy, replacing it with the ideal, difficult to maintain in practice, of comradely collectivism.[48]

As leading Bolshevik intellectuals became personally involved in exposing the "alien" goals of academic freedom and institutional autonomy, something they also attempted to do on a theoretical level to "neutrality" in the social sciences, the academy was drawn to an alternate set of values. In the years of expansion after 1922, these values were linked to missions that meshed with claims to one-party monopoly in the political sphere, which promised to harness the power of the regime for party scholarship.

Hegemonic Missions and Service to the State

As a counter-ideal, the Communist Academy embraced service to the party-state. In March 1922, the academy's presidium, headed by Pokrovskii with Preobrazhenskii as his deputy, resolved to work "in the closest manner" with Gosplan, the commissariats, and other organs of the Party and the state which the Socialist Academy could aid. A special commission including Preobrazhenskii and Bubnov, the head of Agitprop, was formed to work on the project.[49] A year later, Bubnov graphically demonstrated how far certain academy members were willing to go in promoting the institution's service function. The Agitprop department was concerned about the "unlimited quantity of all types of deviations" among youth, he recalled, including the influence of the tract by the ultra-materialist Enchmen. As Bubnov put it: "We needed to mobilize several comrade-specialists with the task of defeating this book in

48. On the struggle in academia after 1917 from the non-Bolshevik perspective of university participants, see Mikhail M. Novikov, *Ot Moskvy do N'iu Iorka: Moia zhizn' v nauke i v politike* (New York: Izdatel'stvo im. Chekhova, 1952), and Sergei Zhaba, *Petrogradskoe studenchestvo v bor'be za svobodnuiu shkolu* (Paris: I. Povolozky, 1922). On Bolshevik rejection of "liberal" academic ideals, S. A. Fediukin, *Bor'ba s burzhuaznoi ideologiei v usloviiakh perekhoda k Nepu* (Moscow: Nauka, 1977), 95–96 and passim. The breakdown of this communitarian ideal is a major theme in Shapiro's dissertation.

49. "Protokol zasedaniia Prezidiuma Sotsialisticheskoi Akademii Obshchestvennykh Nauk, 26/III-22 g.," RTsKhIDNI f. 17, op. 60, d. 230, l. 4–5.

nine days time. That should be the affair of the Academy. . . . But this was not done. I consider this one of the shortcomings in the work of the Academy."[50] Bubnov seemed to view the academy's mission as that of a kind of short-order theorist for the party high command.

Such sentiments formed the backdrop to the resolutions of the Twelfth Party Congress in April 1923, which sanctioned several new tasks for the academy in the first such pronouncement about the institution. In theses drafted by Bubnov's Agitprop department, the academy was charged with moving beyond the boundaries of social science, connecting its work "in the closest manner" with various "institutions and organs," including the commissariats, thus "gradually turning itself into a scientific-methodological center." In return, the resolution held out the promise that the academy would eventually "unite all scientific-research work."[51]

Pokrovskii gave the congress's resolution the widest possible publicity within the academy, focusing his report of the presidium on the resolution in October 1923. The nature of the academy's work, he predicted, would become "much different from the expectations that obtained at the Academy at the beginning of its existence." Changes would occur because "the Academy has been given a specific party function, assigned to it by the resolution of the congress." Pokrovskii did not interpret this function in Bubnov's narrow sense of simply fulfilling ideological assignments important to the Party. Rather, the Bolshevik mandarin called it "perfectly clear" that the academy's party function included a "struggle with the views of the bourgeois professoriat" and the role of arbitrating methodological differences within the Marxist camp.[52] Characteristically, in this variation on the congress's theme Pokrovskii once again brought out the connection between the expanding service role of the academy and the promise of future monopolistic powers.

It might seem that this reorientation of 1922–23 consisted more of paper resolutions than of dramatic change. The Institute of Scientific Methodology, which was founded directly as a result of the Twelfth Congress, never developed into the influential center of theory coordination which was at first envisaged; however, an official redefinition of the academy's goals in the direction of service was itself an important

50. "Protokol obshchego sobraniia chlenov Sotsialisticheskoi Akademii," 11 October 1923, *VSA*, no. 6 (October–December 1923): 429–30.

51. "Rezoliutsiia po voprosam Propagandy, pechati i agitatsii priniatsia [*sic*] Agitpropsekts. XII-go parts"ezda 25.4.23," RTsKhIDNI f. 17, op. 3, ed. khr. 367, l. 24–42; *KPSS v resoliutsiiakh i resheniiakh s"ezdov, konferentsii i plenumov TsK*, 5th ed. (Moscow: Politizdat, 1984), 3:106.

52. "Protokol obshchego sobraniia," 11 October 1923, 420–21 (cited in full at note 50).

development. This was dramatized in the academy's next general meeting in 1924. In the wake of Lenin's death, the assembly voted to change the name of the institution to the Communist Academy, a decision which followed on the heels of one of the most revealing public discussions of institutional goals in the academy's history.

The promulgation of the incipient Lenin cult had galvanized party scholarship to codify the discipline of Leninism. The report of the presidium, delivered by Dvoilatskii, adapted the academy's agenda to this upsurge in attention by calling on the academy to become the center of research on Leninism. Since studying the heritage of Lenin raised "the great danger of various deviations," control over scholarly work on Leninism was required: "The Lenin Institute does not propose to fulfill this task," the report concluded, "and none other than the Academy will be able to do so."

The specter of a new area of monopolistic control for the academy sparked off a virtual barrage of motions to expand the institution's power. Riazanov proposed working with Narkompros to examine "various institutions which are organized in an anarchistic way," in order to liquidate them and incorporate them into the academy. Legal theorist Petr I. Stuchka brought up the FONy as examples of institutions that "from the Marxist point of view offer nothing." The talk ranged so far that Lukin spoke out against "those predatory plans which are being developed here," and Pokrovskii backed off from concrete measures to incorporate other institutions. Finally, the meeting returned to Leninism as the proper outlet for the academy's aspirations, and a motion was accepted to lobby for the "unification of all work on the scientific study of Leninism around the Academy."[53]

The renamed Communist Academy no more succeeded in monopolizing theoretical work on Leninism than it did in creating a single center of Marxist methodology, but the resolutions and plans expressed in the general meetings set the tone for the academy's work as a smorgasbord of new institutes, societies, and journals were founded between 1923 and 1925.[54] The additions included Pokrovskii's Society of Marxist Historians, the Society of Marxist Statisticians, and the upgrade of one "section" into the Institute of World Economy and Politics. And 1925–26 marked the founding of the section on economics, an agrarian commission (including a cooperative commission), and the Institute of

53. "Protokol obshchego sobraniia," 17 April 1924, 373–93 (cited in full at note 38).
54. "10 let Kommunisticheskoi Akademii," 17.

Higher Neural Activity, among others. Three of these organizations deserve special mention as instrumental in augmenting the Communist Academy's function of state service.

In 1925 an Institute of Soviet Construction (*Sovetskogo Stroitel'stva*, a term that carried roughly the same connotation as state-building) was approved by the Orgburo with rising party functionary Lazar M. Kaganovich at its head, and including prominent politician and science administrator Enukidze. This represented a qualitatively new kind of "practicality" within the academy: a program headed by high-level party *praktiki*, conferring on them the prestige of association with the Communist Academy. The institute was charged by its charter with conducting research "according to the assignments of leading state institutions." It was divided into sections on federal government, local government, and local economy and began to promote such papers as "The Latest Mass Campaigns and the Low-Level Soviet Apparat" and "The Condition and Development of Local Budgets."[55]

The reference "leading state institutions" in fact meant the Worker-Peasant Inspectorate (RKI, or Rabkrin), which in 1923 was joined to the TsKK and was "transformed into the control arm of the Politburo over both the party and the state apparatus," as well as a preserve of the emergent Stalin faction.[56] At an inaugural speech at the Institute of Soviet Construction Valerian V. Kuibyshev, the head of TsKK-RKI and a leading Stalin loyalist, defined the new institute as a research wing of the RKI. Indeed, the deputy director of the institute, A. V. Ivanov, was also a deputy commissar of the inspectorate. The low level of the institute's work was exacerbated by problems at both the top and the bottom: in 1927 the fearless Riazanov protested against the "abnormal" situation in which the head of the institute, Kaganovich, was almost never in Moscow; and the institute staff (*sotrudniki*) were mostly young law students with no research experience.[57]

Although in public the academy leaders loudly trumpeted the value of the soviet construction institute to the state, behind closed doors they

55. "Vypiska iz protokola No. 70 zasedaniia Orgbiuro TsK ot 13/III-25 g.," RTsKhIDNI f. 147, op. 1, d. 33, l. 15; "Polozhenie ob Institute Sovetskogo Stroitel'stva pri Kommunisticheskoi Akademii," no date, ARAN f. 350, op. 1, d. 33, l. 57; "Institut sovetskogo stroitel'stva," *Informatsionnyi biulleten'*, no. 9 (March–May 1928): 33.

56. E. A. Rees, *State Control in Russia: The Rise and Fall of the Workers' and Peasants' Inspectorate, 1920–34* (London: Macmillan, 1987), 93.

57. Unititled speech by Kuibyshev, no date, prob. 1925, ARAN f. 350, op. 1, d. 39, l. 1–34; "Stenogramma Zasedaniia Prezidiuma Kommunisticheskoi Akademii, 11/VI-27," ARAN f. 350, op. 1, d. 97, l. 18–27; "Zasedanie Prezidiuma Kommunisticheskoi Akademii. 2/IV-27 g.," ibid., d. 93, l. 19–23.

were acutely aware that their institute's output was according to their conceptions "publicistic" as opposed to "scientific-research work." What passed as research there, one presidium member scoffed, most frequently resembled "an article of a newspaper-like character." Yet by 1927, according to the institute's administrator (*uchennyi sekretar'*), Vetoshkin, it had become the "largest institution at the Communist Academy." When Vetoshkin complained that despite its size the institute's budget was lower than other units of the academy, Miliutin cut him off curtly by replying that those other units were "worth more in terms of scholarly work than your Institute."[58]

A second area that led the development of policy studies in Soviet academia was the academy's efforts to advise the formulation of Soviet foreign policy. Rotshtein's foreign affairs section in the academy evolved between 1922 and 1925 into what one scholar calls the "scholarly-technical arm" of the Commissariat of Foreign Affairs. In April 1925 the Institute of World Economy and Politics was founded with Rotshtein as director, followed by Jenő Varga in 1927. Another observer has speculated that foreign policy consulting developed first within the discipline of "orientology" in the early 1920s largely because Bolshevik leaders considered themselves experts on Europe; but by the mid-1920s the Stalin leadership needed a group of experts that would go beyond Comintern reports on the "situation of the working class" to study finance and politics in Europe and the United States. The Institute of World Economy filled this gap, from the days of its foundation fielding queries from the party leadership and the editorial board of *Pravda*. The institute seemed likely to become a mere service organization. Indeed, Riazanov sardonically suggested that if Budennyi, the famed cavalry commander of the Red Army and a crony of Stalin, discovered the institute he would tie all its work to horses.[59]

Finally, the academy's agrarian section, established in July 1925 under Lev N. Kritsman, quickly became the major center of scholarship of the agrarian Marxists and their school of rural sociology.[60] The agronomists were highly concerned with carving out a consulting and policymaking role, and their work typified the manner in which active

58. "Stenogramma Zasedaniia Prezidiuma Akademii, 11/VI-27," l. 18–19, 26, and d. 91, l. 10 (cited in full at note 57).

59. Oded Eran, *The Mezhdunarodniki: An Assessment of Professional Expertise in Soviet Foreign Policy* (Tel Aviv: Turtledove Publishing, 1979), 17–43; Gerhard Duda, *Jenö Varga und die Geschichte des Instituts für Weltwirtschaft und Weltpolitik in Moskau, 1921–1970* (Berlin: Akademie Verlag, 1994), 45–71.

60. Solomon, *Soviet Agrarian Debate*; on consulting see 26, 215–16 n. 73.

service became incorporated into the everyday functioning of the academy's various parts, especially during the expansion of the mid-1920s. For example, on 24 November 1927 Molotov gave Kritsman a week to come up with a decade's worth of statistical information on peasant taxes, with interpretation of their effects on the poor, middle, and kulak strata. The following September, Molotov informed Kritsman of the necessity to help draft the theses for the party resolution "On Work in the Countryside" for the upcoming Fifteenth Party Congress.[61]

Such activities threatened to overwhelm basic research. During the course of the 1920s, the academy's "service functions sometimes predominated over its research. . . . [S]tate and party organs assumed that the Academy was always on tap, usually at short notice, to do minor or esoteric work."[62] Yet service increased its allure to the party scholars, because work done under the auspices of the academy was often considered in high state and party councils.[63]

Communist Academy of Sciences? The Foray into Natural Science

Like the preoccupation with consulting and policymaking, the academy's expansion into natural science research was an attempt to increase its general authority. It challenged an unwritten "division of labor" between the Communist Academy as a bastion of Marxist social sciences and the Academy of Sciences as the preserve of the natural sciences (with humanities divisions, although clearly resented by the Marxist scholars, that could be justified by proficiency in noncontemporary topics and specialized subfields). Each step the Communist Academy took to bolster the natural sciences within its walls, then, could be interpreted as an implicit threat to the coexistence of the two academies, as well as an attempt to expand the domain of Marxist methodology into virgin soil.

After the Twelfth Congress authorized the Socialist Academy to go beyond the bounds of social science in 1923, it quietly dropped the reference to "Social Sciences" in its name. Since then, the foundation of the natural and exact science section—and later the physiological labo-

61. Viacheslav M. Molotov to Kritsman, 24 November 1927, ARAN f. 528, op. 4, d. 45, l. 1; Molotov to Kritsman, 2 September 1927, ibid., l. 2.

62. Shapiro, "Communist Academy," 112–13; see also 43–48.

63. For example, see Knorin to Stalin, Molotov, Kossior, 22 April 1926, RTsKhIDNI f. 17, op. 60, d. 800, l. 4.

ratory, the Society of Marxist Biologists, and the Institute of Higher Neural Activity—provoked controversy on purely theoretical grounds. The Society of Marxist Biologists in 1926 defined its task as "elaboration of biological problems from the point of view of dialectical materialism" and "propaganda among biologists of the methods of dialectical materialism in the life sciences."[64] This program at the academy in the mid-1920s, in its move beyond the debate over applied versus natural science that was in part prompted by the publication of Engels's *Dialectics of Nature* in 1925, anticipated and indeed represented the first swelling of the movement to apply dialectical methods to natural science that came to the fore in the party Marxist camp in the late 1920s.[65]

It was possible to maintain, as most "mechanists" among Marxist philosophers did in the 1920s, that the methodologies of natural science required no "working over" by Marxism, because Marxism was compatible with all genuine science. The physicist Arkadii K. Timiriazev and Skvortsov-Stepanov, academy members who headed the mechanist school, intensively opposed the Deborin group of philsophers over the applicability of "dialectical method" to natural science. The varying degrees of reductionism inherent in the mechanists' stress on material forces were countered by the Deborin-led school of "dialecticians," who denounced the mechanists for allegedly ignoring the dialectical structure of nature and the importance of Hegelian dialectics for Marxism in general. The Deborinites emerged triumphant for a time in the field of philosophy in the late 1920s. Some Marxists, especially the younger "dialecticians" in the 1920s, actively advocated a kind of proletarianization of natural science by "filtering" it through the core methodology of dialectical materialism. Such a project, however, met more resistance in the 1920s than the causes of proletarian art or literature. Although it was hardly without consequences, it proved far more problematic to effect even after the victory of the Deborinites—in comparison to the hegemony achieved during the Great Break by proletarian culture groups after their own triumph—since, few could forget, natural sci-

64. "Ustav Obshchestva Biologov-Marksistov," no date, ARAN f. 350, op. 1, d. 163, l. 6.

65. Although "important professionals who genuinely believed that science could be enriched by a dialectical perspective" joined the materialist-biologists in the early days, by 1930 I. I. Prezent, who in fact graduated with a social science degree from Leningrad University in 1926 and later became Lysenko's closest partner, was president of the Society of Materialist-Biologists and a major force in the Leningrad branch of the Communist Academy (LOKA). See Douglas R. Weiner, *Models of Nature: Ecology, Conservation, and Cultural Revolution in Soviet Russia* (Bloomington: Indiana University Press, 1988), 123–33.

ence and technology held one of the immediate keys to industrialization.[66]

The academy's embrace of natural science, modest though it remained, gained support primarily because of its political importance to the institution. Riazanov was bitterly opposed to "infecting" Marxism with methods from natural science, but he was virtually alone in actively opposing what he derogatively called the "dog institute," the Institute of Higher Neural Activity, which he charged was simply duplicating work done in Leningrad by academician Ivan P. Pavlov's laboratory.[67]

Other leading academy members countered Riazanov's salvos not out of a commitment to research on dogs or perhaps even to a dialectic of nature, but primarily because the extension into natural science, like the services rendered to state and party organs, enhanced the academy's plans for securing preeminence among scholarly institutions. Pokrovskii underlined that the academy was not "only a social science institution—that is certain." He continued:

> [It is] the seeds of a Communist Academy of Sciences. Attempts to narrow the work of the Academy in any way would be attempts to weaken the significance of this "scientific-methodological center." And since there is only one center in any circle, then it follows—we will not be afraid of words—that our Academy has a certain monopoly on the leadership of party-scientific work in all its dimensions.[68]

The implications of the academy's excursion into natural science were revealed when a proposal surfaced in the bureau of the academy's presidium in 1927 to hand over the Institute of Higher Neural Activity, which was apparently staffed by an embarassingly low number of qualified Marxists, to the Commissariat of Health. Pokrovskii strenuously objected that this would create the impression that the academy had

66. See V. Egorshin, "K voprosu o politike marksizma v oblasti estestvoznaniia," *PZM*, no. 7–8 (June–August 1926): 123–34, esp. 134. The classic work on the subject is Joravsky's *Soviet Marxism and Natural Science*. Loren Graham emphasizes the creative role Marxism played in the work of some scientists in "The Role of Dialectical Materialism: The Authentic Phase," in his *Science in Russia and the Soviet Union: A Short History* (Cambridge: Cambridge University Press, 1993), 99–120. On natural science policy and institutional development in the natural sciences during NEP (focusing on physics) see especially Paul Josephson, *Physics and Politics in Revolutionary Russia* (Berkeley: University of California Press, 1991), and (centering on ecology and the life sciences) Weiner, *Models of Nature*.

67. "Pervaia konferentsiia," 252–53, 263; Joravsky, *Soviet Marxism*, 119–69.

68. M. N. Pokrovskii, "O deiatel'nosti Kommunisticheskoi Akademii," no date, 1928, ARAN f. 540, op. 4, d. 31, l. 8.

failed in its involvement in natural science, and this would "overjoy both the All-Union Academy of Sciences and similar institutions." In a revealing monologue, Pokrovskii raised the larger issues at stake:

> Where are we going, what course are we taking? Are we planning to transform the Communist Academy into a Communist Academy of Sciences? This would mean the creation of a whole range of institutes, laboratories, etc. We have taken this path up until now. . . . Or are we only trying to concentrate Marxist natural scientists in the Communist Academy in order to create a kind of methodological "fist," which through criticism and so on can influence the general course of natural science in the country as well as the work of other institutions, including the same All-Union Academy of Sciences.[69]

Pokrovskii here clearly favored the more ambitious task, but in practice the natural science section in the second half of the 1920s was pursuing the more modest attempt to create a Marxist foothold in new fields. In 1926, for example, the section reported that it chose research problems that "had the most relevance toward supporting the materialistic worldview" and was engaged in such tasks as collating excerpts from Marxist classics that related to the natural sciences.[70] Yet Pokrovskii's two alternatives were not mutually exclusive; the academy, as usual, pursued modest, short-term goals and still harbored large long-term ambitions.

The tensions between the aggressive extension of Marxism, on the one hand, and the relative insulation of the natural and technological sciences against remaking of their core methodologies, on the other, were never fully resolved by the academy or, for that matter, in Soviet higher learning. The academy's entry into natural science nevertheless bolstered Marxist demands that natural scientists should master Marxism and that dialectical materialism be incorporated into their work. At the same time, the more radical exponents of the academy's embrace of natural science were dealt a blow at the 1927 Orgburo meeting on the academy at which Stalin spoke three times. According to Miliutin: "When I talked about the work of the section of natural and exact sciences, Stalin said: it is hardly worth it to develop strongly in that direction, you should pay attention primarily to social problems." Krits-

69. "Stenograficheskii otchet Zasedaniia Biuro Prezidiuma Kommunisticheskoi Akademii. 24/XII-27," ARAN f. 350, op. 1, d. 119, l. 36.

70. "Osnovnye momenty godovoi raboty sektsii estestvennykh i tochnykh nauk Komakademii," no date, 1926, ARAN f. 350, op. 1, d. 58, l. 8–9.

man responded by actually brandishing a copy of the Twelfth Party Congress resolution authorizing the academy to expand into natural science, but Stalin only retorted that this was not a basic part of the academy's work.[71] This blunt rejoinder may have prompted academy leaders to consider the benefits of merging party scholarship's dominance in social science with the Academy of Science's preeminance in natural science.

"Scholarly Organ": The Making of a Central Committee Resolution

The academy evolved not only as a result of long-term shifts in party scholarship, but also through the institution's direct negotiation with the Party's top leadership. In 1927 leaders of the United Opposition who were members of the academy brought their struggle against the leadership into academy forums in the half-year leading up to their expulsion from the Party. At the same time, the first plans for industrialization were laid. With these two developments commanding their attention, the Orgburo and Politburo conducted a review of the Communist Academy that resulted in the first party position statement on the institution since 1923. Published in *Pravda* in the name of the Central Committee, the declaration gave new import both to the institution's service functions and its ideological accountability by declaring that "the Communist Academy must pay special attention to the theoretical preparation of vital [*aktual'nye*] contemporary economic and political problems on the agenda of the Comintern and the Party." In a clause with even more potential resonance, the resolution declared the Communist Academy to be the "scholarly organ" of the Central Committee.[72]

The story of how this influential decision came to be made reveals how the academy leadership balanced disparate political and scholarly concerns as it strove to secure maximum benefit from its interaction with the top party organs. On 2 April 1927 Kritsman gave a detailed report to the academy presidium on an Orgburo meeting he and Miliutin had attended. In the lengthy Orgburo discussion following Krits-

71. "Zasedanie Prezidiuma Kommunisticheskoi Akademii 2/IV-27 g.," ARAN f. 350, op. 1, d. 93, l. 3. During a 1931 reorganization of the academy, the Politburo ordered the natural science section to be eliminated, provoking a protest from Pokrovskii. M. N. Pokrovskii, "Politburo TsK VKP(b). Kopiia L. M. Kaganovichu," no date, RTsKhIDNI f. 147, op. 1, d. 33, l. 73.

72. "O rabote Komakademii (Postanovlenie TsK VKP(b) ot 22 iiulia 1927 g.)," *Pravda*, 26 July 1927, 6.

man's report on the academy, Molotov and Stalin had expressed their views of the academy's work. "In particular," Kritsman revealed with a dramatic touch, "Stalin took the floor three times on this report": "It became clear from the speeches of the Orgburo members [Stalin and Molotov] that they perceive insufficient ties with the work of the Central Committee of the Party. . . . Comrade Molotov formulated this by saying that of course one cannot even talk about the Academy becoming a department of the TsK, but the Academy nevertheless must become the scholarly organ of the TsK." At this point Riazanov interjected: "Maybe then they'll give us the privileges [*prava*]." Kritsman rejoined: "They said it is necessary that the Academy become the organ of scholarly work for the Central Committee and that in this sense it would get the rights of a department [*otdela*]."[73]

The party leadership was thus dangling in front of these ambitious Bolshevik intellectuals the prospect of converting the Communist Academy into an official party administrative center for academia and science. Such a step was never implemented, but the academy seemed closer than ever before to securing a formal role in making personnel, fiscal, and doctrinal policy in higher learning.

As the academy leadership met to discuss the designation of the academy as the "scholarly organ of the Central Committee," the concrete advantages of such status could not be far from anybody's mind. The academy's potential reward for drawing closer to the Central Committee's administrative apparat included not only heightened political authority but also access to classified, censored, or unpublishable information. In 1925, for example, Sovnarkom had neglected to include the academy's library on the list of institutions authorized to receive so-called secret editions, probably because nonparty scholars were employed as researchers in various branches of the academy. The academy stopped receiving these works, which the censorship agency Glavlit defined to include those that bore the stamp "only for members and candidates" of the Party. In his protest to Sovnarkom, Pokrovskii tellingly defended his institution's rights by invoking the stock formula that the academy represented "the highest scientific institution of the USSR, called upon to produce scientific work on the basis of Marxism and Leninism."[74]

73. "Zasedanie Prezidiuma Kommunisticheskoi Akademii 2/IV-27 g.," l. 1–2 (cited in full at note 71).

74. "M. N. Pokrovskii. V Upravlenie delami Sovnarkom 12 maia 1926," ARAN f. 1759, op. 4, d. 170, l. 3–4. Materials from the academy library in 1928 refer to a "secret office" where

The trade-off in 1927, however, was that the academy would have to commit itself, at least on paper, to those "vital questions" on the agenda of the Party and Comintern. A heated discussion in the academy presidium erupted on this wording and all that it implied. Kritsman strongly opposed such a subordination of the academy's scholarly mission: "I believe that this formulation is misguided, not only in the sense that one should not write it, but that it is wrong in essence." Kritsman cited Einstein's theory of relativity, the subject of controversy among physicists and philosophers, as a "genuine problem for us" that was hardly vital to the Central Committee. "If you try to turn the Academy into an apparat, which compiles answers for the Central Committee on current problems, then you won't have an Academy; you will have just that, an apparat."[75]

Miliutin, the second most influential member of the academy after Pokrovskii, took a sophistic but evidently persuasive tack against Kritsman's arguments. The Central Committee was not proposing to adopt a new academy charter, he argued, but only a resolution. Thus the overall tasks of the academy would not change even if such a directive emphasized current goals of analyzing politically relevant issues. Compromise was necessary, Miliutin urged, if "you want to receive a directive from the Central Committee."[76] In his eagerness to secure political capital, Miliutin expressed confidence that the directive would not irrevocably change the academy's course.

Kritsman bowed to this reasoning; the process for approving the official resolution on the academy was set in motion. The Orgburo formed an ad hoc commission that included not only high Agitprop officials but the academy troika of Pokrovskii, Kritsman, and Miliutin to prepare a report on the academy for the Politburo. A draft Politburo resolution, virtually identical to the Central Committee pronouncement later published in *Pravda*, can be found in Kritsman's papers, with Kritsman's handwritten additions. This paper trail confirms that the "Central Committee resolution" of 1927 was really a published version of a Politburo directive that originated, moreover, in an Orgburo commission that

---

such editions were perhaps shelved. "Plan rabot Biblioteki Kom. Akademii na 1928/29 akademicheskii god," no date, ARAN f. 528, op. 3, d. 5, l. 6.

75. "Zasedanie Prezidiuma Kommunisticheskoi Akademii. 2/IV-27 g.," l. 14–15 (cited in full at note 71).

76. Ibid., l. 16.

acted with significant input from the academy presidium.[77] As this implies, the process of channeling the academy into more "practical work" encompassed a subtle process of adaptation on the part of the academy to the blandishments and perceived desires of the Stalin leadership.

The danger of this 1927 gamble was that the academy, having traded its commitment to address the Party's "vital questions" in return only for vague promises, would instead of gaining monopolistic powers cede influence over the fundamental direction of its own work. Service to the Party was now the official standard by which the academy's work would be judged. The principle of validating party scientific-research work outside the scholarly world was enhanced by the long-standing academy practice of underlining service rather than science as a way of enhancing its prestige.[78]

The academy leadership thus swallowed its misgivings and once again reoriented its mission. By 1929, public explanations of the Communist Academy's role had progressed further to assert that all theoretical problems must have practical implications for socialist construction.[79] The academy now could hardly retreat into neutrality when it came to the most "vital questions" of all, the inner-party oppositions and accompanying ideological disputes.

Orthodoxy, Oppositions, and a New *Partiinost'*

In the history of Marxism, "orthodox" trends cannot be assigned a single programmatic core. Orthodoxy was to no small degree a state of mind, a determination to avoid revisionism or deviation. The Bolsheviks, moreover, interpreted orthodoxy to mean an acceptance of the axiom that there is only one correct view. When orthodoxy became the official mantle of the party-state, a web of other factors also intruded on its definition. To be orthodox was to become open to pressures, the most obvious of which were the codified positions of and the outright

77. "Vypiska iz protokola No. 100 zasedaniia Orgbiuro TsK ot 28.III.27 goda," RTsKhIDNI f. 147, op. 1, d. 33, l. 19; "Proekt Politbiuro," no date, 1927, ARAN f. 528, op. 3, d. 31, l. 19–20. See also ARAN f. 1759, op. 1, d. 317, l. 1. The Politburo approved the text drafted by the Orgburo commission in its meeting of 27 June 1927; see RTsKhIDNI f. 17, op. 3, ed. khr. 641, l. 5. Miliutin's copy can be found in GARF f. 3415, op. 2, d. 4, l. 22–23.

78. Pokrovskii, "O deiatel'nosti Kommunisticheskoi Akademii," 1–17 (cited in full at note 68); and "Kommunisticheskaia akademiia (kratkii ocherk)," 5.

79. S. Lopatkin, "Kommunisticheskaia akademiia—tsentr nauchnoi kommunisticheskoi mysli," *Kommunisticheskaia revoliutsiia*, no. 14 (June 1929): 83–84.

ideological directives issued by the Party,[80] the least obvious being, of course, self-censorship. Between these two extremes, the institutional environment in which party science developed could mediate the definition of orthodoxy.

By the expansion beginning in 1922, as we have seen, the academy's membership was largely Bolshevik and its interests were identified with party scholarship. The next year marked one of the most significant controversies over orthodoxy at the academy since this reorientation. The affair centered around Lenin's old rival Bogdanov, the former Vperedist and Proletkul't leader who had been widely attacked in 1920 when the proletarian culture movement was brought under the wing of the Party. A more sustained round of attacks came in 1922–23 in connection with the suppression of the left-wing Bolshevik opposition group the Workers' Truth, which, it was charged in a party-wide campaign, had been inspired by Bogdanov.[81] Because Bogdanov was a founding member of the academy and one of the most active members of its presidium, the problem for the academy was acute. The Bogdanov affair of 1923 is a case study of how a party-wide political campaign impinged on the definition of orthodoxy publicly maintained in the actions of the institution.

In two handwritten letters dated 6 and 7 November 1923, Bogdanov challenged the academy to respond to the campaign against him. At the time, academy members may have been uncomfortable to learn that Bogdanov had been arrested in connection with the Workers' Truth and held by the secret police from 8 September to 23 October of that year. Bogdanov's main line of defense both to his GPU interregators and later to the academy drew heavily on a kind of theoretical elitism that is interesting because it may have been calculated to appeal to his audience. Comparing himself to Galileo, he derided the notion that a theorist as advanced as he was connected to the opposition group's "juve-

80. One of the more spectacular ideological directives of NEP can be reconstructed from Riazanov's letter of resignation to the presidium of the academy in 1931; he gave as his reason for leaving the editorial board of *Pod znamenem marksizma* the ban on criticizing Bukharin's *Historical Materialism*, a chief party textbook. See Riazanov, "V prezidium Kommunisticheskoi Akademii," 8 February 1931, RTsKhIDNI f. 147, op. 1, d. 33, l. 52–59. Riazanov appears to have left the editorial board between issue 4–5 in 1923 and the third issue of 1924. If Riazanov's description of this interdiction is accurate, it explains Vucinich's puzzled exclamation about Bukharin's treatise: "It had no competition. The Communist Academy could not find either an individual or a team to prepare a comprehensive textbook on historical materialism." Vucinich, *Empire of Knowledge*, 82–83.

81. For example, Ia. Iakovlev, "Menshevizm v proletkul'tovskoi odezhde," *Pravda*, 4 January 1923, 2.

nile" theories of an exploiting Soviet "new bourgeoisie" drawn from the "organizing intelligentsia." As he outlined his position on the most controversial of theoretical questions, the nature of the regime, he demonstrated he had moved away from his civil-war era theories of the October Revolution as a barracks communist worker-soldier "uprising" (*vostanie*) (as early as November 1917 he applied the term "war communism" in a letter to Lunacharskii). In 1923, he denied ever having referred to "anything resembling" a "worker-soldier rebellion [*bunt*]"; a "communist block" of workers, working peasantry, and working intelligentsia was the basis of the Soviet order.[82]

"My arrest," he wrote to the academy, "was the result of three years of literary-political persecution, during which I kept my own mouth shut. During this persecution my clear yet undisseminated ideas were distorted and perverted to such a degree that it became possible to attribute to me a childishly naive article in the 'Workers' Truth,'" whose adherents were the target of a wave of arrests in September 1923.[83]

Bogdanov appealed in writing to GPU chief Dzerzhinskii, his former colleague in the Bolshevik underground, who at one point appeared in person at one of the interrogations. In lengthy statements addressed to the GPU and its head, Bogdanov repeatedly emphasized that he was now an "apolitical," a nonparty theoretician and researcher; the academy, he claimed, "was considered . . . not a political but a scientific organization" that studies political phenomena. It is noteworthy, however, that Bogdanov in several ways distanced himself ironically from these distinctions even as he made them, not least by always putting "apolitical" in quotation marks. Later, Bogdanov maintained he convinced Dzerzhinskii he was innocent of underground political work, but the press campaign against him had not stopped; provincial reports linked him to anarcho-syndicalism, opposition to Soviet power, and

82. Antonova and Drozdova, *Neizvestnyi Bogdanov*, 2:190–92, 198, 209; Petr Alexandrovich Pliutto, "Alexandr Bogdanov on the Period of 'War Communism,'" *Revolutionary Russia* 5 (June 1992): 46–52; John Biggart, "Alexandr Bogdanov and the Revolutions of 1917," *Sbornik*, no. 10 (Summer 1984): 8–10, and "Alexander Bogdanov and the Theory of a 'New Class,'" *Russian Review* 49 (July 1990): 265–82. Bogdanov's 1923 formulations to the GPU, it hardly needs to be said, undoubtedly cast his newer theoretical stance toward the Soviet state in a favorable light.

83. A. A. Bogdanov, "V Prezidium Sots. Akademii," 6 November 1923, RTsKhIDNI f. 259, op. 1, d. 63, l. 1–7. Lengthy statements to his interrogators from the former KGB archives have been published in "'Delo' A. A. Bogdanova (Malinovskogo)," *Voprosy istorii*, no. 9 (1994): 6–11, 14–15, but the journal failed to supply archival identification information for these documents. His diary notes of "five weeks with the GPU," composed on his release on 25 October 1923, has been published in Antonova and Drozdova, *Neizvestnyi Bogdanov*, 1:34–44.

even the Polish secret service. Bogdanov turned to the presidium of the Socialist Academy as the only institution that could clear his name.[84]

Bogdanov's letter to the academy was directed solely against distortions in the party journals. The anonymous "materialist" of *Pod znamenem marksizma* had branded him a political renegade and "theoretical opportunist . . . having no relation to the working class": "Can the Socialist Academy ignore a statement . . . that one of its members has 'long been a political renegade?' Can it allow itself to be considered a refuge for political renegades? . . . The Academy must answer all these questions, whether it wants to or not. Even silence is an answer—and the worst possible one for it." Bogdanov called on the presidium either to expel or defend him.[85]

The academy presidium, however, chose not to accept this challenge; it passed a curt resolution professing no need to react to polemical attacks on Bogdanov or to discuss "in connection to such attacks" whether the academy should maintain his membership.[86] In a second letter dated November 7 Bogdanov took up the subject of the academy's own conduct. Bogdanov charged that during the campaign against him the academy declined to give him normal lecture assignments, had not published his article because of "political-tactical considerations," and had even refrained from inviting him to formal academy functions.

"I have acted honestly and seriously toward the Socialist Academy," Bogdanov wrote. "It has remained my last organizational connection after I left Proletkul't two years ago, convinced that my participation jeopardized that organization. And now it is truly not only in my own personal interests that I hope that [the academy] will rise to the heights of that historical role which it can and must fulfill."[87]

One of the only pieces of evidence of how the academy leadership responded to the Bogdanov affair is a 1927 report to the VTsIK by Miliutin. The academy's new second-in-command at that time reported that Bogdanov, along with Bazarov, Ermanskii, and Sukhanov, were

84. "'Delo' A. A. Bogdanova," 7–10, 14–16; Bogdanov, "V Prezidium," 6 November 1923 (cited in full at n. 83).

85. "Materialist," review of N. Lenin and G. Plekhanov, *Protiv A. Bogdanova* (Moscow: Krasnaia nov', 1923), in *PZM*, no. 8–9 (August–September 1923): 285–86; Bogdanov, "V Prezidium," 6 November 1923 (cited in full at n. 83).

86. "Protokol zasedaniia prezidiuma Sotsialisticheskoi akademii 17-go noiabria 1923," ARAN f. 350, op. 1, d. 20, l. 25.

87. A. A. Bogdanov, "V Prezidium Sotsialisticheskoi Akademii," 7 November 1923, RTsKhIDNI f. 259, op. 1, d. 63, l. 8–13.

still the only prominent non–party members left in the academy. In the early part of the decade, Bogdanov and Ermanskii especially had "a certain influence, if you will," especially in the academy's *Vestnik*. But the "line" at the journal was tightened up to permit only "more or less trustworthy Marxism," and their active participation in academy affairs "somehow annulled itself."[88]

In 1923, in the full glare of publicity, the academy ostracized one of its founders from its affairs; it would take no action to swim against the tide. In at least one respect, however, Miliutin's later report was not accurate; in 1927, Bogdanov's papers at the academy were still being respectfully received.[89] How can we explain the differing conduct in the academy in 1923 and 1927? The answer to this question points to another dimension of the problem of orthodoxy.

Even when his life depended on it in the prisons of the secret police, Bogdanov could argue that *nauka* was apolitical only with irony. Party scholarship as a movement was even less willing to invoke a division of spheres between science and politics. But this did not prevent the Bolshevik intellectuals from nonetheless remaining deeply convinced that *nauka* was higher, more rigorous in its forms and methods, and hence qualitatively different from mass Marxism and political work. In academy policies a distinction—troubled, blurry, but perceptible nonetheless—was maintained between the realm of *nauka* and the realm of party politics. Bogdanov's very presence as a politically disreputable nonparty Marxist at the academy testified to the enduring validity of this distinction.

The academy leadership in the early 1920s was consciously determined to maintain scholarship at the institution on a plane distinct from party publicistics. The editorial board of the academy's *Vestnik*, for example, took a formal resolution at the end of 1922 to "consider it essential to delimit the functions of the journal *Pod znamenem marksizma* so that the latter takes on the character of a "fighting Marxist polemical organ, as opposed to a scientific-research one." This resolution reveals a belief in a hierarchy of publications, with research and high theory distinct from more propagandistic genres. A kind of protected forum for scholarly discussions was given institutional form in the academy's tra-

88. "Zasedanie komissii uchenogo komiteta TsIK Soiuza SSR po obsledovaniiu nauchnykh uchrezhdenii pri Kommunisticheskoi Akademii. 17 fevralia 1927," ARAN f. 350, op. 1, d. 145, l. 5–6.

89. See the discussion in A. A. Bogdanov, "Peredely nauchnosti rassuzhdeniia," 14 May 1927, ARAN f. 350, op. 2, d. 144, l. 1–67.

dition of giving papers (*doklady*) that could be both public disputations and scholarly presentations followed by discussions. The discussions, unlike many of the papers, were rarely published and have survived only in the academy archives.[90]

Since this belief system, which conceived of *nauka* as a special preserve, was itself riddled with tensions, with its concomitant urge to declare that knowledge could never be neutral and must be made to serve the revolution, the conception of "scientific-research work" as a privileged genre not fully identified with politics was vulnerable. The evolution of orthodoxy at the academy is to a large extent the story of the continued erosion of the privileged conception of *nauka* in the party institution.

The distinction between scholarship and propaganda, for example, did not negate the Bolshevik intellectuals' wholehearted acceptance of responsibility for the academy's ideological line. The controversy over "revisionist" translations of György Lukács's 1923 *Geschichte und Klassenbewußtsein* in the *Vestnik* in 1924 is instructive in this regard. On the one hand, the proposition that in a scholarly as opposed to a "mass" publication it was possible to be more lax in publishing heterodox views was closely related to the conception of *nauka*'s higher sphere. This at least was the argument advanced when the presidium was criticized in the cell for publishing the translations. Interestingly enough, however, a month before the academy presidium had already instructed the philosopher Deborin to compose a response; the latter then attacked Lukács for idealism and overestimation of the role of consciousness.[91] With the academy not hesitant to commission official commentary on sensitive questions of theory, it could be lobbied or pressured to make such pronouncements. In 1924, for example, one academy member, exasperated by Timiriazev's swipes against Einstein's Theory of Relativity, petitioned the presidium to pass a resolution certifying that Einstein's theory was not reactionary![92]

This delicate, contradictory situation—in which Bolshevik intellectuals embraced the high calling of *nauka* yet could conceive of the most

90. "Protokol zasedaniia redaktsii 'Vestnika,'" 30 December 1922, ARAN f. 370, op. 1, d. 1, l. 10; for example, see the discussion of censorship in A. V. Lunacharskii, "Teatral'naia politika sovetskoi vlasti," 2 October 1926, ARAN f. 350, op. 2, d. 90, l. 1–68.

91. "Protokol no. 64 Otkrytogo sobraniia iacheiki RKP(b) Komakademii ot 17 dekabria 1924," RGAODgM f. 477, op. 1, d. 4, l. 124–26; "Protokol zasedaniia prezidiuma Sotsialisticheskoi Akademii, l. 25 (cited in full at note 86); A. Deborin, "G. Lukach i ego kritika marksizma," *PZM*, no. 6–7 (June-July 1924): 49–69.

92. Ia. Metunovskii, "Sekretariu Sotsakademii. 19/II-1924," ARAN f. 370, op. 1, d. 1, l. 15.

contested scientific problems being resolved by decree—shifted above all under the influence of the inner-party political-ideological battles of the decade. This occured primarily after 1924; in 1923–24 the Trotskyist opposition had less impact at the academy than at other institutions, causing less overt restructuring than, for example, at IKP.[93]

This stemmed in part from the circumstance that the academy's party cell was far less important than those of the other party educational institutions.[94] The prominent members of the academy rarely if ever appeared at the cell; their primary party organization affiliation was invariably elsewhere. Until the influx of young *nauchnye sotrudniki* into the academy in the latter half of the 1920s, the cell was dominated by students from the academy's courses in Marxism. Given the fact that the academy was a sprawling institution to begin with, the cell at first was of negligible significance. Until the latter part of the decade, this situation freed the Bolshevik intellectuals at the academy from the pressures of party cell politics so palpable at IKP and Sverdlov; in a way it institutionalized the generational division between Old Bolshevik theorists and the red professors.

After 1923–24, for example, Preobrazhenskii and Radek, Trotskii's closest oppositionist colleagues, continued to play leading roles at the academy. Preobrazhenskii was not officially listed as main editor of the academy's *Vestnik*; but a presidium resolution from January 1926, appointing Dvoilatskii as temporary "leader" of the journal during Preobrazhenskii's absence from Moscow, confirms that as late as 1926 the oppositionist theoretician was the de facto head of the editorial board.[95]

At the Communist Academy, developments surrounding the suppression of the United Opposition represent the major turning point that was reached three or four years before at institutions lower in the hierarchy. As the political fight with the opposition wore on in 1926, Preobrazhenskii lost his influence in the presidium. But his book *Novaia*

93. Trotskii's adherents did achieve a significant degree of support in the academy cell, but outright opposition majorities like those found at other party schools did not materialize there. "Protokol No. 28 zakrytogo sobraniia iacheiki pri Sots. Akademii 12/XII-23 g.," RGAODgM f. 477, op. 1, d. 2, l. 25 ob.-26; for other cell protocols from 1923–24, see l. 33, and d. 4, l. 107–12, l. 50–51.

94. Until the mid-1920s the cell united the party organizations of the academy with the Marx-Engels Institute and the Lenin Library, because of the small numbers of Communists at those institutions. The cell thus spent an inordinate amount of time on the professional disputes and other problems outside the academy. See RGAODgM f. 477, op. 1, d. 2, l. 1; d. 6, l. 14; and d. 9, l. 57.

95. "Protokol zasedaniia Prezidiuma Kommunisticheskoi Akademii ot 30/I-1926 g.," ARAN f. 350, op. 1, d. 46, l. 21.

Ekonomika still went through two editions in the academy publishing house in 1926. In the meantime, Pokrovskii and the academy press took pains to disassociate the academy as an institution from Preobrazhenskii's oppositionist views. Finally, in 1927 the academy presidium voted not to publish a third edition of this work after Miliutin warned that copies had been snapped up as part of an "oppositionist sensation." The contrary Riazanov unsuccessfully supported a third edition by appealing to the perogatives of scholarship: the book was "a serious work by a person who seriously studies economic problems." Riazanov was voted down, but Preobrazhenskii's other work was still being published in the *Vestnik* as late as 1927.[96]

Between 1924 and 1926, however, cell politics at the academy, as well as the balance of forces preserving scholarship outside the immediate nexus of party politics, shifted noticeably. Those years can be regarded as the time when a younger generation of party scholars, educated with different traditions and priorities, launched its career at the academy. The numbers are striking: before 1 January 1925 there were only 20 *nauchnye sotrudniki* at the academy; by 1 May 1926 there were 67, and by 1928 the number had jumped to 156. Of these young scholars at the academy in 1927, a full 75 percent had graduated from the Institute of Red Professors.[97] This represented a significant change in the life of the academy; the red professors brought with them their distinctively combative political culture. The younger generation, not as heavily taxed with the time-consuming responsibilities the older Bolshevik intellectuals had assumed outside the academy, was capable of altering the tone of the institution as a whole.

The academy's party school, the courses in Marxism, also contributed to changes in the atmosphere at the institution. As the courses expanded from about sixty students in 1921 to over a hundred in 1926, the party qualifications and percentage of students listed as proletarian increased dramatically. This was due to the fact that by the mid-1920s the courses were geared toward promising and experienced party workers mostly from the regional party committees, who were rising politicians in their own right.[98] Among the students with the highest party

96. "Zasedanie Prezidiuma Kommunisticheskoi Akademii. 2/IV-27 g.," l. 36–37 (cited in full at note 71); Shapiro, "Communist Academy," 167–69.

97. Cherepnina, "Deiatel'nost'," 70–71.

98. "Kursy po izucheniiu marksizma pri S. A.," *VSA*, no. 4 (April–June 1923): 459–64; "Khronika," *VKA*, no. 12 (1925): 369–70; "Khronika," *VKA*, no. 15 (1926): 338; Shapiro, "Communist Academy," 114–17; "Protokol zasedaniia Biuro iacheiki i Kurskoma [Kursov marksizma] Komakademii 29-go Maia 1925," RGAODgM f. 474, op. 1, d. 6, l. 43.

posts were several who actively used the academy cell as a base for their work in support of the United Opposition. As the cell increased in importance and as new, unprecedented measures were taken to defeat the opposition, the political struggles within the cell came to affect the entire institution.

In 1926 two students from the courses in Marxism, Bakaev and Nikolaeva, the first a member of the Central Control Commission, traveled to Leningrad to speak at factories on behalf of the United Opposition, causing an uproar in the cell. A separate investigation was launched into the distribution of secret factional documents at the academy, with which Bakaev was also involved. These and other materials from 1926–27 reveal the political tactics of the party majority. To force the hand of active oppositionists, the Central Committee passed a barrage of regulations so stringent that oppositionists either had to recant their views or violate party disciplinary rules.[99]

For example, it was illegal for Bakaev and Nikolaeva to travel to Leningrad because TsK-TsKK resolutions forbade opposition speeches in front of other party cells, as well as travel without permission of the cell leadership. In September 1927, distribution of the opposition's "new platform" at the academy was interpreted by the cell as an antiparty act. In a move reminiscent of what Bogdanov had experienced in 1923, the academy cell reportedly segregated the oppositionists into a separate group which was deprived of its outside teaching and lecturing assignments. In 1927 the cell required all potential sympathizers of the opposition to answer questions about their political beliefs in written form, resulting in a wave of recantations.[100]

Meanwhile, the position of the opposition leaders at the academy was in grave jeopardy. Pokrovskii paved the way for the academy's disassociation from them by invoking the axiom of party scholarship that science was never neutral. In early 1927 the historian avowed that

99. According to one informer, these documents included articles by Zinov'ev and Trotskii on international and inner-party questions. "Protokol 39 Zasedaniia Biuro iacheiki VKP(b) Kommunisticheskoi Akademii ot 12-go oktiabria 1926 g.," RGAODgM f. 477, op. 1, d. 9, l. 62–64; "Otvetstvennyi sekretar' iacheiki Kom. Akademii Mutnov. V Tsentral'nuiu kontrol'nuiu komissiiu VKP(b). Kopiia: V Sekretariat TsK VKP(b)," 22 October 1926, ibid., l. 70. On the Central Committee measures, "Po Rossii," *Sotsialisticheskii vestnik*, 16 October 1926, 14, and 1 November 1926; "Posles"ezdovskaia bor'ba s oppozitsiei," *Sotsialisticheskii vestnik*, 31 March 1926, 13–14.

100. "Protokol 23 zasedaniia Biuro iacheiki VKP(b) Kom. Akademii ot 26/IX-27 g.," RGAODgM f. 477, op. 1, d. 15, l. 83–85; "Protokol obshchego zakrytogo sobraniia iacheiki VKP(b) Kom. Akademii 28/IX-27 g.," ibid., d. 13, l. 28–29; and RGAODgM f. 477, op. 1, d. 15, l. 37–39, 175–76, 179–83, 187–89.

bourgeois scholars were eclectics, "But with us there is one line, one scientific method. If in our midst two opinions are encountered, then for us it is completely clear that one of them is undoutedly wrong." He also added: "At least I did not hear a single indication even from the opposition that such an important scholarly institution should be neutral in high politics. Thank God, all of us are sufficiently Marxist, Leninist, and communist that no one said that."[101]

With the opposition demonstrations at the tenth anniversary of October, grounds were finally available for expulsion of oppositionists from the Party. On 24 October 1927 a large meeting of the academy and Lenin Library voted its symbolic approval for the exclusion of Trotskii and Zinov'ev from the Central Committee in a vote reported as 197–1. On 12 November, the academy presidium—made up of Pokrovskii, Miliutin, Kritsman, Pashukanis, Timiriazev, and Krinitskii—held a meeting to discuss the expulsion of Preobrazhenskii and Radek from the academy. Other leading academy members such as Deborin, Varga, and Friche were also present. Pokrovskii justified expulsion of the oppositionists by citing the newly passed 1927 Central Committee directive that anointed the academy "the scholarly organ" of the Central Committee (raising the possibility that this directive had been conceived with the oppositionist academy members in mind). "Some comrades have declared war on what the Party officially calls Marxism and Leninism. We support this official opinion and cannot support any other, since the Party supports it, and the Academy is, as it is said in the directive . . . the scientific organ of the Party, the center of communist science."[102]

Almost half the academy membership had always been filled symbolically by leading party figures who in fact rarely or never took part in the academy's work. In early 1927 Miliutin had reported that of sixty-seven "academicians" only thirty participated regularly in academy affairs. Accordingly, the general assembly of the academy had to approve the dismissal of Trotskii, Smirnov, and Rakovskii along with Preobrazhenskii and Radek. At around the same time, the assembly proffered new, equally symbolic memberships in the academy to Molotov, Rykov, and Stalin.[103]

101. "Stenograficheskii otchet Plenuma Kommunisticheskoi Akademii. 29-go ianvaria 1927 goda," ARAN f. 350, op. 1, d. 85, l. 21–22.

102. RGAODgM f. 477, op. 1, d. 13, l. 57; "Stenogramma zasedaniia Prezidiuma. 12 noiabria 1927 g.," ARAN f. 350, op. 1, d. 99, l. 52.

103. "Zasedanie komissii uchenogo komiteta TsIK," l. 8 (cited in full at note 88); "Plenum Komm. Akademii 20 marta 1928 g.," *Informatsionnyi biulleten'*, no. 9 (March–May 1928): 3; "Plenum Kommunisticheskoi Akademii," ibid., no. 5 (January–March 1927): 1.

The struggle with the opposition undermined the tradition of unpublicized scholarly disputation when the 1927 debates degenerated into partisan confrontations and Miliutin had transcripts of opposition comments in the question and answer periods distributed outside the academy.[104] Explicit curtailment of the tradition followed in 1928. The presidium resolved that "as a rule, if a paper is scheduled at the Communist Academy with which it, as institution, does not agree, then it must propose its own co-speaker."[105] The more the affairs of party scholarship became the affair of the entire Party, the more the privileged position of *nauka* slipped away.

It was not just political affiliation with opposition groups that came to be monitored, but ideas voiced in theoretical debates that could be connected with oppositionist platforms. Questionnaires from purges conducted at the academy cell in 1929 about membership in opposition groups demanded to know "your relationship to the discussion on industrialization at the Institute of World Economy" or simply queried, "Participation in controversial historical questions?"[106]

Since the academy cell acted as the main agent in the struggle against the United Opposition, it emerged after 1927 for the first time as a major player in academy affairs. The internal dynamics of academy politics altered as the academy cell became noticeably more capable of exerting pressure on the presidium. The cell chided the academy leadership for avoiding the self-criticism campaign, shirking planning in scholarly affairs, employing non–party members in academy work, and even for failure to heed cell recommendations on financial affairs.[107] As the senior generation of Bolshevik intellectuals found itself suddenly vulnerable to militant atack in 1929, the cell even staged a power play

104. "Protokol zasedaniia Biuro iacheiki VKP(b) Kom. Akademii ot 11/III-1927 g.," RGAODgM f. 477, op. 1, d. 15, l. 26. Pokrovskii charged that in 1927 some papers had been "masked" or "half-masked" statements for the opposition; neither in the realm of theory or politics would the academy become a "parliament of opinions." Pokrovskii, "O deiatel'nosti Kommunisticheskoi Akademii," l. 16 (cited in full at note 68).

105. "Protokol No. 14/31 zasedaniia Prezidiuma Kommunisticheskoi Akademii ot 8/XII-1928 g.," ARAN f. 350, op. 1, d. 172, l. 36–37.

106. "Protokol No. 4 obshchego otkrytogo sobraniia iacheiki Kom. Akademii ot 16/VIII-29 g. po chistke t. Arutiuniana," RGAODgM f. 477, op. 1, d. 26, sviazka 2, l. 76–77, also l. 78–79, 82–85, 108–9, 111.

107. "Otchet Biuro iacheiki VKP(b) Kom. Akademii za vremia s oktiabria 1926 po mai 1927 g.," RGAODgM f. 477, op. 1, d. 15, l. 55–59; "Protokol No. 12 sobraniia iacheiki Kom. Akademii, 23/IX-27," ibid., d. 26, sviazka 2, l. 122–38; "Rezoliutsiia biuro iacheiki Kom. Akademii po dokladu uchenogo sekretaria prezidiuma K. A.," no date, late 1928, ibid., d. 22, l. 226–27; "Protokol no. 7 zasedaniia Biuro iacheiki VKP Kom. Akademii 20 fevralia 1928," l. 56–57; "Protokol no. 8 zasedaniia biuro iacheiki VKP(b) Kom. Akademii 27 fev. 1928," ibid., l. 64–66.

by demanding the presidium present all plans and reports to the cell before issuing them.[108]

Finally, the conception of *nauka* standing above current politics faltered under the overriding political imperative for the party majority to endow its pronouncements with an air of infallibility. As one oppositionist resolution at a general meeting of the academy cell in 1928 charged: "Party members are being taught the lesson that the Central Committee cannot make mistakes, that one can in no circumstances criticize it and everything that it says must be accepted by the Party as 100 percent Leninist truth." Only three people out of the two hundred present dared to vote in favor of such a resolution.[109] Around the same time, official formulations of the academy's theoretical and scholarly responsibilities were being touched up to include a novel component, the active defense of majority party policy.

In a striking fashion, defense of the party line was tied into the academy's service role as it had been articulated earlier in the decade. Active advancement of the Party's interests through *nauka* was portrayed as one additional obligation of the institution, a new service added to the list that had already been drawn up. As one commentator phrased it: "The Academy represents the scholarly opinion of the Party and it will not hide behind so-called objectivity in disputed questions; attack on all perversions of the party line enters into its responsibilities."[110] In essence, this represented a new ideological service function.

The emergence of the basic component of Stalinist-type *partiinost'* at the Communist Academy—the notion that scholarship and theory must actively advance the interests of the Party—thus occurred not after Stalin's 1931 letter to *Proletarskaia revoliutsiia*[111] but before Stalin had consolidated power as undisputed party leader. It emerged in part out of party scholarship's embrace of service to the party-state and was facilitated by the slow collapse of the Bolshevik intellectuals' privileged conception of *nauka*.

These origins of the new party-mindedness at the leading center of party social science say something about its nature. This was not merely an ideological *diktat*, which in moments of crisis could force obedience

108. Untitled report on party cell activities, probably May 1929, RGAODgM f. 477, op. 1, d. 28, sviazka 2, l. 64.

109. "Rezoliutsiia na obshchem sobranii iacheiki pri Komakademii 15/IX-28 g.," RGAODgM f. 477, op. 1, d. 13, l. 20–21.

110. Lopatkin, "Kommunisticheskaia akademiia," 84.

111. Stalin's famous intervention on the historical front is discussed, among others, by George Enteen, in his *Soviet Scholar-Bureaucrat*, 160.

to an officially sanctioned line. As we have seen, such "reconciliations with reality" had happened before. Rather, *partiinost'* began to supersede *nauchnost'* as the organizing principle of party scholarship. The identity of party scholarship began to revolve more around service—including ideological service—than its special capabilities for conducting "scientific-research work." The shift deepened as party scholarship struggled more fully to distinguish itself from bourgeois scholarship, to cast itself as an intellectual movement that accorded fundamentally with the new socioeconomic order.

Collectivism, Planning, and Marxist Scholarship

Like the new orthodoxy, the innovations the academy attempted to make in introducing "collective" work in the 1920s cannot be understood outside the perspective of the academy's aspirations. Collectivism would set party scholarship apart in its methods as well as methodology. Advancement of collective endeavors in academy scholarship, which began around 1924, became a way of boosting the institution's credentials.[112] Collective research was touted as efficient and intrinsically suited to a socialist economy; nonparty scholars who believed in the creativity of genius were indicted for individualism.

In fact, many of the first "collective" projects from the Communist Academy in the 1920s—bibliographies, reference works, and specialized encyclopedias—represent some of the institution's most enduring scholarly work. Most notably, the presidium of the separately administered *Bol'shaia Sovetskaia Entsiklopediia* (Great Soviet Encyclopedia, or *BSE*), one of the most ambitious projects of the Bolshevik intellectuals of NEP, was virtually identical with the academy's top leadership.[113]

The idea for a "socialist encyclopedia," so attractive to the Bolshevik intellectuals because of the images it raised of the Enlightenment *Encyclopédie*, first took shape in a Communist Academy resolution of 1923. By 1925 the society "Soviet Encyclopedia" was formed by the academy to administer the project; the first volume appeared in 1926 under the general editorship of Otto Shmidt. The project showcased some of the academy's most cherished ideals for a new *nauka*. As the opening editorial proclaimed, it was based on collaborative work, was intended as

112. See Miliutin's report in "Zasedanie komissii uchenogo komiteta TsIK," l. 7–8 (cited in full at note 88).

113. See the materials on the *BSE* from 1924–29 in ARAN f. 1759, op. 2, d. 7.

"scientific" yet accessible to a broad audience (at the level of someone with a secondary or *rabfak* education), and social science entries were thoroughly Marxist. Special emphasis was given to "practical" areas: economics, current politics, the Soviet system in the social sciences, and agriculture and technology in the natural and exact sciences.[114]

The party historian Nevskii, reviewing the first volume of the encylopedia in 1926, coyly professed uncertainty whether Pokrovskii or Shmidt would go on to play the role of Diderot or d'Alembert, although he favorably compared the Soviet encyclopedia to its Enlightenment predecessor. In the privacy of the academy presidium, Kritsman asserted in 1927 that "of all the large projects which the *Komakademiia* has undertaken, [the encyclopedia] is the only one that can to some degree strengthen the prestige of the Academy in comparison to the All-Union Academy of Sciences." But in one sense this impressive achievement became something of an embarassment for the academy. According to the annoyed activists of the academy's party cell, of the 160 scholars working on the project in 1928 only 13 were Communists.[115] The true labor force behind the Great Soviet Encyclopedia was despised "bourgeois" science. The editorial board was made up of the leading lights of the academy, and the social science topics were controlled by them, but the weakness of party scholarship was nonetheless glaringly apparent. Perhaps because of this predominance of nonparty scholars, the Communist Academy never took formal credit for the project, and the name of the institution did not appear in the published volumes.

If the encyclopedia taxed the academy's capabilities, other forms of collective work interfered with the institution's research capacity. In the latter half of the 1920s collective work increasingly came to mean textbooks, compilations, and anthologies (*khrestomatiia*).[116] Like consulting work, these projects began to inhibit advanced research. Work linked to "political enlightenment" insulated the academy from association with

114. "Zapiska Komakademii v Prezidium TsIK SSSR ob izdanii Bol'shoi Sovetskoi Entsiklopedii," in Ostrovitianov, *Organizatsiia nauki*, 222–23; "Ot redaktsii," in *BSE*, 1st ed., 1:i–ii.

115. V. Nevskii, "Bol'shaia sovetskaia entsiklopediia," *Pechat' i revoliutsiia*, no. 7 (October–November 1926): 113; "Zasedanie Prezidiuma Kommunisticheskoi Akademii 2/IV-27 g.," l. 7 (cited in full at note 71); "Protokol No. 7 Zasedaniia Biuro iacheiki," l. 56–57 (cited in full at note 107).

116. See, for example, the request from Glavlit censor and academy member Lebedev-Polianskii to compile an anthology on cultural questions as a favor to the MK. "V Prezidium Komm. Akademii. 18/II-28," ARAN f. 597, op. 3, d. 7, l. 1; "Protokol No. 8 Zasedaniia Prezidiuma Kommunisticheskoi Akademii ot 12-go maia 1928 g.," ARAN f. 1759, op. 2, d. 12, l. 40–42.

"scholasticism." Pokrovskii's maxim was ostensibly a startling declaration for the head of an academy: "The Communist Academy is distinguished from all other 'academic' institutions by the fact that there has to be as little academicism as possible in its activities."[117] Yet the academy's preoccupation with textbooks also reflected party scholarship's concern with official mass publications that increasingly, in the words of one historian, came to play the "special role" of providing the "point of orientation for researchers" and marking the "boundaries of the permissible." Miliutin touted textbooks as a major job for the academy, and in early 1928 Pokrovskii announced that a textbook was no less important than "the most profound Marxist monographic research."[118]

Collective work assumed an important place in the academy's pantheon of tasks to be fulfilled. The quantity of collective work and practical projects—like statistics on the percentages of party members or proletarians—became a standard element of any academy report after around 1924. A firm acceptance of the necessity of planning science became widespread among Marxist academics as well as among many party and government officials. A literature on the "scientific organization of scientific labor" (*nauchnaia organizatsiia nauchnogo truda*, or NONT) centered around issues ranging from collectivized research to efficient note-taking.[119]

The irony was that planning of scholarship, supposedly intrinsic in the new collectivism, was feeble at best before 1927. Limited ties were established with a few other institutions, such as the department of Marxism-Leninism at the Ukrainian Academy of Sciences.[120] To improve this record, a series of special commissions beginning in October 1927 and continuing through 1928 examined the issue of coordinating the activities of Marxist-Leninist research institutes.[121]

No matter how little planning actually occurred, the issue was intimately tied to the academy leadership's oft-repeated certainty that the

117. Quoted in Lopatkin, "Kommunisticheskaia akademiia," 84.

118. "Pervaia konferentsiia," 246, 273; on textbooks, Enteen, "Soviet Historiography."

119. Graham, *Soviet Academy of Sciences*, 43–79.

120. "Otchet o rabote kafedry Marksizma-Leninizma pri U.A.N. za vremia s 1-go aprelia 1926 g. po 1 marta 1928 g.," ARAN f. 350, op. 1, d. 170, l. 111–66; "Pervaia konferentsiia," 246.

121. These committees, manned by virtually the entire Communist Academy leadership, were largely limited to discussing the Communist Academy and its closest neighbors, the Lenin Institute and the Marx-Engels Institute. "Pom. Direktora Instituta Lenina Vl. Sorin. V Prezidium Kommunisticheskoi Akademii. 29 oktiabria 1927," ARAN f. 350, op. 1, d. 138, l. 2; "Protokol No. 11 Zasedaniia komissii po soglasovaniiu deiatel'nosti nauchno-issledovatel'skikh uchrezhdenii ot 28 aprelia 1928," ARAN f. 1759, op. 2, d. 10, l. 23–24; M. N. Pokrovskii, "V sekretariat TsK. 31/V-28 g.," RTsKhIDNI f. 147, op. 1, d. 33, l. 26.

academy could become the future center of planning, hence organizing and controlling, the world of higher learning. The problem was that the academy, as was suggested at the outset, never rigorously distinguished between dominating party-Marxist institutions and academia as a whole. It had never needed to; yet the distinction assumed critical importance once planning became, as it were, an all-union question in 1928. A 1928 Orgburo commission under Pokrovskii met with few results, but in 1929 the Orgburo nevertheless designated the Communist Academy a "planning center" of Marxist-Leninist scientific-research institutions. The first and second conferences of Marxist-Leninist Scientific-Research Institutions in 1928 and 1929, initiated and orchestrated by the Communist Academy, included Ukrainian and Belorussian delegations and featured much discussion of planning. These gatherings also presented the Communist Academy with a degree of control over coordinating research plans, if only for the "Marxist-Leninist" institutions.[122] Yet if all higher learning were up for grabs, the far greater question was who would gain control of scientific planning on an all-union level.

It was still hard to predict whether a single central planning agency for science and scholarship would emerge from the bureaucratic cacophony of NEP (none ever did). But already in 1928, all signals prompted academy leaders to surmise that if such an agency were set up, Gosplan or a party organ would assume priority over the Communist Academy.[123] Nonetheless, new vistas were rapidly appearing. An unmistakable signal for an assault on bourgeois specialists and the non-party intelligentsia was given in the wake of trumped-up charges of specialist sabotage in the coal-mining region of Shakhtii. A Central Committee circular announcing the affair to all party members rang with a novel intensity of anti-specialist rhetoric; this clarion call was proposed by Stalin, Bukharin, and Molotov for Politburo consideration and approved with corrections on 7 March 1928, three days before the

122. "Vypiska iz protokola No. 122 zasedaniia Orgbiuro TsK ot 27.V.29," RTsKhIDNI f. 147, op. 1, ed. khr. 33, l. 28–29; "Pervaia konferentsiia"; "Protokol zasedaniia komissii po sozyvu 2-i konferentsii marksistsko-leninskikh nauchno-issledovatel'skikh uchrezhdenii ot 28 ianvaria 1929," ARAN f. 350, op. 1, d. 247, l. 1, also l. 22, 31, 101; "2-aia konferentsiia marksistskikh-leninskikh nauchnykh uchrezhdenii. 8-go aprelia 1929. Stenogramma," ibid., d. 250, l. 2–79.

123. This seems why Pokrovskii continued to push the TsK Secretariat for a "party commission" to found an "all-union scientific Gosplan, if not an all-union Glavnauka," in which the Communist Academy would be given a leading role along with Agitprop. Pokrovskii, "V Sekretariat TsK VKP(b). Kopiia APO TsK," no date, probably March 1929, RTsKhIDNI, f. 147, op. 1, ed. khr. 33, l. 75–77.

Mikhail Nikolaevich Pokrovskii speaks from the podium at the First All-Union Conference of Marxist-Leninist Scientific-Research Institutions, organized by the Communist Academy in 1928. Reprinted by permission of the Museum of the Revolution, Moscow, Russia.

Shaktii affair became public with a front-page *Pravda* editorial.[124] In the new atmosphere of sanctioned specialist-baiting this unleashed, the real prize that the planning campaign proferred party scholarship was the suddenly vulnerable institutions of nonparty academia.

A curious phenomenon began to manifest itself in the midst of the discussions of planning. In the name of rational planning, academy members plotted the appropriation and dismemberment of other institutions. This proclivity is present in an especially blunt policy docu-

124. RTsKhIDNI f. 17, op. 3, ed. khr. 676, l. 7, 11–12. Kendall Bailes, *Technology and Society under Lenin and Stalin: Origins of the Soviet Technological Intelligentsia* (Princeton: Princeton University Press, 1978), 76.

ment, resembling more a manifesto for party scholarship, sent to the Central Committee by the executive secretary (*Upravliaiushchii delami*) of the Communist Academy.

The recommendations began conventionally enough: "It is necessary to introduce planning in the realm of scientific research. . . . We need to end this anarchistic disorder and outlive all unneeded parallelism in scholarly work." In this text, however, planning became but one new, brightly colored thread to be woven in to the academy's traditional tapestry of orthodoxy and hegemony. The Communist Academy must lead a "merciless struggle" against all deviations, first of all in its own midst; "The Communist Party must seize science just like in its own time it seized the Soviets, the Trade Unions, and the Cooperatives. . . . The Communist Academy must become the headquarters of the new front."[125]

The academy's reorientation around service, the new *partiinost'*, the erosion of *nauka*'s privileged sphere within the Party, and the tendency for collective forms to undermine research brought party scholarship to the brink of a potentially fatal crisis as the NEP era drew to a close. But instead of perceiving danger, academy leaders saw the anti-specialist offensive as a golden opportunity. After a decade of pursuing hegemonic goals, with endless internal ramifications but to little outward effect, it suddenly became possible to believe they might actually be achieved.

Denouement: RANION and the Academy of Sciences

One of the academy's assaults targeted a mixed institution, a symbol of uneasy coexistence with the nonparty intelligentsia. RANION, which by the end of NEP included fifteen social science research institutes where many nonparty scholars were based, originated in a coalition of institutes first formed in 1921–22 around the social science faculty (FON) of Moscow University.[126] The presidium of the association and the collegia of the member institutes had been stacked with leading party Marxists since 1923, which of course colored all pronouncements put out in the association's name. Although Communists took administrative control, the foundation of RANION nonetheless represented a

125. S. Melent'ev, "Chem dolzhna byt' Kommunisticheskaia Akademiia," no date, GARF f. 3316, op. 45, d. 34, l. 1–5.

126. On the successive changes in RANION's structure, see G. D. Alekseeva, "Rossiiskaia assotsiatsiia nauchno-issledovatel'skikh institutov obshchestvennykh nauk (RANION), 1924–1929," in Nechkina et al., *Ocherki istorii*, 4: 233–37.

concession to the nonparty professoriat after the imposition of the 1922 university charter. At that time, many of Moscow's communist student and teacher activists were outraged by the degree of autonomy the nonparty professors were offered in these research institutes.[127] During the course of the 1920s, the scientific-political section of GUS, led by Pokrovskii, carried out an incremental but persistent policy of boosting the percentage of Communists at RANION and attempting to strengthen Marxist scholarship there.[128]

RANION thus ended up in a weakened position as it slowly twisted under a two-pronged assault. At the center of the institution, leading lights of party scholarship were imported into the presidium of the association (by 1927, thirteen of the fourteen presidium members were party Marxists). As one spokesman admitted, however, before 1925 the subordination of the institutes to the presidium was "purely nominal." Those institutes not formerly associated with the First Moscow University (including four in Leningrad) were even financially independent from the presidium and controlled personel and graduate admissions. But a series of measures, beginning in the fall of 1925 and culminating in a May 1927 order from Glavnauka, substantially strengthened the presidium's powers and created a central admissions committee.[129]

The second prong of the assault came from within. The association was beset by a growing contingent of young communist students who viewed their mission as a struggle against the nonparty professors in their institutes. "There is a constant battle there, sometimes assuming fairly heated forms," Lunacharskii acknowledged. Indeed, a report by the RANION communist faction sharply criticized the association's "tendency to study anti-Marxist problems." The faction derided RANION's publication of the prominent agronomist Chaianov: "The

127. "Protokol obshchego sobraniia professorov, prepodavatelei i nauchnykh sotrudnikov-chlenov RKP," 12 January 1923, RTsKhIDNI f. 17, op. 60, d. 492, l. 1–3. The RANION charter is in RTsKhIDNI f. 17, op. 60, d. 486, l. 30–31. On the circumstances in which RANION was organized as a concession to the nonparty professoriat, which were apparently known to only a few of the top Bolsheviks involved in academic affairs, see "Stenogramma vystupleniia Riazanova D. B. na soveshchanii pri Agit-prop TsK," no later than 6 March 1928, RTsKhIDNI f. 301, op. 2, d. 14, l. 2–3.

128. "Soveshchanie Narkomprosov Soiuznykh i Avtonomnykh Respublik. I-e zasedanie–27 oktiabria 1924," ARAN f. 1759, on. 2, d. 5, l. 64. Pokrovskii, Udal'tsov, and Friche were also on the presidium of RANION in the mid-1920s and helped shape admission policies there. "Instruktsiia o priemnoi i stipendial'noi komissiiakh pri Prezidiuma RANION na 1926 g.," ARAN f. 1759, op. 2, d. 10, l. 21–22.

129. D. A. Magerovskii, "Rossiiskaia assotsiatsiia nauchno-issledovatel'skikh institutov obshchestvennykh nauk (RANION)," *Pechat' i revoliutsiia*, no. 7 (October-November 1927): 276–84.

usual authors are . . . Chaianov and X, Chaianov and Y, etc."[130] Before the fall of 1925, there were only nine communist graduate students of seventy in RANION; but in the following years both the graduate program and the number of Communists was boosted rapidly. In contrast, only 25 percent of the "scientific workers" at RANION as late as 1928 were party members; and this figure was inflated, because the number of communist faculty who actually took part in the life of the institution was "significantly lower."[131]

Perhaps the decisive factor in the demise of RANION, after it suddenly became vulnerable because of the deteriorating position of nonparty intellectuals in 1928, was the enactment of long-standing hegemonic goals within the Communist Academy. In an assault on RANION, the causes of party scholarship, promoting Marxism, and aggressive expansion of the academy happily coincided. In a meeting of leading academy scholars in April 1928, Volgin termed the lack of party members at RANION "alarming."[132] Yet an influx of Marxists was no solution, since it would leave little justification for the association's continued existence: rational scientific planning could not sanction wasteful institutional "parallelism."

As various party figures, Marxist societies, and disciplinary groups whipped up criticism against RANION, a special commission on reorganization at the Communist Academy worked behind the scenes. Among its first decisions were to incorporate RANION's Philosophy Institute and History Institute into the academy. RANION's Timiriazev Agrarian Academy, the major center for non-Marxist agrarian scholars, was divided up in a process beginning in September 1928 and in part transferred to the academy as well. In May 1928 a special meeting convened by the bureau of the Communist Academy presidium (with Pokrovskii, Miliutin, Kritsman, Shmidt, Friche, Deborin, and fifteen other high-level academy members present), met to hear Pashukanis's report on the "reorganization of the academy's institutions." The resolution, giving the example of RANION's philosophy institute, came to the understated but unambiguous conclusion that "parallel existence"

130. "Zapiska Biuro Fraktsii Nauchno-Issledovatel'skogo Instituta (RANION)," no date, ARAN f. 528, op. 3, d. 2, l. 2; A. V. Lunacharskii, "Nauka v SSSR," transcript of lecture, no date, prob. 1928, RTsKhIDNI f. 142, op. 1, d. 179, l. 47.

131. "Pervaia konferentsiia," 257–60; "Sostav nauchnykh rabotnikov nauchno-issledovatel'skikh institutov, vkhodiashchikh v RANION na 1 ianvaria 1928 g.," RTsKhIDNI f. 150, op. 1, d. 92, l. 42.

132. "Protokol No. 11," l. 23 (cited in full at note 121).

of such institutions with those of the Communist Academy was undesirable.[133]

In 1929–30 the Communist Academy absorbed RANION's Institute of Economics, Institute of Soviet Law, and three divisions of its Academy of Artistic Studies. By 1930, RANION had ceased to exist. One historian suggests that the Academy's absorption of the Leningrad Institute of Marxism (which became the Leningrad Branch of the Communist Academy, or LOKA) was also an act against RANION, since the takeover was carried out just after Narkompros had merged that institute with RANION's history institute.[134]

The Communist Academy, and hence party scholarship, was strengthened by the demise of RANION. The academy in most cases quickly absorbed the budgets and incorporated personnel that its nonparty rivals had formerly enjoyed. It was in part on the ruins of the institutional base of mixed communist and nonparty social science scholarship that the academy entered into a period of rapid expansion from 1928 through 1932. For example, the academy's constituent parts numbered 16 in 1927, 22 in 1928, 29 in 1929 and 34 in 1930. Excluding clerical and other staff, the total number of its "scientific workers" increased from 140 in 1927–28 to 378 by the end of 1930.[135]

Yet the expansion of the Communist Academy, reaching its height in 1930, did not lead to the consolidation of its preeminence in the academic world. On the contrary, this moment of organizational triumph coincided with the academy's decline as a research center. In February 1930 the presidium resolved to transform the *Vestnik* into an "informational . . . organ" focusing on Marxist-Leninist research institutions and the training of cadres.[136] The Communist Academy had reaped the fruits

133. "Protokol zasedaniia Biuro Prezidiuma Kommunisticheskoi Akademii ot 19-go maia 1928 g.," ARAN f. 1759, on. 2, d. 12, l. 19. On the Institute of History, "Vypiska iz protokola No. 105 zasedaniia Orgbiuro TsK ot 8 marta 1929 g.," RTsKhIDNI f. 147, op. 1, d. 33, l. 27; T. I. Kalistratova, *Institut istorii FON MGU-RANION (1921–1929)* (Nizhnii Novgorod: Izdatel'stvo "Nizhnii Novgorod," 1992).

134. "Skhema otchetnogo doklada o rabote Komm. Akademii na konferentsii marksistsko-leninskikh nauchno-issledovatel'skikh uchrezhdenii 8-go aprelia 1929 g.," ARAN f. 350, op. 1, d. 248, l. 1, 6; "Proekt Reorganizatsii RANION-a," no date, 1929, ARAN f. 1759, op. 2, d. 10, l. 27–30; Shapiro, "Communist Academy," 215–16. On the Timiriazev Academy, see Solomon, *Soviet Agrarian Debate*, 156–57, and "Protokol soveshchaniia po voprosu o Timiriazevskom nauchno-issledovatel'skom institute, 3/VII-29," ARAN f. 350, op. 1, d. 240, l. 94.

135. "Vypiska iz protokola No. 2 zasedaniia Biuro Prezidiuma Kommunisticheskoi Akademii ot 16-go fevralia 1929 g.," ARAN f. 350, op. 1, d. 240, l. 5–6; Shapiro, "Communist Academy," 218; Alekseeva, "Kommunisticheskaia akademiia," 206.

136. "Protokol No. 8 Zasedaniia Prezidiuma Kom. Akademii ot 31 fevralia 1930 g.," ARAN f. 1759, op. 2, d. 12, l. 59–61; Shapiro, "Communist Academy," 258–61. The *Vestnik* also

of quick victory over RANION. But in the course of the campaign to transform the Academy of Sciences, the ultimately more decisive question of the future preeminent center of scientific-research work was also determined, and not in the favor of the Communist Academy.

The "bolshevization" of the Academy of Sciences became a pivotal moment in the establishment of the Soviet organization of science. It began with the ratification of new election rules in that institution's charter in 1927 and 1928, continued in the campaign to elect Communists and new regime-approved members in 1928–29, and culminated in the expansion and thoroughgoing reorganization of the institution in 1929–30, accompanied by widespread arrests and dismissals.[137]

Despite a flood of recent archival materials, the roots of bolshevization in the decade-long rivalry of the Communist Academy have remained obscure. While key roles in the complex and drawn-out drama were played by the Politburo, the secret police, and the Leningrad party organization, among others, the major impetus behind the vast expansion and takeover of the Academy of Sciences, which also sealed the fate of the Communist Academy, can be traced to the aspirations of party scholarship centered at the *Komakademiia*.[138]

The Communist Academy leadership's involvement in the affairs of its venerable rival can be traced to oversight committees beginning as early as 1924, when bids to curtail the unique autonomy enjoyed by the Academy of Sciences began. In September 1924 Pokrovskii wrote to Rykov, the head of Sovnarkom, to lobby for a draft Academy of Sciences charter put out by Narkompros's Glavnauka, which would have placed the rival academy tightly under the jurisdiction of Glavnauka over the protests of Academy of Sciences permanent secretary Ol'denburg and vice-president Steklov. This attempt to subordinate the Academy of Sciences failed, and in 1925 the Politburo decision to confer all-union status coincided with the its 200th jubilee; the whole extrava-

---

resolved that the academy must respond to "current political campaigns" in addition to conducting "scientific-research work." "Ob itogakh raboty i novykh zadachakh, stoiashchikh pered Komakademiei na novom etape," *VKA*, no. 37–38 (1930): 11.

137. Graham's *Soviet Academy of Sciences* remains the classic work on the topic. See also Aleksey E. Levin, "Expedient Catastrophe: A Reconsideration of the 1929 Crisis at the Soviet Academy of Sciences," *Slavic Review* 47 (Summer 1988): 261–80. The most important piece of scholarship to date in Russian is by the late F. F. Perchenok, "Akademiia nauk na 'velikom perelome,'" in *Zven'ia: Istoricheskii almanakh*, vypusk 1 (Moscow: Feniks, 1990), 163–235.

138. A full-fledged exploration of the relationship between the two academies is contained in Michael David-Fox, "Symbiosis to Synthesis: The Communist Academy and the Bolshevization of the Soviet Academy of Sciences, 1918–1929" (forthcoming).

ganza, for which the Politburo approved 60,000 rubles, produced a windfall of publicity for the older academy.[139]

The public triumph for the Academy of Sciences galvanized its rivals; new plans to subdue it emanated from party scholars. The Politburo had created a special commision to oversee the jubilee headed by Communist Academy second-in-command Miliutin, who took the opportunity to recommend the formation of a new commission for "oversight of the work of the Academy of Sciences."[140] This led to the creation of the so-called Enukidze commission that eventually ran the bolshevization campaign.

Miliutin was already the head of yet another commission, this one under Sovnarkom, which worked from July 1925 to March 1926 on changes to the Academy of Sciences charter. It was this commission which first conceived the crucial rules governing the election of academicians; these were approved by the Politburo in May 1927 and, with further changes in April 1928, provided the basis for the election of the first Communists and party-backed candidates to the academy.[141] As early as October 1927 Communist Academy members Pokrovskii, Miliutin, Volgin, Lunacharskii, and Riazanov received top secret copies from the head of Sovnarkom's Section on Scientific Institutions, Voronov, listing suggested candidates for election to the Academy of Sciences and the openings of new places at the academy (which were later in part reserved for the Marxist social sciences and technical and applied sciences).[142] Party scholars, especially Pokrovskii and Miliutin, who unofficially played the roles of president and vice-president of the

139. "M. N. Pokrovskii. Predsedateliu Sovnarkoma RSFSR A. I. Rykovu. 25.XI.1924," ARAN f. 1759, op. 4, d. 96, l. 1–2; "Tezisy po dokladu Glavnauki o Rossiiskoi Akademii Nauk," no date, 1925, ibid., op. 2, d. 18, l. 4–5; "Protokol No. 70 zasedaniia Politbiuro TsK RKP(b) ot 8 iiulia 1925 goda," RTsKhIDNI f. 17, op. 3, ed. khr. 510, l. 6; also ed. khr. 509, l. 3, and ed. khr. 516, l. 1.

140. "Protokol No. 86 zasedaniia Politbiuro ot 29-go oktiabria 1925 goda," RTsKhIDNI f. 17, op. 3, ed. khr. 526, l. 5. A new set of theses from Glavnauka called for close "ideological and organizational ties" between the Academy of Sciences and the Narkompros organs Glavnauka and GUS (the State Scholarly Council headed by Pokrovskii). "Tezisy po dokladu Glavnauki o Rossiiskoi Akademii Nauk," l. 4–5 (cited in full at n. 139).

141. "Ustav Akademii Nauk SSSR. Proekt komissii SNK SSSR—Pred. V. P. Miliutin," 3 March 1926, ARAN f. 350, op. 1, d. 284, l. 14–27; "Protokol zasedaniia Politbiuro TsK VKP(b) ot 26-go maia 1927 goda," RTsKhIDNI f. 17, op. 3, ed. khr. 636, l. 4–5. At this meeting the Politburo ordered the number of academicians to be boosted from forty to seventy and ratified the infamous clause in the AN charter that allowed for dismissal of academicians if their activities "were clearly to the detriment of the USSR." See also Graham, *Soviet Academy of Sciences*, 87–91.

142. E. Voronov to V. P. Miliutin, October 1927, GARF f. 3415, op. 2, d. 5, l. 29. Twelve copies of this document were sent. Others who received it were Gorbunov, Krinitskii, Litvinov, and Vyshinskii.

Communist Academy, were key players in the oversight of the Academy of Sciences.

The most striking aspect of this monitoring of the Academy of Sciences by the party scholars beginning in the mid-1920s was that the Bolsheviks at first were determined to undermine the stature of the older academy. In 1927 Miliutin was again put in charge of still another Sovnarkom commission to review the Academy of Sciences' newly required annual report; Pokrovskii and Riazanov were also included.[143] Pokrovskii produced an alternately witty, sarcastic, and bitter broadside against the nonparty institution. Depicting the academy as a bastion of "truth-seekers, observing a well-intentioned neutrality toward Soviet power," he condemned it as unable to meet the scientific needs of the present and unwilling to engage in planning. "It is necessary either to radically reorganize the composition and activities of the humanities division of the Academy or to shut it down altogether," Pokrovskii concluded. In a special plea with fundamental implications for his own academy, the Marxist historian called for consideration of whether the Academy of Sciences should be confined to study of the natural and exact sciences.[144]

The other reports of the 1927 Miliutin commission comprised a powerful indictment designed to curtail the old academy's activities. For example, Vyshinskii, the jurist and former rector of Moscow University who would later preside over the show trials of the 1930s, pointed to a "whole range of institutions" at the Academy of Sciences that "do not have any right to exist altogether." Volgin, himself later the permanent secretary of the Academy of Sciences from 1930 to 1935 and its vice-president from 1942 to 1953, charged that the humanities division at that institution suffered from "some kind of organic defect" and was characterized by "vulgar, atheoretical empiricism." The Communist Academy stalwart added pointedly: "If we compare the publications of the Academy of Sciences with those of the Communist Academy, despite all the scholarly-technical advantages of the Academy of Sciences publications, . . . the works of the Communist Academy are noteworthy for the fresh scientific thought that runs through them." It is especially noteworthy that Volgin opposed filling the humanities sections of the

143. "Protokol No. 1 Zasedaniia Komissii SNK SSSR po rasmotreniiu otcheta Akademii Nauk SSSR," 21 June 1927, ARAN f. 1759, op. 2, d. 18, l. 49.

144. M. N. Pokrovskii, "K otchetu o deiatel'nosti Akademii Nauk za 1926 g.," ARAN f. 1759, op. 2, d. 18, l. 88–102; published in *Zven'ia*, 2d ed. (Moscow–St. Petersburg: Feniks, 1992), 580–99.

Academy of Sciences with Marxists, because "in current conditions" this would weaken institutions such as the Communist Academy and the Marx-Engels Institute. Instead, Volgin proposed dismembering the Academy of Sciences and attaching its humanities institutions to various VUZy.[145]

It seems evident that party scholars used the new situation in 1927, coinciding with the first plans for a new socialist offensive and the rise of the Communist Academy as the Party's scholarly organ, to press more concretely for measures that would diminish the Academy of Sciences. In this effort they united with party-oriented allies in the technical sciences grouped in the newly founded All-Union Association for Workers in Science and Technology for Advancement of Socialist Construction (VARNITSO), the establishment of which was overseen by Molotov and Bukharin. The agenda enunciated at the first convocation of VARNITSO's founders on 7 April 1927 minced no words, resolving to work to "strengthen the material base" of research institutes under Narkompros, the Scientific-Technical Administration of VSNKh and other agencies and "weaken" that of the Academy of Sciences.[146]

Communist Academy leaders like Shmidt took part in VARNITSO's founding events, but the organization's guiding light was the soon-to-be academician A. N. Bakh, who not coincidentally was also a member of the 1927 Miliutin commission. Bakh, a biochemist and VSNKh official who was brought into the Academy of Sciences in 1929, punctuated his report to Miliutin by calling for a cap on the Academy of Sciences budget and "unburdening" the academy of "a whole range of institutions."[147] VARNITSO became a willing ally, but still a fledgling junior partner, to the Communist Academy scholars who were pursuing their long-standing preoccupation with the Academy of Sciences.

As concrete plans to reorganize the membership and activities of the Academy of Sciences materialized in 1927, the same group of prominent Bolshevik intellectuals emerged to spearhead the effort. In August 1927 Miliutin, in the name of the Sovnarkom Section on Scientific Institutions, sent out the top secret list of forty-six potential candidates for

145. V. P. Volgin, report for 1927 Miliutin commission (untitled), GARF f. 3415, op. 2, d. 3, l. 29–30.

146. I. A. Tugarinov, "VARNITSO i Akademiia nauk SSSR (1927–1937 gg)," *Voprosy istorii estestvoznaniia i tekhniki*, no. 4 (1989): 46–55.

147. A. N. Bakh, "Otzyv ob otchete o deiatel'nosti Akademii Nauk za 1926 g.," GARF f. 3415, op. 2, d. 3, l. 40–42.

membership in the Academy of Sciences, with a request that Pokrovskii write evaluations of each one.[148]

Perhaps the most important body dealing with the Academy of Sciences for the entire period 1925–29, however, was the so-called Enukidze commission. Designed as a special Sovnarkom link to the old academy after the jubilee, it met irregularly in 1926, to the chagrin of the old academy's leadership, primarily to discuss budgetary issues and foreign travel. Its membership (apart from its namesake and chair) in 1926 included Miliutin as a representative of the Communist Academy and top Agitprop official Knorin, as well as Lunacharskii and Gorbunov. Yet the Enukidze commission was not as idle as the academicians believed. Although it was formed as a Sovnarkom organization, this affiliation seems to have been a fiction put out for the public and the academicians; Politburo protocols show the oversight body in fact became a special commission of the Party's highest organ. By 1928 it defined its role as "political leadership over the Academy of Sciences." Along with the Leningrad obkom of the Party, it directed the election campaign to the Academy of Sciences and took the crucial decision to unleash a "broad campaign" in the press on the elections.[149]

In March 1928 the Enukidze commission submitted its final report to the Politburo, which approved the commission's list of potential candidates for membership in the Academy of Sciences. The list was divided into the party candidates, the first group of Communists later to be elected to the academy; figures "close to us"; and "acceptable candidacies." The commission was authorized to change the list as circumstances dictated; the press campaign and an overhaul of the academy apparat (which took place in the major purge of 1929) were also approved. Given the persistent efforts of the party scholars to undermine the activities of the Academy of Sciences, one of the most striking resolutions the Politburo approved was to "decline the request of comrades Pokrovskii

148. "Zav. Otedelom nauchnykh uchrezhdenii pri SNK SSSR M. N. Pokrovskomu. 29/VIII-27 g.," ARAN f. 1759, op. 2, d. 18, l. 378–80. Pokrovskii's responses are on l. 381–83.

149. "Protokol No. 91 zasedaniia Politbiuro ot 19-go noiabria 1925 goda," RTsKhIDNI f. 17, op. 3, ed. khr. 531, l. 9; "Povestka zasedaniia komissii SNK SSSR po sodeistviiu rabotam Akademii Nauk Soiuza SSR," 9 December 1926, GARF f. A-2306, op. 1, d. 3438, l. 79–80; for other materials, see l. 18–41, 47, 70–73, 77; M. N. Pokrovskii to A. S. Enukidze, June 1928 (no day given), RTsKhIDNI f. 147, op. 1, d. 33, l. 80. It seems that a troika of party scholars was also closely involved with the Enukidze commission: the ubiquitous Pokrovskii; Sverdlov Communist University rector Martyn N. Liadov; and Otto Iul'evich Shmidt, a prominent figure in the Communist Academy and its leading authority in the natural sciences. "K voprosu o rashirenii funktsii Komissii A. S. Enukidze," no date, ARAN f. 1759, op. 2, d. 18, l. 384–85.

and Riazanov to remove their candidacies and to require them to agree to their election to the Academy [of Sciences]."[150] Could it be that the two Communist Academy leaders were reluctant to defect to the rival academy and undermine their own party institutions?

The Politburo had recognized the need for tactical flexibility in upcoming elections to the Academy of Sciences; and the special disciplinary commissions took on the character of protracted negotiations between the academicians and a delegation of party scholars, disingenuously styled "representatives of the Union republics," who insisted on narrowing down the number of candidates to the exact number of vacancies before the elections.[151] Thus all-out crisis erupted when the three most controversial Marxist candidates—the dialectician Deborin, the French Revolution scholar (and Bukharin's brother-in-law) Lukin, and the Marxist literary critic Friche—failed to receive the requisite two-thirds vote in a secret ballot of the academy's general assembly on 12 January 1929. This inflammatory rejection of the tacit arrangements between party and academy leaders was in an underlying sense logical and in its immediate manifestation accidental. Tolz has convincingly shown that majority of the old core of academicians from before 1917—and not just the most prominent scientists like Pavlov and Vernadskii—were more openly and resolutely critical of Marxism and Bolshevism up until 1929 than has previously been assumed. In addition, academicians seem to have underestimated the regime's response as well as overestimated their own importance to it. But this famous episode was also an unexpected result of the Academy of Sciences' traditional secret ballot, since academicians were determined not to sanction the ignomy of electing the three unanimously. Ironically, party scholars had traded so many concessions to get their handful of Marxists elected that the new post-election composition of the Academy of Sciences was even more inclined toward resistance, providing motivation for further reorganization and the secret police action known as the "academic affair" of 1929–30.[152]

150. "Protokol No. 16 zasedaniia Politbiuro TsK VKP(b) ot 22-go marta 1928 goda," RTsKhIDNI f. 17, op. 3, ed. khr. 678, l. 3; "Postanovlenie komissii Politbiuro po voprosu o vyborakh akademikov," approved by Politburo 22 March 1928, ibid., l. 11–13.

151. The "republican" representatives included Moscow-based Communist Academy members Miliutin, Shmidt, the rising Marxist legal theorist Pashukanis, and younger members I. K. Luppol and P. M. Kerzhentsev. The voluminous stenographic reports of the commissions are in GARF f. 3316, op. 45, d. 1–34.

152. Tolz, "Combining Professionalism and Politics"; Perchenok, "Akademiia nauk," 186 and passim; Elena Grigor'evna Ol'denburg, "Zapiska o rabote Sergeia Fedorovicha Ol'denburga v kachestve nepremennogo sekretaria Akademii Nauk v 1928–1929," in ARAN (St. P.) f.

During the siege of the Academy of Sciences following the rejection of three communist candidates, the threat to dissolve the institution into its component parts became a distinct possibility, which might have given the Communist Academy an unprecedented opportunity to step into its place. Dissolution was certainly used as a threat both before and after the rejection of the three communist candidates. In negotiations, the "representatives of the union republics" had raised the specter of the break-up of the institution as leverage. After the election debacle, a delegation of academicians was summoned from Leningrad to an emergency meeting in the Kremlin to convince the authorities to allow the three blackballed Communists to be reelected. While the conciliation was successful, Politburo member Kuibyshev still demanded the old academy be treated to "fire and sword."[153]

It is unlikely the Academy of Sciences was genuinely close to destruction in 1929, but the fact that the Communist Academy was waiting in the wings did give the threat some bite. It is again ironic that what may have tilted the balance was the resolution of the new "faction of communist academicians," the party scholars who had just established a communist bulwark at the venerable academy. The faction's deliberations, sent to the Politburo in February 1929, argued that "the task in regard to the Academy of Sciences consists not in the *destruction* of this institution, but in its lengthy reconstruction."[154]

In an extraordinary volte-face, the newly elected communist academicians, including Communist Academy luminaries Pokrovskii, Riazanov, Deborin, Bukharin, and Friche, now gave their imprimatur to a defense of the old academy.[155] Moreover, it is in the deliberations of the "faction of communist academicians," the leading representatives of party scholarship, that the future course of the *Communist Academy* first became perceptibly linked to a sudden shift in attitudes toward the Academy of Sciences. After establishing a bulwark for party scholarship within the venerable Academy of Sciences, the party scholars obviously began to perceive the decade-long institutional rivalry in an altered light.

208, op. 2, ed. khr. 57, l. 120 and passim. I am grateful to Daniel Todes for presenting me a copy of this unique diary.

153. Perchenok, "Akademiia nauk," 184–85, 183, 188.

154. "V Politbiuro TsK VKP(b). Protokol zasedaniia fraktsii kommunistov-akademikov ot 25.II.29 g.," RTsKhIDNI f. 147, op. 1, d. 33, l. 105; original emphasis.

155. After the application of enormous pressure on the Academy of Sciences, the three blackballed party scholars were elected in a hastily called second vote in early 1929. In this meeting of communist academicians, then, only Lukin and another Communist Academy member, G. M. Krzhizhanovskii, were absent.

The restructured older academy, not its communist counterpart, was now for the first time portrayed as the Soviet Union's dominant scholarly institution of the future. "From the point of view of long-term prospects, it is imperative to hold the course for a single scientific institution, embracing various disciplines with a single method," the communist academicians advised the Politburo. "The Academy of Sciences must be radically reformed, remade, and reconstructed." It was simultaneously resolved that "the Communist Academy . . . must remain a scholarly center of communism in, so to speak, its pure culture."[156] Although the party intellectuals were perhaps unwilling to spell out the full implications for the Communist Academy so soon after their assumption of the title of academician, this formulation was damaging enough for an institution that had for a decade groomed itself for hegemony. The significance of this vote by the communist academicians was accentuated when the Poliburo terminated the Enukidze commission in March 1929 and in its place appointed the faction of communist academicians to a new Politburo commission, headed by Pokrovskii, which would plan the reorganization of the academy.[157]

The startling "change in landmarks" in the attitudes of the Bolshevik intellectuals is brought into sharp relief by successive statements by Riazanov. Immediately following the initial rejection of the three blackballed Bolsheviks by the academy assembly, Riazanov addressed the academicians in the tone frequently heard before at the Communist Academy. "We hypnotized ourselves with the name of the Academy of Sciences," Riazanov provocatively phrased it. Referring to the closure of the French academy in an earlier revolution, he claimed that "we forgot that the bourgeoisie was considerably more daring than we. At the end of the eighteenth century they reckoned with the Academy in the cruelest, the most ferocious way."[158] Of course, Riazanov was likely to unleash this harsh attack immediately following the academicians' initial rejection of the three communist candidates. But in a private letter to permanent secretary Ol'denburg shortly afterward, Riazanov was still unwilling to countenance a long-term commitment to the Academy

156. "V Politbiuro Tsk," (cited in full at note 154). Academicians Pokrovskii, Riazanov, Friche, Bukharin, Deborin, and Gubkin and Sovnarkom's Gorbunov took part in the discussion. Of these communist academicians all but Gubkin were leaders of the Communist Academy.

157. "Protokol No. 68 zasedaniia Politbiuro TsK VKP(b) ot 14-go marta 1929," RTsKhIDNI f. 17, op. 3, ed. khr. 730, l. 5.

158. "Stenogramma vystupleniia Riazanova D. B. na zasedanie Akademii Nauk," no earlier than 12 January 1929, RTsKhIDNI f. 301, op. 1, d. 80, l. 1–14.

of Sciences. While he retracted his previously discussed statements that "the time of Academies is past, they have outlived their epoch," he now affirmed that only time would tell if the Academy of Sciences could live up its new all-union, Soviet role.[159]

Soon after the elections were over, Riazanov radically changed his attitude. He now assured his new colleagues that having spent "colossal energy" on the "winning" of the Academy of Sciences, he and his communist compatriots were unlikely to destroy it from within. Rather, they were interested in reforming and strengthening the institution. Most startling of all, Riazanov now permitted himself to disparage the achievements of the Communist Academy, in which he had been a guiding force from the beginning. This, he now said, was only a "pale copy of the organization of the Academy of Sciences."[160] It is likely Riazanov's disillusionment with the Communist Academy, and by the same token that of other communist academicians, was stimulated by the increasingly militant infighting of the younger generation of academy workers and red professors, who were gathering strength in the institution and stepping up attacks on the Marxist authorities of the 1920s.[161]

Long-held attitudes about the future of the Communist Academy did not vanish overnight. Indeed, for several reasons they would persist for a few more years. For one thing, the Communist Academy retained its significance as a counterweight in scholarship as campaigns continued against the Academy of Sciences, its membership was overhauled, and calls for cultural revolution continued. During the wave of arrests that hit the Academy of Sciences in the "academic affair," Communist Academy members justified the fabricated charges ideologically. A mass of as yet circumstantial evidence has linked Pokrovskii in particular to the

159. D. B. Riazanov to S. F. Ol'denburg, no date, RTsKhIDNI f. 301, op. 1, d. 80, l. 41–50. Of the party scholars, Ol'denburg and other academicians judged Riazanov and Bukharin as least inclined to radically disrupt the work of the Academy of Sciences and viewed Pokrovskii as the most hostile. The political fortunes of the former two, of course, were at their low ebb in 1929–30. Elena Ol'denburg, "Zapiska," 105, 108, 149–50, 166, esp. 177.

160. Untitled letter by Riazanov, RTsKhIDNI f. 301, op. 1, d. 80, l. 57–69.

161. In his remarkable letter of resignation to the presidium of the Communist Academy in February 1931, Riazanov claimed he had not taken part in its work in two years. Outspoken until the end, he scathingly indicted the Communist Academy for its role in vilifying the philosopher Deborin and accepting a subservient *partiinost'*, and he openly mocked the cult of Stalin in Marxist scholarship. Riazanov, "V prezidium Kommunisticheskoi Akademii," 8 February 1931 (cited in full at note 80). Ten days later, Riazanov's former assistant at the Marx-Engels Institute signed confessions to GPU interrogators about Riazanov's "anti-party" activities—the harboring of Menshevik documents. "Materialy o D. B. Riazanove," 18 February 1931, RTsKhIDNI f. 17, op. 85, d. 378, l. 2–14. See also "Teoreticheskoe zaveshchanie akademika D. B. Riazanova," *Vestnik Rossiiskoi akademii nauk* 63, no. 11 (1993): 1035–44, and Rokitianskii, "Tragicheskaia sud'ba akademika D. B. Riazanova," 107–48.

suppression of his nonparty rivals. Yet the persecution of nonparty scholars had the effect of further opening up the Academy of Sciences to party scholarship, since two-thirds of the approximately 150 scholars known to have been arrested were in the humanities.[162] With the influx of party Marxists, it became virtually impossible for the Communist Academy to justify dominance over its former competitor.

It is difficult to escape the ironic conclusion that for the Communist Academy, the bolshevization of the Academy of Sciences was a Pyrrhic victory. Although it would not become apparent to all until after the upheaval of the Great Break, much of the party institution's purpose, and its drive, had in one stroke withered away. As the Academy of Sciences vastly expanded, taking on an influx of young graduate students in 1929–30, admitting a flood of Marxist scholars, and boosting the number of communist staff members from 2 in 1928 to almost 350 by 1933, the Communist Academy's claim to primacy among all Soviet scholarly institutions lost much of its political significance and practical allure.[163] For the first time, the academy lost its place as chief institutional outlet for the aspirations of party scholarship. The quest for hegemony had become a double-edged sword.

The full Sovietization of academia would not occur, however, until after the downfall of its leading Marxist authorities of the 1920s. The group of Bolshevik intellectuals at the helm of the Communist Academy—Riazanov, Pashukanis, Friche, Kritsman, and the others—were virtually all overthrown in their disciplines, and their authority, like the careers of many of their younger followers, was wrecked. The old leadership of the Communist Academy lost most of its power in June 1930.[164] The physically ailing Pokrovskii tenaciously weathered the storm, but met a similar, if delayed (and in his case, posthumous), fate.

The Communist Academy soon spiraled into rapid decline. The sudden political zig-zags of the Great Break—such as the escalation of the collectivization drive, which had caught the agrarian Marxists at the academy completely unprepared—undermined the institution's position

162. V. S. Brachev, "'Delo' Akademika S. F. Platonova," *Voprosy istorii*, no. 5 (May 1989): 117–29, and "Ukroshchenie stroptivoi, ili kak AN SSSR uchili poslushaniiu," *Vestnik Akademii nauk SSSR*, no. 4 (1990): 120–27; Perchenok, "Akademiia nauk," 209; B. V. Anan'ich, "O vospominaniiakh N. S. Shtakel'berg," in A. I. Dobkin and M. Iu. Sorokina, eds., *In Memoriam: Istoricheskii sbornik pamiati F. F. Perchenka* (Moscow: Feniks, 1995), 85; "'Mne zhe oni sovershenno ne nuzhny' (Sem' pisem iz lichnogo arkhiva akademika M. N. Pokrovskogo)," *Vestnik Rossiiskoi akademii nauk* 62, no. 6 (1992): 103–14.

163. Graham, *Soviet Academy of Sciences*, 148.

164. Shapiro, "Communist Academy," 248–53; "Dokladnaia zapiska k Proektu Rezoliutsii TsK o deiatel'nosti Kom. Akademii," no date, 1930, RTsKhIDNI f. 147, op. 1, d. 33, l. 89–94.

as the Party's "scholarly organ." Moreover, the rampant factionalism of the Great Break ended by "discrediting and demoralizing the participants," making a mockery of the Communist Academy's vaunted service role. While the reckoning inherent in the bolshevization of the Academy of Sciences could be partially postponed during the upheaval of 1930–32, the rehabilitation of the bourgeois specialists in the latter year stripped the Communist Academy of its former prominence. In its twilight existence in the 1930s its staff and institutions were whittled away; its own leaders increasingly abstained from the notion of methodological or organizational control over other institutions. In a stroke of supreme irony, the Communist Academy, by Sovnarkom decree of 8 February 1936, was finally swallowed by the Academy of Sciences.[165]

The bolshevization of the Academy of Sciences signaled that the movement of party scholarship—which had emerged toward the end of the civil war as its champions claimed the Communist Academy as its own—could no longer define itself as the opposite of a domestic, bourgeois, nonparty rival; the demise of RANION signaled that nonparty scholarship in the social sciences, as well, was no longer possible in the non-Marxist, semi-autonomous guise that had persisted there in the 1920s. These twin developments laid the groundwork for the emergence of a more integrated Soviet higher learning.[166] In the merger of party and nonparty traditions, the Communist Academy's monopolistic goals were conveniently forgotten; but were they not in a sense achieved in the gargantuan, dominant new Academy of Sciences? Values the Communist Academy had embraced in the course of its protracted NEP-era quest for hegemony, such as the primacy of a service role and the principal of party-mindedness, were now proclaimed official standards for Soviet science as a whole.

165. On the agrarian Marxists, see Susan Gross Solomon, "Rural Scholars and the Cultural Revolution," in Fitzpatrick, *Cultural Revolution*, 148–49; Fitzpatrick, "Cultural Revolution as Class War," in Fitzpatrick, *Cultural Revolution*, 36; on the Communist Academy from 1931 to 1936, see Shapiro, "Communist Academy," 291–331.

166. But the 1920s bifurcation of academia into party and nonparty camps never fully disappeared, since certain fields, institutions, and a powerful segment of the intelligentsia remained either more party-oriented or closer to the party leadership than others.

CONCLUSION / THE GREAT BREAK IN HIGHER LEARNING

The upheaval that overtook all of higher learning in the Soviet Union in 1928–32, which in 1929 Stalin dubbed the Great Break (*velikii perelom*), swept away the dualistic order in organized intellectual life. Defunct was the NEP dynamic that opposed Bolshevik Party institutions and their plethora of revolutionary missions to half-altered old institutions, still dominated by nonparty groups but surviving under the auspices of the Soviet state. In part to overcome the awkward constraints and pervasive contradictions of that phase of the Revolution, in part because of them, a general assault on the nonparty intelligentsia was unleashed and a frenzy of institutional and sectoral reorganization begun.[1] Above all within the camp of communist intellectuals, the new "socialist offensive" was accompanied by the apotheosis of the battles for hegemony and against deviationism; there was a resurgence of "hare-brained schemes," which in their militant utopianism were sometimes reminiscent of war communism.[2] What was novel, however, was that a decade of Bolshevik involvement on the third front had already forged a discrete constellation of communist traditions, policies, institu-

1. A valuable collection for the study of these reorganizations are the records of TsIK's Uchenyi Komitet, GARF f. 7668. The primary Soviet work is V. D. Esakov, *Sovetskaia nauka v gody pervoi piatiletki* (Moscow: Nauka, 1971).

2. The preeminent work remains Fitzpatrick's collection *Cultural Revolution*.

tions, constituencies, and culture in higher learning which now adapted to the turmoil of the "second revolution."

At the end of 1929 the party philosopher Luppol penned a noteworthy narrative about the course of the Revolution on what he referred to interchangeably as the "scientific" and the "ideological" front (but which he might as well, following the slightly different terminology favored in the early 1920s, have called the third or cultural front). The article represents an important window into Bolshevik conceptions of the academic order on the eve of the new era. After the Revolution, Luppol wrote, the front was divided into two poles, represented by the Academy of Sciences and the Socialist Academy. "We" took our first steps there and at IKP, he wrote, creating primarily social scientific journals and beginning to reform higher education; "we" promoted a "worker-peasant" *studenchestvo* and confined professors who could not be trusted as teachers to research institutes. Yet as the "gradual offensive" of Marxism-Leninism continued in the 1920s, the original communist institutions grew and spread to "daughter organizations," producing a dislocation between the two camps that now demanded resolution. The new "assault of revolutionary Marxism-Leninism" would represent the "forced victory of the socialist sector of science."[3]

This striking argument—so easily identifying the institutions, intellectuals, and causes of party academia with the regime, the Revolution, and the ruling ideology—in many ways recalled the Fifteenth Party Congress of 1927, which ratified both the early plans for the industrialization drive and a directive for a "special strengthening of the struggle on the ideological and cultural front." At that gathering, as well, Pokrovskii—*eminence grise* of party scholars, whose own militance, power, and orthodoxy would help him ride out the coming storm until his death in 1932—talked of the experience of the communist academic "sector" and the reconstruction of science on an all-union scale in the same breath.[4] On the eve of what was to be an era of confrontations and ceaseless reorganizations in intellectual life, calls were issued not simply for the forcible expansion of the communist academic system but for the "socialist reconstruction of scientific institutions themselves."[5] The revolution pursued by the party camp in the 1920s and

3. I. K. Luppol, "Rekonstruktivnyi period i nauchnyi front," *Nauchnyi rabotnik*, no. 11 (1929): 3–8.

4. Esakov, *Sovetskaia nauka*, 72–75.

5. This was taken to mean the introduction of planning, self-criticism, the regulation of

identified most closely with those party institutions which have been at the center of attention in this book, was now to be brought to every corner of higher learning.

Communist intentions going into the Great Break, of course, cannot be confused with its results; it is hard to disagree with the proposition that "between 1930 and 1932 the [higher educational] system was so fluid institutionally and numerically that it seems to have been substantially out of control."[6] The opening phase of the Stalin era was marked by an upheaval along the entire cultural front that now embraced its own, new set of paradoxes and contradictions. Among them were the coincidence of a virulent assault on authority (one that swept up many Bolshevik intellectuals predominant in the 1920s) and the great extension of central party power in science, culture, and scholarship; the balancing of extremes of egalitarian and proletarianizing "leveling" with the birth of rigid hierarchy topped by a leader cult; the outburst of fanciful utopian dreaming along with highly orchestrated repressions.[7] Such quintessential features of the Great Break on the cultural front even now remain largely unexplored within the deep context of individual settings and on the basis of archival investigation. Nonetheless, the chaos of the upheaval and the now familiar phenomenon of sudden reversals and unexpected outcomes should not obscure the fact that in higher learning the Great Break involved a coherent program—or, to recall the term employed for the third front a decade earlier, a discernible project. Its main features were articulated in instantly canonical party resolutions and directives, reiterated in Central Committee plenums, repeated tirelessly in newspaper and journal discussions, embodied in constant attempts to plan and restructure activities and institutions, and manipulated and contested in the rampant struggles the upheaval unleashed.

The communist experience of mobilizing students and distributing cadres on all the various levels of higher learning was now turned into an operation of vast scale. The twin rubrics under which this influx and breakneck expansion occurred were proletarianization and communization.[8] The mobilization of "thousanders" of proletarian origin into

---

social composition, and even the "active mastery of dialectical materialism as a method by scientific workers." P. Sergeev, "Bol'nye voprosy nauchnoi raboty," *Revoliutsiia i kul'tura*, no. 9–10 (31 May 1929), 34–43.

6. Kneen, "Higher Education," 47.

7. For a different formulation of the paradoxes of the Plan years, focusing on aesthetic culture, see Clark, *Petersburg*, 261–83.

8. The Orgburo directive of December 1928 on IKP admissions for the coming academic year gives an interesting insight into the combination of attempted social and political engineer-

higher education marked the onset of what became the heyday of proletarianization, and from 1928 through 1931–32 virtually all institutions boasted annually increasing percentages of workers.[9] This proletarianization went hand in hand with the rise of party members into new positions in all areas of academia. A Central Committee directive in 1929 set the goal of reaching no less than 60 percent of party members among "scientific cadres" in the social sciences.[10] The directives put out by the scientific section of Gosplan on compiling a "five-year plan for scientific-research work" called for the compilation of far more detailed data on the class origin, political "worth," and scholarly value of scientific cadres and also set the goal of achieving no less than 25 percent party members among all "scientific workers" by the plan's end.[11] Areas that had been under the *de facto* control of nonparty professors and scholars, such as graduate student selection and most "scientific-technical disciplines," were now deliberately exposed to what Pokrovskii in 1929 openly called social and political criteria.[12] The sheer scope and "tempo" of the initiatives launched to solve the "problem of cadres"—if hardly its centrality within the Bolshevik approach to higher learning—were novel in this period. Yet these momentous efforts were still mounted in the name of the now venerable, still multifaceted Bolshevik project of creating "red specialists," "our" leadership forces, and a new intelligentsia.

One of the best-known features of the Great Break, and a distinct departure from the troubled preservation of nonparty academia that had persisted since 1922, can be called the inverse of cadre promotion: the open assault and widespread repression mounted against a wide

---

ing. It was ordered that the IKP preparatory section should consist of no less than 80 percent workers, and no fewer than forty comrades in the entering class were to be picked by Agitprop from the central party apparat and party committees. At the same time, it was strictly ordered that there would be no lowering of academic standards or evasion of entrance testing. "Vypiska iz protokola No. 89 zasedaniia Orgbiuro TsK VKP(b) ot 28.XII.28 g.," RTsKhIDNI f. 147, op. 1, ed. khr. 35, l. 39.

9. For the academic year 1929–30, for example, Kul'tprop and Narkompros jointly ordered a nationwide program of crash four-month courses for preparing literate, politically active "workers from production" and "batraks" with at least 2.5 years of party membership for entry into *komvuzy*. See "Vsem otdelam kul'tury i propagandy Obl(krai)komov VKP(b), Vsem Obl(krai)ONO i komvuzam," no later than 1 April 1929, RTsKhIDNI f. 12, op. 1, ed. khr. 614, l. 9.

10. Cherepnina, "Deiatel'nost'," 46.

11. "Direktivy po sostavleniiu piatiletnego plana nauchno-issledovatel'skogo dela," no date, GARF f. 7668, op. 1, d. 234, l. 5–8.

12. M. N. Pokrovskii, "O podgotovke nauchnykh rabotnikov," *Nauchnyi rabotnik*, no. 1 (January 1929): 20–21; M. Riutin, "Rukovodiashchie kadry VKP(b)," *Bol'shevik*, no. 15 (August 15, 1928), 18–29.

array of nonparty groups in the intelligentsia in all academic and cultural professions. What has not normally been recognized about the post-Shakhtii attacks on nonparty specialists—which ushered in an era of sanctioned "specialist-baiting"—is that the purges, takeovers, reorganizations, and similar measures that accompanied the imposition of the forms of Bolshevik organization and political culture had frequently been first applied to higher learning in party institutions.

To employ only one example, professorial and teaching personnel went through "reelections" in 1929 and again in 1930. In the first round, according to the party legal specialist Vyshinskii, who was in charge of the operation, 219 of 1,062 professors were either purged or replaced. But less quantifiable yet far more significant than the number removed—many of the professors, just as in party purges, may have later been reinstated or found other positions—was the use of the opportunity to break down what Vyshinskii termed the corporate "conspiracy of silence" and introduce "proletarian self-criticism" for the first time into higher schools.[13] Repressive measures were only the most visible and convenient "weapons" in the attempt to extend the Bolshevik revolutionary system in higher learning, which had been limited in reach in the 1920s. Replicating the conventions of political culture, in forums such as the purge meetings and self-criticism sessions, were intrinsic parts of "sovietization" and "bolshevization."

Another constituent part of extending the franchise, so to speak, of what might be called the cultural revolutionary project was a large-scale effort to remake conceptions and agendas in science, scholarship, and learning. This took place in several distinct forms. The earlier championing of standards of "practicality," service, and planning, which grew up with party scholarship itself in the 1920s, blossomed into the insistent demand of the Five-Year Plan era, repeated in the most varied contexts and with ubiquitous vehemence, that all science serve "socialist construction."[14] The years 1929 and 1930 were extraordinary ones, but this shift was in many cases not as sudden as has sometimes been imagined. In the administration of natural science, for example, one historian has convincingly located the period between 1925 and 1927 as the

13. A. Ia. Vyshinskii, "O nashikh kadrakh," *Nauchnyi rabotnik*, no. 1 (January 1930): 32–36. On purging and expansion in higher education in this period, see Fitzpatrick, *Education*, 193–98.

14. For example, the second Soviet-era charter of the Academy of Sciences of 1930 introduced the proclamation that the highest academic institution would utilize "one scientific method on the basis of the materialist worldview" and pursue "the servicing of the needs of socialist reconstruction of the country." Esakov, *Sovetskaia nauka*, 200.

"turning point" when the Party settled on a science policy that stressed the "science-production tie" and gave precedence to applied over basic research.[15] Yet as we have seen from the growing service function of party scholarship born in antiliberal reaction to the twin notions of pure science and institutional autonomy, there was no one transparent meaning to "practicality," and it could be reconciled with the most abstract Marxist-Leninist theory. The demand that knowledge serve socialist construction should be seen above all as giving expanded currency to an official rationale for the purpose of scholarship, what might well be called an academic ideology that unambiguously defined *nauka* in all its manifestations as subordinate to state, revolution, and Party.

This drive to make learning serve socialist construction affected the party scholarship that embraced it most ardently as much as it did the nonparty scientists at whom it was directed. It transformed higher education perhaps even more immediately and decisively than research. To again cite only one example, the Central Committee's renamed Kul′t-prop department instructed the institutes of red professors to introduce "production practice" in lower party organs, kolkhozes, and Machine-Tractor Stations of up to half of all instruction time by the third year of study. The red professor in philosophy, Garber, dispatched in a brigade to the countryside, became the butt of the now-exacerbated anti-intellectualism of the new red intellectuals when he demonstrated ignorance of the anatomy of a cow: as the student newspaper jeered, "He didn't suspect that all his 'scholarly qualifications' weren't worth a wooden nickle." In that same year of 1930, in many ways the apogee of the Great Break upheaval, the Communist Academy actually declared that the role of research would be to "help the Party in implementing policies that lead to the building of tractors and organization of collective farms."[16]

Among the practitioners of Marxism-Leninism, a related part of the Great Break mission was to establish and elaborate the new conception of *partiinost′*, which we saw emerge in party scholarship's search for relevance and standing, and which led it to adopt an ideological service

15. Paul R. Josephson, "Science Policy in the Soviet Union, 1917–1927," *Minerva* 26 (Autumn 1988): 356.

16. "XVI Parts″ezd i nauchno-issledovatel′skaia rabota," *VKA*, no. 39 (1930): 3–7; P. Shabalkin, "'Beremennaia korova,' ili kak ne nuzhno udariat′," *Za leninskie kadry*, no. 1 (March 1930), 4; "Vypiska iz protokola No. 23 zasedaniia Orgbiuro TsK ot 11.XI.30 g.," RTsKhIDNI f. 147, op. 1, ed. khr. 35, l. 47–48. For a typical summary from 1930 of the "current tasks" of red scholarship, see "Nashi zadachi" (unsigned editorial), *Za leninskie kadry*, no. 1 (March 1930), 1.

role. In what has been called his unpublished "theoretical testament" of 1931, the besieged Riazanov on the eve of his downfall lashed out at the "citation-seeking" of the young "red seminarians" and a brand of Marxism that could transform both the resolutions of the IKP party cell and the "general line" into the last word in wisdom.[17]

In sum, the Great Break incorporated a vast expansion and intensification of the Bolshevik cultural project. In higher learning it took the form of a radical program forcibly to bring the Bolshevik Revolution—closely identified with an entire communist system that had already been operating in party institutions—to "virgin soil." This involved a reconstitution of the third front missions that had risen to prominence a decade before and which had been pursued, hardly exclusively, but most intensively in the party institutions during the 1920s. In both the 1920s and the early 1930s the project as applied to higher learning was held together by the comprehensive sweep of its multifaceted, contested, yet coherent program that flowed from the knitting together of manifold Bolshevik missions on the cultural front. In both the 1920s and the early 1930s this program encompassed the construction of institutions, the politics of cadres, the engineering of social composition, the attempt to create red experts, the spread of party Marxism, the reorientation of science, and the growth of a Bolshevik cultural system as applied to higher learning.[18] Although itself caught in the upheaval, the fundamental position of party higher learning remained analogous to what it had been since it was constituted as a unified entity in 1920. It still represented an arm and extension of the Party in the academic world, integrated into the broader polity and sensitive to regularized links to the party leadership and administrative organs. At the same time, as it has been depicted in the 1920s, it represented a full-fledged, institutionalized, and by now highly developed enterprise and movement in its own right within academia.[19]

17. "Teoreticheskoe zaveshchanie akademika D. B. Riazanova," *Vestnik Rossiiskoi Akademii nauk* 63 (1993): 1035–44.

18. The elements, of course, could be extended: I have omitted, for example, the continuing pursuit of revolutionary pedagogy. "Active methods," collectivism, group evaluations in what were now dubbed study brigades, became an intrinsic part of the revolutionary/party/proletarian program, while any criticism was linked to rightist/reactionary/bourgeois opposition. For example, see E. V. Mikhin, "Klassovaia bor'ba i nauchnye rabotniki," *Nauchnyi rabotnik*, no. 3 (1930): 16–18.

19. Pokrovskii's correspondence between 1929 and February 1932 (RTsKhIDNI f. 147, op. 1, d. 30, 33, 35, 37, 42), although too voluminous to treat here, provides a window into the lines of communication and command between party scholarship and the broader party polity in this period. It includes letters to the Politburo, Central Committee secretaries, especially Mo-

Another feature of the Great Break in higher learning that was also a primary characteristic present at the birth of the third front was the organic interconnectedness of the disparate missions on the cultural front. Once again, they were pursued and discussed together, conceptualized and fused as the single process of bringing the Revolution and socialism to the cultural realm. At a different tempo and in a different fashion, the party camp itself continued to be transformed as it spearheaded the effort. An overriding difference was that the academic order of NEP had erected boundaries and constraints on the pursuit of revolutionary missions within nonparty institutions and sectors; now the field of play for the pursuit of revolutionary missions was extended to, indeed purposefully concentrated on, those areas and aspects of academia which had largely remained outside its scope in the 1920s.

In the ensuing melee, as might have been expected given the inherent conflicts built into the third front regulatory bureaucracy and the divided academic order of NEP, a primary realm of contestation was, once again, "sectoral." In the Great Break, the consequences of the struggles touched off among the range of administrations (*vedomstva*) in higher learning were frequently lasting. Here again, some of the main developments can be seen to have had their roots in the evolution of the 1920s order: the growth of the party sector into a key actor in the fray, the rise of the Academy of Sciences in the wake of bolshevization, and the assault on universities hitherto dominated by the nonparty professoriat.

In the Great Break the central party institutions we have followed achieved their organizational apex and their moment of eclipse simultaneously. The Communist Academy expanded to its greatest breadth, as we have seen; a network of Institutes of Red Professors, with preparatory sections in cities around the country, mushroomed out of the departments of the original IKP. Whereas the combined budgets of the Communist Academy and IKP in 1929–30 were significantly less than that of the Academy of Sciences, in 1930–31 the budget for the five separate IKPs alone exceeded that of the Academy of Sciences.[20] Para-

---

lotov and Kaganovich, and above all to Stetskii at Kul'tprop TsK; it contains not only situation reports (*dokladnye zapiski*) on the "historical front" but routine updates concerning struggles at the Communist Academy, theoretical disputes, and editorial appointments.

20. "Otchet o rabote Uchenogo komiteta TsIK SSSR za 1929–30 gg.," GARF f. 7668, op. 1, d. 209, l. 6; "Smeta raskhodov nauchnykh i uchenykh uchrezhdenii TsIK Soiuza SSR na 1929–1930 g.g.," GARF f. 7668, op. 1, d. 209, l. 54, and "Spisok nauchno-issledovatel'skikh uchrezhdenii, sostoiashchikh v sisteme Uchenogo komiteta TsIK SSSR na 15/1-33 g.," ibid., d. 210, l. 3–21. On the IKP reorganization, "Postanovlenie o reorganizatsii Instituta krasnoi pro-

doxically—and as I intimated in the case of the Communist Academy—this opportunity for the most rapid expansion, the loudest attacks, and the most savage polemics on the "ideological" and "theoretical" fronts arose just as the revolutionary potential to supplant fully what had been until now "bourgeois" higher learning slipped away. Of the many explanations for this fresh irony, several have already been suggested. The increasingly vociferous insistence of the communist intellectuals that the Party was the supreme court of all affairs stripped them of their claim to leadership in intellectual life; the destructive wave of infighting discredited them in light of their own much-vaunted standards of service and "practicality."[21] The Great Break widened the front to bring the Revolution to hitherto "nonparty" groups, areas, institutions, and sectors, with the unintended consequences that many of the Party's own institutions were discredited as revolutionary alternatives. Finally, the entire metamorphosis of Marxist-Leninist social science itself deprived the theory and *nauka* of party intellectuals (as opposed to the pronouncements of the Central Committee) of the authority they had enjoyed in the 1920s. A most substantial blow was the shift in emphasis and prestige to technical training in the era of the Five-Year Plan, which undermined the prospects of the Communist Academy and the party schools that, despite their wider ambitions, had historically made the social sciences their special preserve. All this occurred even as the practices and, it might be said, the legacy of the network of party institutions that rose up in the 1920s were being forcibly applied to a still raggedly integrated Soviet higher learning. In this sense, the Great Break was the period of the greatest triumph and greatest failure for Bolshevik higher learning.

If the party sector met a kind of defeat in victory, there were other far more clear-cut winners and losers in the sectoral realignment that began

---

fessury. Utverzhdeno 18.VIII.30 g.," GARF f. 7668, op. 1, d. 255, l. 5; Vovsy, "Preduprezhdaem i predlagaem: Nikto nichego ne znaet o reorganizatsii IKP," *Za leninskie kadry*, no. 2 (May 1930), 3. The new IKPs created in 1930 were in economics, philosophy, history and law, history of the Party, and the Institute for Preparing Cadres.

21. For examples of how the Communist Academy was paralyzed by intrigues and infighting, see Pokrovskii's parries to the attacks by Pashukanis and younger academy leaders in "Vsem chlenam prezidiuma Komm. Akademii," January 1931, copy sent to A. I. Stetskii, Kul'tprop TsK, RTsKhIDNI f. 147, op. 1, ed. khr. 33, l. 34–35, and on the historical profession, "Dokladnye zapiski v TsK o polozhenii na istoricheskom fronte," no day given, January 1931, RTsKhIDNI f. 147, op. 1, ed. khr. 42, l. 10–23. For a typical polemic generated by the ferocious battles between the "proletarian culture" camp and IKP, see "Obrazets fal'sifikatsii nauchno-politicheskikh dokumentov; Chto sdelala b. gruppa pereverzevtsev s otchetom disskussii o Plekhanove i Pereverzeve. Soobshchenie sekretariata RAPP," 1930, ARAN f. 1759, op. 2, d. 12, l. 63–69.

in the late 1920s. It is enough to consider the fortunes of several other academic sectors. The industrialization drive, coupled with the suspicion cast on the old specialists and the urgency invested in creating new ones, led to an explosion of higher education in general. In the orgy of reorganization various sectors seized their chance to increase their standing. A chief beneficiary was "branch science," encompassing the commissariat-run institutes, which rode the crest of "practicality" and the breakneck expansion of higher technical education after 1928. In 1930 in the wake of Central Committee decrees of 1928 and 1929, the traditionally large, multidisciplinary faculties in higher schools were broken up into independent institutes that often developed narrowly specialized and applied profiles, and many were attached to the economic commissariats. The number of VUZy shot up from 152 in 1929–30, to 579 in 1930–31, to 701 in 1931–32.[22]

For the Academy of Sciences, the Janus face of the Stalin era for the scientific elite was never so starkly apparent. The newly bolshevized academy was racked by arrests, purges, and expansion in this period, but as has already been suggested, the blueprint for its emergence as a dominant, all-union "empire of knowledge" was already ratified.[23] Perhaps this explains why the "Academy Affair," the web of fabricated charges and repressions that continued into 1931, never came to trial. Yet it has been plausibly suggested that the affair was originally planned by the OGPU as one of a series of other show trials of 1930–31 that did take place—for example, the "Industrial Party" trial featuring engineers, the "Laboring Peasant Party" (TKP) trial spotlighting agronomists—designed to target those segments of the nonparty intelligentsia that had been of particular importance to the regime in the 1920s and had thus retained unusual influence and autonomy.[24]

If the harsh repressions experienced in the "academy" sector coincided with its rise to an extraordinary position of dominance, a less ambiguous blow was dealt to the university system. The upheaval and reorganization corresponded to calls for the withering away of the uni-

22. See especially Sh. Kh. Chanbarisov, *Formirovanie sovetskoi universitetskoi sistemy* (Moscow: Vysshaia shkola, 1988), 193–94.

23. For the report of permanent secretary Volgin to the Uchenyi Komitet on the expansion and reorganization of the Academy of Sciences in this period, see "Akademiia nauk za 1928–1933," GARF f. 7668, op. 1, d. 178, l. 1–28.

24. Perchenok, "Akademiia nauk," 232–33. The literature treating the "Academic" or "Platonov Affair" has become voluminous; for the most recent examples see I. G. Aref'eva, ed., *Tragicheskie sud'by: Repressirovannye uchenye Akademii nauk SSSR* (Moscow: Nauka, 1995), and V. S. Kaganovich, *Evgenii Viktorovich Tarle i peterburgskaia shkola istorikov* (St. Petersburg: Dmitrii Bulanin, 1995).

versities as feudal relics and attacks on them as anachronisms in the technological age. Even the rector of Moscow University, in an article "A 175-Year-Old Oldster" (*175-letnii starets*), called for the death of the institution over which he presided. Universities began to be broken up into their component parts, which in turn formed the bases of institutes. In January 1930 the deans (*dekanaty*) and collegial organs of universities were relieved of their duties. Departments (*fakul'tety*) and *kafedry* were shortly thereafter disbanded and "sectors of cadres" or "divisions" were created in their place. The commissar of education, Bubnov, who had replaced Lunacharskii in 1929, noted after the storm had passed (weakened universities were reconstituted in 1932) that his agency had not resisted these "clearly liquidationist moods" (*iavno likvidatorskim nastroeniiam*).[25] Opponents of such "reorganizations" were not only lumped together as "rightists" and class enemies, interestingly enough, but portrayed as opponents of an entire Great Break agenda in the higher school: *vydvizhenie*, "active" methods of teaching, and the remaking of science and learning to fit the needs of socialist construction.[26] It should be apparent that the "organic" thrust of this portrait of the enemy fits squarely into the third front tradition.

As part of the dismemberment of the universities in 1930–31 disciplines such as history, languages, philosophy, art history, pedagogy, economics, and law were for years banished from the university curriculum, which on one level, underscored the predominance of the technological, engineering, and natural sciences begun during the First Five-Year plan and persisting much later. More immediately, however, this weakening of the universities, particularly in the social and humanistic disciplines, reflected the political and institutional struggles between the universities, on one side, and leftist and party forces, on the other.[27] The demise of the research university in Soviet Russia should be attributed, not only to the rise of the scientific-research institutes of the Academy of Sciences to crown the edifice of the academic hierarchy, but also and

25. Chanbarisov, *Formirovanie*, 198. See also G. M. Krzhizhanovskii, ed., *Universitety i nauchnye uchrezhdeniia. K XVII s"ezdu VKP(b)* (Moscow-Leningrad: Gosudarstvennoe tekhniko-teoreticheskoe izdatel'stvo, 1934), 13–15.

26. For example, E. V. Mikhin, "Klassovaia bor'ba i nauchnye rabotniki," *Nauchnyi rabotnik*, no. 5–6 (May-June 1930): 15–18.

27. It should be added, however, that in one of the few archival studies relevant for this topic, Peter Konecny argues that one reason Leningrad State University survived the ordeal was that "communists, having assumed positions of leadership, adopted managerial strategies and defensive institutional tactics which their non-communist rivals employed in the past." See Konecny, "Conflict and Community at Leningrad State University, 1917–1941" (Ph.D. diss., University of Toronto, 1994), 130.

in no small part to the all-out assault by party forces on the nonparty professoriat, an assault either restricted or impossible between 1922 and the Great Break.

This brief sketch, a cataclysmic postscript to the history of higher learning among the Bolsheviks, should not be taken to imply that the Great Break involved a simple, mechanical imposition of the model that rose with the party institutions of the 1920s. The "sectoral" consequences of the Great Break for party higher learning alone—defeat in victory—suggest a more complicated resolution. Nevertheless, several explanations can be advanced to explain why the "socialist offensive" applied to all of higher learning processes that had been pursued first or most avidly in the evolving party camp of the 1920s. This can be attributed to the unusual opportunity for the party sector in the 1920s to pursue revolutionary missions within its own educational and "scientific-research" institutions, even as the academic order imposed constraints on reconstructing nonparty areas. This is hardly to downplay the significance of changes the Revolution brought for the nonparty academic intelligentsia and above all for students in the 1920s. Yet many factors, notably the Bolsheviks' own Manichaean thinking—combined with their "sectoral" interests and the manner in which party institutional structures had assumed the status of symbols of the revolutionary—in fact exaggerated the dualistic features of the NEP academic order on the eve of the much-anticipated revolutionary upsurge. Perhaps most important was that within higher learning the socialist offensive was spearheaded by groups, actors, and entire institutions from the party sector. The decade of channeling revolutionary missions through party institutions in higher learning helped ensure that the Great Break on this "front" encompassed an outgrowth, adaptation, or intensification on a hitherto unimagined scale of the constellation of communist missions and policies that in higher learning had been pursued above all in party institutions in the 1920s.[28] In this sense, the term "bolshevization," used at the time, acquires a special relevance for the Great Break in academia.

With the end of the deepest NEP-style divisions between party and nonparty camps, a much more unified Soviet academic order could arise. The end of the two-camp, two-culture division of NEP academia

28. For an argument with a different focus on the lasting impact of patterns and precedents set in the 1920s, see Katerina Clark, "The Quiet Revolution in Intellectual Life," in Sheila Fitzpatrick et al., eds., *Russia in the Era of NEP: Explorations in Soviet Society and Culture* (Bloomington: Indiana University Press, 1991), 210–30.

might be viewed as a kind of forced merger, in which the practices, conventions, personnel, institutions, and values from the communist and nonparty camps were meshed—if hardly completely, then much more tightly than in the 1920s. The notion of such a new Soviet synthesis beginning with the Stalin era is strongly suggested by manner in which the bifurcated academic order of NEP met its demise in the communist-led "general offensive." For even after former "bourgeois specialists" were rehabilitated, order was restored, and the militants and proletarianizers of the Great Break were reined in during the course of 1932, there could be no return to a status quo ante.

THE history of Bolshevik higher learning lends a new perspective to our understanding of cultural revolution in Soviet Russia. The creation of party educational and scholarly institutions after 1917 and their unification after 1920 into an academic system that rose up to play a crucial role in the course of postrevolutionary higher learning exemplify some of the most concrete and consequential results flowing from the early articulations of a Bolshevik cultural project as a locus of revolutionary activity. To identify "*the* cultural revolution" with the Great Break of the late 1920s and early 1930s or to use the term to encompass all cultural processes under socialism obscures the discrete history and rapid evolution of the Bolshevik cultural project, of which party higher learning formed a significant part. Yet these two extremes in understanding cultural revolution have in fact been dominant, the narrow one in recent Western historiography and the universalistic one in the post–Great Break USSR.

From the 1930s to the 1980s, Soviet writers, following an orthodoxy that drew on the writings of Lenin in the early 1920s, used the concept of cultural revolution to refer to the rising tide of cultural progress and mass enlightenment that followed the October Revolution. For two decades, following the cultural revolution in China, Western historians have linked the term, and hence the process in revolutionary Russia, all but exclusively with the period 1928–1931, that is, with the upheaval on the "cultural front" during the Great Break. This divergence—and the use of "cultural revolution" as a synonym for the entire Great Break by more than one generation of Anglo-American historians of the Soviet Union—can be traced to a group of historians in the 1970s and 1980s who made the signal contribution of first exploring that period as a distinctive episode of militant "class war" and iconoclastic communist utopianism in culture. "In the First Five-Year Plan period, the term 'cultural revolution' was used in a special sense," writes Sheila Fitzpatrick, the most influential of those historians, "different from earlier or later Soviet usages." In a definition with lasting resonance, she takes "cultural revolution" in this period to mean "class war" in culture, a connotation supposedly introduced "abruptly" in 1928 and denoting the surrogate class struggle between "proletarian" Communists and "bourgeois" intellectuals.[29]

But the enterprise of party higher learning in the 1920s demonstrates how vigorous and well developed was the attempt not simply to champion a set of Bolshevik revolutionary missions in culture, education, and science but to implement them in the midst of NEP. A driving motivation behind this earlier project was to create an institutionalized and hence deeply rooted challenge to the nonparty establishment, to develop a new kind of education and pedagogy rooted in revolutionary and Bolshevik culture, and to inculcate Bolshevik practices and traditions. Insofar as the resulting conflicts were an intrinsic part of the cultural front in the 1920s, the Bolshevik cultural project encompassed but reached far beyond a struggle between social groups, between party intellectuals and the nonparty intelligentsia, from the first. It represented the goal of creating a full-fledged revolutionary alternative to all "bourgeois" science and education—with many far-reaching consequences above and beyond the confrontation between groups of communist and nonparty intellectuals portrayed in class terms. Communist higher learning launched as a part of the "cultural front" after the Revolution also encompassed the creation of new kinds of institutions, redefinition of the purpose and orientation of science and scholarship, and the development of higher learning within the communist political system. The question remains whether the notion of cultural revolution should be associated exclusively with 1928–31, and if so, then whether it should be identified so intimately with surrogate class war.[30]

Those who would apply "cultural revolution" exclusively to the

29. Sheila Fitzpatrick, "Editor's Introduction" and "Cultural Revolution as Class War," in *Cultural Revolution*. To distinguish this class-war concept of cultural revolution—and by extension also the phenomenon—from the period before 1928, Fitzpatrick pointed to its departure from Lenin's concept of cultural revolution: "Lenin's idea of cultural revolution was a gradual and nonmilitant raising of cultural standards, achieved without direct confrontation with the old intelligentsia and involving above all the expansion of mass education and the spread of basic literacy."

30. A notable plea for understanding cultural revolution as a "single, long-term process"—and a warning that separating out 1928–31 as "*the* cultural revolution" would lead to "confusion and question-begging"—was made by David Joravsky, "The Construction of the Stalinist Psyche," in Fitzpatrick, *Cultural Revolution*, 107.

Great Break of 1928–31 must believe that this notion of "cultural revolution" changed abruptly in 1928 from its original Leninist incarnation. This belief warrants further examination. Lenin did indeed place overwhelming (but not exclusive) stress on what the most extended analysis terms "culture-as-knowledge"—universal know-how and expertise to be acquired by the proletariat from whatever "bearers" could teach it. This was part of what became Lenin's "virtual obsession" with inculcating the habits of "civilized" societies, overcoming backward "barbarism," and mastering science and technology.[31] Nevertheless, Lenin's employment of the slogan of cultural revolution coincided with, indeed was a part of, the Bolshevik advance on the the third front of culture, which has been traced here as a major, overlooked aspect of the transition to the 1920s order. As such it entered into the party arena and, appropriated by others, added greatly to the importance of a "cultural" agenda for revolutionary forces.

No matter how far removed Lenin's use of the term "cultural revolution" appears from the meaning given to it by those forces on the Bolshevik Left urging, even then, the destruction of bourgeois culture through militant confrontation in the culural arena, there were points of contact between them. For Lenin also stressed the assimilation of culture through the prism of Marxism, as well as its adaptation to the proletarian dictatorship.[32] The concept of cultural revolution, moreover, like most of Lenin's theoretical output, had a lengthy history of its own during the course of the 1920s, when various forces modified it or adapted it to their own agendas.

The concept of cultural revolution became one of many notions that informed activity on the third front in the 1920s. John Biggart, for example, has convincingly analyzed Bukharin's writings on cultural revolution in 1923 and 1928 as a middle ground between Lenin's "developmental" process and the class-war definition of the Great Break.[33] In the

31. Carmen Claudin-Urondo, *Lenin and the Cultural Revolution*, trans. Brian Pierce, (Hassocks, Sussex: Harvester Press, 1977), 1–64. The many compilations include *V. I. Lenin o kul'ture* (Moscow: Politizdat, 1980).

32. This comes through even in Lenin's anti-Proletkul't "theses" of 1920: "Not the *invention* of a new proletarian culture, but the *development* of the best models, traditions, and results of the *existing* culture, *from the point of view* of the Marxist world outlook and the conditions of life and struggle of the proletariat in the period of its dictatorship." Claudin-Urondo, *Lenin and the Cultural Revolution*, 45.

33. John Biggart, "Bukharin's Theory of Cultural Revolution," in A. Kemp-Welch, ed., *The Ideas of Nikolai Bukharin* (Oxford: Clarendon Press, 1992), 131–58. The evolution of the concept of cultural revolution needs to be explored not only in terms of the ideas of its articulators but in terms of the changed context of the "third front" in the course of the 1920s as well.

mid-1920s, in a more explicit elaboration of the cultural assimilationism, the communist civilizing mission, inherent in Lenin's usage, we encounter cultural revolution as a program for the acculturation of "backward" national groups, whose "wild" ideological and religious views have to be plowed by a "cultural tractor." Even here, however, the implication of revolutionary and ideological class struggle is not absent: for example, it was asserted that cultural revolution means not only raising the cultural level of the masses of general, but of the poor batraks in particular, in order to create a "consciousness of the revolutionary, socialist-thinking proletariat."[34] The party scholar Luppol, in his 1925 survey of Lenin's thought on culture, made a not uncommon acknowledgment that culture in the "transition period" could not be simply "reorganized" by violence either today or tomorrow. Just as typical, however, was his blunt formulation of rivalry with nonparty specialists and the depiction of expertise as something to be seized from the enemy: carrying out cultural revolution required the taking of "all of science, all of technology, all knowledge and art. . . . And this science, technology, and art is in the hands of specialists and in their minds."[35]

Most significantly, the militants of the "proletarian culture" camp well before 1928 pursued a radical conception of cultural revolution they claimed was Leninist. As Averbakh proclaimed, "The problem of proletarian culture is above all the question of Lenin's cultural revolution." He agreed that the "liquidation of illiteracy" was a primary task, but insisted that "the process of cultural revolution encompasses not only the tasks of teaching reading and writing, but also the entire area of the ideological superstructure" through a process of "class struggle."[36] If this proletarianizing incarnation of "Leninist cultural revolution" was the property of the Bolshevik Left, it becomes easier to understand how and why it was adopted immediately when the Party "turned left" in 1928. A key moment in the official adoption of a voluntaristic and iconoclastic definition of the term came in an Agitprop conference in the

---

Biggart, for example, unconvincingly portrays Bukharin's notion of cultural revolution, which focused not only on raising the mass cultural level but training the most able party and working-class cadres at institutions like IKP and Sverdlov, as somehow at odds with (and not part of) the "NEP system" (131).

34. I. Arkhincheev, "Na putiakh kul'turnoi revoliutsii," *Bol'shevik*, no. 17–18 (30 September 1925), 60–74.

35. I. Luppol, "Problema kul'tury v postanovke Lenina," *Pechat' i revoliutsiia*, no. 5–6 (July–September 1925): 16–18.

36. Leopol'd Averbakh, "O proletarskoi kul'ture, 'napostovskoi putanitse,' i bol'shevistskikh aksiomakh," *Bol'shevik*, no. 6 (31 March 1926), 101–14.

summer of 1928, when the "class content of cultural construction" was defined as "the task of constructing proletarian culture."[37] We have encountered Agitprop, of course, as the agency that won oversight of the party schools. In the formative third front power struggles it embraced a notion of "pure" party propaganda while rejecting what was again widely attacked in the late 1920s as "enlightenment for its own sake," and it came to represent the left wing of the divided NEP-era cultural bureaucracy. Even the official reformulation of "cultural revolution" in the Great Break, then, was introduced, not as a negation or abrupt shift from the NEP order, but as an outgrowth of the agenda of the Bolshevik cultural Left. Cultural revolution became the rubric signifying the entire project of implementing communist missions on the cultural front. In this light, the rise of a militant definition of cultural revolution during the Great Break reflects a new phase in a continuing long-term Bolshevik project on what had long before been constituted as a primary arena of the Revolution, the third front of culture.

USING the vehicle of party higher learning, I have traced several phases in the history of Bolshevik institution-building and revolutionary missions in culture. A seminal moment in the emergence of a Bolshevik cultural program was the formulation by the Vperedist wing of the Party in the prerevolutionary underground of an agenda involving the creation of a new intelligentsia, a new culture, and a new science. Achievement of these missions was linked closely to party schools and education from 1909 on; and while cultural questions remained the special territory of intellectuals in this wing of the Party, the new enterprise of formal party education proved attractive and influential to the Leninists as well. A second phase, during the explosion of "enlightenment" activity after 1917, culminated in the emergence of a unified system of institutions that developed a specifically party identity, coopted or superseded other movements, and rose up as the primary and self-proclaimed rival of "bourgeois science" and the nonparty intelligentsia.

The third and most critical phase came during the 1920s, when an attempt to implement a complex of Bolshevik missions shaped the evolution of a flourishing new network of party institutions. The result was a sweeping and many-leveled transformation during the course of NEP, which proved of lasting significance because of some basic features of

37. Cited, for example, as an iconic text by A. Maletskii, "Problema kul'turnoi revoliutsii v programme Kominterna," *Revoliutsiia i kul'tura*, no. 19 (15 October 1928), 9. The conference is noted by Fitzpatrick in "Cultural Revolution as Class War," 10.

the enterprise. Bolshevik higher learning became more than a base for certain groups of communist scholars, students, and intellectuals, or certain factions within academic disciplines and cultural professions. In no small part because the contradictory NEP order seemed to stall revolutionary change elsewhere, Bolshevik higher learning became a formative attempt at implementing revolutionary missions on the third front through institution-building, during which party models of institutional organization were first applied to academia. It became the champion of a new party-approved curriculum and a new pedagogy. It became a branch of the Party in academia, tied organically to the broader polity and power structure to which it belonged. It became the forum for the growth and spread of an elaborate Bolshevik political and academic culture that spread outward in academia. All these features ensured that the intentions and actions of the party leadership must be considered as only one, albeit crucial factor in the "revolution of the mind." Looming larger was the decade of experience in a sprawling new enterprise that itself was part and parcel of the Party.

No aspect of Soviet history, it is fair to say, has produced so much attention as the history of the Communist Party. Yet the overwhelming majority of accounts, in confronting the one-party monopoly on power, have considered the Party almost exclusively as the agent of change. Certainly it has appeared in that guise here as well. Yet the view afforded from within the enterprise of party higher learning suggests that many levels of change within the 1920s transformation cannot be reduced to the intentions of even the most powerful leaders. In this account, the Party has appeared not only as an agent and a victimizer but also as a movement in a very immediate sense caught in a web of its own making, gripped in a powerful vice of party political practices and culture. The Bolshevik cultural system not only developed but inculcated on a large scale new ways of speaking, acting, and thinking; it evolved in ways that went far beyond individual agency even as the Bolsheviks were launching their most voluntaristic attempts to transform the cultural sphere, for all the while, the structures and traditions the Party had erected in the everyday life of its institutions had come to dominate its members' lives. In ways in which contemporaries may have been scarcely aware, the intense pressures and habits of the emergent system mastered even the activist, interventionist Party that had created it.

It is perhaps fitting to end with a reflection on one of the more subtle yet fundamental of the transformations of the 1920s. When Bolshevik higher learning rose up for the first time to become the direct competitor to "bourgeois" science and its institutions, it was still cast in the role of revolutionary outsider beating on the walls of established academe. The 1920s order at once perpetuated this role, because the "present" of the "bourgeois" academic establishment during NEP was relatively assured even as its future was uncertain, and inversed it, as a result of the party camp's powerful position and the entrenchment of a system of party education and research. Even as the fires of the Great Break raged, capping a decade of continuous evolution on the third front, the outsider stance of party institutions of higher learning was being much more fundamentally negated—a "negation of the negation" that is perhaps the most ironic and indeed uncontrollable transformation we have witnessed. No longer was it the underdog, the alternative, the revolutionary force pressing for a wholesale revolution of the mind. In the decades that followed, party schools retreated to the spheres of training cadres, producing ideologists, and preserving certain "party" disciplines. Bolshevik higher learning itself had finally become part of the establishment.

Selected Bibliography

I. Archival Sources

1. Rossiiskii tsentr khraneniia i izucheniia dokumentov noveishei istorii (RTsKhIDNI). Formerly the Central Party Archive of the Institute of Marxism-Leninism of the Central Committee of the CPSU (TsPA IML).

Fond 12. Lichnyi fond of Krupskaia, Nadezhda Konstantinovna.

Fond 17, op. 3. Protokoly zasedanii Politbiuro TsK RKP(b)—VKP(b) (Politburo protocols), 1919–41.

Fond 17, op. 60. The Central Committee's department of Agitation and Propaganda (Agitprop TsK), 1921–28.

Fond 17, op. 85c. Materials from the Central Committee's Secret Documents Department (Sekretnyi otdel TsK), 1926–34.

Fond 89. Lichnyi fond of Iaroslavskii, Emel'ian Mikhailovich.

Fond 142. Lichnyi fond of Lunacharskii, Anatolii Vasil'evich.

Fond 147. Lichnyi fond of Pokrovskii, Mikhail Nikolaevich.

Fond 150. Lichnyi fond of Skvortsov-Stepanov, Ivan Ivanovich.

Fond 259. Lichnyi fond of Bogdanov, Aleksandr Aleksandrovich.

Fond 296. Lichnyi fond of Miliutin, Vladimir Pavlovich.

Fond 323. Lichnyi fond of Kamenev, Lev Borisovich.

Fond 329. Lichnyi fond of Bukharin, Nikolai Ivanovich.

Fond 338. Longjumeau Party School (Partiinaia shkola v Lonzhiumo), 1910–11.

Fond 531, op. 1. Lenin School of the Communist International (Mezhdunarodnaia Leninskaia shkola pri Kominterne).

Fond 559. Lichnyi fond of Adoratskii, Vladimir Viktorovich.

Fond 613. Central Control Commission (Tsentral'naia kontrol'naia komissiia, or TsKK).

2. Rossiiskii gosudarstvennyi arkhiv obshchestvennykh dvizhenii goroda Moskvy (RGAODgM). Formerly the Archive of the Institute of History of the Moscow Party Committee and the Moscow Control Commission of the CPSU (MPA).

Party Cell Collections (Fondy pervichnykh partorganizatsii):

Fond 459. Sverdlov Communist University (Kommunisticheskii universitet imeni Ia. M. Sverdlova).

Fond 474. Institute of Red Professors (Institut krasnoi professury, or IKP).

Fond 477. Communist Academy (Kommunisticheskaia akademiia).

3. Arkhiv Rossiiskoi Akademii Nauk, Moskovskoe otdelenie (ARAN). Formerly the Archive of the Academy of Sciences of the USSR (AAN).

Fond 350. Kommunisticheskaia akademiia.

Fond 370. Redaktsiia zhurnala Vestnik Kommunisticheskoi Akademii.

Fond 453. Lichnyi fond of Rotshtein, Fedor Aronovich.

Fond 496. Lichnyi fond of Shmidt, Otto Iul'evich.

Fond 528. Lichnyi fond of Kritsman, Lev Natanovich.

Fond 597. Lichnyi fond of Lebedev-Polianskii, Pavel Ivanovich.

Fond 643. Lichnyi fond of Friche, Vladimir Maksimovich.

Fond 1759. Lichnyi fond of Pokrovskii, Mikhail Nikolaevich.

4. Gosudarstvennyi arkhiv Rossiiskoi Federatsii (GARF). Formerly Central State Archive of the October Revolution (TsGAOR). Collections with the prefix "A" are located at the filial of GARF, the former Central State Archive of the RSFSR (TsGA RSFSR). The prefix "R" indicates a declassified collection.

Fond A-2306. Commissariat of Education (Narkompros).

Fond A-2313. Main Committee on Political Enlightenment (Glavpolitprosvet).

Fond 3316. Council of People's Commissars (Sovnarkom).

Fond 3415. Sotsialisticheskaia akademiia (1918–21).

Fond R-3415. Kommunisticheskaia akademiia (1925–29).

Fond 5221. Kommunisticheskii universitet imeni Ia. M. Sverdlova.

Fond R-5221. Kommunisticheskii universitet imeni Ia. M. Sverdlova (1925–38).

Fond 5284. Institut krasnoi professury.

Fond 7668. Komitet po zavedyvanii uchenymi i uchebnymi uchrezhdeniiami pri TsIK SSSR (Uchenyi komitet).

5. Trotsky Archive, Houghton Library, Harvard University.

II. *Journals, Serials, Newspapers*

Biulleten' zaochnoi konsul'tatsii (IKP). Continues *Biulleten' zaochno-konsul'tatsionnogo otdel. IKP* [Institute of Red Professors].

Bol'shevik.

Informatsionnyi biulleten' [Communist Academy].

Izvestiia Akademii nauk SSSR.

K leninskoi uchebe. Continues *Leninskaia ucheba* [Sverdlov Communist University].

Kommunisticheskaia revoliutsiia. Continues *Vestnik agitatsii i propagandy*.

Kommunisticheskoe prosveshchenie.

Komsomol'skaia letopis'.

Komsomol'skii rabotnik.
Krasnaia nov'.
Krasnyi student.
Kratkii otchet o rabote [Communist Academy].
Leninskii sbornik.
Molodaia gvardiia.
Molodoi Bol'shevik.
Na putiakh k nove shkole.
Narodnoe prosveshchenie.
Narodnoe prosveshchenie v RSFSR v osnovnykh pokazateliakh; statisticheskii sbornik.
Nauchnyi rabotnik.
Nauka i ee rabotniki.
Nauka i nauchnye rabotniki SSSR: Spravochnik.
Novyi mir.
Otchet [Communist Academy].
Pechat' i revoliutsiia.
Plan rabot [Communist Academy].
Pod znamenem marksizma.
Pravda.
Proletarskaia kul'tura.
Proletarskaia revoliutsiia.
Proletarskoe studenchestvo.
Rabfakovets.
Revoliutsiia i kul'tura.
Sotsialisticheskii vestnik.
Sovetskoe studenchestvo. Continues *Krasnoe studenchestvo* and *Krasnaia molodezh'.*
Spravochnik partiinogo rabotnika.
Sverdlovets [Sverdlov Communist University].
Sverdloviia [Newspaper, Sverdlov Communist University].
Vestnik Kommunisticheskoi Akademii.
Za leninskie kadry [Newspaper, Institute of Red Professors].
Zapiski Kommunisticheskogo Universiteta im. Ia. M. Sverdlova.

III. Specialized Bibliographies and Encyclopedias

Apanasewicz, Nellie. *Education in the U.S.S.R.: An Annotated Bibliography of English Language Materials 1965–1973.* Washington: U.S. Government Printing Office, 1974.

Brickman, William W., and John T. Zepper. *Russian and Soviet Education, 1731–1989: Multilingual Annotated Bibliography.* New York: Garland Publishing, 1992.

Lebedev, V. F. *Pedagogicheskaia bibliografiia. Sistematicheskii ukazatel' knizhnoi i zhurnal'noi literatury po voprosam narodnogo prosveshcheniia za 1917–1924 gg.* 3 vols. Leningrad: Gosizdat, 1926.

Nauchnaia literatura SSSR: sistematicheskii ukazatel' knig i zhurnal'nykh statei, 1928. Vol. 1, *Obshchestvennye nauki.* Moscow: OGIZ RSFSR, 1932.

Nevskii, Vladimir Aleksandrovich. *Predmetnyi ukazatel' izbrannoi literatury po politprosvetraboty*. Moscow-Leningrad: "Gudok," 1925.

Nevskii, Vladimir Ivanovich. *Deiateli revoliutsionnogo dvizheniia v Rossii: Bio-bibliograficheskii slovar'*. Moscow: OGIZ, 1931.

Pedagogicheskaia bibliografiia. Vol. 1, 1924–1930. Moscow, "Prosveshchenie," 1967.

Pedagogicheskaia entsiklopediia. 3 vols. Moscow: Rabotnik prosveshcheniia, 1927–30.

Piskunov, A. I. *Sovetskaia istoriko-pedagogicheskaia literatura 1918–1957. Sistematicheskaia ukazatel'*. Moscow: Izdatel'stvo Akademii pedagogicheskikh nauk RSFSR, 1960.

IV. Unpublished Dissertations

Andreev, E. G. "Deiatel'nost' RKP(b) po organizatsii politicheskogo obrazovaniia, sovershenstvovaniia i razvitiia form i metodov partiinogo prosveshcheniia, 1921–1925 gg." Doctor of Sciences diss., Kirov University, Alma-Ata, 1974.

Charbonneau, Ronald G. "Non-Communist Hands: Bourgeois Specialists in Soviet Russia, 1917–1927." Ph.D. diss., Concordia University, Montreal, 1981.

Cherepnina, Bronislava I. "Deiatel'nost' Kommunisticheskoi Partii v oblasti podgotovki nauchno-pedagogicheskikh kadrov po obshchestvennym naukam v SSSR za 1918–1962 gg. (na materialakh vysshei shkoly)." Candidate of Sciences diss., Institut narodnogo khoziaistva im. Plekhanova, Moscow, 1964.

Clark, Katerina. "The Image of the Intelligent in Soviet Prose Fiction, 1917–1932." Ph.D diss., Yale University, 1971.

Doroshenko, Viktoriia A. "Kommunisticheskaia akademiia i ee rol' v razrabotke voprosov otechestvennoi istorii (1918–35 gg)." Candidate of Sciences diss., Moscow State University, 1964.

Ferdinand, C. I. P. "The Bukharin Group of Political Theoreticians." D. Phil. diss., Oxford University, 1984.

Gorsuch, Anne. "Enthusiasts, Bohemians, and Delinquents: Soviet Youth Cultures, 1921–1928." Ph.D. diss., University of Michigan, 1992.

Katz, Zev. "Party-Political Education in Soviet Russia." Ph.D. diss., University of London, 1957.

Mikhailov, Dmitrii A. "Podgotovka rukovodiashchikh i teoreticheskikh kadrov partii v usloviiakh stroitel'stva sotsializma, 1918–1932 gg." Candidate of Sciences diss., Akademiia obshchestvennykh nauk pri TsK, Moscow, 1968.

Morrissey, Susan. "More 'Stories about the New People': Student Radicalism, Higher Education, and Social Identity in Russia, 1899–1921. Ph.D. diss., University of California at Berkeley, 1993.

Shapiro, Joel. "A History of the Communist Academy, 1918–1936." Ph.D. diss. Columbia University, 1976.

Solovei, V. D. "Rol' Instituta krasnoi professury v stanovlenii sovetskoi istoricheskoi nauki." Candidate of Sciences diss., Moscow State University, 1987.

Swanson, James. "The Bolshevization of Scientific Societies in the Soviet Union." Ph.D. diss., Indiana University, 1968.

Tandler, Fredrika M. "The Workers' Faculty (Rabfak) System in the USSR." Ph.D. diss., Columbia University, 1955.

Tolz, Vera. "Russian Academicians under Soviet Rule." D. Phil. diss., University of Birmingham, 1993.

Yu, Miin-ling. "Sun Yat-sen University in Moscow, 1925–1930." Ph.D. diss., New York University, 1995.

V. Collections of Documents

Antonova, N. S., and N. V. Drozdova, comps. *Neizvestnyi Bogdanov*. 2 vols. Moscow: ITs "AIRO-XX," 1995.

Anweiler, Oskar, and Klaus Meyer, eds. *Die sowjetische Bildungspolitik 1917–1960: Dokumente und Texte*. Berlin: Osteuropa-Institut, 1979.

Boldyrev, N. I., ed. *Direktivy VKP(b) i postanovleniia sovetskogo pravitel'stva o narodnom obrazovanii. Sbornik dokumentov za 1917–47*. 2 vols. Moscow: Izdatel'stvo Akademii pedagogicheskikh nauk RSFSR, 1947.

Direktivy VKP(b) po voprosam prosveshcheniia. Moscow: Gosizdat, 1929.

Fogelevich, Leonid Grigor'evich. *Deistvuiushchee zakonodatel'stvo o pechati: sistematicheskii sbornik*. Moscow: Izdatel'stvo Narkomtruda SSSR, 1927.

Iaroslavskii, Emilian Mikhailovich, ed. *TsKK-RKI v osnovnykh postanovleniiakh partii*. Moscow-Leningrad: Gosizdat, 1927.

Kim, M. P., ed. *Protokoly soveshchanii narkomov prosveshcheniia soiuznykh i avtonomnykh respublik 1919–1924*. Moscow: Nauka, 1985.

Levshin, B. V., ed. *Dokumenty po istorii Akademii nauk SSSR*. 2 vols. 1917–25, 1926–34. Leningrad: Nauka, 1986.

Makarevich, M. A., ed. *Partiinaia etika: Dokumenty i materialy diskussii 20-x godov*. Moscow: Politizdat, 1989.

Nenarokov, Al'bert Pavlovich, ed. *Kul'turnoe stroitel'stvo v SSSR, 1917–1927. Razrabotka edinoi gosudarstvennoi politiki v oblasti kul'tury: Dokumenty i materialy*. Moscow: Nauka, 1989.

Soskin, V. N., ed. *Sud'by russkoi intellegentsii. Materialy diskussii, 1923–25*. Novosibirsk: Nauka, sibirskoe otedelenie, 1991.

VI. Published Primary Sources

Adoratskii, Vladimir Viktorovich. *Istoricheskii materializm: Khrestomatiia dlia komvuzov, sovpartshkol*. Moscow: Gosizdat, 1925.

Biblioteka Kommunisticheskoi Akademii: ee organizatsiia i deiatel'nost', 1918–1928. Moscow: Izdatel'stvo Kommunisticheskoi akademii, 1928.

Bobryshev, I. *Melkoburzhuaznye vliianiia sredi molodezhi*. 2d rev. ed. Moscow-Leningrad: Molodaia gvardiia, 1928.

Bubnov, Andrei Sergeevich, et al. *Na ideologicheskom fronte: Bor'by s kontrrevoliutsii*. Moscow: Krasnaia nov', 1923.

Bukharin, Nikolai Ivanovich. *Bor'ba za kadry: Rechi i stat'i*. Moscow-Leningrad: Molodaia gvardiia, 1926.

——. *K novomu pokoleniiu: Doklady, vystupleniia i stat'i, posviashchennye problemam molodezhi.* Moscow: Progress, 1990.
——. *Proletarskaia revoliutsiia i kul'tura.* Moscow: "Priboi," 1923.
Chem dolzhen byt' Kommuniversitet. Moscow: Izdatel'stvo Kommunisticheskogo universiteta im. Sverdlova, 1924.
X [Desiat'] let Kommuniversiteta im. Ia. M. Sverdlova. Moscow: Izdatel'stvo Kommunisticheskogo universitita im. Sverdlova, 1928.
Dewey, Evelyn. *The Dalton Laboratory Plan.* New York: E. P. Dutton, 1922.
El'iashevich, V. B., et al., eds. *Moskovskii Universitet, 1755–1930: Iubileinnyi sbornik.* Paris: Sovremennye zapiski, 1930.
Ermilov, V. I. *Protiv meshchanstva i upadochnichestva.* Moscow-Leningrad: Gosizdat, 1927.
Gonikman, Solomon L'vovich. *Partiinaia ucheba.* Kharkov: Proletarii, 1926.
Gorev, Boris Isaakovich. *Na ideologicheskom fronte: Sbornik statei.* Moscow-Leningrad: Gosizdat, 1923.
Gusev, Sergei Ivanovich, ed. *Kakova zhe nasha molodezh'? Sbornik statei.* Moscow-Leningrad: Gosizdat, 1927.
Iaroslavskii, Emilian Mikhailovich. *Kakim dolzhen byt' kommunist. Staraia i novaia moral'.* Moscow: Molodaia gvardiia, 1925.
——. *O chistke i proverke chlenov i kandidatov VKP(b).* Moscow-Leningrad: Gosizdat, 1929.
Intelligentsiia i revoliutsiia. Sbornik statei. Moscow: Dom pechati, 1922.
Intelligentsiia i sovetskaia vlast'. Moscow, 1919.
Itogi chistki partii. Moscow: Gosizdat, 1930.
Ivanov, P. *Studenty v Moskve. Byt, nravy, tipy.* Moscow: Tip. obshchestva rasprostraneniia poleznykh knig, 1903.
K XIV s"ezdu RKP(b). Moscow: Gosizdat, 1925.
Kanatchikov, Semen. *Istoriia odnogo uklona.* 5th ed. Leningrad: Priboi, 1925.
Katalog izdanii Kommunisticheskoi Akademii, 1923–26. Moscow: Kommunisticheskaia Akademiia, 1926.
Kommunisticheskii Universitet imeni Ia. M. Sverdlova: X-mu Vserossiiskomu S"ezdu Sovetov. Moscow: Izdatel'stvo Kommunisticheskogo universiteta im. Sverdlova, 1922.
Kommunisticheskii Universitet imeni Ia. M. Sverdlova. Sostav studenchestva v 1923–24 uchebnom godu. Moscow, [1924?].
Komsomol'skii byt. Moscow-Leningrad: Molodaia gvardiia, 1927.
Kosarev, V. "Partiinaia shkola na ostrove Kapri. Pochemu voznikla mysl' o zagranichnoi part-shkole." *Sibirskie ogni,* no. 2 (May–June 1922): 62–75.
Krupskaia, N. K. *Zadachi i organizatsiia sovpartshkol.* Moscow: Krasnaia nov', 1923.
Lenin, Vladimir Il'ich. *Pol'noe sobranie sochinenii.* 5th ed. 55 vols. Moscow: Politizdat, 1958–65.
Liadov, Martyn Nikolaevich. *Voprosy byta.* Moscow: Izdatel'stvo Kommunisticheskogo universiteta im. Sverdlova, 1925.
Lifshits, S. "Kapriiskaia partiinaia shkola (1909)." *Proletarskaia revoliutsiia,* no. 6 (1924): 33–73.
——. "Partiinaia shkola v Bolon'e (1910–1911 gg.)." *Proletarskaia revoliutsiia,* no. 3 (March 1926): 109–44.

Lopatkin, S. "10 let Kommunisticheskoi akademii." *Revoliutsiia i kul'tura*, no. 21 (15 November 1928), 39–47.

——. "Kommunisticheskaia akademiia—tsentr nauchnoi kommunisticheskoi mysli." *Kommunisticheskaia revoliutsiia*, no. 14 (July 1929): 83–90.

Lunacharskii, Anatolii Vasil'evich. *Neizdannye materialy*. Vol. 82 of *Literaturnoe nasledstvo*. Moscow: Nauka, 1970.

——. *Problemy narodnogo obrazovaniia: Sbornik*. Moscow: Rabotnik prosveshcheniia, 1923.

——. *Prosveshchenie i revoliutsiia. Sbornik statei*. Moscow: Rabotnik prosveshcheniia, 1926.

——, ed. *Tretii front. Sbornik statei*. Moscow: Rabotnik prosveshcheniia, 1924.

Magerovskii, D. A. "Rossiiskaia assotsiatsiia nauchno-isseldovatel'skikh institutov obshchestvennykh nauk." *Nauchnyi rabotnik*, no. 11 (November 1927): 51–61.

Massovoe partprosveshchenie. Moscow-Leningrad: Gosizdat, 1926.

Milchakov, A. *Komsomol v bor'be za kul'turnyi byt*. Moscow: Molodaia gvardiia, 1927.

Nevskii, Vladimir Ivanovich. *Otchet rabochego-krestianskogo kommunisticheskogo universiteta im Sverdlova*. Moscow: Gosizdat, 1920.

O chistke i proverke riadov RKP. Moscow: Moskovskii rabochii, 1929.

O rabote iacheek RKP(b). TsK. Soveshchanie sekretarei iacheek. Moscow, 1924.

O rabote iacheek RKP(b) Vysshikh uchebnykh zavedenii (Materialy soveshchanii Vuzovskikh iacheek pri TsK RKP[b]). Moscow: Izdanie TsK, 1925.

Plan rabot Kommunisticheskoi Akademii na 1929–1930 god. Moscow: Kommunisticheskaia Akademiia, 1930.

Pokrovskii, Mikhail Nikolaevich. *Lenin i vysshaia shkola*. Leningrad: Gosizdat, 1924.

——, ed. *Trudy Instituta krasnoi professury*. Moscow: Gosizdat, 1923.

Politicheskoe vospitanie Komsomola. Moscow-Leningrad: Gosizdat, 1925.

Popov, Konstantin A. "Partprosveshchenie v nachale nepa i teper'." *Kommunisticheskaia revoliutsiia*, no. 24 (December 1925).

Preobrazhenskii, Evgenii Alekseevich. "Blizhaishie zadachi Sotsialisticheskoi Akademii." *Vestnik Sotsialisticheskoi Akademii*, no. 1 (November 1922).

Ruzer-Nirovaia, N. A., ed. *Sovpartshkoly i komvuzy. Sbornik*. Moscow: Gosizdat, 1926.

Ryndich, Adrian Filippovich. *Partiino-sovetskie shkoly: k voprosu o metodike zaniatii so vzroslymi*. Moscow: Gosizdat, 1925.

——, ed. *Laborotornyi plan i ego znachenie v metodike kommunisticheskogo vospitaniia*. Moscow: Izdatel'stvo Kommunisticheskogo universiteta im. Sverdlova, 1926.

——, ed. *Metodika i organizatsiia partprosveshcheniia*. Moscow: Izdatel'stvo Kommunisticheskogo universiteta im. Sverdlova, 1926.

——, ed. *Sovpartshkoly i komvuzy*. Moscow: Gosizdat, 1926.

Sbornik po voprosam partprosveshcheniia. Moscow: Izdatel'stvo Kommunisticheskogo universiteta im. Sverdlova, 1924.

Selishchev, A. M. *Iazyk revoliutsionnoi epokhi: Iz nabliudenii nad russkim iazykom poslednikh let (1917–1926)*. Moscow: Rabotnik prosveshcheniia, 1928.

Semashko, N. A. "O dvukh zagranichnykh partiinykh shkolakh." *Proletarskaia revoliutsiia*, no. 3 (March 1928): 142–51.

Stalin, Iosif Vissarionovich. *Sochineniia*. 13 vols. Moscow: OGIZ, 1946–1951.
Subbotin, Anatolii Aleksandrovich. *Kak rabotaet Tsentral'naia Kontrol'naia Kommissiia*. Moscow-Leningrad: Gosizdat, 1926.
Sud'by sovremennoi intelligentsii. Moscow: Moskovskii rabochii, 1925.
Teoreticheskaia rabota kommunistov v 1924 g. Moscow: Izdatel'stvo Kommunisticheskoi akademii, 1925.
Udal'tsov, A. D. "Ocherk istorii Sotsialisticheskoi Akademii, 1918–1922 gg." *Vestnik Sotsialisticheskoi Akademii*, no. 1 (1922).
Upadochnoe nastroenie sredi molodezhi: Eseninshchina. Moscow-Leningrad: Izdatel'stvo Kommunisticheskoi akademii, 1927.
Valentinov, N. [N. Vol'skii.] *Novaia ekonomicheskaia politika i krizis partii posle smerti Lenina. Gody raboty v VSNKh vo vremia NEP. Vospominaniia*. Moscow: Sovremennik, 1991.
Valk, S. N., et al., eds. *Sankt-Peterburgskie Vysshie zhenskie (Bestuzhevskie) kursy (1878–1918 gg.). Sbornik statei*. Leningrad: Izdatel'stvo Leningradskogo Universiteta, 1965.
Vol'fson, Miron Borisovich. *Politgramota*. Moscow: Rabotnik prosveshcheniia, 1929.
Vol'fson, Semen Iakovlevich. *Intelligentsiia kak sotsial'no-ekonomicheskaia kategoriia*. Moscow: Gosizdat, 1926.
Voprosy kul'tury pri dikature proletariata. Sbornik. Moscow: Gosizdat, 1925.
Zalkind, Aaron Borisovich. *Revoliutsiia i molodezh'. Sbornik statei*. Moscow: Izdatel'stvo Kommunisticheskogo universiteta im. Sverdlova, 1925.
Zander, S. "Vysshaia shkola i proletarskii universitet." *Proletarskaia kul'tura*, no. 20–21 (January–June 1921): 19–27.
Zhaba, Sergei P. *Petrogradskoe studenchestvo v bor'be za svobodnuiu shkolu*. Paris: I. Povolozky, 1922.

VII. Secondary Sources

Alekseev, P. B. *Revoliutsiia i nauchnaia intelligentsiia*. Moscow: Politizdat, 1987.
Andreeva, M. S. "Glavpolitprosvet—organ gosudarstvennoi propagandy kommunizma." In V. G. Chufarov, ed., *Kul'turnaia revoliutsiia v SSSR*. Sverdlovsk: Ural'skii gosudarstvennyi universitet, 1974.
Anweiler, Oskar. *Geschichte der Schule und Pädagogik in Rußland vom Ende des Zarenreiches bis zum Beginn der Stalin-Ära*. Berlin: Quelle & Meyer Verlag, 1964.
Anweiler, Oskar, and Karl-Heinz Ruffman, eds. *Kulturpolitik der Sowjetunion*. Stuttgart: Alfred Kröner Verlag, 1973.
Bailes, Kendall. "Alexei Gastev and the Soviet Controversy over Taylorism." *Soviet Studies* 29 (July 1977): 373–94.
——. *Science and Russian Culture in an Age of Revolutions: V. I. Vernadskii and His Scientific School, 1863–1945*. Bloomington: Indiana University Press, 1990.
——. *Technology and Society under Lenin and Stalin: Origins of the Soviet Technological Intelligentsia, 1917–1941*. Princeton: Princeton University Press, 1978.
Barber, John. "The Establishment of Intellectual Orthodoxy in the U.S.S.R., 1928–1934," *Past and Present* 83 (May 1979): 141–64.

——. *Soviet Historians in Crisis, 1928–1932.* London: Macmillan, 1981.
Biggart, John. "Alexander Bogdanov and the Theory of a 'New Class.'" *Russian Review* 49 (July 1990): 265–82.
——. "'Anti-Leninist Bolshevism': The *Forward* Group of the RSDRP." *Canadian Slavonic Papers* 23 (June 1981): 134–53.
——. "Bukharin and the Origins of the 'Proletarian Culture' Debate." *Soviet Studies* 39 (April 1987): 229–46.
——. "Bukharin's Theory of Cultural Revolution." In A. Kemp-Welch, ed., *The Ideas of Nikolai Bukharin.* Oxford: Clarendon Press, 1992.
Blank, Stephen. "Soviet Institutional Development during NEP: A Prelude to Stalinism." *Russian History/Histoire Russe*, 9:2–3 (1982): 325–46.
Brachev, V. S. "'Delo' Akademika S. F. Platonova." *Voprosy istorii*, no. 5 (May 1989): 117–29.
——. "Ukroshchenie stroptivoi, ili kak AN SSSR uchili poslushaniiu." *Vestnik Akademii nauk SSSR*, no. 4 (1990): 120–27.
Brusnikin, E. M. "Iz istorii bor'by Kommunisticheskoi partii za vuzovskuiu intelligentsiiu v 1917–1922 gg." *Voprosy istorii KPSS*, 8 (1972): 81–93.
Chanbarisov, Sh. Kh. *Formirovanie sovetskoi universitetskoi sistemy.* Moscow: Vysshaia shkola, 1988.
Cinella, Ettore. "État 'prolétarien' et science 'bourgeoise': Les *specy* pendant les premières années du pouvoir soviétique." *Cahiers du monde russe et soviétique* 32 (October–December 1991): 469–500.
Clark, Katerina. *Petersburg, Crucible of Cultural Revolution.* Cambridge: Harvard University Press, 1995.
Cohen, Stephen F. *Bukharin and the Bolshevik Revolution: A Political Biography, 1888–1938.* Oxford: Oxford University Press, 1980.
Daniels, Robert Vincent. *The Conscience of the Revolution: Communist Opposition in Soviet Russia.* Cambridge: Harvard University Press, 1960.
David-Fox, Michael. "The Emergence of a 1920s Academic Order in Soviet Russia." Forthcoming.
——. "Memory, Archives, Politics: The Rise of Stalin in Avtorkhanov's *Technology of Power.*" *Slavic Review* 54 (Winter 1995): 988–1003.
——. "Symbiosis to Synthesis: The Communist Academy and the Bolshevization of the Russian Academy of Sciences, 1918–1929," forthcoming.
David-Fox, Michael, and David Hoffmann. "The Politburo Protocols, 1919–1940." *Russian Review* 55 (January 1996): 99-103.
De George, Richard T. *Soviet Ethics and Morality.* Ann Arbor: University of Michigan Press, 1969.
Dobkin, A. I., and M. Iu. Sorokina, eds. *In Memoriam: Istoricheskii sbornik pamiati F. F. Perchenka.* Moscow: Feniks, 1995.
Duda, Gerhard. *Jenö Varga und die Geschichte des Instituts für Weltwirtschaft und Weltpolitik in Moskau, 1921–1970.* Berlin: Akademie Verlag, 1994.
El'kina, D. *Ocherki po agitatsii, propagande i vneshkol'noi rabote v dorevoliutsionnoi Rossii.* Moscow-Leningrad: Gosizdat, 1930.
Elwood, Ralph Carter. "Lenin and the Social-Democratic Schools for Underground Party Workers, 1909–1911." *Political Science Quarterly* 81 (September 1966): 370–91.

Emmons, Terrence, ed. *Time of Troubles: The Diary of Iurii Vladimirovich Got'e*. Princeton: Princeton University Press, 1988.

Engelstein, Laura. *The Keys to Happiness: Sex and the Search for Modernity in Fin-de-Siècle Russia*. Ithaca: Cornell University Press, 1992.

Enteen, George. *The Soviet Scholar-Bureaucrat: M. N. Pokrovskii and the Society of Marxist Historians*. University Park: Pennsylvania State University Press, 1978.

Eran, Oded. *The Mezhdunarodniki: An Assessment of Professional Expertise in Soviet Foreign Policy*. Tel Aviv: Turtledove Publishing, 1979.

Fediukin, S. A. *Bor'ba s burzhuaznoi ideologiei v usloviiakh perekhoda k Nepu*. Moscow: Nauka, 1977.

——. *Partiia i intelligentsiia*. Moscow: Politizdat, 1983.

——. *Sovetskaia vlast' i burzhuaznye spetsialisty*. Moscow: Mysl', 1965.

——. *Velikii Oktiabr' i intelligentsiia: Iz istorii vovlecheniia staroi intelligentsii v stroitel'stvo sotsializma*. Moscow: Nauka, 1972.

Ferro, Marc, and Sheila Fitzpatrick. *Culture et révolution*. Paris: École des Hautes Études en Science Sociales, 1989.

Fil'chenikov, M. P. "Iz istorii partiinykh uchebnykh zavedenii." *Voprosy istorii KPSS*, no. 1 (1958): 108–22.

Fitzpatrick, Sheila. "Ascribing Class: The Construction of Social Identity in Soviet Russia." *Journal of Modern History* 65 (December 1993): 745–70.

——. *The Commissariat of Enlightenment: Soviet Organization of Education and the Arts under Lunacharsky, October 1917–1921*. Cambridge: Cambridge University Press, 1971.

——. *The Cultural Front: Power and Culture in Revolutionary Russia*. Ithaca: Cornell University Press, 1992.

——. *Education and Social Mobility in the Soviet Union, 1921–1934*. Cambridge: Cambridge University Press, 1979.

——. "The Emergence of Glaviskusstvo: Class War on the Cultural Front, Moscow 1928–29." *Soviet Studies* 23 (October 1971): 236–53.

——. "New Perspectives on Stalinism," and responses. *Russian Review* 45 (October 1986): 357–413; 46 (October 1987): 375–431.

——, ed. *Cultural Revolution in Russia, 1928–1931*. Bloomington: Indiana University Press, 1978.

Fitzpatrick, Sheila, et al., eds. *Russia in the Era of NEP: Explorations in Soviet Society and Culture*. Bloomington: Indiana University Press, 1991.

Fülöp-Miller, René. *The Mind and Face of Bolshevism: An Examination of Cultural Life in Soviet Russia*. New York: Alfred A. Knopf, 1928.

von Geldern, James. *Bolshevik Festivals, 1917–1920*. Berkeley: University of California Press, 1993.

Gill, Graeme. *The Origins of the Stalinist Political System*. New York: Cambridge University Press, 1990.

Gleason, Abbott, et al., eds. *Bolshevik Culture: Experiment and Order in the Russian Revolution*. Bloomington: Indiana University Press, 1985.

Gorzka, Gabrielle. *Arbeiterkultur in der Sowjetunion. Industriearbeiterklubs, 1917–1929. Ein Beitrag zur sowjetischen Kulturgeschichte*. Berlin: Verlag Arno Spitz, 1990.

Graham, Loren R. "The Formation of Soviet Research Institutes: A Combination of

Revolutionary Innovation and International Borrowing." *Social Studies of Science* 5 (August 1975): 303–29.
——. *Science in Russia and the Soviet Union: A Short History.* Cambridge: Cambridge University Press, 1991.
——. *The Soviet Academy of Sciences and the Communist Party, 1927–1932.* Princeton: Princeton University Press, 1967.
——, ed. *Science and the Soviet Social Order.* Cambridge: Harvard University Press, 1990.
Groys, Boris. "The Birth of Socialist Realism from the Spirit of the Avant-Garde." In Hans Günther, ed., *The Culture of the Stalin Period.* New York: St. Martins Press, 1990.
——. *The Total Art of Stalinism: Avant-Garde, Aesthetic Dictatorship, and Beyond.* Trans. Charles Rougle. Princeton: Princeton University Press, 1992.
von Hagen, Mark. *Soldiers in the Proletarian Dictatorship: The Red Army and the Soviet Socialist State, 1917–1930.* Ithaca: Cornell University Press, 1990.
Hans, Nicholas. *The Russian Tradition in Education.* London: Routledge & Kegan Paul, 1963.
Hans, Nicholas, and Sergius Hessen. *Education Policy in Soviet Russia.* London: P. S. King & Son, 1930.
Hardeman, Hilde. *Coming to Terms with the Soviet Regime: The "Changing Signposts" Movement among Russian Émigrés in the Early 1920s.* DeKalb: Northern Illinois University Press, 1994.
Harper, Samuel N. *Civic Training in Soviet Russia.* Chicago: University of Chicago Press, 1928.
——. *Making Bolsheviks.* Chicago: University of Chicago Press, 1931.
Hayashida, R. H. "Lenin and the Third Front," and reply from Frederic Lilge. *Slavic Review* 28 (June 1969): 314–27.
Heller, Michel. "Premier avertissement: un coup de fouet. L'histoire de l'expulsion des personalités culturelles hors de l'Union Soviétique en 1922." *Cahiers du monde russe et soviétique* 20 (April–June 1979): 131–72.
Holmes, Larry E. *The Kremlin and the Schoolhouse: Reforming Education in Soviet Russia, 1917–1931.* Bloomington: Indiana University Press, 1991.
Holmes, Larry E., and William Burgess. "Scholarly Voice or Political Echo? Soviet Party History in the 1920s." *Russian History/Histoire Russe* 9:2–3 (1982): 378–98.
Iaroshevskii, M. G., ed. *Repressirovannaia nauka.* Leningrad: Nauka, 1991.
Ivanov, A. E. *Vysshaia shkola Rossii v kontse XIX–nachale XX veka.* Moscow: Institut Istorii SSSR, 1991.
Ivanova, Liudmila Vasil'evna. *Formirovanie sovetskoi nauchnoi intelligentsii, 1917–27 gg.* Moscow: Nauka, 1980.
——. *U istokov sovetskoi istoricheskoi nauki: Podgotovka kadrov istorikov-marksistov v 1917–1929 gg.* Moscow: "Mysl'," 1968.
——, ed. *Istoricheskii opyt planirovaniia kul'turnogo stroitel'stva v SSSR.* Moscow: Institut istorii SSSR AN SSSR, 1988.
Izmozik, V. S. *Glaza i ushi rezhima: Gosudarsvennyi politicheskii kontrol' za naseleniem Sovetskoi Rossii v 1918–1928 godakh.* St. Petersburg: Izdatel'stvo Sankt-Peterburgskogo Universiteta Ekonomiki i Finansov, 1995.
Jarausch, Konrad H., ed. *The Transformation of Higher Learning, 1860–1930: Ex-*

pansion, Diversification, Social Opening, and Professionalization in England, Germany, Russia, and the United States. Stuttgart: Klett-Cotta, 1983.

Johnson, William H. E. *Russia's Educational Heritage*. New Brunswick, N.J.: Rutgers University Press, 1950.

Joravsky, David. "Cultural Revolution and the Fortress Mentality." Washington, D.C.: Kennan Institute Occasional Paper, 1981.

——. *Russian Psychology: A Critical History*. London: Basil Blackwell, 1989.

——. *Soviet Marxism and Natural Science, 1917–1932*. London: Routledge & Kegan Paul, 1961.

——. "The Stalinist Mentality and the Higher Learning." *Slavic Review* 42 (Winter 1983): 575–600.

Josephson, Paul. *Physics and Politics in Revolutionary Russia*. Berkeley: University of California Press, 1991.

——. "Science Policy in the Soviet Union, 1917–1927." *Minerva* 26 (Autumn, 1988): 342–69.

Kagarlitsky, Boris. *The Thinking Reed: Intellectuals in the Soviet State from 1917 to the Present*. Trans. Brian Pierce. London: Verso Press, 1988.

Kassow, Samuel D. *Students, Professors, and the State in Tsarist Russia*. Berkeley: University of California Press, 1989.

Kelly, Aileen. "Empiriocriticism: A Bolshevik Philosophy?" *Cahiers du monde russe et soviétique* 22 (January–March 1981): 89–118.

Kenez, Peter. *The Birth of the Propaganda State: Soviet Methods of Mass Mobilization, 1917–1929*. Cambridge: Cambridge University Press, 1985.

Kinelev, V. G., ed. *Vysshee obrazovanie v Rossii. Ocherk istorii do 1917 goda*. Moscow: NII VO, 1995.

Kirstein, Tatjana. "Das sowjetische Parteischulsystem." In Boris Meissner et al., eds., *Einparteisystem und bürokratische Herrschaft in der Sowjetunion*. Cologne: Markus Verlag, 1979.

Kneen, Peter. "Higher Education and Cultural Revolution in the USSR." CREES Discussion Papers. Soviet Industrialization Project Series, no. 5. University of Birmingham, 1976.

Kol'tsov, Anatolii Vasil'evich. *Razvitie Akademii nauk kak vysshego nauchnogo uchrezhdeniia SSSR, 1926–1932*. Leningrad: Nauka, 1982.

Konecny, Peter. "Chaos on Campus: The 1924 Student *Proverka* in Leningrad." *Europe-Asia Studies* 46:4 (1994): 617–36.

Korzhikhina, T. P., and Iu. Iu. Figatner. "Sovetskaia nomenklatura: stanovlenie, mekhanizmy deistviia." *Voprosy istorii*, no. 7 (1993): 25–38.

Kotkin, Stephen. *Magnetic Mountain: Stalinism as a Civilization*. Berkeley: University of California Press, 1995.

Krementsov, Nikolai. *Stalinist Science*. Princeton University Press, in press.

Lampert, Nicholas. *The Technical Intelligentsia and the Soviet State*. New York: Holmes & Meier, 1979.

Lane, David. "The Impact of Revolution: The Case of Selection of Students for Higher Education in Soviet Russia, 1917–1928." *Sociology* 7 (May 1973): 241–52.

Lapidus, Gail. "Socialism and Modernity: Education, Industrialization, and Social Change in the USSR." In Paul Cocks et al., eds., *The Dynamics of Soviet Politics*. Cambridge: Harvard University Press, 1976.

Lazitch, Branko. "Les écoles de cadres du Comintern: Contribution à leur histoire." In Jacques Freymond, ed., *Contributions à l'histoire du Comintern*. Geneva: Librairie Droz, 1965.

Lee, David Currie. *The People's Universities of the USSR*. New York: Greenwood Press, 1988.

Leikin, A. Ia., ed. *Intelligentsiia i sotsialisticheskaia kul'turnaia revoliutsiia*. Leningrad: Gosudarstvennyi pedagogicheskii institut imeni A. Ia. Gertsena, 1975.

Leikina-Svirskaia, V. R. *Russkaia intelligentsiia v 1900–1917 godakh*. Moscow: Mysl', 1981.

Leonova, Lira Stepanova. *Istoricheskii opyt KPSS po podgotovke partiinykh kadrov v partiinykh uchebnykh zavedeniiakh, 1917–1975*. Moscow: Izdatel'stvo Moskovskogo universiteta, 1979.

——. *Iz istorii podgotovki partiinykh kadrov v sovetsko-partiinykh shkolakh i kommunisticheskikh universitetakh (1921–1925)*. Moscow: Izdatel'stvo Moskovskogo universiteta, 1972.

——. "'Perepiska Sekretariata TsK RSDRP(b)-RKP(b) s mestnymi partiinymi organizatsiiami' kak istochnik osveshcheniia problemy podgotovki partiinykh kadrov v pervye gody sovetskoi vlasti." *Vestnik Moskovskogo Universiteta*, 8th ser., no. 6 (1987): 3–14.

Levin, Alexey E. "Expedient Catastrophe: A Reconsideration of the 1929 Crisis at the Soviet Academy of Sciences. *Slavic Review* 47 (Summer 1988): 261–80.

Lewin, Moshe. *The Making of the Soviet System: Essays in the Social History of Interwar Russia*. New York: Pantheon Books, 1985.

Lewis, Robert. "Science, Nonscience, and the Cultural Revolution." *Slavic Review* 45 (Summer 1986): 268–92.

Lilge, Frederic. "Lenin and the Politics of Education." *Slavic Review* 27 (June 1968): 230–57.

Maguire, Robert. *Red Virgin Soil: Soviet Literature in the 1920s*. Princeton: Princeton University Press, 1968.

Mally, Lynn. *Culture of the Future: The Proletkult Movement in Revolutionary Russia*. Berkeley: University of California Press, 1990.

Marot, John Eric. "Alexander Bogdanov, Vpered, and the Role of the Intellectual in the Workers' Movement." *Russian Review* 49 (July 1990): 241–64.

——. "Politics and Philosophy in Russian Social Democracy: Alexander Bogdanov and the Sociotheoretical Foundations of *Vpered*." *Canadian Slavonic Papers* 33 (September–December 1991): 263–84.

McClellan, Woodford. "Africans and Black Americans in the Comintern Schools, 1925–1934." *International Journal of African Historical Studies* 26:2 (1993): 371–90.

McClelland, James. *Autocrats and Academics: Education, Culture and Society in Tsarist Russia*. Chicago: University of Chicago Press, 1979.

——. "Bolshevik Approaches to Higher Education, 1917–1921." *Slavic Review* 30 (December 1971): 818–31.

——. "The Professoriate in the Russian Civil War." In Diane P. Koenker et al., eds., *Party, State, and Society in the Russian Civil War*. Bloomington: Indiana University Press, 1989.

——. "Proletarianizing the Student Body: The Soviet Experience During the New Economic Policy." *Past and Present* 80 (August 1978): 122–46.

——. "The Utopian and the Heroic: Divergent Paths to the Communist Educational Ideal." In Abbott Gleason et al., eds., *Bolshevik Culture*. Bloomington: Indiana University Press, 1985.

——. "Utopianism versus Revolutionary Heroism in Bolshevik Policy: The Proletarian Culture Debate." *Slavic Review* 39 (September 1980): 403–25.

McNeal, Robert H. *Bride of the Revolution: Krupskaia and Lenin*. Ann Arbor: University of Michigan Press, 1973.

Merridale, Catherine. *Moscow Politics and the Rise of Stalin: The Communist Party in the Capital, 1925–1932*. London: Macmillan, 1990.

——. "The Reluctant Opposition: The Right 'Deviation' in Moscow, 1928." *Soviet Studies* 41 (July 1989): 382–400.

Mickiewicz, Ellen Propper. *Soviet Political Schools: The Communist Party Adult Instruction System*. New Haven, Conn.: Yale University Press, 1967.

Naiman, Eric. "The Case of Chubarov Alley: Collective Rape, Utopian Desire, and the Mentality of NEP." *Russian History/Histoire Russe* 17 (Spring 1990): 1–30.

——. "Revolutionary Anorexia (NEP as Female Complaint)." *Slavic and East European Journal* 37 (Fall 1993): 305–25.

Nechkina, M. V., et al., eds. *Ocherki istorii istoricheskoi nauki v SSSR*. Vol. 4. Moscow: Nauka, 1966.

Nilsson, Nils Åke, ed. *Art, Society, Revolution: Russia, 1917–1921*. Stockholm: Almqvist & Wiksell, 1979.

Nötzold, Jürgen. "Die deutsch-sowjetischen Wissenschaftsbeziehungen." In Rudolf Vierhaus and Bernhard von Brocke, eds., *Forschung im Spannungsfeld von Politik und Gesellschaft: Geschichte und Struktur der Kaiser-Wilhelm-/Max-Plank-Gesellschaft*. Stuttgart: Deutsche Verlag, 1990.

Perchenok, F. F. "Akademiia nauk na 'velikom perelome.'" In *Zven'ia: Istoricheskii almanakh*, vypusk 1 Moscow: Feniks, 1990.

Pethybridge, Roger. "Concern for Bolshevik Ideological Predominance at the Start of NEP." *Russian Review* 41 (October 1982): 445–53.

——. *One Step Backwards, Two Steps Forward: Soviet Society and Politics in the New Economic Policy*. Oxford: Clarendon Press, 1990.

Pinegina, L. A. "Nekotorye dannye o chislennosti i sostave intelligentsii k nachalu vosstanovitel'nogo perioda (po materialam perepisei 1922 i 1923 gg.)." *Vestnik Moskovskogo universiteta*, 8th ser., no. 3 (1979): 12–20.

Price, Jane. *Cadres, Commanders, and Commissars: The Training of the Chinese Communist Leadership, 1920–1945*. Boulder, Colo.: Westview Press, 1976.

Read, Christopher. *Culture and Power in Revolutionary Russia: The Intelligentsia and the Transition from Tsarism to Communism*. London: Macmillan, 1990.

Rigby, T. H. *Communist Party Membership in the USSR, 1917–1967*. Princeton: Princeton University Press, 1968.

——. "Staffing USSR Incorporated: The Origins of the Nomenklatura System." *Soviet Studies* 40 (October 1988): 523–37.

Rittersporn, Gábor Támas. "The Omnipresent Conspiracy: On Soviet Imagery of Politics and Social Relations in the 1930s." In J. Arch Getty and Roberta Manning, eds., *Stalinist Terror: New Perspectives*. Cambridge: Cambridge University Press, 1993.

Rokitianskii, Ia. G. "Tragicheskaia sud'ba akademika D. B. Riazanova." *Novaia i noveishaia istoriia*, no. 2 (March–April 1992): 107–48.
Rosenfeldt, Niels Erik. *Knowledge and Power: The Role of Stalin's Secret Chancellery in the Soviet System of Government.* Copenhagen: Rosenkilde & Bagger, 1978.
Rosenthal, Bernice, ed. *Nietzsche in Russia.* Princeton: Princeton University Press, 1986.
——, ed. *Nietzsche and Soviet Culture.* Cambridge: Cambridge University Press, 1994.
Scherrer, Jutta. "La crise de l'intelligentsia Marxiste avant 1914: A. V. Lunačarskij et le bogostroitel'stvo." *Revue des études slaves* 51: 1–2 (1978): 207–15.
——. "Les écoles du Parti de Capri et de Bologne: La formation de l'intelligentsia du Parti." *Cahiers du monde russe et soviétique* 19 (July–September 1978): 258–84.
——. "'Ein gelber und ein blauer Teufel': Zur Entstehung der Begriffe 'bogostroitel'stvo' und 'bogoiskatel'stvo.'" *Forschungen zur osteuropäischen Geschichte* 25 (1978): 319–29.
Scherrer, Jutta, and Georges Haupt. "Gor'kij, Bogdanov, Lenin: Neue Quellen zur ideologischen Krise in der bolschewistischen Fraktion, 1908–1910." *Cahiers du monde russe et soviétique* 19 (July–September 1978): 321–34.
Service, Robert. *The Bolshevik Party in Revolution: A Study in Organizational Change, 1917–1923.* New York: Barnes & Noble, 1979.
Shatz, Marshall. *Jan Wacław Machajski.* Pittsburgh: University of Pittsburgh Press, 1989.
Sheng, Yueh. *Sun Yat-sen University in Moscow and the Chinese Revolution: A Personal Account.* Lawrence: University of Kansas, Center for East Asian Studies, 1971.
Shimoniak, Wasyl. *Communist Education: Its History, Philosophy, and Politics.* New York: Rand McNally, 1970.
Shteppa, Konstantin. *Russian Historians and the Soviet State.* New Brunswick, N.J.: Rutgers University Press, 1962.
Siegelbaum, Lewis, and Ronald Grigor Suny, eds. *Making Workers Soviet: Power, Class, and Identity.* Ithaca: Cornell University Press, 1994.
Sochor, Zenovia A. *Revolution and Culture: The Bogdanov-Lenin Controversy.* Ithaca: Cornell University Press, 1981.
Solomon, Susan Gross. *The Soviet Agrarian Debate: A Controversy in Social Science, 1923–1929.* Boulder, Colo.: Westview Press, 1977.
Solovei, V. D. "Institut krasnoi professury. Podgotovka kadrov istorikov partii v 20–30-e gody." *Voprosy istorii KPSS*, no. 12 (1990): 87–98.
Stites, Richard. *Revolutionary Dreams: Utopian Vision and Experimental Life in the Russian Revolution.* New York: Oxford University Press, 1989.
——. *The Women's Liberation Movement in Russia: Feminism, Nihilism, and Bolshevism, 1860–1930.* Princeton: Princeton University Press, 1978.
Thomson, Boris. *Lot's Wife and the Venus of Milo. Conflicting Attitudes to the Cultural Heritage in Modern Russia.* Cambridge: Cambridge University Press, 1978.
Tucker, Robert C. *Political Culture and Leadership in Soviet Russia.* Brighton: Wheatsheaf Books, 1987.

Tugarinov, I. A. "VARNITSO i Akademiia nauk SSSR (1927–1937 gg.)." *Voprosy istorii estestvoznaniia i tekhniki*, no. 4 (1989): 46–55.
Tumarkin, Nina. *Lenin Lives! The Lenin Cult in Soviet Russia*. Cambridge: Harvard University Press, 1983.
Ul'ianovskaia, V. A. *Formirovanie nauchnoi intelligentsii v SSSR, 1917–1937 gg.* Moscow: Nauka, 1966.
Vucinich, Alexander. *Empire of Knowledge: The Academy of Sciences of the USSR, 1917–1970*. Berkeley: University of California Press, 1984.
——. *Science in Russian Culture, 1861–1917*. Stanford: Stanford University Press, 1970.
——. *Social Thought in Tsarist Russia: The Quest for a General Science of Society*. Chicago: University of Chicago Press, 1976.
Williams, Robert C. *Artists in Revolution: Portraits of the Russian Avante-Garde, 1905–1925*. Bloomington: Indiana University Press, 1977.
——. "The Nationalization of Early Soviet Culture." *Russian History/Histoire Russe* 9:2–3 (1982): 157–72.
——. *The Other Bolsheviks: Lenin and His Critics, 1904–1914*. Bloomington: Indiana University Press, 1986.
Zepper, John T. "Krupskaya on Dewey's Educational Thought." *School and Society* 100 (January 1972): 19–21.
——. "N. K. Krupskaya on Complex Themes in Soviet Education." *Comparative Education Review* 9 (February 1965): 33–37.
Znamenskii, O. N. *Intelligentsiia nakanune velikogo oktiabria (fevral'–oktiabr' 1917 g.)*. Leningrad: Nauka, 1988.

Index

Studies of the Harriman Institute

Selected Titles in Russian Literature and Culture

Through the Glass of Soviet Literature. Views of Russian Society by Ernest J. Simmons (Columbia University Press, 1953).

Russian Classics in Soviet Jackets by Maurice Friedberg (Columbia University Press, 1962).

Red Virgin Soil. Soviet Literature in the 1920s by Robert A. Maguire (Princeton University Press, 1968; reprint Cornell University Press, 1987).

Mayakovsky. A Poet in the Revolution by Edward J. Brown (Princeton University Press, 1973).

The Familiar Letter as a Literary Genre in the Age of Pushkin by William Mills Todd III (Princeton University Press, 1976).

Sergei Aksakov and Russian Pastoral by Andrew A. Durkin (Rutgers University Press, 1983).

Russian Metaphysical Romanticism. The Poetry of Tiutchev and Boratynskii by Sarah Pratt (Stanford University Press, 1984).

Leo Tolstoy. Resident and Stranger by Richard Gustafson (Princeton University Press, 1986).

Andrey Bely. Spirit of Symbolism, edited by John Malmstad (Cornell University Press, 1987).

Russian Literary Politics and the Pushkin Celebration of 1880 by Marcus C. Levitt (Cornell University Press, 1989).

Alien Tongues. Bilingual Russian Writers of the "First" Emigration by Elizabeth Klosty Beaujour (Cornell University Press, 1989).

Russianness: In Honor of Rufus Mathewson, edited by Robert L. Belknap (Ardis Publishers, 1990).

In Stalin's Time by Vera Dunham (Cambridge University Press, 1976; reprint Duke University Press, 1990).

Folklore for Stalin by Frank Miller (M. E. Sharpe, 1990).

Vasilii Trediakovsky. The Fool of the New Russian Literature by Irina Reyfman (Stanford University Press, 1990).

Ilya Repin and the World of Russian Art by Elizabeth Kridl Valkenier (Columbia University Press, 1990).

The Genesis of "The Brothers Karamazov" by Robert L. Belknap (Northwestern University Press, 1990).

Autobiographical Statements in Twentieth-Century Russian Literature, edited by Jane Gary Harris (Princeton University Press, 1990).

The Paradise Myth in Eighteenth-Century Russia. Utopian Patterns in Early Secular Russian Literature and Culture by Stephen Lessing Baehr (Stanford University Press, 1991).

Andrei Bitov. The Ecology of Inspiration by Ellen Chances (Cambridge University Press, 1993).

The Pragmatics of Insignificance. Chekhov, Zoshchenko, Gogol by Cathy Popkin (Stanford University Press, 1993).

Exploring Gogol by Robert A. Maguire (Stanford University Press, 1994).

Abram Tertz and the Poetics of Crime by Catharine Theimer Nepomnyashchy (Yale University Press, 1995).

Scenarios of Power. Myth and Ceremony in Russian Monarchy by Richard S. Wortman (Princeton University Press, 1995).

Revolution of the Mind. Higher Learning among the Bolsheviks, 1918–1929 by Michael David-Fox (Cornell University Press).